Multicultural Odysseys

Multicultural Odysseys

Navigating the New International Politics of Diversity

Will Kymlicka

OXFORD
UNIVERSITY PRESS

OXFORD

UNIVERSITY PRESS

Great Clarendon Street, Oxford OX2 6DP

Oxford University Press is a department of the University of Oxford.
It furthers the University's objective of excellence in research, scholarship,
and education by publishing worldwide in

Oxford New York

Auckland Cape Town Dar es Salaam Hong Kong Karachi
Kuala Lumpur Madrid Melbourne Mexico City Nairobi
New Delhi Shanghai Taipei Toronto

With offices in

Argentina Austria Brazil Chile Czech Republic France Greece
Guatemala Hungary Italy Japan Poland Portugal Singapore
South Korea Switzerland Thailand Turkey Ukraine Vietnam

Oxford is a registered trademark of Oxford University Press
in the UK and in certain other countries

Published in the United States
by Oxford University Press Inc., New York

British Library Cataloguing in Publication Data

Data available

Library of Congress Cataloging in Publication Data

Data available

Typeset by SPI Publisher Services, Pondicherry, India
Printed in Great Britain
on acid-free paper by
Biddles Ltd., King's Lynn, Norfolk

ISBN 978–0–19–928040–7

1 3 5 7 9 10 8 6 4 2

Acknowledgements

This book covers a lot of territory, intellectually and geographically, much of it some distance from my initial training as a political philosopher. I would not have been able to write it without the advice and encouragement of many friends and colleagues who have helped me navigate through unfamiliar waters.

I've had the good fortune of working with some wonderful colleagues on projects closely related to this book, including three edited volumes: *Can Liberal Pluralism Be Exported? Western Political Theory and Ethnic Relations in Eastern Europe*, co-edited with Magda Opalski; *Multiculturalism in Asia*, co-edited with Baogang He; and *Ethnicity and Democracy in Africa*, co-edited with Bruce Berman and Dickson Eyoh. Special thanks to my co-editors, and the contributors, for introducing me to the global dimensions of these issues.

The ideas in this book were first tried out in a number of conferences, seminars, and workshops over the past few years, and I'm grateful to the organizers who invited me, and to the colleagues and audiences who provided very helpful feedback. There are too many to list individually, but I owe a special thanks to the following people and institutions for arranging particularly informative and challenging trips that might not otherwise have been possible: Rupak Chattopadhyay at the Forum of Federations and Rohan Edrisinha at the Centre for Policy Alternatives for an invitation to Sri Lanka; Carlos Mendoza at the United Nations Development Program for a visit to Guatemala; Brian Selmeski at the Canadian Defense Academy and Ricardo Calla Ortega at the Bolivian Ministry of Indigenous Affairs for a visit to Bolivia; Christopher Hull at the Canadian Embassy in Damascus and Sari Hanafi at the American University in Beirut, who helped arrange an unforgettable lecture series in Syria and Lebanon; David Turton and the British Council for an invitation to Ethiopia; Ishiyama Fumihiko, Morigiwa Yasutomo and Sakurai Tetsu at IVR Japan, who arranged a lecture series in Japan; Daniel A. Bell, who arranged talks at the City University of Hong Kong and Fudan University in Shanghai; Chusnul Mar'iyah and Rosa Evaquarta at the University of Indonesia; and Serguei Koutznetsov at the European Commission on Democracy through Law for a conference in Moldova.

I've had the privilege of participating in several comparative projects on state–minority relations, including the Carnegie Foundation's 'Comparative Citizenship Project' directed by Alexander Aleinikoff and Douglas Klusmeyer; the Friedrich Naumann Foundation's project on international minority rights, directed by Gerhart Raichle, and the United Nations Human Development Report on 'Cultural Liberty', directed by Sakiko Parr-Fukada. I'd like to thank them, and their colleagues, for inviting me to participate.

Over the years, I have benefited from extended discussions and assistance from several colleagues, particularly Marc Weller, François Grin, Graham Holliday and Tove Malloy at the European Centre for Minority Issues; Sally Holt and John Packer at the Office of the High Commissioner on National Minorities of the Organization for Security and Cooperation in Europe; Levente Salat at the Ethnocultural Diversity Resource Centre in Cluj, Romania; Donna Lee Van Cott, Maria Kovacs, Joseph Carens, Avigail Eisenberg, Bashir Bashir, and Jacob Levy. Special thanks to my colleagues in the Canadian Institute for Advanced Research's Successful Societies program. Our discussions have been invaluable in helping me situate these issues in a broader historical and social perspective.

Closer to home, I'd like to thank several people here at Queen's with whom I have been working closely, including Keith Banting in the School of Policy Studies, my co-author in several projects relating to diversity, citizenship and the welfare state; Margaret Moore, John McGarry, and Bruce Berman in the Political Studies department, my colleagues in the new 'Ethnicity and Democratic Governance' project; and my supportive colleagues in the Philosophy Department.

My work on this topic has been made possible by a Killam Fellowship from the Canada Council for the Arts, fellowships from the Trudeau Foundation and the Canadian Institute for Advanced Research, as well as by research grants from the Social Sciences and Humanities Research Council of Canada, and the Canada Research Chairs program. I'm very grateful for their support.

I've had excellent research assistance from Lisa Vanhala, Siobhan Byrne, Michael Kocsis, and Omid Hejazi. For helpful comments on earlier drafts of this manuscript, many thanks to Corinne Lennox, Stefan Ehrentraut, Alexander Osipov, Peter Hall, Wayne Norman, Rainer Baubock, and especially Sue Donaldson, whose comments and suggestions have profoundly shaped this project from the initial proposal to the final edits.

Thanks, as always, to my wonderful editor at OUP, Dominic Byatt, who has patiently waited for this book, Kate Hind for shepherding it through the production process, and to Virginia Williams for her careful copy-editing.

I'm very grateful to Gary Fiegehen and the Nisga'a Lisims government for permission to use the beautiful cover image. The carving was one of several artifacts repatriated to the Nisga'a under the terms of their 1998 Treaty with the Canadian government, which is an important example and hopeful symbol of the new politics of diversity discussed in this book. (The carving depicts one of the strictest moral laws - Uks T'is'a - wherein an individual is ostracized from the community as a 'discontinued' member of his or her clan. This is why there are no oars in the boat.)

Finally, and most importantly, thanks to Sue, my partner on this intellectual odyssey.

Contents

Part I

The (Re-)Internationalization of State–Minority Relations

1

Introduction

In the last forty years, we have witnessed a veritable revolution around the world in the relations between states and ethnocultural minorities. Older models of assimilationist and homogenizing nation-states are increasingly being contested, and often displaced, by newer 'multicultural' models of the state and of citizenship. This is reflected, for example, in the widespread adoption of cultural and religious accommodations for immigrant groups, the acceptance of territorial autonomy and language rights for national minorities, and the recognition of land claims and self-government rights for indigenous peoples.

This shift has often been the result of endogenous domestic political processes. After a period of internal debate and negotiation in response to intense mobilization by particular minorities, a number of countries have concluded that the older models were not appropriate given their specific demographic or historical circumstances.

But increasingly this shift has an international dimension to it. International intergovernmental organizations are encouraging, and sometimes pressuring, states to adopt a more multicultural approach. Those states that are prepared to consider adopting models of multicultural citizenship will find an array of international organizations willing to provide support, expertise, and funding. Those states that cling to older assimilationist or exclusionary models find themselves subject to international monitoring, criticism, and sanction. In short, we are witnessing the increasing 'internationalization' of state–minority relations, and the global diffusion of multiculturalism as a new framework for reforming those relations.

We can distinguish two levels at which multiculturalism is being globalized. First, there is the global diffusion of the *political discourse* of multiculturalism. A set of ideas about the importance of accommodating diversity

is being circulated by international networks of non-governmental organizations (NGOs), scholars, and policy-makers. On virtually any given
day of the year, somewhere in the world an international organization
is sponsoring a seminar or publishing a report intended to publicize the
ideals and practices of multiculturalism. These activities often involve
sharing knowledge about 'best practices' in various countries, building
transnational networks of experts and advocates, creating space for the
safe expression of politically sensitive topics, and training local educators,
bureaucrats, NGOs, and media personnel in the challenges of accommodating a multiethnic and multicultural population.

Second, there is the codification of multiculturalism in certain international *legal (or quasi-legal) norms*, embodied in declarations of minority
rights. The last fifteen years in particular have seen a proliferation of
efforts to develop international norms of minority rights, at both the
global and regional levels. Globally, the United Nations (UN) adopted
a Declaration on the Rights of Persons Belonging to National or Ethnic, Religious and Linguistic Minorities in 1992, and is debating a Draft
Declaration on the Rights of Indigenous Peoples. Other international
intergovernmental organizations, such as the United Nations Educational, Scientific and Cultural Organization (UNESCO), the International
Labour Organization, and the World Bank, have also developed norms
on minority or indigenous rights. Declarations have also been drafted by
organizations at the regional level, such as the Council of Europe's 1995
Framework Convention for the Protection of National Minorities, or the
Organization of American States' 1997 draft Declaration on the Rights of
Indigenous Peoples. In most cases, these Declarations and Conventions
are not in fact judicially enforceable—that is, individuals or groups cannot
go to any international court to force their government to comply with
these norms. But these norms do have some bite. States are increasingly
monitored and judged for how well they comply with these norms, and
failure to comply has resulted not only in criticism, but also, in some
cases, in tangible consequences.

If the first level involves the diffusion of a set of ideals and best practices
to which all states should aspire, the second involves the codification of
a set of minimum standards below which no states should fall. These
twin processes of diffusing multiculturalism and minority rights are fundamentally reshaping the traditional conceptions of state sovereignty,
nationhood, and citizenship that have underpinned the international system of nation-states. Not surprisingly, they have generated considerable
anxiety and resistance. The global diffusion of multiculturalism has been,

and remains, deeply contested. And yet, despite the significance of these trends, and the resistance they have generated, there has been surprisingly little scholarly work done on the international diffusion of multiculturalism and minority rights.[1] The wording of these international declarations and conventions has been exhaustively parsed by international lawyers,[2] but we know little about the underlying causes and consequences of these trends. We do not know about the social forces that have generated these trends, or about their potential benefits and risks, or about the alternatives to them that have been rejected or foreclosed. These trends rest on certain assumptions about the 'problem' raised by ethnicity and ethnic politics, and about the appropriate 'solutions', but these assumptions are rarely made explicit, let alone defended.

My aim in this book is to identify some of the moral dilemmas and political complexities raised by these international efforts to diffuse multiculturalism. I believe that these developments are potentially progressive. For one thing, they offer the promise of protecting some of the most vulnerable groups in the modern world from serious injustices. Ethnic minorities have not fared well under the Westphalian system of sovereign 'nation-states'. Various policies of assimilation and exclusion have been directed at minorities in the name of constructing homogenous nation-states, and the international community has historically turned a blind eye to these injustices. Today, however, there is a growing commitment to remedy this situation, and it is increasingly accepted that the treatment of minorities is a matter of legitimate international concern, and should be subject to international norms and standards. At a minimum, these evolving standards set limits on the means that Westphalian nation-states can use to pursue their visions of national homogenization. But these norms also, implicitly at least, offer an alternative vision to the Westphalian state, one which views diversity as an enduring reality and defining feature of the polity, and which views tolerance as a core value. Viewed in this light, the trend towards diffusing models of multiculturalism is a desirable one.

---

[1] See n. 6 below for a fuller discussion of how this issue has fallen outside the mainstreams of the existing academic literatures on issues of ethnicity and ethnic politics.

[2] For detailed analysis of these legal texts, see Thornberry 1991, 2002; Dinstein 1992; Henrard 2000; Alfredsson and Ferrer 1998; Bowring and Fottrell 1999; Akermark 1997; Cumper and Wheatley 1999; Wheatley 2005; Woehrling 2005; Weller 2005b; Lerner 1991; Phillips and Rosas 1995; Rehman 2000; Welhengama 2000; Pentassuglia 2002; Council of Europe 2004; Gayim 2001; Crawford 1998; Ghanea and Xanthaki 2005; Alston 2001; Musgrave 1997; Anaya 1996; Lam 2000; Letschert 2005; Meijknecht 2001; Thornberry and Estebenez 2004.

Moreover, the particular conception of multiculturalism being promoted by international organizations is, I believe, a morally progressive extension of existing human rights norms. There are many examples around the world in which the language of multiculturalism and minority rights is invoked by local elites to perpetuate gender and caste inequalities, or to legitimize unjust cultural practices and traditions.[3] However, international organizations have been careful to avoid such illiberal or oppressive conceptions of multiculturalism. The political discourses and legal norms of multiculturalism being advanced by international organizations and international law are a natural and logical evolution of the norms of universal human rights, and operate within the constraints of those norms. In that sense, they serve to deepen and consolidate the larger human rights revolution.

Not everyone agrees. Some critics see the general movement to diffuse multiculturalism and minority rights as a betrayal of the founding ideals of the international community. According to Alain Finkielkraut, for example, the UN's embrace of multiculturalism has involved abandoning Enlightenment universalism for cultural relativism:

The United Nations, founded to propagate the universalist ideals of Enlightened Europe, now speaks on behalf of every ethnic prejudice, believing that peoples, nations and cultures have rights which outweigh the rights of man. The 'multicultural' lobby dismisses the liberal values of Europe as 'racist', while championing the narrow chauvinism of every minority culture (Finkielkraut 1988).

In fact, however, the UN's documents are unambiguous that norms of multiculturalism cannot be used to 'outweigh the rights of man' (or woman). The UNESCO Universal Declaration on Cultural Diversity states that 'No one may invoke cultural diversity to infringe upon human rights guaranteed by international law, nor to limit their scope' (Article 4). The UN's Declaration on minority rights states that any rights or duties recognized in the Declaration 'shall not prejudice the enjoyment of all persons of universally recognized human rights and fundamental freedoms' (Article 8(2)). The International Labour Organization's Convention on the rights of indigenous peoples says that the right of indigenous people to maintain their cultural practices should be respected 'where these are not incompatible with fundamental rights defined by the national legal

---

[3] There is now an extensive literature on the way multiculturalism can be invoked to limit the rights of women and other vulnerable 'internal minorities'. For influential discussions, see Okin 1999, Shachar 2001, and Eisenberg and Spinner-Halev 2005.

system and internationally recognized human rights' (Article 8(2)). The Council of Europe's Framework Convention on the rights of national minorities says that the Convention must be interpreted in a way that complies with the European Convention on Human Rights (Article 23). In fact, every international declaration and convention on these issues makes the same point—the rights of minorities and indigenous peoples are an inseparable part of a larger human rights framework, and operate within its limits.

Finkielkraut's critique fundamentally misconstrues both the motivations of international organizations for becoming involved in this field and the content of the minority rights being promoted. As I will show, the emerging international discourses and norms are fundamentally *liberal* in character. As such, they are broadly consistent with theories of 'liberal multiculturalism' that have been developed by recent Western political theorists, in which multiculturalism is understood as a concept that is both guided and constrained by a foundational commitment to principles of individual freedom and equality.[4]

Having defended this ideal of liberal multiculturalism in my own work—particularly my 1995 book *Multicultural Citizenship: A Liberal Theory of Minority Rights*—I have been struck by the way it has come to inform the work of many international organizations, and I would like to believe that its global diffusion is desirable and beneficial. Indeed, I have happily served as a foot soldier in this process. While my earlier work focused primarily on domestic debates within the Western democracies, I have since been asked to discuss the relevance of these ideas for the formulation of international norms of minority rights, and for the global diffusion of models and best practices of multiculturalism. Much of my work in the past decade has involved participating in seminars, workshops, and advisory groups on these topics in some two dozen countries, from Ethiopia to Estonia, from Syria to Sri Lanka, from Mexico to Moldova. As a result, I have watched first-hand the processes by which a set of concepts and discourses are circulating around the world—primarily (though not exclusively) from West to East, and from North to South—diffusing through academia, civil society, and the bureaucracy, under the watchful eye and guiding hand of international organizations.[5]

[4] See e.g. Spinner 1994; Taylor 1992; Tamir 1993, Raz 1994. For an overview, see Kymlicka 2001, chap. 2.

[5] While the circulation of ideas is asymmetric, it is not unidirectional. Indian intellectuals, for example, have been influential in shaping contemporary international discourse on human and minority rights. As Anant shows, they have been active shapers, and not just passive recipients, of international norms (Anant 2003).

While still hopeful about this general trend, I have become increasingly perplexed about the way these processes are unfolding, and uncertain about where they are heading, or indeed where they should be heading. Attempts to internationalize multiculturalism and minority rights are running into a veritable minefield of conceptual confusions, moral dilemmas, unintended consequences, legal inconsistencies and political manipulation, and it's not clear that there is a road map for navigating around these obstacles. Faced with these obstructions, international efforts have sometimes come to a dead-end, and sometimes been deflected off-course. My aim in this book is not to offer magic solutions for overcoming all of these difficulties—some of them, I suspect, are unsolvable in the foreseeable future—but to more clearly identify the challenges they raise, and the pitfalls ahead of us if we ignore them.

I will discuss a number of these difficulties over the course of the book, but they generally fall under three headings. First, there is a problem of categories. Is the goal to formulate norms and standards that apply to all minorities, or is the goal to formulate different norms for different types of minorities—for example, different norms for immigrant groups, national minorities, and indigenous peoples? International organizations have alternated between these two options, which I will call the 'generic' and 'targeted' approaches. This in itself is not necessarily a problem, since any plausible conception of liberal multiculturalism will almost certainly combine both generic and targeted elements. But the particular way in which targeted categories have been defined and distinguished is, I will argue, arbitrary and unsustainable. Current international norms rely almost exclusively on three categories—minorities, national minorities, and indigenous peoples—and these categories cannot do the work that is required of them.

Second, there is the problem of conditions and sequencing. To state the obvious, liberal multiculturalism is easier to adopt where liberal democracy is already well established, and where the rule of law and human rights are well protected. In countries where these basic foundations of liberal democracy are not yet present or consolidated, some level of democratization and liberalization may be needed before it makes sense to push for the full implementation of liberal multiculturalism. Yet the problem of violent ethnic conflict, and the need to find paths to ethnic co-existence, is often most severe precisely in countries that are not consolidated democracies. Is the goal then to formulate norms that apply once a certain level of democratic consolidation has taken place, or is the goal to formulate norms that can help prevent or resolve ethnic conflict in countries with varying levels of democracy and freedom? International organizations have alternated between these two approaches—sometimes articulating the 'highest standards' of minority protection for a free and democratic society, sometimes articulating minimal rules of ethnic co-existence that can be expected of any country. Here again, this is not inherently a problem—any sensible approach to the governing of ethnic diversity will need to combine both long-term ideals and short-term prag-matic recommendations. But the particular way in which they have been combined is, I will argue, incoherent, and potentially counter-productive.

The inability of the international community to address these two prob-lems of categories and conditions reflects a third, even deeper, dilemma: namely, the relationship between justice and security. Implicit in current international norms and standards is a hopeful picture of a future where ethnic minorities and indigenous peoples are recognized as legitimate actors and equal partners in the governing of democratic societies. But this optimistic desire to create more space for a democratic multicultural politics is mixed with powerful fears that ethnic politics is too often a destabilizing force, undermining democracy and development, and hence needs to be contained if not suppressed. Is the goal to open up space for a vibrant democratic multiethnic politics, or is the goal to suppress and contain destabilizing ethnic mobilization? International organiza-tions alternate between these approaches, as indeed is appropriate, since both perspectives identify aspects of the complex reality of contemporary ethnic politics. But too often, security fears have driven out considerations of justice, distorting decisions about both categories and conditions, with results that are detrimental not only to justice, but also, paradoxically, for security.

On all of these issues, international organizations have made decisions that made sense at a particular point in time, as pragmatic responses to immediate challenges, but the cumulative result has been to create a structure of international norms that is unsustainable in the long term. There are no simple or risk-free solutions to any of these dilemmas. If current approaches sacrifice justice for short-term pragmatism, some of the proposed alternatives pose too high a risk to peace and security. The best way forward is not clear, an uncertainty that is not helped by the virtual absence of any serious academic discussion on these topics.[6]

---

[6] There is an impressive academic literature on most aspects of ethnic diversity and ethnic politics, but surprisingly little of it directly addresses the dilemmas international organizations face in formulating norms and standards. For example, there is a sophisticated literature within normative political theory on ideals of multicultural justice in consolidated

What is clear, however, is that the status quo is unsustainable in the long term. Indeed, the cracks are already showing. If we wish to preserve the experiment of internationalizing multiculturalism and minority rights, we need to think long and hard about what goals we are trying to achieve in this experiment, and what risks are worth taking in their pursuit.

* * * * *

The internationalization of multiculturalism is a vast topic, which I cannot hope to cover in all its complexity. So I need to say a few words about the specific focus of my arguments, and to define some key terms, in relation to both 'internationalization' and 'multiculturalism'. I have already talked loosely about 'international actors', 'international networks', 'international organizations', and even 'the international community', and readers may wonder what these nebulous terms refer to. In this book, my main focus is on international intergovernmental organizations (or 'IOs') established by treaties amongst the world's nation-states, either at the global level (such as the UN, the World Bank, the International Labour Organization) or at a regional level (Organization of American States, the European Union, the African Union), with a mandate to speak and act on behalf of their member-states. The decision of these international organizations to formulate norms and standards regarding ethnic diversity, and to use the various carrots and sticks at their disposal to promote certain models for governing diversity, is a fateful one, I believe, and raises the dilemmas and paradoxes I have just mentioned.

Of course, even if these IOs had not attempted to formulate norms and standards in this area, there would still be many informal channels by which models of multiculturalism would diffuse around the world.

liberal democracies, but it typically says nothing about how attempts to codify these norms should deal with problems of conditions and sequencing and security fears (see the literature cited in n. 3). Conversely, there is an equally impressive literature exploring the causes and possible solutions to violent ethnic conflict, including issues of peacebuilding and post-conflict reconstruction (for a good overview, see Wimmer et al 2004), but it typically says nothing about how international norms and standards should integrate these short-term strategies with long-term goals of multicultural justice. Within the field of international relations, a few political scientists have examined the efforts of international organizations to secure compliance with minority norms, but the focus has not been on how these norms were formulated, but rather on the tools used to promote them—e.g. whether these organizations have sought compliance through 'socialization' or 'conditionality' (e.g. Kelley 2004a, 2004b). The norms themselves are just taken as given. There is of course a voluminous international law literature on minority and indigenous rights (cited in n. 2), but it is remarkably insular, almost entirely disconnected from either the normative political theory debates about multiculturalism or the social science debates about ethnic politics (for a notable exception, see Knop 2002). As a result, none of these literatures systematically confronts the dilemmas involved in formulating international norms and standards on issues of ethnic diversity.

With or without the support of IOs, various actors in each country would scan the experience of other countries looking for relevant ideas and examples and potential allies, in ways that have been well studied in the 'policy transfer' literature (e.g. Weyland 2005; Stone 2004; Dolowitz and Marsh 1996, 2000; James and Lodge 2003). However, the fact that IOs are seen as speaking for 'the international community', and have a mandate to establish 'international norms', raises the moral and political stakes.

The claim that these IOs speak for 'the international community' is of course problematic. Indeed, the very term 'international community' is a misnomer, insofar as if conjures up an image of a world in which states have friendly relations with each other based on mutual respect and shared values. In reality, the world order is characterized by ideological cleavages, and by relations of mistrust and mutual antagonism if not exploitation, underpinned by dramatic inequalities of power and influence. Leaders of the UN may claim to speak on behalf of 'We the Peoples' (UN 2000), and to reflect the consensus of the world's societies and peoples. But the vast majority of the world's peoples have little or no say in shaping the UN's policies. The UN's activities and policies reflect asymmetries in global power, privileging the views and interests of the West. This is certainly true in the sphere of multiculturalism, where the emerging norms and standards are heavily shaped by Western experiences and expertise, with minimal input from the rest of the world. And, as we will see, in many parts of the world, norms that are advanced in the name of 'the international community' are resisted and resented as reflecting simply the prejudices or preoccupations of the West.

These global asymmetries have led some commentators to suggest that we should replace talk of the 'international community' with, say, 'Western powers', or even 'American hegemony'. On this view, IOs are essentially tools for advancing the geo-political interests of the most powerful (Western) states, not mechanisms for identifying and promoting the shared values of the world's peoples. And their diffusion of multiculturalism is, therefore, part of the 'cunning of imperialist reason' (Bourdieu and Wacquant 1999). But if it would be naïve to assume that the norms of multiculturalism adopted by IOs reflect some sort of authentic global consensus, it would equally be a mistake to treat them as merely the expression of Western hegemony. For one thing, Western states are themselves deeply divided over the merits of international norms of minority rights, and are not always in control of how these norms develop. For example, when the Draft Declaration on the Rights of Indigenous Peoples came to a vote at the UN's Human Rights Council (HRC) in July 2006, it was adopted with the support of developing countries over the objection of several Western countries including the United States, Canada, New Zealand, and Australia.[7]

While the multiculturalism-promotion policies of IOs do not reflect the values of a united 'international community',[8] nor are they simply ciphers for the foreign policy of a hegemonic country or power bloc. The fact is that IOs have often developed these norms for their own internal reasons, to fulfil their own mandates and advance their own institutional agendas. In many cases, IOs have been authorized or encouraged by their powerful member-states to 'do something' about ethnic diversity, often in response to some dramatic international event or crisis (such as the crisis in the Balkans in the early 1990s). But what they ended up doing about diversity was not pre-ordained. It was not inevitable that they would attempt to formulate norms and standards, or that these standards would use the categories and concepts that have recently emerged. IOs are constrained by larger geo-political realities, but within those constraints, they have significant room to respond to issues of ethnic diversity according to their own institutional logic. And this is reflected in the way different IOs have approached issues of diversity. The World Bank's approach to ethnic diversity is different, for example, from that of UNESCO, which is different again from that of the International Labour Organization, even though all are beholden to the same set of powerful member-states. While all of these organizations have moved to some extent in a more 'pro-multicultural' direction, they perceive the 'problem' of ethnic diversity in different ways, and hence offer different 'solutions', reflecting their different institutional mandates and bureaucratic cultures.

In a recent study, Michael Barnett and Martha Finnemore have shown that the autonomy of IOs has consistently been under-estimated by scholars and commentators, who treat their policies as simply the outcome of negotiations between their most powerful member-states (Barnett and Finnemore 2004). In reality, these policies are often the outcome of struggles within the organization itself, as staff attempt to make sense of

---

[7] Of these countries, only Canada was a voting member of the HRC, but it expressed its opposition in the name of all four countries.

[8] An apparent exception is the Declaration on the Rights of Persons Belonging to National or Ethnic, Religious and Linguistic Minorities, which was passed unanimously by the UN General Assembly in 1992, but this may reflect its toothless quality.

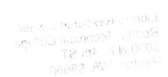

their mandate, defend their turf, and advance their careers and ideals. IOs not only help to determine what are acceptable solutions to the world's problems, they also help to define what these problems are in the first place, by developing the conceptual frameworks used to describe issues and to identify risks and opportunities.

The recent evolution of international norms and standards regarding ethnic diversity provides many examples of this dynamic. One example, which I will discuss at length in Chapter 7, is the dramatic variations in the way different IOs understand the category of 'indigenous peoples', and in the way they do or do not distinguish the rights of indigenous peoples from other types of ethnocultural groups. So far as I can tell, these decisions reflect each IO's internal priorities and procedures, rather than the diktat of powerful member-states. In fact, IOs appear to have had considerable autonomy to define their own position in relation to all three of the dilemmas I raised earlier—that is, how to categorize minorities and to combine generic and targeted rights; how to combine short-term conflict prevention with longer-term ideals; and how to integrate hopes for greater justice with fears of insecurity. None of these decisions was pre-ordained by forces outside of the respective IOs—they emerged from the way IOs themselves analysed the problem of ethnic diversity and framed possible solutions to it.

Unfortunately, I believe that IOs have often exercised their autonomy in ways that box them into moral conundrums and political dead-ends, complicating the prospects for the global diffusion of liberal multiculturalism. Or so I will argue in this book. I don't want to exaggerate the scope of this autonomy. Given the deep inequalities and antagonisms in the global order, there are structural limits to the extent to which IOs can serve as vehicles for progressive change, including on issues of ethnic diversity. But within these limits, IOs are influential international actors, with enough autonomy to make a significant contribution, for good or bad, to how issues of ethnic diversity are understood and resolved around the world.

While I have picked IOs as the primary focus for studying the internationalization of multiculturalism, these organizations do not make their decisions in isolation. In fact, they typically have relatively few people on staff with expertise in the relevant fields. Their efforts to identify and promote 'norms' and 'best practices' have therefore been heavily dependent on the participation of other actors. IOs recruit academics, think-tanks, philanthropic foundations, and professional advocacy groups to sit on advisory groups, serve as consultants, write working papers, and act as partners for joint projects and programmes.[9] These linkages have created what Kofi Annan calls 'global policy networks' (UN 2000), centred around IOs but extending into academia and civil society, working on a common set of problems with a common set of assumptions and goals. In fact, the interconnections and interdependence amongst these actors is so strong that it is often difficult to distinguish them. Distinctions between 'NGO officials', 'academics' and 'international bureaucrats' start to break down when we look at the actual individuals involved. Elites move between these different roles with surprising ease (or indeed occupy them simultaneously). In his study of the 'democracy-makers' in the United States (i.e. the main actors involved in shaping US policies of international democracy-promotion), Nicolas Guilhot shows that elites circulate freely between academia, philanthropic organizations, government agencies, and the boards of major NGOs (Guilhot 2005; cf. Dezalay and Garth 2002). To my knowledge, no one has conducted a similar study of the people shaping multiculturalism-promotion policies at the international level, but anecdotal evidence suggests a very similar pattern of elite circulation across the different types of international actors, from academia and civil society to IOs and back again.

In short, we can think of IOs as the spine of a larger network of actors who have been recruited to (or volunteered for) the project of formulating norms and standards regarding the governance of ethnic diversity. And if IOs have stumbled in their efforts—if they have mishandled questions of categories and conditions—at least part of the explanation is that they have received bad advice from this network of academics, advocates, and donors. Or perhaps more accurately, they have received short-sighted advice, focusing exclusively on immediate challenges, without much attention to underlying goals and long-term sustainability.

I hasten to add that I include myself in this critique. If not a card-carrying member of these global policy networks, I am at least a

---

[9] The role of philanthropic foundations is particularly interesting. For example, the World Bank's new programme to help the Roma minority in Eastern Europe (the 'Decade of Roma Inclusion') is a joint initiative with George Soros's Open Society Institute; the UN's efforts to promote anti-discrimination policies in Latin America have been supported by the Rockefeller Foundation, which has also publicized the work of the High Commissioner on National Minorities at the Organization of Security and Cooperation in Europe (OSCE); and so on. According to Alistair Bonnet, these foundations have played an important role in the diffusion of American-style models of anti-discrimination policies around the world (Bonnett 2006), and indeed have been more active proponents than the American government itself. A systematic study of how these foundations make decisions in this field would be very valuable. As this example suggests, their role is unlikely to offset any tendency of IOs to privilege Western experiences. Virtually all of the actors in this diffuse network—including the academic experts, NGOs, and philanthropic organizations—are Western-dominated.

fellow-traveller, and one motivation for this book is growing uncertainty about how I or other academics can best contribute to these international efforts. There have been instances when, in the hope of being constructive in the short term, I have found myself suppressing difficult questions about the underlying goals and long-term sustainability of the emerging framework of minority rights norms and standards. In the various meetings and workshops I've attended, I've often sensed an unspoken agreement to ignore the elephant under the table.

In fact, I remain hesitant to raise some of these worries, since this is not an auspicious time for advocates of the internationalization of multiculturalism. As we will see in Chapter 2, it was somewhat of an accident that IOs ever ventured down the road of formulating norms and standards regarding ethnic diversity, and there are many people who would welcome an excuse to cancel the experiment. After an initial period of optimism about the prospects for an ever-strengthening international regime of minority rights, most defenders now hope only to preserve the status quo, whatever its limitations. They worry that if we ask IOs to revisit the underlying goals and assumptions of their norms and standards, the result will be to weaken not strengthen them.[10] On this view, the status quo is as good as it gets, at least for the foreseeable future, and we should work for incremental improvements within it, rather than re-opening debates about the very categories and concepts being used.

As it happens, I share this pessimism about the likelihood of a fundamental rethinking of the international framework of minority rights. And if I thought that the status quo could in fact be maintained, I might continue to keep my worries to myself. The current framework of norms and standards has undoubtedly helped some historically marginalized groups, most notably indigenous peoples in Latin America, and more generally has helped to legitimize claims-making by ethnic groups as a normal and legitimate part of democratic politics. These are not insignificant achievements, and are worth defending. But I'm increasingly convinced that the status quo is not sustainable, and that we need to start thinking about how we will respond when the cracks emerge.

So when discussing the 'internationalization' of multiculturalism, I am focusing in the first instance on IOs that have been formulating norms and standards in the field of ethnic diversity, and secondarily on the affiliated global policy networks which help IOs in this endeavour. These IOs have a mandate to speak on behalf of their member-states, and in

---

[10] For examples, see p. 53 below.

that sense represent 'the international community'. If it would be naïve to take this claim at face value, it would equally be a mistake to ignore the significance of this claim. In Jeffrey Checkel's terminology, IOs are 'norm-makers', and countries around the world are expected to be 'norm-takers' (Checkel 1999), and this relationship is key to understanding the paradoxes of the new international politics of diversity.

A second clarification concerns my use of the term 'multiculturalism', and my claim that IOs are engaged in 'multiculturalism-promotion'. I am using multiculturalism as an umbrella term to cover a wide range of policies designed to provide some level of public recognition, support or accommodation to non-dominant ethnocultural groups, whether those groups are 'new' minorities (e.g. immigrant and refugees) or 'old' minorities (e.g. historically settled national minorities and indigenous peoples). This covers many different types of policies for different types of minority groups, and much of the book is concerned with examining how international norms address these differences. What they all have in common, however, is that they go beyond the protection of the basic civil and political rights guaranteed to all individuals in a liberal-democratic state, to also extend some level of public recognition and support for ethnocultural minorities to maintain and express their distinct identities and practices.

Several recent declarations and conventions adopted by IOs, as well as their lists of recommendations and best practices, promote multiculturalism in this sense. While they affirm the principle that individuals should not be discriminated against on the basis of their race or ethnicity, they go beyond this to also encourage policies that provide positive protection or promotion of ethnocultural diversity. If IOs simply wished to reaffirm the principle of non-discrimination, there would have been no need to adopt new declarations or conventions, since that principle is already clearly stated in several earlier international instruments, from the founding 1948 Universal Declaration on Human Rights to the 1966 International Convention on the Elimination of All Forms of Racial Discrimination. What these newer declarations and conventions add is some form of positive recognition of or support for ethnocultural diversity, which qualifies them as 'multicultural' on my definition of that term.

Admittedly, IOs themselves rarely use the term 'multiculturalism' in the texts of their norms and standards. They use a range of other terms, such as 'the protection and promotion of cultural diversity', the 'protection and promotion of minority and regional languages', the 'protection and promotion of the rights of persons belonging to national or ethnic, religious and linguistic minorities', the duty to 'recognize, accommodate, promote and strengthen the role of indigenous people', or to 'empower indigenous people and their communities', and so on. All of these are examples of multiculturalism, as I am using the term, even if IOs themselves do not use it.

One reason why IOs do not use the term 'multiculturalism' is that in many countries it has more limited connotations. In Europe, for example, 'multiculturalism' is often seen as a distinctly New World term that does not cover older European ideas of 'minority protection'. Even within the New World, 'multiculturalism' is sometimes used only in the context of immigrant groups, and does not cover policies towards indigenous peoples. (This is true, for example, in both New Zealand and Canada.) In Latin America, by contrast, 'multiculturalism' (or 'pluriculturalism') is almost exclusively used in reference to claims of indigenous peoples, rather than immigrant groups.

Given these diverse understandings of the term, using 'multiculturalism' as an umbrella term risks misunderstanding. It would be preferable to find a more widely shared umbrella term. Unfortunately, all of the alternatives run into similar difficulties. Some people, for example, use the term 'minority rights' to cover the claims of all non-dominant ethnocultural groups, whether new or old (as I myself did in earlier work). But that too has proven to be a contested term. For one thing, not all of the policies being promoted by IOs are easily captured in the language of 'rights'. Moreover, the term 'minorities' is problematic. In some countries, like the United Kingdom, the term 'minorities' is only used to refer to immigrant groups, not to older historic groups, such as the Scots or Welsh. In Austria, by contrast, the term 'minorities' is typically used to refer to historically settled groups, like the Slovenes, not to newly settled groups. And in many countries, indigenous peoples reject the term 'minorities', and prefer the term 'nations' or 'peoples', for reasons I discuss below.

Other scholars have suggested yet other options to serve as umbrella terms that can encompass the issues raised by different types of ethnocultural diversity—for example, 'diversity policies', 'cultural rights', 'community rights', 'group rights', 'differentiated citizenship', 'pluralist constitutionalism', 'liberal pluralism', to name but a few. All of these terms suffer from their own potential for misunderstandings, which I won't rehearse here, and in any event are even less commonly used by IOs than 'multiculturalism'. And so, in the absence of any commonly accepted alternative, I will stick with 'multiculturalism', despite its limitations. But I hope readers will keep in mind that I am using this solely as a shorthand umbrella term for a very wide range of policies adopted or demanded by many different types of ethnocultural groups, including 'immigrants', 'minorities', 'national' groups, and 'indigenous peoples'.

In fact, IOs themselves sometimes end up using multiculturalism in just this way. When the UN's Working Group on Minorities wanted to explore the implications of UN norms and standards for different types of ethnocultural groups in Africa, it organized a series of workshops called 'Multiculturalism in Africa'.[11] Similarly, when the United Nations Human Development Report issued its report on cultural diversity, looking at immigrants, substate national groups, and indigenous peoples, it summarized its recommendations as a call for 'multicultural democracy' (UNHDR 2004). In these and other cases, 'multiculturalism' is used by IOs as a kind of overarching label that incorporates the more specific policies directed at different types of minority groups, a usage I am following in this book.

For those who dislike the term, and who prefer another one, such as 'minority rights', 'diversity policies', 'interculturalism', 'cultural rights', or 'differentiated citizenship', feel free to substitute it as you go along. Nothing important rests on the label. What does matter, and what may be more controversial, is my claim that IOs are promoting a distinctly *liberal* form of multiculturalism and minority rights. By this, I mean not only that these norms operate within the constraints of human rights standards—that 'no one may invoke cultural diversity to infringe upon human rights guaranteed by international law', in the words of UNESCO quoted earlier—but also that these norms are inspired by underlying liberal values of freedom, equality, and democracy. Liberal multiculturalism rests on the assumption that policies of recognizing and accommodating ethnic diversity can expand human freedom, strengthen human rights, diminish ethnic and racial hierarchies, and deepen democracy.

This assumption was central to the way IOs formulated their norms and standards. To be sure, as we will see, IOs had other, more pragmatic, motives for 'doing something' about issues of ethnic diversity. But without a belief in the ideal of liberal multiculturalism, they would not have adopted the particular standards they did, and indeed might not have adopted 'norms' and 'standards' at all, as opposed to more flexible, case-by-case tools of ethnic conflict prevention and conflict resolution.

I believe that adopting multiculturalism can indeed contribute to freedom, equality, and democracy, as I will discuss in Chapters 4–5 below.

---

[11] See, for example, the 'Report on the Second Workshop on Multiculturalism in Africa', Kidal, Mali, 8–13 January 2001 (E/CN.4/Sub.2/AC.5/2001/3). See also UNESCO's *International Journal on Multicultural Societies*.

But the link between multiculturalism and these underlying values is not simple or risk-free. Much depends on the underlying conditions, the nature of the ethnic groups involved, and the types of policies being considered. To be effective, international norms and standards need to recognize and reflect this complexity. And this, in turn, requires grappling with the dilemmas I mentioned earlier—about the nature of the categories we are using, the conditions and sequencing of minority rights, and the relationship between justice and security.

* * * * *

The experiment in promoting liberal multiculturalism is a recent one—most of the relevant declarations and conventions have only been around for at most ten to fifteen years—and it may be too early to draw definitive conclusions about how well the experiment is going, or where it is heading. Some of the worries I raise in this book are, admittedly, speculative. But enough time has passed, I think, to make some preliminary assessments. And one lesson we can safely draw is that liberal multiculturalism has proven to be a tough sell.

The hard reality is that attempts by IOs to diffuse ideals of liberal multiculturalism beyond the Western democracies have had limited success to date. Outside of a small circle of activists and intellectuals, these efforts have largely fallen on deaf ears. In those few cases where post-colonial or post-communist states seem to have followed the advice of IOs to shift in a more multicultural direction, it has rarely been because state leaders have been convinced of the merits of the argument for liberal multiculturalism. Rather, IOs mobilized sufficiently powerful sanctions or incentives to compel these leaders to adopt policies they did not believe in. This is true, for example, of many of the pro-minority policies adopted by post-communist countries under pressure from European organizations. When IOs relied solely on powers of persuasion to promote liberal multiculturalism, they generally failed. They only gained traction when persuasion was backed up with the threat that post-communist countries would not gain entry into the European Union or NATO without meeting minority rights standards (Kelley 2004*a*).

As always, there are exceptions to this generalization—the international promotion of indigenous rights in some Latin American countries has been a more successful story, with multiculturalist (or 'interculturalist', as it is often called in the region) ideals diffusing more widely into the local political cultures. But in general, liberal multiculturalism has received a cool reception.

It was perhaps predictable that ideas of liberal multiculturalism would be resisted by state elites, who do not want to share their power with minorities. What is more striking, however, is how little support there is for such ideas within the liberal/democratic/reform opposition in many post-communist and post-colonial states, or within the civil society organizations that are supposed to provide the seed-bed for progressive reform. Even those social forces that one might have expected to be the natural allies of the international community in this field are often lukewarm about it, if not outright hostile.[12] The assumption that multiculturalism should be seen as an intrinsic part of a larger process of liberalization and democratization is simply not widely accepted in many countries.

Any plausible strategy for diffusing liberal multiculturalism needs to understand the sources of this scepticism and resistance. Unfortunately, an all-too-common response, particularly in the popular press but also in some academic and policy circles, has been to moralize and psychologize the situation. Resistance to multiculturalism is attributed to the persistence of pre-modern identities and attitudes of 'tribalism' (in Africa/Asia) or 'ethnic nationalism' (in post-communist Europe). On this view, the problem is that many societies lack the political sophistication to deal constructively with issues of diversity, and so cannot appreciate the merits of the models of multiculturalism that have emerged within 'mature' Western democracies. To remedy this perceived problem, programmes are established to teach the value of tolerance in the schools and media, to initiate cross-cultural and inter-faith dialogue and understanding, and more generally to promote modern (or post-modern) ideas of fluid, multiple and overlapping identities in place of (pre-modern) conceptions of a static and binary opposition between 'us' and 'the other'.

Not surprisingly, these programmes are often perceived by their intended beneficiaries as reflecting a condescending and paternalistic attitude towards non-Western societies and cultures, and so are resented and resisted. Moreover, they do not address the real problem. Opposition to liberal multiculturalism is not solely the result of prejudice, ignorance or xenophobia. The reality is that liberal multiculturalism has costs, and imposes risks, and these costs vary enormously both within and across societies. Multiculturalism not only challenges people's traditional

---

[12] NGOs that depend on foreign funding know that they are expected to use the buzz-words of diversity and tolerance, and obligingly comply. But this provides little indication of their actual attitudes towards issues of multiculturalism and minority rights. See Ditchev 2004 for the phenomenon of Bulgarian NGOs and government officials mimicking a commitment to multiculturalism for foreign donors while preserving 'monoculturalism as prevailing culture'.

understandings of their cultural and political identity, but also has potential implications for processes of democratization, economic development, respect for human rights, and even for geo-political security. Liberal multiculturalism, in some times and places, can be a high-risk choice. It is these implications, and not simply an irrational attachment to pre-modern identities, which underpins much of the opposition to liberal multiculturalism in post-colonial and post-communist states.

The current strategies of the international community for diffusing liberal multiculturalism do not adequately address these concerns. As a result, several aspects of the political discourses and legal norms being promoted by the international community appear naïve, arbitrary, and even dangerous to many people in post-colonial and post-communist states. The standard arguments given in favour of liberal multiculturalism—often little more than platitudes about the value of diversity and tolerance—simply do not connect with people's perceptions of the potential risks and costs involved in the management of state–minority relations.

One reason why the international community has failed to adequately address these anxieties about the risks of liberal multiculturalism is that insufficient attention has been paid to how these anxieties have been addressed in the West. Insofar as multiculturalism has taken (uneven) root in the West, it is not because Westerners have some distinctive moral virtue of tolerance, or some sophisticated understanding of the nature of their cultural and political identities. Rather, as we will see in Chapter 4, a fortunate set of circumstances has lowered the risks of liberal multiculturalism, allowing Western countries to frame and channel ethnic politics in a way that is compatible with the robust protection and promotion of democracy, economic prosperity, human rights and regional security. Multiculturalism is never entirely risk-free, but where these fortunate circumstances exist, it becomes '*la belle risque*'—a modest and manageable risk worth taking in the pursuit of a fairer and more inclusive society.

A more honest account of the origins of liberal multiculturalism in the West—one which focuses less on alleged civic virtues or mature attitudes and more on contingent circumstances—would help us better understand the obstacles to its global diffusion, and perhaps design more constructive ways of overcoming them. Such an account would also help us understand and address the lingering opposition to liberal multiculturalism within the West. After all, liberal multiculturalism is still perceived as a high-risk venture in some Western countries, at least with respect to certain types of ethnic diversity, and has been subject to periods of backlash and retreat. This suggests that the emergence and consolidation of liberal multiculturalism is always a contingent and somewhat fragile achievement. Sustaining the political will and public support for liberal multiculturalism, in the West or elsewhere, depends on our ability to carefully attend to these risks, real or perceived, and to find ways of mitigating them.

In short, the long-term success of the global diffusion of multiculturalism requires a more nuanced understanding of the social and political conditions that sustain and enable different models of state–minority relations, and how these conditions vary across time and space. Both the political discourses of liberal multiculturalism and the international legal norms of minority rights need to be grounded in a more realistic political sociology. This will almost certainly require changes not only in the way liberal multiculturalism is described and promoted internationally, but also in our expectations about what forms or aspects of liberal multiculturalism are genuinely appropriate and relevant in different parts of the world.

Some commentators think these sorts of changes will emerge spontaneously. The international community's commitment to diversity is relatively recent, and we can already see a process at work of 'filling the frame', as various actors and institutions start to learn what sorts of discourses and norms are effective under what conditions, and as precedents are established that fill gaps and resolve ambiguities and inconsistencies.[13]

My own view, however, is that these difficulties will not spontaneously sort themselves out. Any attempt to address them will require a number of difficult and controversial decisions about the nature and purpose of multicultural policies and minority rights, and about the role of international organizations in protecting them. While a wide range of IOs have adopted the discourse of multiculturalism, this common rhetoric conceals deep disagreements about how issues of ethnic diversity relate to issues of human rights, democratization, and development. Given these disagreements, and the ineffectiveness of existing discourses and norms, the long-term prognosis may not be a filling of the frame, but rather an

---

[13] For the 'filling the frame' analogy, see Weller 2003. This Whiggish interpretation of the evolution of minority rights norms is implicit in most discussions by international lawyers on these issues. See, for example, Henrard's discussion of the 'ever-increasing synergy towards a stronger level of minority protection' between human and minority rights norms (Henrard 2005).

emptying of the frame, as international organizations retreat from the project of internationalizing multiculturalism. As we will see below, there are hints of such a retreat already.

This suggests we are at a critical point in the evolution of the internationalization of multiculturalism. If we are to achieve the progressive potential inherent in this process, we need to move beyond platitudes about the value of 'diversity' and 'tolerance' and examine hard questions about how different aspects of liberal multiculturalism relate to issues of democratization, human rights, development, and regional security, both in the West and elsewhere. On this basis, we might be able to identify more realistic and consistent norms and practices of liberal multiculturalism for global diffusion. Otherwise, we are likely to witness the gradual abandonment of the bold but sometimes bewildering fifteen-year experiment in internationalizing multiculturalism.

* * * * *

My aim in this book is not to provide a detailed blueprint for the future, but rather to explore the current process of internationalizing multiculturalism, and to identify the difficult challenges and choices it is raising for us. To that end, I begin in the next chapter by discussing why the international community has become so concerned with trying to shape state–minority relations, particularly in the post-Cold War era. As we will see, this is partly the result of a pessimistic view of the dangers that ethnic politics can pose to peace and stability in post-communist and post-colonial states, combined with an equally optimistic view about the way that liberal multiculturalism has helped pacify and normalize ethnic politics in much of the West. The various ideas of 'best practices' and 'legal norms' developed by the international community in the past fifteen years reflect this somewhat unstable mix of fear and hope.

In Part II, I explore the hopeful side of the equation, by unpacking the logic of liberal multiculturalism. I identify the different forms that liberal multiculturalism has taken in the West, and defend the view that multiculturalist policies have indeed helped to pacify ethnic politics, and to deepen democracy and strengthen human rights. However, I also argue that their success in this regard has depended on a number of very special conditions relating to democratic consolidation, the human rights revolution, and geo-political security. The uneven and/or fragile nature of these conditions helps to explain the varying record of liberal multiculturalism for different groups in different Western countries.

In Part III, I explore how fears of destabilizing ethnic conflict in post-colonial and post-communist states have motivated IOs to become more involved in the field of state–minority relations, and in particular to promote liberal multiculturalism. It was always clear that the details of particular Western models of liberal multiculturalism could not simply be transplanted into other countries with very different histories, demographics, and institutional structures. So the task has been to try to identify more general aspects of liberal multiculturalism—its underlying ethos, principles, or strategies—and on this basis to formulate lessons that are potentially universalizable. This has proven to be an exceptionally difficult task, and the results often reflect a paradoxical mix of pessimism and optimism. At times, the international community promotes a naïve, almost utopian, ethos of liberal multiculturalism that tells citizens not to fear ethnic diversity. On the other hand, the international community itself is powerfully driven by the fear of destabilizing ethnic conflict, and this has influenced how it defines the categories of minorities that are entitled to claim different kinds of rights, and the conditions under which they are entitled to claim them. In order to prevent ethnic politics from 'getting out of control', the international community has attempted to limit and constrain the 'legitimate' forms of multiculturalism in ways that do not always reflect, and may indeed contradict, the principles of liberal multiculturalism. To some extent this was inevitable and appropriate, given that the circumstances which enabled the adoption of liberal multiculturalism in the West do not yet exist in many post-communist and post-colonial states. But the unintended result has been a schizophrenic approach to ethnic political mobilization, simultaneously affirming and discouraging minority claims, generating a raft of inconsistencies, double-standards, and perverse effects. And these, in turn, are generating the perception in much of the world that the international promotion of liberal multiculturalism lacks any principled foundation.

I explore these tensions in two main contexts: the attempt by IOs to develop norms and standards regarding the treatment of 'national minorities' in Europe, particularly by the Council of Europe and the Organization for Security and Cooperation in Europe (Chapter 6); and the attempt by IOs to develop norms and standards regarding the treatment of 'indigenous peoples' at a global level, particularly by the United Nations, the World Bank, and the International Labour Organization (Chapter 7). In both cases, I will argue that initial successes are at risk because of the failure to grapple with the underlying dilemmas about categories, conditions, and goals.

I conclude with some tentative suggestions about how to re-conceive the global diffusion of liberal multiculturalism. I do not think these difficulties can be entirely resolved, but they can be more successfully managed, partly by rethinking the roles of different international actors in promoting liberal multiculturalism, and partly by rethinking the substantive content of the discourses and norms being promoted. We need changes in both the message and the messengers.

I remain convinced that liberal multiculturalism is the best hope for building just and inclusive societies around the world, and that its diffusion cannot be achieved without the assistance of international organizations. Just for that reason, it is important to step back and make sure that the enormous efforts invested by the international community in this field in the last fifteen years are still on course.

2

The Shifting International Context: From Post-War Universal Human Rights to Post-Cold War Minority Rights

The recent wave of international activity in the field of minority rights rests on a simple but striking assumption—namely, that issues regarding the treatment of minorities are 'matters of legitimate international concern and consequently do not constitute exclusively an internal affair of the respective State'.[1] This assumption has been stated explicitly by several international organizations since 1990 to justify the formulation of new norms and monitoring mechanisms.

I will discuss the details of some of these norms and mechanisms below, but the first task is to explore this underlying assumption. Why is the treatment of minorities a matter of 'legitimate international concern'? Why aren't state–minority relations 'exclusively an internal affair', a domestic matter to be resolved in accordance with each state's own traditions or priorities? Of course, few people would argue that there should be no limits whatsoever on how states treat minorities. Even before the new wave of minority rights norms, there were already prohibitions on gross violations of human rights such as genocide, ethnic cleansing, and racial discrimination. But if a country meets these minimal standards, why is there a legitimate international interest in formulating additional minority rights standards? Why does the international community care whether countries adopt assimilationist or multiculturalist models of nationhood and citizenship?

The claim that the international community has a legitimate interest in the treatment of minorities is sometimes described as a dramatic break

---

[1] Report of the OSCE, Meeting of Experts on National Minorities (Geneva, 19 July 1991), Section II, para. 3 (<http://www.osce.org/item/14125.html>).

with tradition, reversing the long-standing assumption that states should have a relatively free rein to manage ethnic diversity as they see fit. In reality, however, the international community has always been acutely aware of 'the minority problem', and concerned that it be managed properly. Disaffected minorities have been a source of conflict since the mid-nineteenth century, and the struggles of secessionist and irredentist minorities have repeatedly redrawn the map of Europe, often in violent and destabilizing ways. Awareness of this fact has never been far from the surface in the mind of the international community. When Woodrow Wilson in 1919 said 'Nothing, I venture to say, is more likely to disturb the peace of the world than the treatment which might in certain circumstances be meted out to minorities', he was repeating commonly accepted wisdom.[2]

What has changed over time is the way this 'minority problem' is conceptualized, and hence the proposed remedies. We need to understand these changes if we want to make sense of the current activities of the international community, and the dilemmas it has run into. As we will see, historical legacies are profoundly shaping how contemporary conflicts are addressed.

The Post-War Settlement

For the first few decades of the twentieth century, the 'minority problem' was seen primarily as an issue of irredentist minorities. As the Habsburg, Russian, and Ottoman multination empires in Europe broke apart into several newly independent countries, the 'minority problem' focused on those people who ended up on the 'wrong' side of a new international border—for example, the ethnic Hungarians who found themselves in Romania; or the ethnic Germans who found themselves living in Poland.

In response to this problem, bilateral treaties were established to ensure reciprocal protection of co-nationals in neighbouring countries. For example, Germany agreed to accord certain rights and privileges to ethnic Poles residing within its borders, so long as Poland provided reciprocal rights to ethnic Germans in Poland. This treaty system of minority protection was extended, and given a more secure international legal basis, under the League of Nations.

---

[2] Quoted in Krasner 1999: 93.

However, after World War II, this approach was decisively rejected. For one thing, it only protected minorities who had a 'kin-state' nearby which took an interest in them. Moreover, the treaties were potentially destabilizing, because where such kin-states did exist, they could invoke the treaty to justify invading or intervening in weaker countries. For example, Nazi Germany justified its invasion of Poland and Czechoslovakia on the grounds that these countries were violating the treaty rights of ethnic Germans on their soil.

So as the foundations for a new international order were being built after World War II, an alternate approach was adopted. This new approach was to substitute universal human rights for minority-specific rights. Rather than protecting vulnerable groups directly, through special rights for the members of designated groups, minorities would be protected indirectly, by guaranteeing basic civil and political rights to all individuals regardless of their group membership. Basic human rights such as freedom of speech, association, and conscience, while attributed to individuals, are exercised in community with others, and so provide protection for a minority's group life. Where these individual human rights are firmly protected, it was felt, no further minority-specific rights are needed. Inis Claude nicely captured the thinking involved:

the general tendency of the postwar movements for the promotion of human rights has been to subsume the problem of national minorities under the broader problem of ensuring basic individual rights to all human beings, without reference to membership in ethnic groups. The leading assumption has been that members of national minorities do not need, are not entitled to, or cannot be granted rights of a special character. The doctrine of human rights has been put forward as a substitute for the concept of minority rights, with the strong implication that minorities whose members enjoy individual equality of treatment cannot legitimately demand facilities for the maintenance of their ethnic particularism. (Claude 1955: 211)

In short, the very idea of 'minority rights' was discredited after World War II, on the grounds that it was both unnecessary and destabilizing. In a few short years, minority rights virtually disappeared from the international vocabulary. As Jozef Kunz put it in a famous quote from 1954,

At the end of the First World War international protection of minorities was the great fashion: treaties in abundance, conferences, League of Nations activists, an enormous literature. Recently, this fashion has become nearly obsolete. Today, the well dressed international lawyer wears 'human rights'. (Kunz 1954: 282)

As a result, there were no references to minority rights in either the Charter of the United Nations, or the Universal Declaration of Human Rights of 1948.[3] And this silence was replicated in various post-war regional charters of human rights, whether in Europe (e.g. the European Convention on Human Rights of 1950), the Americas (e.g. the American Declaration of the Rights and Duties of Man of 1948, or the American Convention on Human Rights of 1969), or Africa (e.g. the African Charter on Human and Peoples' Rights of 1981).

The construction of a system of universal human rights under the UN is one of the great moral achievements of the twentieth century, inspired and pursued by moral visionaries, and committed to attacking the prejudice and intolerance that have poisoned ethnic relations around the world (Glendon 2001). But in relation to minority issues, the post-war replacement of targeted minority rights with universal human rights was not only, and perhaps not primarily, the result of moral idealism or a sincere desire to find an alternative means of protecting minorities. It also reflected a desire to control and disempower minorities. As Claude notes, the Nazi manipulation of the League of Nations system of minority protection, and the willing cooperation of German minorities in it, had created 'a strong reaction against the concept of international protection [of minorities] . . . the hard fact was that statesmen, generally backed by a public opinion which was deeply impressed by the perfidy of irredentist and disloyal minorities, were disposed to curtail, rather than to expand, the rights of minorities' (Claude 1955: 57, 69, 81). For post-war statesmen, it was essential to find an approach that would weaken the capacity of minorities to challenge state power, either domestically or internationally (Jackson Preece 1998: 43). This meant denying minorities any international standing, and also undermining the domestic institutional basis on which minorities had historically sustained themselves as cohesive communities and organized to contest for state power. The human rights approach seemed to fit the bill: it protected the members of minority groups as individuals, but did not protect their institutions, and so disempowered them as collective actors.

It was well understood in Europe at the time that the human rights approach would not give minorities what they needed to be able to

---

[3] According to Morsink, there was some support for including minority rights in the UN's 1948 Convention against Genocide, which was being negotiated at the same time as the UDHR, and indeed minority rights were only left out of the genocide convention on the expectation that they would be included in the UDHR. But in the end, they were left out of the UDHR as well (Morsink 1999).

maintain their languages and cultures, such as the right to use their language in public institutions (schools, courts, or public media), or to exercise some form of local or regional autonomy. Without these minority rights, centuries-old communities and regional cultures would be unable to resist the nation-building and assimilationist policies of the larger state. For some people, the fact that human rights norms did not protect minorities from this long-term assimilationist outcome was a regrettable limitation, but for many others it was in fact an important virtue. The experience of the League of Nations, it was felt, showed that the needs of minorities must be subordinated to the larger interest 'in making the national state secure, and its institutions stable, even at the cost of obliterating minority cultures and imposing homogeneity upon the population' (Claude 1955: 80–1). In short, it was *raison d'état*, as much as moral principle, which determined the rejection of pre-war traditions of minority rights.

The Rebirth of Minority Rights

Whatever its underlying rationale, this opposition to the idea of international norms of minority rights held sway for most of the next forty years, despite periodic attempts by some countries (particularly in the Soviet bloc) to revive the idea. Starting in the 1980s, however, attitudes started to change. At the global level within the United Nations, these changes have followed two tracks: there is one track for the specific case of 'indigenous peoples', and another track for 'minorities' in general.

Let me start with the indigenous track. In one sense, indigenous peoples have always had a unique standing within international law.[4] Even in the heyday of the post-war opposition to any idea of group-specific minority rights, there was still some acknowledgement of the special status of indigenous peoples. This was reflected, for example, in the International Labour Organization's Convention 107 on the 'Protection and Integration of Indigenous and Tribal Populations', adopted in 1957. This was the clearest exception to the post-war rule that international law would not recognize any rights based on group membership. However, it was the exception that proved the rule. The Convention endorsed certain special

---

[4] For helpful overviews, see Anaya 1996 and Keal 2003, who both point out the central role that the European conquest of indigenous peoples had in shaping the historical evolution of international law.

measures for indigenous people, but only as temporary paternalistic protections for a vulnerable population that was seen as unable to cope with the rigours of modern life, until such time as they were ready to stand on their own as equal and undifferentiated national citizens. For example, Article 3 of the Convention states:

1. So long as the social, economic and cultural conditions of the [indigenous and tribal] populations concerned prevent them from enjoying the benefits of the general laws of the country to which they belong, special measures shall be adopted for the protection of the institutions, persons, property and labour of these populations.

2. Care shall be taken to ensure that such special measures of protection—

   (a) are not used as a means of creating or prolonging a state of segregation; and

   (b) will be continued only so long as there is need for special protection and only to the extent that such protection is necessary.

There is no suggestion here that states have a duty to recognize indigenous peoples as historic societies and self-governing communities, or to accommodate their pre-existing cultural, legal, and political institutions and traditions. Rather, the goal was to encourage the adaptation and assimilation of indigenous peoples to the pre-existing institutions of the nation-state. In that sense, it actually fitted quite well with the standard post-war orthodoxy.

However, by the 1980s, attitudes towards the rights of indigenous peoples started to change. The paternalistic and assimilationist premises of the ILO's 1957 Convention became an embarrassment, and a decision was made to redraft it, resulting eventually in a new ILO Convention on indigenous peoples adopted in 1989 (Convention 169). In the preamble to this new Convention, drafted in cooperation with the United Nations, the ILO stated that the time had come to adopt new international standards with a view to 'removing the assimilationist orientation of the earlier standards', and to 'recognizing the aspirations of these peoples to exercise control over their own institutions'. The new Convention covered a gamut of rights that were seen as specific to indigenous peoples, including land claims, language rights, and customary law.

This was perhaps the first real example of a 'multiculturalist' international norm in the post-war era, unambiguously accepting the principle of positive, group-specific rights (Rodriguez-Pinero 2005). But this

Convention quickly became seen as an inadequate articulation of the rights of indigenous peoples, and there has been further norm-setting at the United Nations. A crucial text here is the Draft Declaration on the Rights of Indigenous Peoples, formulated in 1993, and slowly working its way through the process of gaining state approval. The Draft Declaration not only reaffirms and strengthens the ILO Convention's defence of indigenous rights regarding land, language, and customary law, but also asserts that indigenous peoples have a right to internal self-determination (i.e. to extensive self-government within the boundaries of the larger state, although not to 'external self-determination' or secession). Any reference to self-determination is notoriously sensitive in the international arena, even if secession is expressly ruled out, and it is unclear whether or when the Draft Declaration will be formally approved by the UN General Assembly. Arguably, though, it only makes explicit what is already implicit in the 1989 ILO Convention, and these core ideas have rapidly diffused throughout the international community. We see echoes of the Draft Declaration, for example, in the norms on indigenous peoples adopted by the United Nations Development Program,[5] the World Bank,[6] the UN Human Rights Committee,[7] the UN Committee on the Elimination of Racial Discrimination,[8] UNESCO,[9] and recent UN World Conferences (e.g. the 1993 World Conference on Human Rights in Vienna, or the 2001 World Conference Against Racism in Durban).[10]

Moreover, the UN has established a raft of specialized instruments for monitoring and addressing the rights of indigenous peoples, including the declaration of the International Decade of Indigenous Peoples from

[5] See 'UNDP and Indigenous Peoples: A Practice Note on Engagement', which specifically mentions indigenous claims to 'self-determination' as an issue for the UNDP (<http://www.undp.org/cso/resource/policies/IPPolicyEnglish>).

[6] See the World Bank's Operational Policy 4.10 on Indigenous Peoples (2005). <http://www.worldbank.org/indigenouspeoples>

[7] When countries report to the Human Rights Committee on their implementation of the ICCPR, they often discuss the rights of indigenous peoples under Article 27's 'right to culture'. But the HRC responds by encouraging states to explain whether or how they are fulfilling indigenous peoples' Article 1 right to self-determination—see, for example, the HRC's Concluding Observation on Russia's Periodic Report (UN Doc. E/C.12/1/Add.50, September 2000, para. 10), and the discussion in Wheatley 2005: 118–19.

[8] See Committee on the Elimination of Racial Discrimination, 'General Recommendation XXIII' on the rights of indigenous peoples (1997) GR XIII (51) HRI/GEN/1/Rev.5. The International Convention on the Elimination of all Forms of Racial Discrimination, adopted in 1965, did not itself refer to indigenous peoples, but the Monitoring Committee has interpreted it to cover indigenous rights, and the World Conference Against Racism in 2001 also affirmed this connection between fighting racial discrimination and protecting indigenous rights.

[9] See UNESCO's 'Universal Declaration on Cultural Diversity', 2001, paras 4–5.

[10] See 'Vienna Declaration and Programme of Action', World Conference on Human Rights, Part 1, para. 20; Part 2, paras 28–32 (A/CONF.157/23 (1993)).

1995 to 2004; the appointment of a Special Rapporteur on the Situation of Human Rights and Fundamental Freedoms of Indigenous People in 2001, the creation of an Inter-Agency Support Group on Indigenous Issues in 2002; and the creation of the Permanent Forum on Indigenous Issues in 2003.

In short, in the context of indigenous peoples, we see a clear trend towards recognizing the necessity for certain targeted rights, although the content of these rights remains contested, particularly in relation to natural resources and political governance. This trend is often said to be 'unique' and 'exceptional'—an anomaly in the international system adopted in response to the specific needs of isolated populations, without any implications for the treatment of minorities generally. On this view, the post-war ground rules, based on universal human rights rather than minority-specific rights, remain unchanged for all other ethnocultural groups. This is a perception that is sometimes promoted by indigenous peoples themselves and their advocates, who assert that the status of indigenous peoples has nothing in common with the claims of 'minorities', and that the ideology of 'indigenism' has no connection with more general theories of 'multiculturalism'.[11]

It is certainly true that the rapid acceptance of the idea of targeted indigenous rights is partly explained by the perception that indigenous peoples are a relatively small and somewhat exceptional case that doesn't set a precedent for other ethnocultural minorities.[12] But the fact is that the shift towards a more 'difference-friendly' approach has not been restricted to indigenous peoples. There have been important developments along a second track focusing on minorities in general that have changed the ground rules for the treatment of all ethnocultural groups.

The reference point for this more general shift is a provision of the UN's International Covenant of Civil and Political Rights (ICCPR) of 1966. Article 27 of the ICCPR states:

In those States in which ethnic, religious or linguistic minorities exist, persons belonging to such minorities shall not be denied the right, in community with the other members of their group, to enjoy their own culture, to profess and practise their own religion, or to use their own language.[13]

---

[11] On 'indigenism' within the international community, see Niezen 2003.

[12] As we will see later, this perception may be mistaken, since the category of 'indigenous peoples' has been expanding to include a wider range of groups in more parts of the world.

[13] A similar clause appears in the UN's Convention on the Rights of the Child (1989), Article 30.

When originally drafted, this article was not necessarily intended to provide any tangible minority-specific rights, as opposed to simply reaffirming the commitment to universal human rights. It can be read as calling on states to ensure that the members of minority groups have the same civil liberties as all other citizens, particularly freedom of speech, freedom of association, and freedom of conscience. As such, it can be seen as essentially an anti-discrimination provision, and in that sense duplicated other provisions in international human rights laws that prohibit discrimination in civil liberties on the basis of race or ethnicity.[14]

However, as occurred in the context of indigenous peoples, attitudes towards the rights of minorities started to change in the 1980s, and Article 27 has gradually been reinterpreted to encompass positive minority rights. This is partly due to some creative jurisprudence by the UN's Human Rights Committee. In its 'General Comment on Article 27', released in 1994, it argued that the Article not only imposes a duty of non-discrimination in the protection of civil liberties, but also may require adopting 'positive measures' to enable and accommodate the minority's exercise of this right to enjoy their culture.[15] This idea was reaffirmed by the UN General Assembly in 1992 when it adopted a Declaration on the Rights of Persons Belonging to National or Ethnic, Religious and Linguistic Minorities. The Preamble to this Declaration asserts that it is inspired by Article 27, but subtly rewords the key phrases to make it clear that they impose positive obligations to enable minorities to be able to enjoy their culture, and not simply the negative duty to respect civil liberties in a non-discriminatory manner.[16]

---

[14] As is usually the case, the wording of this Article reflects a compromise amongst a wide range of views. Some delegates hoped that Article 27 would provide positive rights to minorities, but interpreted the category of 'minorities' narrowly, to refer primarily or exclusively to the kin-state minorities in Europe that had been the subject of the earlier League of Nations scheme. On this view, there were no 'minorities' in the Americas or in post-colonial states, since neither immigrants nor indigenous peoples fit the traditional European conception. Others argued that the category of minorities should be interpreted more broadly, but that Article 27 should be interpreted as simply guaranteeing non-discrimination for such minorities. The wording of Article 27 was (deliberately) ambiguous between these interpretations. For the history underlying the drafting of Article 27, see Thornberry 1991, chap. 15.

[15] Human Rights Committee, 'General Comment 23, The Rights of Minorities (Article 27)', 8 April 1994. Report of the Human Rights Committee, Vol. 1, GAOR, 49th Session, Supplement No. 40 (A/49/40), pp. 107–10.

[16] Interestingly, the main example given of such positive measures concerns the claim of indigenous peoples to ancestral land. See para. 3.2 of General Comment 23 (cited in previous note), and the case of *Kitok v Sweden* (Communication No. 197/1985, reprinted in Philips and Rosas 1995: 286–97). Although the HRC states clearly that the duty of states to positively support the right to enjoy one's culture applies to minorities as such, not just indigenous

This shift is further reflected in the creation of various minority-specific procedures and institutions, such as the establishment of the UN Working Group on Minorities in 1995 under the Sub-Commission on Human Rights of the Human Rights Commission; and the appointment of a UN Independent Expert on Minority Issues in 2005. These reflect the recognition that there is a need to supplement traditional difference-blind human rights norms with minority-specific provisions.

In short, we see developments along two separate tracks at the UN: there is one track for 'minorities' in general, grounded primarily in a 'right to enjoy one's culture', and a separate track for 'indigenous peoples', grounded primarily in a right to (internal) self-determination. This distinction resurfaces in many recent international documents. I will return several times to this important but complicated distinction, which is drawn in different ways for different purposes by different international organizations. But for the moment, the key point is that in both tracks, there is increasing acceptance of the need for some provisions aimed specifically at the needs and aspirations of ethnocultural groups.

This increased acceptance of minority rights is not limited to the UN. We see important developments at the regional level as well, during roughly the same time period, particularly in Europe. Much of Europe today is consumed by an anti-immigrant backlash, and so may not seem like a propitious environment for the development of difference-friendly international norms. But in the European context, it is common to distinguish 'historic minorities', traditionally settled in a country, from 'new minorities' or 'migrants'. The category of historic minorities in Europe includes some groups that are considered as 'indigenous peoples' (such as the Sami in Scandinavia) as well as other long-standing 'national minorities', such as the ethnic Germans in Poland, or the Scots in Britain. It is in relation to these historic 'national minorities' that important developments regarding pan-European norms have taken place.[17]

The idea of a minority rights charter for historic minorities was first debated in the European Parliament in the 1980s, without success (Toggenburg 2004: 5). But since 1990, three of the most powerful European intergovernmental organizations have taken up the cause and made firm minority rights commitments: namely, the Council of Europe, the

peoples, it has in fact been very reluctant to specify what these positive duties might be outside the case of indigenous peoples.

[17] The question of how to distinguish these historic 'national' minorities from 'new' minorities or immigrants—or indeed whether it is appropriate to do so—is a matter of intense controversy, to which I will return in Chapter 6.

main body for promoting human rights and democracy in Europe; the European Union, the locus of European economic integration; and the Organization for Security and Cooperation in Europe (OSCE), a security organization originally set up to defuse tensions during the Cold War, and now more generally focused on maintaining peace and preventing conflict.

The OSCE was the first European body to make an official declaration on minority rights, in its Copenhagen Document of 1990 and the Geneva Document of 1991. It also established the office of the High Commissioner On National Minorities in 1993, and developed a series of important Recommendations relating to minority rights in the sphere of education (1996), language (1998), effective participation (1999), and broadcasting (2003).[18]

Based in part on these OSCE norms, the Council of Europe adopted a European Charter for Regional or Minority Languages in 1992, a Framework Convention for the Protection of National Minorities in 1995, and has subsequently established an Advisory Committee to monitor its implementation, and a 'Committee of Experts on Issues Relating to the Protection of National Minorities'.[19]

The European Union, for its part, declared in 1993 that respect for minority rights was one of the 'accession criteria' that countries (particularly post-communist countries) needed to meet if they wished to join the Union, and issued a series of annual reports assessing how well candidate countries were performing on minority rights issues. In 1994, the EU Parliament also passed a resolution on linguistic and cultural minorities in the European Community, and established the European Bureau for Lesser Used Languages (EBLUL). And in 2004, minority rights were listed as one of the foundational values of the EU in Article 2 of

---

[18] See the Hague Recommendations Regarding the Education Rights of National Minorities (1996); the Oslo Recommendations Regarding the Linguistic Rights of National Minorities (1998); the Lund Recommendations on the Effective Participation of National Minorities in Public Life (1999); and the Guidelines on the Use of Minority Languages in the Broadcast Media (2003) (available at <http://www.osce.org>). The OSCE has also developed specialized instruments for dealing with Roma issues, in particular the Contact Point for Roma and Sinti Issues in 1994.

[19] The Council of Europe has also established specialized instruments to address the particular needs of the Roma minority, including the appointing of a Coordinator for Roma Issues in 1994; the formation of a Specialist Group on Roma, Gypsies and Travellers in 1995; and the establishment of the European Roma and Travellers Forum in 2004. For its part, the Parliamentary Assembly of the Council of Europe, not content with these norms and structures, has established its own Sub-Committee on the Rights of Minorities in 2005, as well as passing a number of Recommendations on the issue, including Recommendation 1492 in 2000 and Recommendation 1623 in 2003, both aimed at strengthening the rights of national minorities.

its (ill-fated) draft Constitution. The EU has also adopted special exemptions for the indigenous Sami peoples within the EU, and declared that respect for indigenous rights will be one of the conditions for developing countries to receive EU development aid.[20]

While Europe has seen the most active developments at the regional level, there have also been developments in other regions. In the Americas, a Proposed Declaration on the Rights of Indigenous Peoples was drafted by the Inter-American Commission on Human Rights in 1997, and the Inter-American Development Bank is working on an Operational Policy on Indigenous Peoples. In Africa, the African Commission on Human and Peoples' Rights endorsed the idea of drafting a declaration on the rights of indigenous peoples in 2003. And in Asia, the Asian Development Bank adopted a regional version of the World Bank's norms on indigenous peoples in 1998.

I could go on for several pages listing all of the international organizations involved in this field, and the alphabet soup of working groups, agencies, declarations, and conventions they have created. I will discuss the details of some of these later in the book, and some of the conceptual puzzles and political obstacles they have run into.

But enough has been said, I hope, to give an indication of the incredible scale and pace of these changes. For almost forty years after World War II, the issue of minority rights was essentially invisible within the international community. But it re-emerged in the 1980s, and reached the top of the UN and European agendas in the early 1990s, leading to a flurry of studies, negotiations, and drafts, the results of which have gradually become institutionally consolidated and diffused around the world over the past fifteen years.

Moreover, this shift has not been limited to one small sector or dimension of the international community. It is perhaps not surprising that a UN organization like UNESCO, whose mandate is to protect the cultural heritage of humankind, would be sympathetic to the claims of indigenous peoples and ethnocultural minorities whose languages and cultures are under threat.[21] But the discourse of multiculturalism is equally found in

---

[20] For the internal exemptions, see the Sami protocol included as part of the accession agreements signed by Finland, Sweden, and Norway (OJ 1994 C41). For the external policies, see the European Union Council Resolution of 30 November 1998 on Indigenous Peoples within the Framework of the Development Cooperation of the Community and the Member States.

[21] If anything, UNESCO has been a follower not a leader in this area. Until recently, UNESCO was as unsympathetic to minority rights as the rest of the international community. It interpreted its mandate of protecting cultural diversity to mean protecting the national cultures of developing countries against the threat of Western (i.e. American) cultural

UN bodies whose mandate relates to human rights, labour conditions, peace and security, development, and the environment.[22]

A similar dynamic can be seen in the European context. The issue of minority rights was first addressed by the OSCE, whose mandate is to protect peace and security. Its ideas were then adopted by the Council of Europe, which is primarily a human rights body, and also by the European Union, whose function is primarily economic integration.

In short, ideas of multiculturalism and minority rights, which one might have expected to be relegated to the peripheral institutions of the international community dealing with 'culture' and 'heritage', have permeated the core institutions relating to security, development, and human rights. There are important variations in the extent to which these different organizations are truly committed to ideas of minority and indigenous rights, and in how they understand and interpret them. And, as we will see, these variations have had powerful consequences for the way the internationalization of multiculturalism has unfolded. But I think it's fair to say that the role of the international community in promoting minority and indigenous rights has expanded more quickly and more widely than anyone could have predicted twenty years ago.

From Rhetoric to Action?

Having said that, it's difficult to measure the real-world significance of these changes. There has undoubtedly been a sea-change in *rhetoric* from

hegemony, in part by strengthening the capacity of post-colonial states to build up their own national systems of schools, media, and cultural institutions. These UNESCO policies had little success in reducing the global hegemony of American culture, but they did have the effect of displacing minority languages and cultures from increasingly 'nationalized' public space. As Eriksen puts it, for many years UNESCO was 'tightly allied with a tiersmondiste outlook whose principal raison-d'étre lies in the dissemination of standardized, state-monitored education and modern means of communication in the Third World'—a post-colonial nation-building project that was often as harmful to minorities as Western colonialism (Eriksen 2001: 138). It is only recently that UNESCO has started to ally itself with the 'Fourth World' of minorities and indigenous peoples against the homogenizing projects of post-colonial Third World states, replacing 'supremacist nationalism' with 'minority identity politics' (ibid. 136). Eriksen's formulation of this shift is somewhat polemical, but UNESCO's own internal review of its policies on cultural diversity describes a similar trajectory (Keitner 2004). This review describes a shift from an earlier era when nation-states were treated by UNESCO as 'unitary entities' within which 'cultural assimilation' was assumed to be desirable, to a post-1990 era which focused on 'the theoretical and practical questions of minority rights and the co-existence of diverse cultural communities' (Keitner 2004: 3, 4, 8).

[22] Recent international declarations on the environment emphasize the necessity of accommodating cultural diversity as a precondition for sustaining the environment and bio-diversity—see e.g. para. 22 of the Rio Declaration on Environment and Development, adopted in 1992, and Chapter 26 of the accompanying Action Plan 'Agenda 21' (A/CONF.151/26).

the immediate post-war era, but the rhetorical commitment to minority and indigenous rights is not always matched by actions. Advocates of minority rights have complained repeatedly that international organizations do not live up to their own declared commitments. For example, while the UN has declared that minority rights will play an integral role in its new conception of conflict prevention (UN 2004), there continues to be virtually no connection between the UN's minority rights branch in Geneva and its conflict prevention branch in New York (MRG 2004; Steiner 2004; Chesterman 2001; Chapman 2005). Similarly, while the UN's Millennium Declaration has noted the importance of minority rights to achieving its Millennium Development Goals (MDG)—the ambitious plan to reduce world poverty by half by 2015—there does not appear to be any mechanism in place to ensure that MDG activities take into account minority concerns (MRG 2005, Quane 2005).

Even when action plans and monitoring mechanisms are adopted to promote minority and indigenous rights, they are often ineffective. For example, the World Bank's Operational Directive 4.20 instructs Bank officials to screen projects for their potential impact on indigenous peoples. But the Bank has been widely criticized for ignoring this directive (Gray 1998; Kingsbury 1999b; Sarfaty 2005; MacKay 2002). Indeed the Bank's own internal audit shows that of the 89 projects where the directive should have been applied, it was only applied in a 'satisfactory' way in 32 cases. In the remaining cases, it was either not applied at all (34 cases) or applied in an unsatisfactory way (23 cases), without a sound diagnosis of the issues or adequate participation by indigenous peoples themselves (World Bank 2003).[23]

Similarly, while the UN has established a number of mechanisms to promote minority rights, including a Working Group on Minorities and an Independent Expert on Minority Issues, critics argue that they are suffering 'death by a thousand cuts', lacking the mandate or resources needed to really make a difference.[24]

And as I noted at the start of this book, the international community has consistently refused to make any of its minority rights norms

[23] Earlier audits of the World Bank had come to similar conclusions—i.e. that the Bank made loans for projects that violated ILO standards of indigenous rights, and that the safeguards for indigenous peoples were applied far less stringently than other forms of conditionality, such as structural adjustment conditions (Gray 1988: 286, 294). The Bank's Operational Directive 4.20 has recently been revised and updated as Operational Policy 4.10.

[24] See 'Minorities unite to maintain and strengthen UN Working Group', Minority Rights Group International e-bulletin, 13 July 2005. See also Eide 2004.

judicially enforceable.[25] Proposals to turn the UN Declaration on Minority Rights into a legally binding Convention, or to incorporate European minority rights norms into the judicially enforceable European Convention on Human Rights, have been consistently rejected.

Faced with these and other examples of the disjunction between official rhetoric and actual practice, it is tempting to conclude that the new international discourse on multiculturalism and minority rights is largely just window-dressing, behind which it is 'business as usual'. And this would hardly be surprising. After all, international intergovernmental organizations are not neutral referees in conflicts between states and minorities. They are precisely clubs of states, all of whose members have an interest in protecting the rights and privileges of states. And, as we will see in Chapters 6 and 7, states have found all sorts of ingenious ways of qualifying the new international norms, and weakening their monitoring and enforcement mechanisms, to ensure that minorities are not substantially empowered in their struggles to achieve greater rights. A cynic might well conclude that all of the international talk about minority rights is just a lot of sound and fury, signifying nothing.

And yet.... The reality is that it is not business as usual. Something really has changed. The development of international norms and mechanisms is making a difference, and perhaps even a profound and epochal difference. In some cases, these effects are clear and direct. The most obvious example is in Europe. The decision of the European Union to make respect for minority rights one of the accession criteria for would-be members has had a clear and immediate impact on the policies of various post-communist countries. The 'carrot' of joining the EU prodded several countries to adopt pro-minority policies that would not have emerged otherwise.[26] Similarly, despite the half-heartedness with which the World

---

[25] Some countries permit individuals to bring complaints to the UN and the UN Human Rights Committee has examined, and sometimes upheld, claims by individuals that their rights under Article 27 of the ICCPR have been violated. However, these judgments are not enforceable.

[26] The literature on the impact of EU conditionality on minority policies in post-communist Europe is extensive. The general consensus seems to be that where the EU was able to credibly persuade states that their accession was jeopardized by the poor treatment of minorities, this often did have an effect. However, there also seems to be a consensus that the EU did not want minority issues to become an obstacle to accession, and so varied the interpretation of this criterion from case to case to minimize the prospects that it would become a problem. See Kelley 2004a, 2004b; Ardrey 2005; Batt and Amato 1998; Burgess 1999; Chandler 1999; DeWitte 2002, 2004; Dobre 2003; Galbreath 2003, 2006; Guglielmo 2004; Hughes and Sasse 2003; Johnson 2006; Malloy 2005; Ram 2001, 2003; Sasse 2004, 2006; Schwellnus 2005; Toggenburg 2004; Vermeersch 2002, 2003; Vizi 2005; Johns 2003; Wilkinson 2005; EUMAP 2001; MacFarlane 2001.

Bank has applied its own Operational Directive to safeguard the rights of indigenous peoples, the reality is that this Directive has given indigenous peoples in some countries (particularly in Latin America) a level of voice and participation that they would not otherwise have had (Brysk 2000).

But it would be a mistake to focus exclusively on these cases of direct international pressure to change national policies. The actions of the international community are also changing the way domestic debates around ethnic politics are conducted, not only by reframing the terms of those debates, but also by changing perceptions about which parties are legitimate actors in the debate. Put simply, the international community has played an important role in 'normalizing' ethnic political mobilization and minority claims-making.

In the past, countries with robust minority rights were often seen as 'exceptions', if not 'deviations', from what a 'normal' state looks like. Throughout much of the twentieth-century, the most influential example of a normal state was France—i.e. a highly centralized state with an undifferentiated conception of republican citizenship and a single official language. In this model, there is no room for minority rights—indeed, the French government and its Constitutional Court have repeatedly asserted that it is conceptually impossible that 'minorities' could exist in the country, since everyone by definition had an identical and undifferentiated citizenship.[27] This was the model that many post-colonial and post-communist states aspired to, in part because it seemed to be the most 'modern'. In relation to this ideal of the state, countries that were officially multilingual, and/or that recognized various forms of substate autonomy or legal pluralism for their minorities and indigenous peoples, were seen as anomalies and anachronisms.

In recent years, however, international organizations have revised their views about what a 'normal' and 'modern' state looks like. Indeed, they have literally reversed the tables. In contemporary international discourse, the idea of a centralized, unitary, and homogenous state is increasingly described as an anachronism, a throwback to the nineteenth century. By contrast, pluralistic, multilingual, and multilevel states with complex internal structures for recognizing and empowering regions and minorities are increasingly seen as representing the more truly 'modern'

---

[27] In the words of the Haut Conseil à l'Intégration, 'The French conception of integration should obey a logic of equality and not a logic of minorities. The principles of identity and equality which go back to the Revolution and the Declaration of the Rights of Man and of Citizens impregnate our conception, this founded on the equality of individuals before the law, whatever their origin, race, religion . . . to the exclusion of an institutional recognition of minorities' (quoted in Bonnett 2000: 59).

(or even 'post-modern') approach. States that rigidly cling to the older centralized and unitary model, and that continue to deny that minorities exist (as in France, Greece, Turkey, or Japan), are increasingly described as backward, unable or unwilling to recognize and deal with the complexity and inherent pluralism of the modern world.[28]

Some countries have had trouble adapting to this new reality. When Romania was first struggling to justify its existence as an independent state after the breakdown of the Habsburg empire, its key strategy was to emphasize that it was (almost) a homogenous nation, with only small and politically inconsequential minorities. When Romania re-acquired independence with the collapse of the Soviet bloc, and sought to 're-join Europe', it reasserted this discourse of homogeneity, not realizing that the times had changed. Today, denying the existence of minorities, or treating them as politically inconsequential, is seen as evidence that one is not yet ready to be a member in good standing of the club of liberal democracies. And so Romania has gradually learned that if it wishes to be treated as a 'normal' and 'mature' European country, it needs to acknowledge its minorities, and to treat them as enduring and constituent elements of the country, rather than as historical aberrations or regrettable blots on the idea of a unitary and homogenous nation.

This change in the international discourse of what a normal state looks like is not merely rhetorical. It has implications for the legitimacy of minorities as political actors. Under the old model, the very idea of ethnic political mobilization was often seen as suspect, and indeed was illegal in many countries, both in the West and elsewhere. Political parties that were founded on ethnic lines, or that questioned the unitary and unilingual nature of the state, were often prohibited, as were other forms of ethnic political mobilization. But today, the visible and active participation of ethnic political actors and movements is seen as an inherent part of a truly free and democratic society.

And here, I think, we get to the heart of the matter. Having officially embraced the idea that a 'normal' and 'modern' state is one that recognizes minority and indigenous rights, the inevitable result has been to legitimize attempts by ethnocultural groups to mobilize politically to claim these rights. Even if the international community has no intention of directly pressuring states to accept particular minority claims—even if international norms exist only on paper, and are not subject to effective

---

[28] Not surprisingly, many French intellectuals, raised on the view that French republicanism is the very origin and epitome of revolutionary modernism, have resented this implication that they are now an anachronism in Europe. See Birnbaum 2004.

international monitoring or enforcement—they nonetheless legitimize a wide range of ethnic political mobilizations. In the past, states might have suppressed ethnic political mobilizations on the grounds that they are 'radical', 'disloyal', 'subversive', or 'unconstitutional'. But today minorities can claim that they are only seeking to apply international standards to which the state itself has subscribed.

And indeed the international community encourages ethnic groups to make claims based on these international norms. International organizations not only adopt pious declarations, they also publicize these norms around the world, translating them into various languages, and distributing them in print and on the internet. In conjunction with sympathetic governments, NGOs, and philanthropic organizations, they also sponsor workshops and training manuals to explain the origins and nature of these norms, to suggest how groups can invoke them, and to give examples of 'best practices' that instantiate them. They also fund fellowships to bring members of minority groups and indigenous communities to work within international organizations, and to learn more about how they can act effectively within the system.

In short, behind each one of these international declarations there is a veritable industry of promotional activities, creating international networks of activists, scholars, and policy-makers, all of whom have a vested interest in further publicizing and promoting these norms. None of this involves making 'hard' legal commitments that minorities can seek to enforce in international courts against their own states. But these activities are changing people's expectations and sense of entitlement, diffusing knowledge, enhancing skills, and building coalitions. More generally, they legitimize efforts to self-organize and mobilize ethnic groups whose political representatives deserve a seat at the table, both in domestic politics and in international forums.

In all of these respects, the international environment today is profoundly more sympathetic to minority claims than thirty or forty years ago. The debate about whether these international norms are 'real' obligations or are 'merely rhetorical' is misconceived. Relations between states and minorities are still fundamentally determined by domestic political processes, with relatively few hard constraints from international law. But the way in which these domestic political processes are framed has been dramatically altered by a new international environment that stigmatizes older assimilationist models while encouraging minority rights activism.

Explaining the Shift

What explains this shift? We can quickly dismiss one explanation. According to some critics, the shift is the result of the creeping influence of cultural relativism, introduced either by cultural anthropologists or postmodernist cultural theorists, which rejects the very idea of universal moral principles. This is supposed to explain why the post-war settlement that relied exclusively on universal human rights is being contested in the name of targeted minority and indigenous rights (e.g. Finkielkraut 1988; Cowan 2001).

In reality, far from challenging these universalist ideas, the justifications given by international organizations for adopting minority rights appeal to these very ideas. What has changed is not people's beliefs about the legitimacy of universal moral norms, but rather people's assumptions about whether minority rights promote or hinder those universal norms. As we've seen, the architects of the UN, and of post-war regional organizations, assumed that minority rights were not only unnecessary for the creation of a viable new international order, but indeed destabilizing of such an order. Today, however, it is widely asserted that the accommodation of ethnic diversity is not only *consistent* with, but in fact a *precondition* for, the maintenance of a legitimate international order. Indeed, it is increasingly asserted that virtually all of the goals and values of the international community—whether it is human rights, peace and security, democracy, or economic development—depend on the recognition of minority and indigenous rights.

Consider a few examples:

According to the Organization for Security and Cooperation in Europe, minority rights are a precondition *for peace and security*:

Stability and security are best served by ensuring that persons belonging to national minorities can effectively enjoy their rights ... Lasting peace and stability on this continent are possible only if the UN Declaration on the Rights of Minorities and the Framework Convention for the Protection of National Minorities are fully implemented. (OSCE 1999)

A similar sentiment about the role of minority rights in reducing conflict is expressed at the global level by the United Nations:

Conflicts are most frequent in poor countries, especially in those that are ill governed and where there are sharp inequalities between ethnic or religious groups. The best way to prevent them is to promote healthy and balanced economic development, combined with human rights, minority rights and political arrangements in which all groups are fairly represented. (UN 2000)

According to the United Nations Development Program, and the UN Millennium Development Goals, minority and indigenous rights are vital to achieving *development* and the reduction of *poverty*:

Campaigns to assimilate indigenous peoples usually ended up worsening their poverty and deprivation.... Protecting indigenous peoples' distinct languages and cultures is of central importance. (UNDP 2000: 86, 88)

[Where] the condition of poverty is coupled with sharp ethnic or religious cleavages...the solution is clear, even if difficult to achieve in practice: to promote human rights, to protect minority rights, and to institute political arrangements in which all groups are represented. (UN 2000: 45)

Similar sentiments about the role of indigenous rights in reducing poverty have been expressed by the International Labour Organization:

The widening of ethnic inequalities in countries with indigenous and tribal peoples reveals that conventional anti-poverty policies fail to tackle the social and economic exclusion facing them...social and economic policies must recognize and accommodate indigenous and tribal peoples' needs, aspirations and rights. As distinct peoples, they have special rights (group rights) that include the right to be different and to influence decisions affecting their livelihoods and future... [Poverty-Reduction programmes] are more likely to address the structural causes of indigenous and tribal peoples' pauperization and social exclusion where (a) legal frameworks recognize indigenous peoples' group rights; (b) institutions and policies respecting and accommodating cultural diversity have been developed; (c) indigenous peoples have organized and mobilized for political change. (Tomei 2005, p. v)[29]

According to UNESCO, minority rights are an inseparable component of *human rights*:

The defence of cultural diversity is an ethical imperative inseparable from respect for human dignity. It implies a commitment to human rights and fundamental freedoms, in particular the rights belonging to minorities and those of indigenous

---

[29] See also the Arusha Declaration adopted at a recent World Bank conference on social policy: 'Fostering an enabling, accessible, responsive and accountable state...entails universal application of the rule of law, and equal rights under the law for all citizens. Universal rights, however, need to be accompanied by legitimate, effective, and accountable institutions for policy formulation and implementation, with rigorous monitoring of outcomes. This implies recognizing and celebrating multiculturalism as a source of strength for societies, and supporting policies that accommodate diversity in the achievement of universal rights' (World Bank Conference on 'The New Frontiers of Social Policy', Arusha Statement, December 2005).

peoples. Cultural rights are an integral part of human rights, which are universal, indivisible and interdependent. (UNESCO, Universal Declaration on Cultural Diversity, 2001)

Finally, according to the OSCE, minority rights are a precondition for *democratization*:

Effective participation of national minorities in public life is an essential component of a peaceful and democratic society. Experience in Europe and elsewhere has shown that, in order to promote such participation, governments often need to establish specific arrangements for national minorities. (OSCE 1999)

In all of these statements, the original universalistic goals of the UN remain the uncontested guidelines. There is not even a hint of cultural relativism in any of these statements, or of a retreat from the commitment to universal values. What has changed are the assumptions about the impact of minority rights on these goals. Today, international organizations assert that minority rights support, rather than inhibit, the achievement of the aspirations underlying the UN Charter.

These are all striking statements, and it is worth pausing to think about them. Is it really true that recognizing minority and indigenous rights is a precondition for achieving peace, development, democracy, and human rights? If so, this would certainly help to explain the recent headlong embrace of minority rights. I suspect, however, that many scholars would be sceptical of such a claim. To be sure, there have been some major academic studies showing a strong link between minority rights and various desirable outcomes, including peace and democracy. The most prominent of these is the mammoth 'Minorities at Risk' (MAR) project directed by Ted Robert Gurr (Gurr 1993, 2000), the most in-depth and comprehensive attempt to statistically examine the relationship between state policies towards minorities and the risks of violent and destabilizing conflict. After examining 275 cases of state–minority conflicts, Gurr concluded that the 'strong global trends' towards greater recognition of minority rights have indeed reduced 'the incidence of new ethno-political conflicts'. He also recommended that the international community should continue to play an active role in diffusing these global trends, including 'continued international support for non-discriminatory policies, recognition of group rights, and provision of sub-state autonomy' (Gurr 2000: 211). Follow-up studies using the MAR database have confirmed this basic conclusion (Bermeo 2002; Saideman and Ayres 2001; Saideman et al 2002). Not surprisingly, the MAR study has been widely cited by international organizations in support of their pro-active efforts to diffuse liberal multiculturalism (e.g. UNHDR 2004; MRG 2004; Chapman 2005).

But the methodology of the MAR study has been questioned (Fearon and Laitin 2000), and there are many highly respected political scientists, sociologists, and anthropologists who argue that the impact of minority rights on peace, democratization, development, and human rights is at best highly contingent. Indeed, some argue that, under many circumstances, the impact is likely to be negative. (I will discuss these arguments in Chapters 6–7 below.) We certainly have nothing like incontrovertible proof that this or that type of minority right, for this or that type of minority group, is a precondition for achieving democratization, respecting human rights, promoting economic development, or sustaining peace and stability. We do not have the sort of systematic cross-national and longitudinal studies needed to confirm or refute these hypotheses, all of which remain deeply contested within the scholarly literature.[30]

Given this uncertainty, why have so many international organizations concluded that minority and indigenous rights are needed to pursue their mandate?[31] There is no single or simple answer here, particularly given the heterogeneity of the institutions involved. The route by which the World Bank became involved in this field is different from that of UNESCO or the Council of Europe. The events that triggered a rethinking of minority issues depended on the specific mandate of each institution, and on the sorts of institutional vulnerabilities and incentives created by the organization's structure. It would take a separate book to trace each of these paths.

But if we step back from these details, I think we can see this shift as resulting from the convergence of two factors: a fear of the spread of ethnic violence after the collapse of Communism, and a hope for the possibility of a viable liberal-democratic form of multiculturalism. Let me start with the fear. With the collapse of the Communist bloc, there was initially great optimism that liberal democracy would emerge around the world. Instead, what emerged in many post-communist countries was violent ethnic conflict, particularly in the Balkans and the Caucasus. Overly optimistic predictions about the rapid replacement of Communism with

---

[30] See, e.g., a recent study commissioned by the World Bank on the effects of adopting more culturally sensitive models for delivering public services, particularly in the areas of health, education, and the legal system (Marc 2005). The study concludes that there is virtually no systematic evidence one way or the other regarding the effects of these policies.

[31] See Wilkinson 2005, who asks 'Why do the EU, the OSCE, and the Council of Europe propose consociational policies when we have so little data in the way of systematic findings about which policies really do prevent or reduce violence?' (Wilkinson 2005: 253).

liberal democracy were supplanted with overly pessimistic predictions about the replacement of Communism with ethnic war. There were fears that violent ethnic conflict would spread from Yugoslavia to Central Europe (particularly Romania and Slovakia with their restive Hungarian minorities), and to the Baltics and Central Asia (with their sizeable Russian minorities), engulfing virtually the entire post-communist world.[32] The collapse of Somalia and Sudan, and the genocide in Rwanda, made clear that this problem was not limited to post-communist Europe, but rather affected much of the developing world.[33] Writing in 1993, Daniel Moynihan, a former US Ambassador to the UN, captured the spirit of the times when he wrote 'nation states no longer seem inclined to go to war with one another, but ethnic groups fight all the time' (Moynihan 1993).

Such conflicts were seen not only as a humanitarian catastrophe for the people within a country, but as having serious international repercussions, in the form of mass refugee flows and the destabilization of neighbouring states. Moreover, ethnic civil wars often create pockets of lawlessness which become havens for the smuggling of arms and drugs, or for terrorist groups (Paris 2004: 1–2).[34] As a result, ethnic conflict came to be seen as a serious threat to international peace and security, and indeed as perhaps the main threat, now that the threat of war between the superpowers had receded. There was a strong feeling that the international community needed to 'do something' to help states manage this 'apparently remorseless rise of ethnic and communal conflict' (Roberts 1994: 6). Given this combination of humanitarian imperatives and geopolitical interests, for the international community to treat these conflicts as purely domestic matters 'is not just heartless, it is foolish' (Collier et al 2003: 11).

So the first factor underlying international initiatives in this field was a pessimistic, even apocalyptic, vision of ethnic politics as a threat to peace, democracy, and development. This perception was, in part, a reaction to the unfolding tragedies in Yugoslavia and Rwanda, but it was reinforced

[32] See Michael Ignatieff's comment in 1993 that 'When the Berlin Wall came down...I thought, like many people, that we were about to witness a new era of liberal democracy... We soon found out how wrong we were. For what has succeeded the last age of empire is a new age of violence' (Ignatieff 1993: 5, quoted in Norman 2006, p. viii, cf. Pfaff 1993.)

[33] Prior to 1990, scholars used to argue that the Cold War had artificially kept alive ethnic conflicts in the Third World, as the United States encouraged ethnic minorities to rebel against states allied to the Soviets, and vice versa. After 1990, however, people started to wonder if the Cold War had in fact artificially suppressed ethnic conflicts, as ethnically heterogeneous states started to fall apart once they lost superpower backing.

[34] Recall that Osama bin Laden set up base first in Sudan and then in Afghanistan, two 'failed states' that had collapsed due, in part, to ethnic conflict.

by a wave of social science studies which seemed to suggest that ethnic heterogeneity was a 'problem' along multiple dimensions. Studies seemed to show, for example, that countries with more ethnic heterogeneity were likely to be less democratic, have lower economic growth, and lower levels of social spending to help the needy.[35] So the high-profile cases of ethnic civil wars seemed to be just the most visible tip of a much broader set of pathologies associated with 'too much ethnic diversity' or 'too much ethnic politics'.

The second factor, however, was the reverse—namely, the emergence within the Western democracies of new and seemingly benign forms of ethnic politics. As we will see in Chapter 3, the West had undergone its own 'ethnic revival' starting in the 1960s, with a dramatic upsurge in ethnic political mobilization by a range of different groups, including immigrant groups, substate nationalist groups (such as the Scots, Catalans, and Québécois), and indigenous peoples.[36] As in post-communist Europe, this Western ethnic revival was initially feared by many people as potentially destabilizing, and a threat to liberal democracy. These fears were partly due to lingering memories of the failure of the inter-war minority protection regime, and partly due to the fact that some of the initial manifestations of this ethnic revival in the late 1960s and early 1970s were indeed inspired by various Marxist or anarchist ideologies that espoused the violent overthrow of the state.[37]

By the early 1990s, however, there was a widespread (though not universal) sense of optimism that these fears were overstated, and that Western countries had found a way to safely contain ethnic political mobilization within the boundaries of peaceful liberal-democratic politics.

In fact, we can go further. Many people argued that ethnic mobilization in the West was not just *constrained* by the rules of liberal democracy and human rights, but was in fact *inspired* by liberal values and human rights ideals. Ethnic politics in the West, on this view, was not a threat to democracy, but was itself a profoundly democratic phenomenon, as historically disadvantaged groups rightly challenged their cultural stigmatization or invisibility in the pursuit of greater freedom and equality. The emergence and institutionalization of ethnic politics, like the rise of feminist and gay

[35] See, e.g., Easterly and Levine 1997 (on the negative impact of ethnic heterogeneity on growth); James 1987, 1993 (on public spending), and Welsh 1993 (on democracy).

[36] For an overview of this Western ethnic revival, see Smith 1981.

[37] Consider the more radical wings of the 'Black Power' movement, or the use of terrorist tactics by minority nationalist groups, such as the FLQ in Quebec, or ETA in Spain. These groups often viewed themselves as part of broader revolutionary struggles.

movements, was a manifestation and consolidation of a broader process of liberalization and democratization, not a threat to it.

This optimistic view of ethnic politics in the West was articulated in new theories of 'liberal multiculturalism' that first emerged in the late 1980s and early 1990s.[38] According to liberal multiculturalists, the sorts of group-differentiated minority policies that had emerged in the West since the 1960s were worthy of our support, and indeed of celebration. This was true of the regional autonomy schemes and language rights adopted for substate national groups, of the multiculturalism policies adopted for immigrants, and of the land claims and self-government rights adopted for indigenous peoples. All were helping to build fairer and more inclusive democratic societies, and should be seen as part and parcel of a free and democratic society.

So the early 1990s witnessed both a profound pessimism about ethnic politics in the post-communist and post-colonial world, and an equally profound optimism about ethnic politics in the West. The attitudes and activities of the international community regarding state–minority relations have been shaped by both of these perspectives. The apocalyptic fear of spiralling ethnic conflict provided the impetus and urgency for the international community to get involved; the hopeful belief in a truly liberal and democratic form of multiculturalism provided the inspiring ideal and sense of moral direction. It is these two factors (and not a sudden embrace of cultural relativism) that help to explain the explosion of international efforts in this area from 1990 to 1995, when virtually all of the major global and regional minority rights instruments were developed.

It's important to repeat that both factors were necessary to generate the sorts of international initiatives that we have seen. Without the sense of urgent danger, IOs would not have overcome traditional state reluctance to sanction international intervention in state–minority relations. But without the belief in an ideal of multicultural justice, the fear of conflict could have easily led to very different kinds of international initiatives. After World War I, for example, fears of ethnic violence led many people to support either partition (to enable each ethnic group to form its own state, wherever possible) or population transfers (e.g. transferring ethnic Greeks from Turkey to Greece, and ethnic Turks from Greece to Turkey). After World War II, similar fears led to another bout of (what we would

---

[38] This 'first wave' of liberal multiculturalism includes Spinner 1994; Taylor 1992; Baubock 1994; Tamir 1993, Raz 1994. I include my own work in this category: Kymlicka 1989, 1995. For more recent accounts, see Carens 2000; Torbisco Casals 2006; Mitnick 2006.

now call) ethnic cleansing, as ethnic Germans were forcibly expelled from Czechoslovakia, Poland, and other countries. And some people today continue to suggest that the international community should consider these options of partition or population transfer, at least as a last resort (e.g. Kaufmann 1996, 1998). In the early 1990s, however, the international community was profoundly committed to the view that it was feasible and desirable to build new forms of multicultural democracy (Manas 1996). And so its response was to try to formulate norms of minority and indigenous rights that would help build liberal multiculturalism.

The timing is important here. Both the apocalyptic fears and the celebratory optimism have faded to some extent since the early 1990s. Few people today fear that ethnic violence will emerge in Central Europe or the Baltics, and recent scholarship has shown that ethnic violence in postcolonial states is far less common, and far more difficult to incite, than earlier commentators supposed (Fearon and Laitin 1996, 2003; Young 2002).[39] Other issues are now seen as more serious threats to international peace and security, from terrorism to AIDS and global poverty. Newer research has also put into question earlier claims that ethnic heterogeneity as such is a barrier to democracy, human rights, economic growth, or the welfare state.[40]

Conversely, the bloom has fallen off the rose of Western liberal multiculturalism, at least with respect to immigrant groups in some countries. There is a widespread perception in Western Europe that multiculturalism 'went too far' in the context of predominantly Muslim immigrants, and there has been a reassertion of more assimilationist or exclusionary policies. (Minority rights provisions for substate national groups and indigenous peoples, by contrast, have not yet suffered any serious backlash in any Western democracy.) Even those who remain supportive of multiculturalist reforms in the west have had growing doubts about whether they are feasible in other regions of the world.

As a result, the efforts of the international community to formulate new norms or new mechanisms have slowed down. There is less of a sense of urgency about the need to avert impending disasters, and less confidence

[39] Fearon and Laitin show, for example, that in Africa (often seen as beset with violent ethnic conflict) for any randomly chosen but neighbouring pair of ethnic groups, on average only five in 10,000 had a recorded violent conflict in any year. As they note, this suggests that it is the pervasiveness of inter-ethnic cooperation, not conflict, that needs explaining.

[40] See, e.g., Alesina and LaFerrera 2005, Collier 2000; Lian and Oneal 1997 (showing that the negative relationship between ethnic heterogeneity and economic growth fades at higher levels of development and in democracies; Walker and Poe 2002 (ethnic heterogeneity is not an obstacle to respect for various categories of human rights); and Fish and Brooks 2004 (ethnic and religious heterogeneity are not correlated with lower levels of democracy).

that we know the ideal we are aiming to achieve. Earlier ambitious plans to strengthen international norms—for example, by strengthening the mandate of various international bodies that monitor minority rights— have been put on the back burner. Indeed, most people think that if the international community were to reconsider these mandates today, the result would likely be to weaken rather than strengthen them.

For example, advocates have backed off their initial hopes of turning the 1992 UN Declaration on Minority Rights into a binding Convention,[41] or of turning the Council of Europe's Framework Convention on minorities into a justiciable part of the European Convention on Human Rights; or of reopening the mandate of the OSCE's High Commissioner on National Minorities to expand the scope of its activities. In each case, many activists and advocates think that the result would be to erode the gains initially made in the crucial 1990–5 period.

And yet, despite some attempts at retrenchment, the basic international architecture of minority and indigenous rights remains in place, and indeed has become more institutionally embedded. Moreover, while the feelings of both urgency and enthusiasm have ebbed, the underlying issues remain unchanged. The reality is that ethnic conflict can cause humanitarian catastrophes and threaten international peace and stability, and this makes the treatment of minorities a legitimate matter of international concern. Moreover, the practices of liberal multiculturalism in the West show that ethnic diversity can be managed in a way that is consistent with the values of human rights and democracy. In that sense, it was appropriate, and indeed inevitable, that both the fear of ethnic violence and the hope of liberal multiculturalism would influence the international community.

What is less clear, however, is whether current international efforts have combined these two influences in the right way. At times, the implicit assumption seems to be that the latter is the solution to the former—that is, that liberal multiculturalism can provide the basis for addressing the problem of ethnic conflict in post-communist and post-colonial states. But it is not obvious that the two can or should be connected in such a direct way. After all, the two perspectives developed quite separately. Theorists of liberal multiculturalism focused almost exclusively on debates

[41] The UN's Working Group on Minorities has repeatedly asked the Human Rights Commission and the office of the High Commissioner on Human Rights to consult with governments to assess their views about the possibility of drafting a UN Convention on Minorities, but little or no support has been forthcoming (e.g. E/CN.4/2002/91/Add.1). Even Minority Rights Group, the main international advocacy group in the field, does not view this as a good time to push for such a Convention (MRG 2003).

within the Western democracies, and few if any suggested that Western models could be transported to post-colonial states. Conversely, few scholars of ethnic conflict in the developing world suggested that Western models of liberal multiculturalism were the solution. Both discourses were influential in the early 1990s, but they operated in separate domains, with little contact.

It is not entirely clear how or when the idea first arose that the international community should appeal to Western liberal multiculturalism when thinking about how to deal with ethnic relations in post-communist or post-colonial states. So far as I can tell, this idea seems to have emerged within international organizations themselves, in a rather unconscious way. Nature abhors a vacuum, and perhaps it was inevitable that the optimistic discourse of liberal multiculturalism would be invoked to counter-balance the pessimistic discourse of destabilizing ethnic conflict. And given the (perceived) urgency of the situation in the early 1990s, there was not time for a sustained or systematic discussion of the extent to which liberal multiculturalism really is appropriate or relevant for post-colonial and post-communist states.[42]

I think the time has come, however, for such a discussion. As I noted earlier, attempts to diffuse liberal multiculturalism around the world are not working well. And this shouldn't be surprising, given what we know about the general difficulty of transferring the institutions of liberal constitutionalism, and given that multiculturalism is one of the most contentious aspects of contemporary liberal-democratic politics. If strategies to promote liberal multiculturalism are to have any chance of success, we need to be more self-reflective about both the hopes and fears that motivate international efforts, and more cautious in how we connect the two.

The rest of the book is intended to provide the first steps in such a rethinking. In Part II, I will explore the logic and preconditions of liberal multiculturalism in the West, focusing in particular on the differentiated

---

[42] It is also possible that liberal multiculturalism simply piggybacked on a more general commitment of IOs to 'liberalization' as the miracle cure for all of the ills of post-communist and post-colonial states. As Paris says, 'Decades from now, historians may look back on the immediate post-Cold War years as a period of remarkable faith in the powers of liberalization to remedy a broad range of social ills, from internal and international violence to poverty, famine, corruption, and even environmental destruction' (Paris 2004: 35). IOs may not have consciously adopted a distinctly multicultural model of liberalism, they simply may have adopted the model of liberalism that was currently in the ascendant. And in the early 1990s, the ascendant form of liberalism was a pluralist one. (Another important feature of the ascendant model of liberalism at the time was its commitment to economic liberalization and free trade. I will discuss the connection between the 'multicultural' and 'neo-liberal' dimensions of liberalization in Chapter 4.)

forms it takes, and the conditions that enable and constrain it. In Part III, I then examine how the international community has attempted to promote liberal multiculturalism in post-communist and post-colonial states. At times, I will argue, the international community has been far too hopeful in the way it has promoted a liberal and democratic form of multiculturalism, ignoring the conditions that make it a viable approach. But at other times, deep-seated fears about the potential for destabilizing ethnic conflict have led the international community to qualify and limit minority rights norms in ways that are ambiguous, inconsistent, and even undemocratic. Naïve optimism alternates with distorting fears. As we will see, a lot of work remains to be done in figuring out how we can bring our hopes and fears regarding ethnic politics into some kind of coherent and realistic framework.

Part II

Making Sense of Liberal Multiculturalism

Introduction to Part II

As we've seen, the international community's efforts in shaping state-minority relations around the world are at least partly inspired and justified by a belief in the possibility of a truly liberal and democratic form of multiculturalism. Some critics doubt that such a possibility exists, on the grounds that 'ultimately liberal democracy and multiculturalism are not compatible' (Delanty 2003: 99). If so, then the international community is trying to export a non-existent phenomenon.

In the next three chapters, I will argue that there is such a thing as liberal multiculturalism, in both theory and practice, and indeed that it has been working well, at least in some contexts. However, I will also argue that it has its own distinctive logic and preconditions that aren't well understood, and that these often get lost in translation when efforts are made to diffuse liberal multiculturalism around the world.

I begin in Chapter 3 by exploring the general idea of liberal multiculturalism, as well as the more specific forms it has taken in the Western democracies since its emergence in the 1960s. In Chapter 4, I discuss the preconditions that enabled liberal multiculturalism to emerge in the West over the past forty years, focusing on both the conditions that encouraged minorities to be more vocal in their claims-making, and the conditions that encouraged dominant groups and state governments to be more open to accepting these claims. In Chapter 5, I explore the strengths and limitations of liberal multiculturalism in practice. As we will see throughout, the practice of liberal multiculturalism is neither simple nor straightforward. It is more contingent than is often realized, in ways that complicate the project of formulating international norms and standards in this field.

3

The Forms of Liberal Multiculturalism

There is no universally accepted definition of 'liberal multiculturalism', and any attempt to provide a single definition to encompass all of its different forms is likely to be too vague to be useful. We could say, for example, that liberal multiculturalism is the view that states should not only uphold the familiar set of common civil, political, and social rights of citizenship that are protected in all constitutional liberal democracies, but also adopt various group-specific rights or policies that are intended to recognize and accommodate the distinctive identities and aspirations of ethnocultural groups. This definition is fair enough, as far as it goes, but doesn't take us very far.

A more helpful approach to understanding the logic of liberal multiculturalism is to understand what it is a response to, or what it is a reaction against. All struggles for multiculturalism share in common a rejection of earlier models of the unitary, homogenous nation-state. In order to understand the idea of a liberal multicultural democracy, therefore, we need first to understand this older model of a homogenous nation-state, and why it has been rejected.

Until recently, most states around the world have aspired to be 'nation-states'. In this model, the state was implicitly (and sometimes explicitly) seen as the possession of a dominant national group, which used the state to privilege its identity, language, history, culture, literature, myths, religion, and so on, and which defined the state as the expression of its nationhood. (This dominant group was usually the majority group, but sometimes a minority was able to establish dominance—e.g. whites in South Africa under the apartheid regime, or *criollo* elites in some Latin American countries.) Anyone who did not belong to this dominant national group was subject to either assimilation or exclusion.[1]

There is nothing 'natural' about such nation-states. Very few countries around the world are historically mono-national (Iceland, Portugal, and the Koreas are the most frequently cited examples). In most countries, this ideal (or illusion) of national homogeneity had to be actively constructed by the state through a range of 'nation-building' policies that encouraged the preferred national identity while suppressing any alternative identities. Public policies were used to promote and consolidate a common national language, national history and mythology, national heroes, national symbols, a national literature, a national education system, a national media, a national military, in some cases a national religion, and so on. Groups which resisted these nationalizing policies were subject not only to political disempowerment, but also, typically, to economic discrimination and to various forms of 'demographic engineering' (e.g. pressuring members of the group to disperse, and/or promoting settlement by members of the dominant group in the homeland of indigenous/minority groups). These and other policies were aimed at constructing the ideal of a nation-state.

The precise character of these nation-building policies has varied from country to country, and region to region. In most Western countries, there has been a single dominant ethnonational group, forming a clear majority of the population (e.g. the Greeks in Greece; the Castilians in Spain, etc.), and nation-building policies have been used to impose this dominant group's language and culture on the rest of the population. Some of the policies adopted to achieve this goal include:

- the adoption of official language laws which define the dominant group's language as the only official 'national' language, and which require this to be the only language used in the bureaucracy, courts, public services, the army, higher education, etc.;

- the construction of a nationalized system of compulsory education promoting a standardized curriculum, focused on teaching the dominant group's language/literature/history (which are redefined as the 'national' language and literature and history);

---

[1] This exclusion could take the form of exclusion from the halls of power within the state (e.g. through denial of the vote, or other forms of political disempowerment), or it could literally involve exclusion from the territory of the state, through racial restrictions on immigration, or through ethnic cleansing.

- the centralization of political power, eliminating pre-existing forms of local sovereignty/autonomy enjoyed historically by minority groups, so that all important decisions are made in a forum where the dominant group forms a majority;
- the diffusion of the dominant group's language and culture through national cultural institutions, including national public media and public museums;
- the adoption of state symbols celebrating the dominant group's history, heroes, and culture, reflected for example in the choice of national holidays, or the naming of streets, buildings, mountains, and so on;
- the construction of a unified legal and judicial system, operating in the dominant group's language and using its legal traditions, and the abolition of any pre-existing legal systems used by minority groups;
- the adoption of settlement policies which encourage members of the dominant national group to settle in areas where minority groups have historically resided, so as to swamp the minorities even in their historic homelands;
- the adoption of immigration policies that require knowledge of the 'national' language/history as a condition of gaining citizenship, and that often give a preference to immigrants who share the same language, religion, or culture as the dominant group;
- the seizure of lands, forests, and fisheries which used to belong to minority groups and indigenous peoples, and declaring them to be 'national' resources, to be used for the benefit of the nation.

This is just a sample of the policies adopted in Western states: one could quickly expand the list.[2] But the intended outcome of these policies is clear: to centralize all political and legal power in forums dominated by the majority group; to privilege that group's language and culture in all public institutions, which are then diffused throughout the territory of the state; and to make minority languages and cultures invisible in public space.

Similar policies have been adopted in most post-communist countries (e.g. Romania, Croatia), and in most post-colonial contexts where there is a numerically dominant ethnic group (e.g. Malaysia, Thailand, Sri Lanka, Ethiopia, Sudan). The situation is somewhat different in those

---

[2] For a more detailed cataloguing of the aims and methods of nation-building, see Norman 2006, chap. 2.

post-colonial states where no single group forms a numerical majority. In such cases, the former colonial language is often chosen as the official national language, and the colonial legal tradition forms the basis for the national legal system, to the exclusion of all indigenous languages and legal traditions. Yet even in these contexts, nation-building policies operate to construct a homogenous national culture, reinforced by the centralization of power, the nationalization of the legal system and education system, the development of national media and national holidays, and so on.

It is difficult to exaggerate the pervasiveness of these nation-building policies. When states periodically engage in particularly virulent or intrusive forms of nation-building, there is often some international publicity and protest. But the more everyday forms of nation-building—what Billig calls 'banal nationalism', in which public institutions and public space are imprinted with a particular national identity—often go unnoticed or unremarked upon (Billig 1995). Nation-building policies have become such a pervasive feature of modern life that most people scarcely even notice them.

Virtually every Western democracy has pursued this ideal of national homogeneity at one point or another, as have virtually all post-communist and post-colonial states. As I discuss below, an increasing number of Western democracies have abandoned this goal in favour of a more multicultural model of the state. But at one point or another, virtually every Western democracy has sought to define itself as a mono-national state. The only exception to this pattern in the West that I know of is Switzerland. Switzerland never attempted to try to construct a single national language on the territory of the state. It has always accepted that the French- and Italian-speaking minorities would exist as distinct linguistic groups into the indefinite future. But every other Western democracy—including some that are very diverse, and that now pride themselves on their diversity, like Canada—has at some point or other had the goal of inculcating a common national language and culture.

A wide range of justifications have been offered historically for this pursuit of national homogeneity. In some contexts, it was argued that the state needed to be more unified in order to effectively defend itself against external or internal enemies, or to build the civic solidarity needed for a welfare state. Or that a culturally unified state was easier to administer, and would have a more efficient labour market. But these sorts of justifications were also typically buttressed by racialist and ethnocentric ideologies which asserted that the language and culture of minority groups and indigenous peoples were backward and inferior, if not barbaric, unworthy of respect or protection. There is widespread variation across time and space in the way these geo-political, economic and ideological arguments have been interwoven, but the same elements recur repeatedly in the 'stories of peoplehood' that dominant groups tell themselves to justify their projects of national homogenization (Smith 2003).

This adoption of this model, and its accompanying policies and underlying justifications, has had profound effects on substate groups. Within the territory of most states there are many groups possessing their own language, their own history, their own culture, their own heroes, their own symbols. Such groups are often excluded entirely by the process of nationbuilding, or included only at the price of accepting assimilation and second-class status, stigmatized by the racialist and ethnocentric ideologies used to justify nation-building. Indeed, minorities are typically the first target of these policies, since they are the greatest obstacle to the goal (or myth) of a unified nation-state, and hence most in need of 'nationalization'. The result, over time, has been the creation of multiple and deeply rooted forms of exclusion and subordination for minorities, often combining political marginalization, economic disadvantage, and cultural domination.

As a result, various substate groups have contested this attempt to construct homogeneous nation-building states, and have advocated instead a more multicultural model of the state.[3] What does a multicultural state look like? The precise details vary from country to country, for reasons I discuss below. The sort of reforms demanded by African-Americans in the United States differs dramatically from the reforms demanded by indigenous Maori in New Zealand or by Chinese immigrants in Canada. However, there are some general principles that are common to these different struggles for a multicultural state. First, a multicultural state involves the repudiation of the older idea that the state is a possession of a single national group. Instead, the state must be seen as belonging equally to all citizens. Second, as a consequence, a multicultural state repudiates any nation-building policies that assimilate or exclude members of minority or non-dominant groups. Instead, it accepts that individuals should be able to access state institutions, and to act as full and equal citizens in political life, without having to hide

---

[3] This struggle has not always been conducted in the name of 'multiculturalism', and some groups may indeed reject the term. For reasons discussed below, the struggle has often instead been conducted in the name of a 'multi*national* state', or various ideals of 'partnership', 'federalism', 'historic rights', or simply 'democracy'.

or deny their ethnocultural identity. The state accepts an obligation to accord recognition and accommodation to the history, language, and culture of non-dominant groups, as it does for the dominant group. Third, a multicultural state acknowledges the historic injustice that was done to minority/non-dominant groups by these policies of assimilation and exclusion, and manifests a willingness to offer some sort of remedy or rectification for them.

These three interconnected ideas—repudiating the idea of the state as belonging to the dominant group; replacing assimilationist and exclusionary nation-building policies with policies of recognition and accommodation; and acknowledging historic injustice and offering amends for it—are common to virtually all real-world struggles for 'multiculturalism'.

Varieties of Liberal Multiculturalism

These points of commonality are very abstract, and as soon as we look at the details of specific countries, enormous differences emerge. The precise way in which minority groups wish to be recognized and accommodated, or to have their historic injustices amended, varies greatly from country to country, as well as between different minorities within a single country.

It would be impossible to provide a comprehensive overview of the different forms that multiculturalism can take, but for the purposes of illustration, let me focus on three general trends within Western democracies.

(a) Indigenous peoples The first trend concerns the treatment of indigenous peoples, such as the Indians and Inuit in Canada, the Aboriginal peoples of Australia, the Maori of New Zealand, the Sami of Scandinavia, the Inuit of Greenland, and Indian tribes in the United States. In the past, all of these countries had the same goal and expectation that indigenous peoples would eventually disappear as distinct communities, as a result of dying out, or intermarriage, or assimilation. A number of policies were adopted to speed up this process, such as stripping indigenous peoples of their lands, restricting the practice of their traditional cultures, languages, and religions, and undermining their institutions of self-government.[4]

---

[4] For the similarities and differences in policies of Aboriginal assimilation across the New World settler states, see Armitage 1995.

However, there has been a dramatic reversal in these policies, starting in the early 1970s. Today, all of the countries I just mentioned accept, at least in principle, the idea that indigenous peoples will exist into the indefinite future as distinct societies within the larger country, and that they must have the land claims, cultural rights, and self-government rights, needed to sustain themselves as distinct societies.

Consider the constitutional affirmation of Aboriginal rights in the 1982 Canadian Constitution, along with the establishment of a land claims commission and the signing of new treaties; the revival of treaty rights through the Treaty of Waitangi in New Zealand; the recognition of land rights for Aboriginal Australians in the *Mabo* decision; the creation of Sami Parliaments in Scandinavia, the evolution of 'Home Rule' for the Inuit of Greenland; and the laws and court cases upholding self-determination rights for American Indian tribes. In all of these countries there is a gradual but real process of decolonization taking place, as indigenous peoples regain rights regarding their lands, legal norms, and self-government (Havemann 1999).

I will call this a shift towards a more 'multicultural' approach, although this term is not typically used by indigenous peoples themselves, who prefer the terminology of self-determination, treaty rights, and aboriginality or indigeneity, for reasons explored in Chapter 7. My colleague Keith Banting and I have developed a 'Multiculturalism Policy Index' which attempts to measure the extent of the shift (Banting and Kymlicka 2006). We first came up with a list of specific policies which can be taken as emblematic or representative of the new multicultural approach. In the case of indigenous peoples, this list includes the following nine policies:

(1) recognition of land rights/title;
(2) recognition of self-government rights;
(3) upholding historic treaties and/or signing new treaties;
(4) recognition of cultural rights (language, hunting/fishing);
(5) recognition of customary law;
(6) guarantees of representation/consultation in the central government;
(7) constitutional or legislative affirmation of the distinct status of indigenous peoples;
(8) support/ratification for international instruments on indigenous rights;
(9) affirmative action for the members of indigenous communities.

We then attempted to identify which of these policies were in force in which Western democracies in the period 1980 to 2000, and on that basis placed countries in one of three categories: those that had decisively shifted towards a multicultural approach, by adopting six or more of the nine policies; those that had made a more modest but still significant shift, by adopting between three and five of the nine policies; and those that had barely shifted in this direction, if at all, with two or fewer of these policies. Of the nine Western democracies with indigenous peoples, we concluded that four could be categorized as strongly multicultural (Canada, Denmark, New Zealand, United States), three were modestly multicultural (Australia, Finland, Norway), and only two had barely shifted (Japan, Sweden).[5] This is admittedly a rather crude way of trying to measure the extent to which Western democracies have adopted a more multicultural approach regarding indigenous peoples, but it does give some indication of a widespread if uneven trend.

(b) Substate/minority nationalisms The second trend concerns the treatment of substate 'national' groups, such as the Québécois in Canada, the Scots and Welsh in Britain, the Catalans and Basques in Spain, the Flemish in Belgium, the German-speaking minority in South Tyrol in Italy, and Puerto Rico in the United States.[6] In all of these cases, we find a regionally concentrated group that conceives of itself as a nation within a larger state, and mobilizes behind nationalist political parties to achieve recognition of its nationhood, either in the form of an independent state or through territorial autonomy within the larger state. In the past, all of the above-mentioned countries have attempted to suppress expressions of substate nationalism. To have a regional group with a sense of distinct nationhood was seen as a threat to the state, putting into question the state's legitimate right to rule all of its territory and population. Various efforts were made to erode any sense of distinct nationhood, often using the same tools that were used against indigenous peoples—for example, restricting minority language rights, abolishing traditional forms of

---

[5] For further details of how we assigned these scores, and the complications involved, see Banting and Kymlicka 2006: chap. 2.

[6] The French and Italian minorities in Switzerland could also be considered here, although some commentators dispute whether they display a 'national' (or 'nationalist') consciousness. I would argue that insofar as they have not displayed such a national consciousness, it's partly because (unlike virtually every other national minority in the West) they did not need to mobilize along nationalist lines in order to achieve territorial autonomy and official language status. Had federalization and multilingualism not been part of their initial terms of entry into the Swiss state, I suspect that they too would have developed the sort of nationalist political mobilization that we see elsewhere in the West.

regional self-government, and encouraging members of the dominant group to settle in the minority group's homeland in an effort to outnumber the minority even in its traditional territory.

However, there has been a dramatic reversal in the way Western countries deal with substate nationalisms. Today, all of the countries I have just mentioned have accepted the principle that substate national identities will endure into the indefinite future, and that their sense of nationhood and nationalist aspirations must be accommodated in some way or other. This accommodation has typically taken the form of what we can call 'multination and multilingual federalism': that is, creating a federal or quasi-federal subunit in which the minority group forms a local majority, and can thereby exercise meaningful forms of self-government.[7] Moreover, the group's language is typically recognized as an official state language, at least within their federal subunit, and perhaps throughout the country as a whole.

At the beginning of the twentieth century, only Switzerland and Canada had adopted this combination of territorial autonomy and official language status for substate national groups. Since then, however, virtually all Western democracies that contain sizeable substate nationalist movements have moved in this direction. The list includes the adoption of autonomy for the Swedish-speaking Aland Islands in Finland after World War I, autonomy for South Tyrol and Puerto Rico after World War II, federal autonomy for Catalonia and the Basque Country in Spain in the 1970s, for Flanders in the 1980s, and most recently devolution for Scotland and Wales in the 1990s.

Indeed, if we restrict our focus to sizeable and territorially concentrated national minorities, this trend is now essentially universal in the West. All groups over 250,000 that have demonstrated a desire for territorial

---

[7] In Spain, Belgium, Canada, and Switzerland, territorial autonomy for national minorities was achieved through a federalizing of the state, so as to create a federal subunit that was dominated by the national minority. The United Kingdom, by contrast, did not federalize the entire country, but created quasi-federal forms of territorial autonomy for Scotland and Wales. A similar quasi-federal autonomy regime exists for the Swedes in Finland, the Germans in South Tyrol, and for Puerto Rico in the United States. I use the term 'multination federalism' to cover both federal and quasi-federal forms of autonomy. It is important to distinguish such 'multination' federations from other federal systems where internal subunits are not designed to enable minority self-government, such as the continental United States, Germany, Australia, and Brazil. In these countries, none of the subunits was designed to enable a national minority to exercise self-government over its traditional territory, although it would have been possible in the American case. Indeed, in the United States, internal boundaries were deliberately drawn in such a way as to prevent the possibility of a minority-dominated subunit. For more on the difference between multination federalism and other forms of federalism, see Kymlicka 2001, chap. 5.

autonomy now have it in the West, as well as many smaller groups (such as the German minority in Belgium).

This, then, is the second major trend: a shift from suppressing substate nationalisms to accommodating them through regional autonomy and official language rights. Amongst the Western democracies with sizeable national minorities, only France is an exception to this trend, in its refusal to grant autonomy to its main substate nationalist group in Corsica. Even here, however, legislation was recently adopted to accord autonomy to Corsica, although this was struck down by a controversial ruling of the Constitutional Court.

There are some other potential exceptions. Northern Ireland is difficult to categorize, since Catholics are clearly a national minority, but are not territorially concentrated, and so the model of multination federalism is not available. Even here, however, we see clear movement in the direction of greater recognition of minority nationalism. Northern Ireland has recently adopted a peace agreement that explicitly accords Catholics a number of guarantees in terms of representation, and acknowledges their identification with co-nationals in Ireland.

Another complicated case is the Netherlands, where the sizeable Frisian minority lacks territorial autonomy or significant language rights, although this is largely because (virtually alone amongst such sizeable national minorities in the West) the group has not in fact mobilized along nationalist lines to acquire such rights. It is not clear that the Netherlands would reject such claims if clearly supported by most Frisians.[8]

Amongst Western countries, perhaps the only country that remains strongly and ideologically opposed to the official recognition of substate

[8] It is entirely appropriate, from a liberal-democratic point of view, to ensure that minority claims for territorial autonomy are only accepted when they do in fact have genuine support, as reflected for example in consistently high levels of support for politicians or political parties that campaign for it. As the Frisian example shows, not all national minorities are mobilized in this way. National minorities do not enter the world with a fully formed nationalist consciousness: they are constructed by political actors who seek to persuade enough of their members that it makes sense to mobilize politically as a national minority for national goals. In the Frisian case, these attempts to generate a nationalist consciousness amongst the members of a minority have failed. From a historical viewpoint, the Frisians have as much claim to be a distinct 'people' as any other ethnonational group in Europe. Yet attempts by Frisian elites to persuade people of Frisian descent or people living in historic Friesland that they should support nationalist political objectives have repeatedly failed. This is fully acceptable from a liberal point of view. National minorities may have a right to claim territorial autonomy, but they certainly have no duty to do so. Whether or not a national minority claims territorial autonomy should be determined by the wishes of the majority of its members, as shaped and expressed through free democratic debate and contestation. Where this mobilization has been successful, the clear trend in the West has been to accommodate claims for territorial autonomy and official language status.

national groups is Greece, where the once-sizeable Macedonian minority has now been swamped in its traditional homeland.

Here again, I call this a shift towards a 'multicultural' approach to substate national groups, although this terminology is rarely used by these groups themselves, who prefer the language of nationhood, self-determination, federalism, and power-sharing. To measure the extent of this shift, Banting and I identified the following six policies as emblematic of a multicultural approach to substate national groups:

(1) federal or quasi-federal territorial autonomy;

(2) official language status, either in the region or nationally;

(3) guarantees of representation in the central government or on constitutional courts;

(4) public funding of minority language universities/schools/media;

(5) constitutional or parliamentary affirmation of 'multinationalism';

(6) according international personality (e.g. allowing the substate region to sit on international bodies, or sign treaties, or have their own Olympic team).

Of the eleven Western democracies that contain sizeable national minorities (over 100,000 people), we concluded that eight have moved in this direction, five of them strongly, and three of them more modestly. The strongly multicultural countries are Belgium, Canada, Finland, Spain, and Switzerland; the modestly multicultural countries are Italy, the United Kingdom, and the United States, while the three hold-outs are France, Greece, and Japan. Here again, we see a clear trend, but with important variations in its depth or scope.

(c) Immigrant groups A third trend concerns the treatment of immigrant groups. Historically, the most important 'countries of immigration' (i.e. Australia, Canada, New Zealand, and the United States) had an assimilationist approach to immigration. Immigrants were encouraged and expected to assimilate to the pre-existing society, with the hope that over time they would become indistinguishable from native-born citizens in their speech, dress, recreation, voting patterns, and way of life generally. Any groups that were seen as incapable of this sort of cultural assimilation were prohibited from emigrating in the first place, or from becoming citizens. This was reflected in laws that excluded Africans and Asians from entering these countries of immigration for much of the twentieth century, or from naturalizing.

Since the late 1960s, however, we have seen a dramatic change in this approach. There were two related changes: first, the adoption of race-neutral admissions criteria, so that immigrants to these countries are increasingly from non-European (and often non-Christian) societies; and second, the adoption of a more 'multicultural' conception of integration, one which expects that many immigrants will visibly and proudly express their ethnic identity, and which accepts an obligation on the part of public institutions (like the police, schools, media, museums, etc.) to accommodate these ethnic identities.

These twofold changes have occurred, to varying degrees, in all of the traditional countries of immigration. All of them have shifted from discriminatory to race-neutral admissions and naturalization policies. And all of them have shifted from an assimilationist to a more multicultural conception of integration. There are important differences in how official or formal this shift to multiculturalism has been. In Canada, Australia, and New Zealand, this shift was marked by the declaration of an official multicultural policy by the central government. But even in the United States, we see similar changes on the ground. The United States does not have an official policy of multiculturalism at the federal level, but if we look at lower levels of government, such as states or cities, we often find a broad range of multiculturalism policies. If we look at state-level policies regarding the education curriculum, for example, or city-level policies regarding policing or hospitals, we'll often find that they are indistinguishable from the way provinces and cities in Canada or Australia deal with issues of immigrant ethnocultural diversity. As in Canada, they have their own diversity programmes and/or equity officers. As Nathan Glazer puts it, 'we are all multiculturalists now' (Glazer 1997), although this perhaps understates the considerable variation across cities and states in the US in their commitment to multiculturalism policies.[9]

Similarly, in Britain, while there is no nation-wide multiculturalism policy, many of the same basic ideas and principles are pursued through their 'race relations' policy.[10] All of these countries have accepted

---

[9] See also Joppke 2002, who notes that many countries have accommodated diversity claims without this being 'written on the forehead of the state' (Joppke 2002: 250). Experts in immigration and integration issues have repeatedly demolished the mythical contrast between the American 'melting pot' and the Canadian 'mosaic', yet the myth endures in the popular imagination. For more on variation in multiculturalism policies at the state level within the United States, see Hero and Preuhs 2006.

[10] For the British model of multiculturalism through race relations, see Favell 2001; Commission on the Future of Multi-Ethnic Britain 2000. Rights of entry into Britain maintain a degree of racial bias, as witnessed by the debate about whether 'British subjects' in Hong Kong would have the right to domicile in the UK itself.

the same twofold change—adopting race-neutral admissions and naturalization policies, and imposing on public institutions a duty to accommodate immigrant ethnocultural diversity—although the degree and formal recognition of the latter change vary from country to country.

This trend applies primarily to countries of immigration—that is, countries which legally admit immigrants as permanent residents and future citizens. Amongst such countries, the main exception to this trend is France, which retains an assimilationist conception of French republican citizenship.[11] It is a different story, however, in those countries that do not legally admit immigrants, such as most countries of northern Europe. These countries may well contain large numbers of 'foreigners', in the form of illegal economic migrants, asylum-seekers, or 'guest-workers', but these groups were not admitted as part of a deliberate immigration policy. As it happens, even some of these countries have adopted aspects of a 'multicultural' approach (e.g. Sweden and The Netherlands). But in general, the trend from assimilation to multiculturalism is one that has taken place most strongly within countries of immigration.

What are the specific policies that reflect this shift in approach? Banting and I identified the following eight policies as the most common or emblematic forms of immigrant multiculturalism:

(1) constitutional, legislative, or parliamentary affirmation of multiculturalism, at the central and/or regional and municipal levels;
(2) the adoption of multiculturalism in school curricula;[12]
(3) the inclusion of ethnic representation/sensitivity in the mandate of public media or media licensing;
(4) exemptions from dress-codes, Sunday-closing legislation etc. (either by statute or by court cases);
(5) allowing dual citizenship;
(6) the funding of ethnic group organizations to support cultural activities;

---

[11] As evidenced by the refusal to allow Muslim girls to wear headscarves to public school.

[12] Not all forms of education that teach about immigrant cultures qualify as 'multicultural education'. In Germany, for example, special education arrangements were set up for the children of Turkish guest-workers with the goal of preparing them to return to their 'home' (even if they were in fact born in Germany), on the assumption that they did not really belong in Germany. This sort of 'preparationist education' clearly differs from what is typically understood as 'multicultural education', and does not count as a multiculturalism policy. As discussed earlier, multiculturalism policies are policies that seek to recognize and accommodate ethnic diversity as a fact of society, not policies that seek to encourage ethnic groups to leave.

(7) the funding of bilingual education or mother-tongue instruction;

(8) affirmative action for disadvantaged immigrant groups. [13]

We then attempted to determine which countries had shifted in the direction of these policies, either strongly (by adopting six or more of the eight policies), or modestly (by adopting three to five of the eight policies). By our calculations, all four of the traditional countries of immigration have made this shift, some strongly (Australia, Canada) and others modestly (New Zealand, United States). However, if we look beyond these traditional immigration countries, the remaining seventeen Western democracies in our study offer a different picture. Of these, none has shifted strongly towards multiculturalism, and only four have made a modest shift (Belgium, The Netherlands, Sweden, United Kingdom), while the vast majority have essentially resisted the trend (Austria, Denmark, Finland, France, Germany, Greece, Ireland, Italy, Japan, Norway, Portugal, Spain, Switzerland).

So the shift to multiculturalism in this context is obviously more contested than in the case of indigenous peoples or substate nationalist groups. Whereas the majority of Western countries have made either a decisive or modest shift towards a multicultural approach for the 'old' minorities, the evidence is more mixed for immigrant groups. While there is a clear trend towards a more multicultural approach in the case of

---

[13] Some commentators have suggested including a ninth policy—namely, a policy of admitting large numbers of immigrants as permanent residents and future citizens. Some people view a pro-immigration policy as itself a form of multiculturalism policy, on the assumption that only a country that is willing to accommodate diversity would voluntarily admit immigrants as future citizens. However, the link between immigration policy and multiculturalism is complex. Some critics of multiculturalism policies are in fact defenders of more open borders: they are happy with the idea of greater ethnic and racial diversity in the population, but simply oppose any government recognition or accommodation of this diversity through multiculturalism policies. This is a long-standing view amongst libertarians. Conversely, in some countries, support for multiculturalism policies is dependent on sharply limiting the number of new immigrants who can take advantage of these policies. This is often said to be the case in Britain. The quasi-multiculturalism policies adopted in the 1970s (under the heading of race relations) were part of a package in which the government said to Britons: 'we will close the door to new immigrants; but we expect you to accept and accommodate the immigrants from the Caribbean and South Asia who have already arrived'. Re-opening the door to immigration was seen as undermining the tenuous support for multiculturalism policies. We see a similar complex relationship between multiculturalism policies and refugee admission policies. While there is a tendency for pro-multiculturalism countries to have more generous policies on the admission of refugees (Kate 2005), this is not always the case, as witnessed by the harsh treatment of refugees in Australia, compared with the (formerly) generous openness to refugees in Germany, even though the former is pro-multiculturalism and the latter not. Policies about whether to admit people as immigrants or refugees, and policies about how to accommodate them once admitted, raise quite distinct issues. I am focusing on policies that concern the treatment of immigrant groups that already reside in the territory of the state, such as the eight policies listed above.

the traditional New World countries of immigration, it has been largely rejected elsewhere, and there are several high-profile cases of a 'retreat' from multiculturalism, to which I will return in the next chapter.

In one sense, it should not be surprising that the idea of multiculturalism for migrant communities has not taken root outside the traditional countries of immigration. After all, the idea of adopting a multicultural conception of citizenship presupposes that the newcomers are in fact 'citizens', rather than simply 'guests', 'visitors', or 'foreigners'. Yet this is precisely what was contested in many countries of continental Europe, until recently. As I noted earlier, post-war migrants in Europe were not typically admitted as permanent residents and future citizens under an explicit immigration policy. Rather, they entered under a variety of other guises. Some migrants entered a country illegally (e.g. North Africans in Italy), others as asylum-seekers (e.g. Kosovars in Switzerland), and yet others as students or 'guest-workers' who renewed (or overstayed) their initial visa (e.g. Turks in Germany). When they entered the country, these people were not conceived of as future citizens, or even as long-term residents, and indeed they would not have been allowed to enter in the first place if they had been seen as permanent residents and future citizens. However, whatever the initial expectations and official rules, they have settled more or less permanently. In principle, and to some extent in practice, some of these migrants may face the threat of deportation if they are detected by the authorities, or if they are convicted of a crime. But they nonetheless form sizeable communities in certain countries, engage in some form of employment, legal or illegal, and marry and form families. Borrowing a term from Ancient Greece, Walzer calls these groups 'metics'—that is, *de facto* long-term residents who are nonetheless excluded from the polis (Walzer 1983).

The issue of adopting multiculturalism can barely arise until such groups move out of the category of temporary foreigners and move into the category of permanent residents and citizens,[14] which is indeed what many of these groups have sought. But this has not been an easy transition to make. Some countries have no established process or infrastructure for integrating immigrants, and so resist accepting that they are now *de facto* 'countries of immigration'. Moreover, many of these metics have

---

[14] As I noted in n. 12, a form of pseudo-multiculturalism has sometimes been adopted for metics, on the assumption that encouraging the members of a group to maintain their language and culture will make it more likely they will return to their country of origin. But this 'preparationist' form of multiculturalism is the antithesis of the idea of multicultural citizenship developed in the traditional countries of immigration.

either broken the law to enter the country (illegal immigrants), or are seen as reneging on their promise to return to their country of origin (students, guest-workers, asylum-seekers), and so are not viewed as worthy of citizenship. Moreover, countries with no tradition of accepting newcomers are often more xenophobic, and prone to view all foreigners as potential security threats, or as potentially disloyal, or simply as unalterably 'alien'. In these countries, of which Austria and Switzerland are the best-known examples, the official policy has not been to try to integrate metics into the national community, but to get them to leave the country, either through expulsion or voluntary return. In short, the hope was that if metics were denied citizenship, so that they only had a precarious legal status within the country, and if they were told repeatedly that their real home was in their country of origin, and that they were not wanted as members of the society, then they would eventually go home.

But it is increasingly recognized that this approach is not viable. Metics who have lived in a country for several years are unlikely to go home, even if they have only a precarious legal status. This is particularly true if the metics have married and had children in their adopted country. At this point, it is their new country, not their country of origin, which has become their 'home'. Indeed, it may be the only home that the metics' children and grandchildren know. Once they have settled, founded a family, and started raising their children, nothing short of expulsion is likely to get metics to return to their country of origin.

So a policy based on the hope of voluntary return is unrealistic. Moreover, it endangers the larger society. For the likely result of such a policy is to create a permanently disenfranchised, alienated, and racially or ethnically defined underclass. Metics may develop an oppositional subculture in which the very idea of pursuing success in mainstream institutions is viewed with suspicion. The predictable consequences can involve some mixture of political alienation, criminality, and religious fundamentalism amongst the metics, particularly the second generation, which in turn leads to increased racial tensions, even violence, throughout the society.

To avoid this, there is an increasing trend in Western democracies, even in non-immigrant countries, to enable metics to regularize their status and to naturalize. Asylum-seekers whose refugee claims are accepted are granted permanent residence and access to citizenship, and not required to return to their country of origin even when the danger of persecution has passed. Guest-workers who have renewed (or overstayed) their visa are often able to gain permanent residence. Periodic amnesties are offered for illegal immigrants. In effect, long-settled metics are increasingly treated as if they had initially arrived as legal immigrants, and are allowed to follow the immigrant path to integration. In some cases, this integration process has been revised in a more 'multicultural' direction—Sweden is a prominent case, declaring 2006 to be The Year of Multiculturalism—although this remains uncommon outside the traditional countries of immigration.

Three Key Features of Liberal Multiculturalism

In relation to indigenous peoples, substate national groups, and immigrants, then, there has been a shift away from historic policies of assimilation or exclusion towards a more multicultural approach that recognizes and accommodates diversity. As we will see in Part III, each of these trends has, to varying degrees, shaped emerging international norms—most strongly in the case of indigenous peoples, more modestly regarding substate national groups, and quite minimally for immigrant groups. Various aspects of this shift will be explored throughout the volume, but for our immediate purposes, three points are worth highlighting, in order to forestall misunderstandings—first, about the different categories of minorities; second, about the content of the rights that are accorded to these minorities; and third, about the relationship between multiculturalism and nation-building.

First, as this brief survey suggests, liberal multiculturalism in the West is highly group-differentiated, or to use the terminology I introduced earlier, it is highly 'targeted'. Liberal multiculturalism guarantees certain generic minority rights to all ethnocultural groups, but it also elaborates a number of targeted categories of minority rights. The precise categories differ from country to country, but they typically fall into the same basic pattern. The most common distinction is between 'old' minorities, who were settled on their territory prior to it becoming part of a larger independent country, and 'new' minorities, who were admitted to a country as immigrants after it achieved legal independence. But within the category of 'old' minorities, a further distinction is typically drawn between 'indigenous' groups and other historic minorities, often called 'national minorities' or 'nationalities'.

We see this basic threefold pattern in several Western democracies. Finland, for example, accords different rights to the Sami, as an indigenous people, than to the Swedes, who are a traditional cross-border national minority, and both of these 'old minorities' have a different set of minority rights from those of 'new minorities' established through recent migration. Similarly, Denmark distinguishes the rights of the indigenous Inuit in Greenland from the rights of the (cross-border) German national minority, and distinguishes both of these from the rights of new immigrants.[15] Canada distinguishes the rights of the indigenous Aboriginal peoples (Indians, Inuit, and Métis) from those of the historic French colonial settlers of New France (Quebec) whose presence predated the British colonization of North America, and distinguishes both of these old minorities from the multicultural rights accorded to ethnic groups formed by immigration to the country. In the United States, indigenous Indian tribes have a different legal status from the historic Spanish colonial settlement of Puerto Rico conquered by the Americans in 1898, and both of these are distinguished from the legal status accorded to immigrant ethnic groups.

Of course, not all countries have all three types of ethnocultural diversity. Australia and New Zealand, for example, have both indigenous peoples and immigrant ethnic groups, but no substate nationalist groups. Belgium, Switzerland, Spain, and Britain, by contrast, all have issues of substate nationalism and immigration, but no indigenous peoples. In all of these cases, however, the framework of liberal multiculturalism remains group-differentiated. Britain, for example, distinguishes the rights of its historic substate 'nations' (the Scots, Welsh, and Irish) from its immigrant-origin 'minorities'.

Indeed, I'm not aware of any Western democracy that relies solely on generic minority rights to govern its ethnocultural diversity, without any element of targeted minority rights. Moreover, this targeted element is not marginal or peripheral. On the contrary, the entire infrastructure of liberal multiculturalism is often built around it. In most countries, the different forms of ethnocultural diversity are governed by different pieces of legislation, which are administered by different government departments, using different concepts and principles. Indigenous peoples, substate nationalist groups, and immigrants all form their own policy 'tracks', and one of the most striking aspects of liberal multiculturalism in the West is how separate these targeted tracks are from each other, administratively and legally.[16] Countries can and do move at very different speeds

[15] For details of how all four Nordic countries distinguish these three categories of indigenous, national minorities, and migrants, see Hannikainen 1996.

[16] In the Canadian case, for example, the guiding concepts used in articulating and negotiating claims within the Aboriginal track include treaty rights, Aboriginal rights, common law title, *sui generis* property rights, fiduciary trust, indigeneity, self-government, and self-determination. The main concepts used in articulating and negotiating claims within the French-Canadian track include bilingualism, duality, (asymmetric) federalism, distinct

along the different tracks. A country can be a trail-blazer in one mode of multiculturalism while a hold-out in another. For example, compared to its Nordic neighbours, Sweden has been unusually supportive of multiculturalism for immigrants, but unusually resistant to land claims and self-government rights for the indigenous Sami. Switzerland has been a model for the accommodation of substate national minorities through official language rights and regional autonomy, but has been perhaps the most exclusionary country in Europe in its treatment of immigrants. Countries can be advancing along one track, while retreating along another.

It is quite surprising how little interaction or spillover there is between these different policy tracks. And when the various struggles for multiculturalism do interact, they are as likely to conflict as to cooperate. Immigrants, national minorities, and indigenous peoples may all seek to challenge their historic subordination to the dominant group, but they don't necessarily support each other's struggles. Immigrants may not instinctively support demands by indigenous peoples and substate national groups for greater self-government, and these historic minorities in turn may not instinctively support demands by immigrant groups for multicultural citizenship (Medda-Windischer 2004). Liberal multiculturalism as it has evolved in the West is the outcome of multiple struggles by different types of ethnocultural groups, mobilizing along different legal and administrative tracks, and not a single unified struggle in the name of 'diversity'.

We cannot hope to understand the theory and practice of liberal multiculturalism without coming to grips with its targeted or group-differentiated character. Any attempt to articulate liberal multiculturalism as if it were purely a matter of generic minority rights is doomed to failure. The logic of liberal multiculturalism cannot be captured in the form 'all minorities have a right to X' or 'all persons belonging to minorities have a right to X'. Different types of minorities have fought for, and gained, different types of minority rights, and this group-differentiated targeting is key both to understanding the challenges involved in adopting liberal multiculturalism and to evaluating its successes and limitations to date. Unfortunately, as we will see in Part III, international organizations, for reasons of both principle and expediency, have had difficulty acknowledging the targeted nature of liberal multiculturalism.

society, and nationhood. And the main concepts used in the immigrant track include multiculturalism, citizenship, integration, tolerance, ethnicity, diversity, and inclusion. For a more detailed discussion of the legal and political separation between these tracks or 'silos' in Canada, see Kymlicka 2007.

The second key point I want to emphasize concerns the content of the minority rights found within Western liberal multiculturalism. Many commentators discuss multiculturalism as if it were primarily focused on issues of symbolic recognition, and hence disconnected from issues regarding the distribution of material resources or political power. It is common, for example, to say that multiculturalism reflects 'the politics of recognition' as opposed to the 'politics of redistribution',[17] or to say that it pursues 'the politics of identity' as opposed to the 'politics of interests'.

These distinctions between 'recognition' and 'redistribution', or between 'identities' and 'interests', are useful for some analytic purposes. But it should be clear that liberal multiculturalism as it has evolved in the West is not restricted to questions of symbolic recognition or identity politics. Liberal multiculturalism also addresses issues of power and resources. This is particularly clear in relation to national minorities and indigenous peoples, where states have been restructured to create new political units that enable minority self-government. In relation to these groups, Western democracies have moved away from older models of unitary, centralized nation-states, and repudiated older ideologies of 'one state, one nation, one language'. Today, virtually all Western states that contain indigenous peoples and substate national groups have become 'multination' states, recognizing the existence of self-governing 'peoples' and 'nations' within the boundaries of the state. This recognition is manifested in a range of minority and indigenous rights that include regional autonomy and official language status for national minorities, and customary law, land claims, and self-government for indigenous peoples.

In the case of immigrants, the changes may be less obvious, since we do not see the same type of devolution or federalization of state power to minority-controlled political units. But if we return to the list of immigrant multiculturalism policies in the West (see p. 73 above), several are intended to enhance access to state power, public services, and economic opportunities. These include affirmative action policies, mechanisms for political participation and consultation, and the development of health care and social service delivery models that are adapted to the needs of minorities.

Taken together, these trends represent a dramatic transformation in the relationship between states and ethnic groups. These changes are not purely token or symbolic. On the contrary, they often involve a significant redistribution of economic resources and political power—something

---

[17] For the *locus classicus* of this distinction, see Fraser 1995, 1998, 2000.

close to a genuine sharing of power—as well as giving non-dominant groups enhanced access to state institutions.

This linking of identities and interests within multiculturalism policies should not surprise us, since it mirrors the way identities and interests are linked in the nation-building policies to which multiculturalism is a response. State nation-building is not just about recognizing a particular majority identity—although it is indeed an example *par excellence* of the 'politics of identity'—but also about building public institutions around that identity, so that it becomes a source of economic opportunity, political power, and social prestige. Liberal multiculturalism has the same aspiration to link identities and interests. It not only recognizes particular minority identities, but seeks to transform the economic opportunities, political powers, and social status available to bearers of that identity.

The precise ways in which 'recognition' and 'redistribution', or 'identity' and 'interests', are combined varies from one multiculturalism policy to another, and from one group to another. If it's a mistake to treat multiculturalism as purely a matter of symbolic recognition, it would equally be a mistake to treat it as purely a disguised form of class politics. While it is common for minorities to suffer simultaneously from political, economic, and cultural exclusion, the links between these different forms of exclusion are complex, and multiculturalism policies track this variability.

Some groups, like indigenous peoples, are disproportionately concentrated in vulnerable economic positions, politically marginalized, and subject to demeaning or silencing cultural representations—and their claims address these multiple forms of subordination. But there are other groups that combine cultural and political exclusion with economic privilege. A striking example is Chinese minorities in South-East Asian countries such as Indonesia, Malaysia, Philippines, or Thailand. In each of these countries, the Chinese minority forms a small percentage of the population, yet often owns a large part—perhaps even the dominant part—of the economy. In Indonesia, for example, the Chinese minority forms around 3 per cent of the population, but is estimated to control 70 per cent of the private economy. Yet, despite their economic privileges, they have faced serious cultural exclusions. Until recently, Chinese-language education was restricted; and it was forbidden to publish in Chinese, or to put Chinese characters on shop signs. In Thailand, the Chinese were pressured to adopt Thai surnames. More generally, Chinese groups in the region are often still defined as 'foreigners' who do not really belong, even if they have been living in the country for generations; they are invisible in the public sphere, and excluded from state symbols and national narratives.[18]

The case of economically privileged but culturally stigmatized traders may seem like a peculiarity of the 'crony capitalism' found in authoritarian regimes (Chua 2003; Riggs 1994). But there are many cases within the established Western democracies of groups that are culturally stigmatized without suffering economic exclusion. A non-ethnic example is that of gays and lesbians in most Western democracies, who enjoy similar per-capita levels of income or education as heterosexuals, but are targets of homophobia. Some well-established immigrant or religious groups, like Arab-Americans, enjoy higher-than-average levels of education and income, but are culturally marginalized or stigmatized. They are typically invisible in public space, except when presented in the media or Hollywood as terrorists or religious fundamentalists.

Or consider a substate nationalist minority like the Catalans. They enjoy the same standard of living as the majority—in fact, somewhat higher—yet they have suffered from cultural exclusion, as their language and culture have been stigmatized as inferior by the majority. They resent the way their language and traditions have been marginalized by the central government, and have mobilized for regional autonomy (or even independence).[19]

So not all multiculturalist claims involve a demand for economic redistribution. But even in these cases, multiculturalism is not purely 'symbolic'—it still centrally involves issues of political power and representation (such as the Catalan demand for autonomy). To be sure, as we will see next chapter, there are political actors who would like to reduce multiculturalism to mere symbolism. In many cases, political elites and government officials may have hoped and expected that token reforms would be sufficient. They may have hoped that it would be enough to put a few words of a minority language on the state currency, for example, or to put an indigenous historical figure on a postage stamp, and this would satisfy aspirations for 'recognition'. However, whatever the original intention of government officials, non-dominant groups have

---

[18] In the Indonesian case, for example, the Chinese are invisible in the authoritative state representations of national history at the main independence monument (Monas) or at the 'Taman Mini' complex that illustrates the cultures of the country. For a general overview of the status of Chinese in South-East Asia, see Ho 2000.

[19] For a refutation of the common view that these movements are a reaction to economic underdevelopment, see Connor 1993.

used multicultural reforms as a springboard for negotiating significantly enhanced access to public resources, powers and offices.

The success of these struggles for a more substantive form of multiculturalism will be evaluated in Chapter 5. But for now, the key point is that multiculturalism is not inherently about recognition rather than redistribution or identities rather than interests. The sorts of policies listed in this chapter cut across these distinctions, addressing issues of legal rights, political decision-making, economic resources, and public services. Indeed, this is why multiculturalism in its various forms has been so controversial, both in the West and in the rest of the world. We can't hope to understand these controversies if we assume in advance that multiculturalism is just about symbols.

A third potential misunderstanding concerns the link between liberal multiculturalism and nation-building. I said earlier that multiculturalism, in all of its different forms, involves a repudiation of older models of homogeneous nationhood. One might assume, therefore, that multiculturalism and nationalism are sworn enemies and inherently contradictory ideologies, and that support for one entails repudiation of the other. On this view, there is a zero-sum relationship between multicultural policies and nation-building policies, such that multiculturalism can only take root in a 'post-national' state and society. In reality, however, the sort of multiculturalism that has emerged within the West has transformed nation-building, not replaced it. All Western countries continue to adopt a range of policies to inculcate overarching national identities and loyalties, including the mandatory teaching of the nation's language, history, and institutions in schools, language tests for citizenship, the funding of national media and museums, and the diffusion of national symbols, flags, anthems, and holidays, to name just a few. This is as true of countries that qualify as 'strongly' multicultural in my lists above as of countries that have made little if any shift in a multicultural direction. However, where multiculturalism policies have been adopted, they operate to supplement and transform these nation-building policies so that the latter are less likely to marginalize or stigmatize minorities—for example, by ensuring that nation-building policies do not exclude metics and racial caste groups, or coercively assimilate immigrants, or undermine the self-government of national minorities and indigenous peoples. In those Western countries that have strongly moved in the direction of multiculturalism, the resulting approach is best described as one in which robust forms of nation-building are combined and constrained by robust forms of minority rights.

My assessment of the strength of multiculturalism in various countries therefore does not track the extent to which these states have repudiated nation-building, but rather, the extent to which nation-building has been transformed in a more pluralistic direction. In this respect, my conception of the difference between 'strong', 'modest', and 'weak' multiculturalism differs from the way these terms are sometimes used. David Miller, for example, also distinguishes between stronger and weaker forms of multiculturalism, which he labels 'radical' and 'moderate'. But on his view, 'radical' multiculturalism involves a commitment to accommodating minorities without simultaneously promoting an overarching identification with (and loyalty to) the larger political community and state (Miller 1995, chap. 5, 2000: 105–6, 2006). He distinguishes this from a 'moderate' multiculturalism that combines multiculturalism with nation-building policies that seek to inculcate an overarching political identity and loyalty. In the British context, for example, moderate multiculturalism would tell citizens that there are many different and legitimate ways of 'being British', and that being British is not inconsistent with the public expression and accommodation of other identities, including 'being Muslim' or 'being Scottish', whereas radical multiculturalism would absolve or discourage minorities from adopting such a pan-ethnic super-ordinate political identity.

This distinction between radical and moderate multiculturalism may be useful for some analytic purposes, but all actually existing forms of multiculturalism in the Western democracies qualify as 'moderate' in Miller's sense, operating to transform rather than repudiate nation-building. No Western democracy has abandoned nation-building policies, whether in the field of official languages, core curricula in schools, citizenship requirements, state symbols, public media, and so on. But these nation-building policies have, to varying extents in different countries, been qualified and transformed by multiculturalism policies.[20]

What we see in the 'real world of liberal democracies', therefore, is a complex dialectic of state nation-building (state demands on minorities) and minority rights (minority demands on the state). The choice

---

[20] Indeed, in the context of substate nationalist groups and indigenous peoples, we can say that multiculturalism has actually multiplied nation-building projects. By acknowledging the presence of these 'nations within', and according them self-governing powers, liberal multiculturalism enables them to adopt their own (substate) nation-building projects, subject to the same limitations and qualifications needed to protect 'internal minorities' within these self-governing territories. For a fuller discussion of how multiculturalism both enables and constrains these nation-building projects, at state and substate levels, see Kymlicka 2001.

is not between nationhood and multiculturalism, but between different packages of policies that combine the enduring aspirations and functional needs for nation-building with the equally enduring demands to accommodate diversity.[21]

In short, liberal multiculturalism is a more complicated phenomenon than many people realize. It is not a single principle or policy, but an umbrella of highly group-differentiated approaches. And each of these approaches is itself multidimensional, incorporating economic, political, and cultural elements in different ways. Each also has its own complex links to policies and practices of nation-building. There is a natural tendency to want to simplify this complexity, and to reduce multiculturalism to a single principle or dimension, as if it was all really about, say, 'protecting endangered cultural traditions', or 'validating stigmatized identities', or 'repudiating nationalism'. But we need to avoid these simplifying presuppositions, and to examine in a more open-minded way why these various policies emerged, what they were intended to achieve, and how they are operating in practice.

* * * * *

In this chapter, I have tried to outline some of the main forms of liberal multiculturalism in the West. I have not yet shown that they are 'liberal' in any meaningful sense, beyond the fact that they emerged within the framework of Western liberal democracies. To show this requires examining the nature of the mobilization that gave rise to these reforms, and the actual effects (intended and unintended) of adopting them. That is my goal in the next two chapters.

Defenders of these reforms have argued that they are needed to overcome deep-seated forms of exclusion and stigmatization, helping Western democracies to become freer, fairer, more inclusive, and indeed more

[21] Far from being inherently mutually contradictory, it might be more accurate to view nation-building and multiculturalism as providing the legitimating conditions for each other. Were it not for the presence of nation-building policies that potentially harm minorities, many claims for multicultural rights would appear as simply 'privileges' or 'special interests'. Conversely, were it not for the presence of minority rights, many nation-building policies would appear as unjust privileges for the majority. After all, we cannot simply take for granted that it is legitimate for liberal-democratic states to insist on common national languages, education systems, citizenship tests, and so on, and to impose these on minorities. As I discussed earlier, there are certain valid purposes that are promoted by nation-building policies, such as civic solidarity. But it is not legitimate to pursue these goals by assimilating, excluding, or disempowering minorities, or by imposing costs and burdens on groups that are often already disadvantaged. Unless supplemented and constrained by minority rights, state nation-building is likely to be oppressive and unjust.

democratic societies. It is on the basis of this perception that various international organizations have publicized the theories and 'best practices' of liberal multiculturalism as a model for other countries. As I hope to show, while there are good grounds to defend this optimistic perception about the effects of liberal multiculturalism, there are also grounds for hesitation about its exportability.

4

The Origins of Liberal Multiculturalism: Sources and Preconditions

Liberal multiculturalism did not emerge out of thin air. It has been built up over time, drawing on a number of sources and facilitating conditions that enabled it to rise out of what John Kingdon famously called the 'primeval policy soup' (Kingdon 1997). Any serious effort to promote liberal multiculturalism needs to attend to these sources and preconditions. And yet we know surprisingly little about them.

One problem is that much of the literature on this issue suffers from 'methodological nationalism' (Wimmer and Glick Schiller 2002). When explaining the emergence of multiculturalism policies, commentators tend to focus on a particular country, and then invoke facts that are specific to that country, such as particular personalities or high-profile events, the strategies of particular organizations or political parties, the nature of the electoral system, and so on. These factors are undoubtedly important in explaining the details of any particular case, but once we recognize the pervasive nature of the trend towards multiculturalism, it seems clear that the main explanation must lie in forces and dynamics that are found across many Western democracies, rather than factors specific to particular countries. There must be underlying structural causes that explain why so many Western democracies have moved in similar directions, despite their different electoral and party systems. Put schematically, we need to explain both why such a broad range of minority groups have become more assertive in advancing rights-claims, and why such a broad range of countries have become more willing to accept these claims.

I do not believe that we have a clear understanding of what these underlying causes are. However, I will try in this chapter to identify several factors that have made the trend towards the greater accommodation of ethnocultural diversity possible, and perhaps even inevitable, in the West.

I will start with the most important ideological factor—namely, the rise of a human rights culture, and the resulting de-legitimation of traditional ethnic and racial hierarchies. As I will try to show, human rights ideals have not only helped to inspire and justify claims for multiculturalism, but also have strongly influenced how these claims are framed, channelling and filtering them to accord with the underlying values of international human rights norms.

There is an obvious irony here. As we saw in Chapter 2, when human rights norms were initially codified by the UN after World War II, they were seen precisely as an alternative to the inter-war system of minority rights, rendering the latter unnecessary. And for several decades after World War II, the assumption that human rights replace minority rights prevailed. But the human rights revolution unleashed a set of ideas about ethnic and racial equality, and a set of political movements contesting ethnic and racial hierarchies, that led naturally to contemporary struggles for multiculturalism and minority rights. In these contemporary struggles, unlike inter-war ideas of minority protection, minority rights are tightly interwoven with human rights ideals. The resulting model of multiculturalism has proven to be an attractive vehicle for converting historic relations of hierarchy or enmity into relations of democratic citizenship.

But having an attractive or compelling moral ideal is rarely enough to generate consensus on significant political reforms. I will therefore also look at some of the more prudential or strategic reasons why dominant groups and states have been willing to support, or at least acquiesce in, the adoption of multicultural reforms. These include changes in the geo-political security situation of the Western democracies, and changes in the nature of the global economy.

There is no way of determining the precise relative weights of the more principled reasons for adopting multiculturalism, as compared to the more strategic reasons. But I believe that both have indeed played a vital role in the rise of multiculturalism in the West, and, just as importantly, both are crucial to assessing the prospects for its diffusion around the world.

The Human Rights Revolution as Inspiration

The first factor to consider is the human rights revolution. The adoption of liberal multiculturalism has been both inspired and constrained by human rights ideals. Indeed, the trend towards liberal multiculturalism can only be understood as a new stage in the gradual working out of the logic of human rights, and in particular the logic of the idea of the inherent equality of human beings, both as individuals and as peoples.

With the adoption of the Universal Declaration of Human Rights (UDHR) in 1948, the international order decisively repudiated older ideas of a racial or ethnic hierarchy, according to which some peoples were superior to others, and thereby had the right to rule over them. It's important to remember how contested this idea of human equality was. In 1919, when Japan proposed that a clause on racial equality be included in the covenant of the League of Nations, this was soundly rejected by the United States, Canada, and other Western powers (MacMillan 2001: 316–21). Assumptions about a hierarchy of peoples were in fact widely accepted throughout the West up until World War II, when Hitler's fanatical and murderous policies discredited them. The whole system of colonialism was premised on the assumption of a hierarchy of peoples, and this assumption was the explicit basis of both domestic policies and international law throughout the nineteenth century and the first half of the twentieth century (including the racially exclusionary immigration laws found in all the New World settler states, mentioned in the previous chapter). In short, prior to World War II, 'racism around the world was largely socially accepted, politically buttressed, economically supported, intellectually justified, and legally tolerated' (Lauren 1996: 144).

Since 1948, however, we have been living in a world where the idea of human equality is unquestioned, at least officially, and this has generated a series of political movements designed to contest the lingering presence or enduring effects of older ethnic and racial hierarchies. (It has also inspired movements to contest other types of hierarchies, such as gender, disability, and sexual orientation.)

In relation to ethnic and racial hierarchies, we can identify a sequence of such movements. The first was decolonization, from roughly 1948 to 1966. Some Western countries that signed the UDHR did not believe that endorsing the principle of the equality of peoples would require them to give up their colonies (e.g. France, Spain, Portugal). But this position was unsustainable, and the link between equality and decolonization was made explicit in the UN's 1960 General Assembly Resolution 1514 on decolonization.

A second stage was racial desegregation, from roughly 1955 to 1965, initiated by the African-American civil rights struggles, and partially inspired by decolonization struggles.[1] When the United States signed the UDHR in 1948, it did not believe that this would require abandoning its segregationist laws. But this position too became unsustainable, and the link between equality and racial discrimination was made explicit in the UN's 1965 Convention on the Elimination of All Forms of Racial Discrimination.

The African-American civil rights struggle subsequently inspired historically subordinated ethnocultural groups around the world to engage in their own forms of struggle against the lingering presence of ethnic and racial hierarchies. We can see this in the way indigenous peoples adopted the rhetoric of 'Red Power', or in the way national minorities (such as the Québécois or Catholics in Northern Ireland) called themselves 'white niggers' (Vallieres 1971), or in the way Caribbean immigrants to the UK adopted the rhetoric and legal strategies of American blacks (Modood 1996, 2003). All of these movements were profoundly influenced by American ideas of civil rights liberalism, and its commitment to defend equality for disadvantaged and stigmatized minorities.

However, as civil rights liberalism spread, it also had to adapt to the actual challenges facing different types of minorities around the world. For American theorists, ideas such as 'civil rights' and 'equality' have been interpreted through the lens of anti-discrimination in general, and racial desegregation in particular. For most American theorists, the sorts of rights that civil rights liberalism must defend are therefore rights to undifferentiated citizenship within a 'civic nation' that transcends ethnic, racial, and religious differences.

In most countries, however, the situation of minorities needing protection differs from that of African-Americans, and so too do the sorts of civil and political rights they require. African-Americans were involuntarily segregated, solely on the basis of their race, excluded from common institutions and opportunities to which they often wanted access. Many minorities, however, are in the opposite position: they have been involuntarily assimilated, stripped of their own language, culture, and self-governing institutions. They too have faced oppression at the hands of their co-citizens, and have had their civil rights denied to them, often with the enthusiastic backing of large majorities, on the grounds of their inferiority or backwardness. They too need counter-majoritarian

---

[1] On the link between decolonization struggles and the African-American civil rights struggles, see Von Eschen 1997; Anderson 2003.

protections. But the form these protections take is not solely anti-discrimination and undifferentiated citizenship, but rather various group-differentiated minority rights. In the Canadian context, for example, these include bilingualism and provincial autonomy (for the Québécois), land claims and treaty rights (for Aboriginal peoples), and various sorts of multicultural accommodations (for immigrant/ethnic groups).[2]

The struggle for these differentiated minority rights must be understood, I believe, as a local adaptation of civil rights liberalism, and hence as a new stage in the unfolding of the human rights revolution. Just as decolonization inspired the struggle for racial desegregation, so racial desegregation inspired the struggle for minority rights and multiculturalism. This third stage is inspired by the civil rights liberalism of the second stage (as well as the decolonization struggles of the first stage), shares its commitment to contesting ethnic and racial hierarchies, and seeks to apply this commitment more effectively to the actual range of exclusions, stigmatizations, and inequalities that exist in Western democracies. Few countries that signed the UDHR expected that endorsing the principle of the equality of peoples would require accepting norms of multiculturalism and minority rights. But that position too has become unsustainable, and the link between equality and multiculturalism has been made explicit in the UN's 1992 Declaration on the Rights of Persons Belonging to National or Ethnic, Religious and Linguistic Minorities.

In all three stages of this struggle against ethnic and racial hierarchy, what matters is not the change in international law *per se*, which has had little impact on most people's everyday lives. The real change has been in people's consciousness. Members of historically subordinated groups today demand equality, and demand it as a *right*. They believe they are entitled to equality, and entitled to it *now*, not in some indefinite or millenarian future.

This sort of rights-consciousness has become such a pervasive feature of modernity that we have trouble imagining that it did not always exist. But if we examine the historical records, we find that minorities in the past typically justified their claims, not by appeal to human rights or equality, but by appealing to the generosity of rulers in according 'privileges', often in return for past loyalty and services (Schwittay 2003). Today, by contrast, groups have a powerful sense of entitlement to equality as a basic human

---

[2] I develop this interpretation of the Canadian experiment in multiculturalism as a local adaptation of civil rights liberalism and human rights norms in greater depth in Kymlicka 2007.

right, not as a favour or charity, and are angrily impatient with any lingering manifestations of older hierarchies.[3]

Of course, there is no consensus on what 'equality' means (and, conversely, no agreement on what sorts of actions or practices are evidence of 'hierarchy'). People who agree on the general principle of the equality of peoples may disagree about whether or when this requires official bilingualism, for example, or consociational power-sharing, or religious accommodations. But there can be no doubt that Western democracies historically privileged a particular national group over other groups who were subject to assimilation or exclusion. This historic hierarchy was reflected in a wide range of policies and institutions, from the schools and state symbols to policies regarding language, immigration, media, citizenship, the division of powers, and electoral systems. So long as leaders of non-dominant groups can identify (or conjure up) manifestations of these historic hierarchies, they will be able to draw upon the powerful rights-consciousness of their members.

The Human Rights Revolution as Constraint

The human rights revolution is important in another way. It constrains as well as inspires the pursuit of multiculturalism, and this constraining function helps to explain why states and dominant groups have become more willing to accept minority claims.

States are unlikely to accept strong forms of minority rights if they fear they will lead to islands of local tyranny within a broader democratic state. The likelihood that multiculturalist reforms will gain popular support depends heavily, therefore, on confidence that these reforms will not jeopardize human rights and liberal-democratic values. And here, the human rights revolution has served a dual function. If it has helped to inspire minorities to push for multiculturalism, it is equally true that the human rights revolution constrains the way in which minorities articulate and pursue their minority rights. In fact, the human rights revolution is a two-edged sword. It has created political space for ethnocultural groups to contest inherited hierarchies. But it also requires groups to advance their claims in a very specific language—namely, the language of human rights,

---

[3] On the 'rights revolution', see Ignatieff 2000; Walker 1998. The development of this rights-consciousness is related, in part, to growing levels of education amongst many minorities.

civil rights liberalism, and democratic constitutionalism, with their guarantees of gender equality, religious freedom, racial non-discrimination, gay rights, due process, and so on. The leaders of minorities can appeal to the ideals of liberal multiculturalism to challenge their historic exclusion and subordination, but those very ideals also impose the duty on them to be just, tolerant, and inclusive.

Of course, the mere fact that minority groups articulate their claims in the language of human rights and liberal constitutionalism is not, by itself, sufficient to generate confidence that these values will be upheld. The use of this language may be merely strategic, adopted purely for public consumption. The traditional leaders of a minority group may wish to contest their subordinate status *vis-à-vis* the dominant group while still hoping to maintain their own dominance over women, religious minorities, migrants, lower caste groups, and so on.

So the question is whether these values will be respected in practice. And in the established Western democracies, there are good grounds for confidence on this score. This confidence arises from two sources: the existence of robust legal mechanisms to protect human rights, and the existence of a consensus on liberal-democratic values that cuts across ethnic lines. Put simply, there is no legal space for minorities to set aside human rights norms in the name of multiculturalism, and, in the case of most minorities, there is no wish to do so.

From a legal point of view, policies of multiculturalism operate within the larger framework of liberal constitutionalism, and as such any powers devolved to autonomous minority institutions are typically subject to the same common standards of respect for human rights and civil liberties as any other public institution. In virtually every case of multination federalism in the West, for example, substate governments are subject to the same constitutional constraints as the central government, and so have no legal capacity to restrict individual freedoms in the name of maintaining cultural authenticity, religious orthodoxy, or racial purity.[4] In many cases, they are also subject to regional and international human rights monitoring, and more generally are integrated into a dense web of rights-protecting mechanisms (including constitutional courts, human rights

---

[4] A partial exception concerns Indian tribal governments in the United States, which have a limited exemption from some provisions of the US Bill of Rights, and this exemption has allowed some tribes to adopt policies that violate liberal norms. But it is worth emphasizing that, while many tribal governments defend this partial exemption from the US Bill of Rights, they typically do not object to the idea that their self-government decisions should be subject to international human rights norms and international monitoring. See, on this, Kymlicka 2001, chap. 4; Cowan 2007.

commissions, ombudsmen, etc.). People who live in the autonomous entities of Scotland, Catalonia, or Quebec have access to some of the most advanced systems of human rights protection in the world.

Not only is it legally impossible for minorities in the West to establish islands of illiberal rule, but in many cases the evidence suggests that they have no wish to do so. In the case of national minorities, for example, as we will see in the next chapter, all of the evidence suggests that their members are at least as strongly committed to liberal-democratic values as members of dominant groups, if not more so. This removes one of the central fears that dominant groups have about minority self-government. In many parts of the world, there is the fear that once national minorities or indigenous peoples acquire self-governing power, they will use it to persecute, dispossess, expel, or kill anyone who does not belong to the minority group. In the established Western democracies, however, this is a non-issue. There is no fear that self-governing groups will use their powers to establish islands of tyranny or theocracy. More specifically, there is no fear that members of the dominant group who happen to live in the territory of the self-governing minority will be subject to persecution or expulsion. The human rights of English residents of Scotland are firmly protected, not only by Scottish constitutional law, but also by European law, and this would be true even if Scotland seceded from Britain. The human rights of English-Canadian residents of Quebec, or of Castilian residents of Catalonia, are fully protected, no matter what political status Quebec or Catalonia ends up having.

Of course, there are illiberal strands within minority nationalist movements—consider the racist and anti-immigrant wings of Basque and Flemish nationalism—as there are within historically dominant groups. And the level of support for liberal-democratic values within some immigrant and indigenous groups is even more contested. There is always the risk that institutions and programmes established in the name of liberal multiculturalism will be captured by such illiberal elements. I will return to this risk in the next chapter, when I discuss how we should evaluate liberal multiculturalism in practice. But the adoption of liberal multiculturalism rests on what Nancy Rosenblum calls the 'liberal expectancy' (Rosenblum 1998: 55–61)—that is, the hope and expectation that liberal-democratic values will grow over time and take firm root across ethnic, racial, and religious lines, within both majority and minority groups, and that in the meantime there are robust mechanisms in place to ensure that multicultural policies and institutions cannot be captured and misused for illiberal purposes.

This liberal expectancy rests, in part, on the assumption that the public structures and principles of a liberal democracy exert a kind of 'gravitational pull' on the beliefs and practices of ethnic and religious groups (Galston 1991: 292). As Rosenblum notes, this metaphor of gravitational pull—an all-pervasive but invisible force—obscures rather than reveals the actual mechanisms at work, and indeed many discussions of the liberal expectancy have a somewhat mysterious air to them. However, there is considerable evidence that such a process has indeed operated historically. When Catholics and Jews first started arriving in the United States in the nineteenth century, for example, it was widely believed that their conservative and patriarchal beliefs and authoritarian practices precluded them from truly embracing liberal democracy. And yet most religious groups in America have become liberalized, gradually incorporating norms of individual freedom, tolerance, and sexual equality into their own self-understandings. Similarly, there were doubts about whether earlier waves of immigrants to the United States and Canada from southern or eastern Europe, where liberal democracy had never taken root, could truly internalize liberal-democratic values. Yet today these groups are often seen as some of the most loyal defenders of constitutional principles. And some substate nationalist groups that had earlier flirted with authoritarian ideologies, such as Quebec between the two world wars, have undergone dramatic liberalization.

These earlier experiences of the liberal expectancy in action have helped generate confidence that multiculturalism can be safely contained within the boundaries of liberal-democratic constitutionalism and human rights norms. In a society permeated by a strong belief in this liberal expectancy, citizens feel confident that however issues of multiculturalism are settled, their own basic civil and political rights will be respected. No matter how the claims of ethnocultural groups are resolved—no matter what language rights, self-government rights, land rights, or multiculturalism policies are adopted—people can rest assured that they won't be stripped of their citizenship, or subject to ethnic cleansing, or jailed without a fair trial, or denied their rights to free speech, association, and worship. Put simply, the consensus on liberal-democratic values ensures that debates over accommodating diversity are not a matter of life and death. As a result, dominant groups will not fight to the death to resist minority claims.[5]

[5] This is an important issue even in contexts where the dominant group does not itself respect liberal-democratic values and human rights. Indeed, it can be especially important in such contexts. In countries where the dominant group has habitually mistreated minorities,

This dual role of human rights—both as inspiration and constraint—has been pivotal in enabling the adoption and acceptance of liberal multiculturalism. It legitimizes the claims of historically disadvantaged minorities, yet reassures members of the dominant group that no matter how debates over minority rights are resolved, basic human rights will be protected.

In this way, liberal multiculturalism in the West can be understood as a process of 'citizenization', in sociological jargon. Historically, ethnocultural and religious diversity has been characterized by a range of illiberal and undemocratic relations—including relations of conqueror and conquered; colonizer and colonized; settler and indigenous; racialized and unmarked; normalized and deviant; orthodox and heretic; civilized and backward; ally and enemy; master and slave. The task for all liberal democracies has been to turn this catalogue of uncivil relations into relationships of liberal-democratic citizenship, in terms of both the vertical relationship between the members of minorities and the state, and the horizontal relationships amongst the members of different groups.

In the past, it used to be assumed that the only or best way to engage in this process of citizenization was to impose a single undifferentiated model of citizenship on all individuals. But liberal multiculturalism starts from the assumption that this complex history inevitably and appropriately generates group-differentiated ethnopolitical claims. The key to citizenization is not to suppress these differential claims, but rather to filter and frame them through the language of human rights, civil liberties, and democratic accountability.[6] And this is precisely what liberal multiculturalism, understood as a third stage in the human rights struggle against ethnic and racial hierarchy, seeks to do.

In my view, the acceptance of liberal multiculturalism in the West, and its attractiveness as a model to be diffused globally, is centrally tied to this process of citizenization. The idea that multiculturalism can serve as an effective vehicle for creating and consolidating relations of

there is likely to be a particularly strong fear that the minority will take revenge on local members of the dominant group once it acquires self-government. (Think about the fate of the Serbs in Kosovo.) In this context, it may be hypocritical for the dominant group to invoke 'human rights' as a grounds for rejecting minority self-government, but fear about the treatment of their co-ethnics living in the minority's self-governing territory is nonetheless a powerful factor.

[6] This distinguishes liberal multiculturalism from other forms of 'multiculturalism' in history that weren't tied to ideas and relationships of democratic citizenship—e.g. the Ottoman millet system, which accorded minorities a number of constitutional guarantees, but defined them in a position of constitutional inequality (e.g. exclusion from visible high offices) and unfreedom (e.g. prohibitions on proselytization).

liberal-democratic citizenship in multiethnic states is contested. Indeed, most commentators writing in the 1950s and 1960s would have rejected this idea, fearing that it would simply reproduce relations of enmity or hierarchy. But we now have close to forty years of experience in the West with various models of liberal multiculturalism, and, as I discuss in the next chapter, there is growing evidence that these models can indeed serve this function.

Multiculturalism is not the only example of this process of citizenization. On the contrary, the rise and spread of liberal multiculturalism in the West has to be situated within the much broader processes of liberalization and democratization that occurred across virtually the entire range of social policy starting in the 1960s—for example, liberalizing reproductive rights (abortion laws, contraception), liberalizing divorce laws, abolishing the death penalty, prohibiting gender and religious discrimination, decriminalizing homosexuality, amongst many other such reforms. All of these were intended to replace earlier uncivil relations of dominance and intolerance with newer relations of democratic citizenship. And these legal and policy reforms, in turn, reflected wider processes of liberalization in civil society and public opinion, with the dramatic displacement of conservative, patriarchal, and deferential attitudes with more liberal, egalitarian, and autonomous values.[7] The rise of multiculturalism is one dimension of this broad-ranging struggle to liberalize society and to implement the ideals of the human rights revolution and of civil rights liberalism.

Multiculturalism and Liberalization

The account I've given so far shouldn't be surprising. I've essentially just said that liberal democracies in the West have adopted a liberal-democratic conception of multiculturalism. Surely that is what one would expect, barring clear evidence to the contrary. And yet it is remarkable how few commentators are willing to contemplate the possibility that multiculturalism is a liberal-democratic phenomenon, and how much intellectual energy has been expended in finding or inventing any number of alternative accounts of the intellectual foundations and moral impulses behind it.

---

[7] The *locus classicus* for this shift in public attitudes is the work of Ronald Inglehart, and the World Values Survey—see e.g. Inglehart et al 1998; Inglehart and Welzel 2005.

As I noted earlier, some commentators have argued that the very idea of multiculturalism is at odds with the logic of liberal democracy, and that the shift towards recognizing group-differentiated rights represents a reaction against human rights and liberalization. On this view, the first two stages in the post-war struggle against ethnic and racial hierarchy—decolonization and racial desegregation—were inspired by Enlightenment liberalism, but the third stage represents a deviation from, and reaction against, civil rights liberalism.

Commentators disagree about the precise nature of this deviation. Indeed, the academic literature is full of various fanciful theories about where and how multiculturalism departed from the liberal tradition. Some say that multiculturalism is based on a cultural-relativist reaction against liberalism, rooted in nineteenth-century German romanticism. According to Finkielkraut, for example, the first two stages were 'conceived under the implicit patronage of Diderot, Condorcet or Voltaire', whereas the third stage is driven by the chauvinistic and relativistic thinking of Herder and Spengler (Finkielkraut 1988: 54, 64). Others argue that multiculturalism is based on a post-modernist and deconstructionist rejection of liberalism, rooted in Nietzschean scepticism. According to Richard Caputo, for example, 'proponents of multiculturalism tend to accept and build upon the Nietzschean rejection of rationalism with its notion of universal truth and justice' (Caputo 2001: 164).

While these interpretations are familiar ones in the academic literature, I simply don't believe there is any credible evidence for them, at least within the Western democracies. I have read literally hundreds of position papers and policy documents produced by the various participants in the policy networks on multiculturalism—governments, professional advocacy groups, philanthropic organizations—as well as the resulting laws and court cases, and I have yet to find a single discussion that expresses any sympathy for either Spengler or Nietzsche, either implicitly or explicitly.

Within the public debate, we can find yet another, more simple, explanation for how multiculturalism has diverged from liberalism. Multiculturalism, it is said, is about 'culture', and culture (at least in the context of ethnic groups) is fundamentally about ancestral 'traditions', so that 'accommodating cultural diversity' is essentially a matter of preserving 'traditional ways of life'. This basic idea can be elaborated in various ways. One familiar form argues that while some degree of cultural change is inevitable, there are certain practices that are vital to the 'authenticity' or 'integrity' of a culture, and which must therefore be protected from change. These 'authentic' practices are said to be essential to the identity of the group, and hence to the identity of its individual members. This link between culture and identity is thought to be particularly strong if the cultural practice is 'traditional'—that is, deeply rooted in a people's history, and not just the result of recent adaptations or outside influences. On this view, cultural rights and policies of cultural inclusion are presented as primarily or exclusively intended to protect such 'authentic' cultural practices from pressures to change.

On this view, multicultural claims are interpreted through a set of ideas relating to cultural authenticity and group identity. 'Culture' is typically interpreted in terms of (or reduced to) a set of discrete practices, preferably 'traditional' and 'authentic' practices. These practices are then said to be essential to the group's identity, and hence to the identity of individual members, and so must be accommodated and protected by multiculturalism policies.

This is a version of what Amartya Sen calls the 'communitarian' or 'conservative' approach to multiculturalism (UNHDR 2004), or what we might simply call a 'traditionalist' approach.[8] It should immediately be clear, I hope, that this account is not only different from, but flatly in contradiction to, the liberal account I have developed. The liberal view of multiculturalism is inevitably, intentionally, and unapologetically transformational of people's cultural traditions. It demands both dominant and historically subordinated groups to engage in new practices, to enter new relationships, and to embrace new concepts and discourses, all of which profoundly transform people's identities and practices.

This is perhaps most obvious in the case of the historically dominant majority nation in each country, which is required to renounce fantasies of racial superiority, to relinquish claims to exclusive ownership of the state, and to abandon attempts to fashion public institutions solely in its

---

[8] The claim that multiculturalism is rooted in cultural conservatism rather than liberalism has a long-standing pedigree. Indeed, many of the earliest academic theorists of multiculturalism in the 1970s and 1980s simply took for granted that multiculturalism arose as a 'communitarian' reaction against liberalisation, and as an attempt to contain its corrosive effects on traditional authorities and practices. On this view, multiculturalism was demanded by communitarian or conservative elites who worried that newly emancipated individuals would use their human rights and civil rights to question and reject traditional authority structures and cultural practices. Multiculturalism, in short, was intended to set communitarian brakes on liberalization. See, e.g., Van Dyke 1977, 1982; Svensson 1979; Addis 1992; Garet 1983; Johnston 1989; McDonald 1991; Karmis 1993. I discuss this 'first wave' of communitarian theories of multiculturalism, and how it has been contested by more recent liberal theories of multiculturalism, in Kymlicka 2001, chap. 2.

own national (typically white/Christian) image. In fact, much of multi-culturalism's 'long march through the institutions' consists precisely in identifying and attacking those deeply rooted traditions, customs, and symbols that have historically excluded or stigmatized minorities. Much has been written about the transformations in majority identities and practices this has required, and the backlash it can create.[9]

But liberal multiculturalism is equally transformative of the identities and practices of minority groups. Many of these groups have their own histories of ethnic and racial prejudice, of anti-Semitism, of caste and gender exclusion, of religious triumphalism, and of political authoritarianism, all of which are delegitimized by the norms of liberal-democratic multiculturalism and minority rights.[10] Moreover, even where the traditional practices of a minority group are free of these illiberal or undemocratic elements, some of these practices may have emerged as a response to the experience of discrimination, stigmatization, or exclusion at the hands of others, and may lose their attractiveness as that motivating experience fades in people's memories. Some minority groups developed distinctive norms of self-help, endogamy, and internal conflict resolution because they were excluded from or discriminated within the institutions of the larger society. Those norms may lose their rationale as ethnic and racial hierarchies break down, and as group members feel more comfortable interacting with members of other groups and participating in state institutions. Far from guaranteeing the protection of the traditional ways of life of either the majority or minorities, liberal multiculturalism poses multiple challenges to them.

So the traditionalist conception of multiculturalism stands in sharp contrast to the liberal conception, with different goals and rationales. Indeed, from a liberal perspective, the traditionalist approach to multi-culturalism is deeply implausible and unattractive, for several reasons:[11]

(1) The traditionalist conception assumes that the cultural practices for which state recognition is being sought are 'timeless' or 'authentic'.

[9] For a discussion of 'white backlash' against multiculturalism, see Hewitt 2005; Hansen 2007; Bulbeck 2004.

[10] John Meyer has noted how contemporary models of a virtuous national society involve abandoning earlier claims to heroic nationalism, racial distinctiveness/superiority, religious missions, or to special historic duties to bring civilization to one's neighbourhood. His focus is on how these ideological changes have 'tamed' the nation-state (Meyer 2001: 6), but we can see the same dynamic with respect to substate groups. They too must abandon claims to racial and religious supremacism and to historic missions, and reframe their demands in the language of ensuring progress, justice, and human rights.

[11] I have discussed the limitations of the traditionalist or communitarian conceptions of multiculturalism in Kymlicka 1989, 1995, 2004c.

In reality, however, studies repeatedly show that so-called traditional practices are fairly recent, often themselves the product of earlier cultural interchanges, and sometimes even 'invented' by elites to legitimize their position.[12] So ideas of 'cultural authenticity' or 'cultural purity' are often anthropologically naïve. They are also politically dangerous. They imply that there is something abnormal and regrettable about cultural evolution and cross-cultural influence, when in fact such changes and influences are normal, inevitable, and essential to the process of human development. It is cultural hybridity, not cultural purity, which is the normal state of human affairs, and fantasies of cultural purity can only be maintained by artificially cutting off groups from interaction with the larger world, and by instilling xenophobic fear of others (Waldron 1995; Cowan et al 2001).[13]

(2) The traditionalist conception assumes that there is a neutral or objective way of determining which practices are 'authentic' to a group. In reality, this is a matter of political contestation *within the group itself.* It is often conservative elites within the group who claim the authority to judge what is authentic and traditional, and they do so precisely to suppress demands for change from reformers within the group. Practices that historically may have been variable, evolving, contested and optional are declared by conservative elites to be 'sacred', a matter of religious or cultural obligation, and essential to group membership. To interpret multiculturalism as protecting traditional or authentic practices has the effect of rewarding such conservative elites: it gives power to those who can claim to be the guardians of ancient traditions, while implying that those people who wish to challenge these traditions are not 'true' or 'proper' members of the group (Parekh 2000). In this sense, the conservative interpretation of multiculturalism is more accurately described, not as according people cultural *rights*, but as imposing cultural *duties*—that is, the duty to maintain one's culture, whether one wants to do so or not—and hence as an abridgement not expansion of individual freedom.

(3) The traditionalist claim that there is a right to preserve one's cultural traditions has been interpreted by some—most famously, by the American

---

[12] The literature on the invention of tradition is huge. For the *locus classicus*, see Hobsbawm and Ranger 1983.

[13] A related mistake is to view our identities as citizens of larger societies as somehow 'inauthentic' and 'artificial', as compared to the 'true' identity tied up with membership in particular ethnic or religious groups. In reality, wider pan-ethnic civic identities are just as normal and natural—just as common in history—as more particularistic ethnic or religious identities.

Anthropology Association (AAA)—to preclude the very idea of universal human rights. According to the AAA's statement to the United Nations in 1947, people's identities and personalities are realized through their cultures, and so everyone has the right to live by their own traditions, which means that the very idea of judging local cultures by universal standards of human rights is unsound (AAA 1947). More recently, anthropologists have backed away from this extreme relativist view, and have attempted to reconcile support for a right to cultural preservation with support for universal human rights.[14] Anthropologists today are more likely to accept the possibility that some cultural traditions are oppressive, and that universal human rights can help to prevent this oppression. So we now find anthropologists talking about 'balancing' human rights and the right to cultural preservation. But this still is a dangerous position if it implies that human rights protection should be sacrificed or compromised (albeit 'not too much') in order to accommodate practices that violate those standards.

(4) The traditionalist claim that respecting a cultural tradition is essential to respecting a person's identity can be invoked as a 'trump' to avoid democratic debate. To say that a particular cultural practice is part of my 'identity' is sometimes a way of inviting others to consider and debate its value and significance. But in other contexts, this claim is invoked as a way of foreclosing that debate, by implying that any questioning of that practice will be interpreted as a sign of disrespect for me as a person. Where identity claims are presented in this way as non-negotiable trumps, the result is to erode the potential for democratic dialogue. In multi-ethnic states where there are diverse and sometimes competing cultural traditions, we need to find a way to talk civilly about our practices, to discuss their benefits and costs, and to think about fair and honourable compromises where these practices conflict.[15]

In short, interpreting multiculturalism as a right to preserve authentic cultural traditions raises several potential dangers: it may inhibit constructive relations between cultures (by privileging cultural purity over cultural hybridity); it may erode the freedom of individuals within groups (by privileging authoritarian or conservative elites over internal reformers);

---

[14] For the evolving and tortured relationship between anthropologists and human rights, see Freeman 2002; Cowan et al 2001; Wilson 1997.

[15] For an eloquent statement of this concern, see Waldron 2000. For other expressions of the concern that (conservative) multiculturalism can imprison people in scripts about identity and culture that impede individual autonomy and democratic deliberation, see Appiah 2004; Markell 2003; Benhabib 2002; Sen 2006; Bayart 2005.

it can be invoked to deny the existence of universal human rights; and it may threaten the space for civil debate and democratic negotiation over cultural conflicts.

Given the profound differences between the liberal and conservative interpretations of multiculturalism, it's crucial to determine which of these in fact underpins the recent shifts towards multiculturalism within the West. One can find echoes of both views in the public debate, but which of them provides the framework for contemporary multicultural-ism policies?

Critics of multiculturalism typically assume that it is the conservative interpretation that underpins the trend towards multiculturalism.[16] I believe, however, that this assumption is implausible, and indeed demon-strably false. For one thing, these critics have not provided any plausible account of how conservative multiculturalism could have become the official public policy of Western democracies, particularly in a forty-year era of wide-ranging liberalization and human rights reforms.[17] How could a 'winning coalition' be built in support of conservative multiculturalism in Western democracies? How could it gain the support of the major political parties, or of a majority of members of the national legislature? It's difficult to make political sense of this scenario, and indeed most critics who discuss the adoption of multiculturalism treat it as a mystery, as if gremlins snuck into national parliaments and drafted multicultural policies while no one was watching.[18]

If we look at the actual process by which multiculturalism policies were adopted, a different picture emerges. In reality, virtually every-one involved in adopting multicultural reforms in the West—from the

[16] Some indeed assume that this is the only possible interpretation of multiculturalism, and that its flaws can only be remedied by rejecting the tyranny of 'culture talk' (Booth 1999; Mamdami 2000).

[17] For example, critics of Canada's Multiculturalism Act have suggested that its conserv-ative logic of cultural preservation entails that female genital mutilation (FGM) should be permitted within those immigrant groups where it is a 'traditional' practice (Bissoondath 1994; Gwyn 1995). But how can we reconcile this with the fact that, at the very same time Canada was adopting its Multiculturalism Act, it also became one of the first countries in the world to accept that a girl should be granted refugee status if she faces a risk of being subject to FGM if returned to her country of origin, even if FGM is 'traditional' in that country of origin (Levine 1999: 40)? It would be self-contradictory for a country like Canada to tolerate FGM within its own borders in the name of cultural preservation, while defining it as persecution overseas. Critics like Bissoondath and Gwyn assume that legislators have in fact embraced this self-contradiction, but they give no plausible interpretation of how or why such a self-contradiction could have emerged. We can avoid this incoherence, and provide a more plausible political explanation for both decisions, if we see both as stemming from liberal values. Indeed, as we will see, the actual text of the Multiculturalism Act makes clear that it is liberal rather than traditionalist in inspiration.

[18] For a clear example, see Barry 2001: 292–9.

political activists and civil society organizations that initially mobilized for these reforms, to the segment of the public that supported them, to the legislators who adopted them, to the bureaucrats who drafted and implemented them, to the judges who interpreted them—were inspired by the ideals of human rights and civil rights liberalism. These actors viewed multicultural reforms as part of a larger process of social and political liberalization, and embedded these reforms legally and institutionally within a liberal rights framework.

To be sure, the fact that the contemporary wave of multicultural reforms originated in the human rights revolution doesn't yet tell us anything about its actual effects, including any unintended effects. Once multicultural policy structures are in place, illiberal conservative or authoritarian elites within various communities have often attempted to gain control over them, or at least to influence their implementation and direction. This is a universal phenomenon: once new powers or resources are made available, competition will inevitably arise for control over them. For example, once multiculturalism funds are made available, and multiculturalism advisory councils established, conservative elites within immigrant groups seek access to them. Once institutions of self-government are established for indigenous peoples or substate nationalist groups, conservatives seek to use these new powers to protect their traditional authority. This sort of political contestation is inevitable. Indeed, it would violate every known law of political science if it didn't happen. It is even possible that multicultural policies have sometimes, unintentionally, served to strengthen the hand of conservative elites against the forces of liberal reform within various communities.

So one important question we need to ask is to what extent conservative/authoritarian elites have been successful in capturing these policies, and what safeguards are in place to ensure that the original emancipatory goals and ideals are not subverted. I will return to this question in the next chapter, when discussing how we should evaluate the actual operation of multiculturalism policies, and their future prospects.

But my focus in this chapter is on the origins of multiculturalism policies—the normative principles and political coalitions that underpinned their adoption. And here I would insist that the actors involved in adopting multiculturalism in the Western democracies viewed themselves as expressing and extending the human rights revolution, not reacting against it.

This is obviously a sweeping generalization, and it would ultimately need to be tested on a case-by-case basis for all of the different types of multiculturalism policies adopted for different groups in different countries. But as a first step, let me focus on the Canadian case, where the connection between liberalization and multiculturalism is particularly clear.

Consider the bases of political support for multiculturalism in Canada. If multiculturalism reflected a reaction against liberalization, we would expect to see two competing political camps: a liberal camp in favour of liberalizing reforms on issues of gender equality, abortion, divorce, and gay rights, so as to emancipate individuals; and then a conservative camp in favour of immigrant multiculturalism, Aboriginal rights, and Quebec autonomy so as to protect these communities from liberalizing reforms. In reality, the situation in Canada is just the opposite.

On the one hand, we have patriarchal cultural conservatives who believe that society is changing too fast, and who believe that more weight should be given to traditional authorities and practices. This is the group Michael Adams has characterized as the 'father knows best' crowd (Adams 1997, 2000), which he estimates at around 35 per cent of the Canadian population.[19] Predictably, they strongly oppose liberalizing reforms about women's equality and gay rights. But they equally oppose immigrant multiculturalism, Aboriginal rights, and accommodating Quebec. Indeed, the emergence of these diversity policies is precisely one of the changes that they find most distressing. There has not been (and is not now) any significant level of public support for any of these forms of multiculturalism amongst cultural conservatives.

Of course, having lost the battle to block these policies, patriarchal conservatives have not simply disappeared. They are regrouping in order to see how they can now exploit the opportunities created by these policies. For example, conservative Protestants in Canada, who initially fought tooth and nail to block multiculturalism in the public schools since it would strip Christianity of its privileged position, are now regrouping to see whether they can invoke multiculturalism to regain some lost privileges (Davies 1999). But this *post-facto* strategic appeal to multiculturalism must be distinguished from support for the policy's adoption, which patriarchal conservatives strongly opposed.

On the other hand, we have the liberal wing of the Canadian populace, which has become increasingly egalitarian, anti-authoritarian, and individualistic. Predictably, they strongly support gender equality and gay

---

[19] Adams subdivides this group into 'traditionalists' and 'Darwinists', but they share the fear that liberal reforms are undermining social order, and include diversity policies amongst these destabilizing liberal reforms.

rights, but they equally endorse multiculturalism policies, and view both sets of reforms as expressions of a single logic of civil rights liberalism.

So both camps have operated on the assumption that multicultural-ism is an integral part and parcel of a larger process of liberalization—although of course they differ on how to evaluate this larger process—and changes in support for multiculturalism policies over time track changes in support for liberal egalitarian values more generally (Dasko 2005).

The link between liberalization and multiculturalism policies can be confirmed by examining the way these policies have been legally drafted and judicially enforced. One of the most striking things about these policies is how tightly and explicitly they are connected to broader norms of human rights and liberal constitutionalism, both conceptually and institutionally.

Consider the preamble to Canada's Multiculturalism Act of 1988. It begins by saying that *because* the government of Canada is committed to civil liberties, particularly the freedom of individuals 'to make the life that the individual is able and wishes to have', and because it is committed to equality, particularly racial equality and gender equality, and because of its international human rights obligations, particularly the international convention against racial discrimination, *therefore* it is adopting a policy of multiculturalism. It goes on, in the main text, to reiterate human rights norms as part of the substance of the multiculturalism policy.[20] You could hardly ask for a clearer statement that multiculturalism is to be understood as an integral part of the human rights revolution, and an extension of, not brake on, civil rights liberalism. There is not a whiff of cultural conservatism, patriarchalism, or post-modernist deconstruction-ism in this statement. It is the very milk of Enlightenment liberalism and universal human rights.

In fact, this point had already been made explicit in the original 1971 parliamentary statement on multiculturalism in Canada, which stated that 'a policy of multiculturalism within a bilingual framework is basically the conscious support of individual freedom of choice. We are free to be ourselves' (Trudeau 1971: 8546).

These formulations are intended as an instruction to the relevant polit-ical actors, from minority activists to bureaucrats to judges, that multi-culturalism must be understood as a policy inspired by liberal norms. Nor was this left to chance, or to the goodwill of political actors. The

---

[20] The Act is reprinted as an appendix in Kymlicka 1998.

Multiculturalism Act is located squarely within the larger institutional framework of liberal-democratic constitutionalism, and hence is legally subject to the same constitutional constraints as any other federal policy. Any federal action done in the name of multiculturalism must respect the requirements of the Canadian Charter of Rights and Freedoms, as interpreted and enforced by judicial bodies such as the Canadian Human Rights Commission and the Supreme Court.

So the way in which multiculturalism in Canada has been legally defined makes clear that it does not exist outside the framework of liberal-democratic constitutionalism and human rights jurisprudence, or as an exception to it, or as a deviation from it. Rather, it is firmly embedded within that framework. It is defined as flowing from human rights norms, as embodying those norms, and as enforceable through judicial institutions whose mandate is to uphold those norms.[21]

Of course, this is just one example from one country, and there may be aspects of the Canadian approach that are not found in other Western democracies. Even so, it's an important case to consider, since Canada was the first country to adopt an official multiculturalism policy, and as a result has played an important role in shaping international conceptions of what multiculturalism is. As Yasmeen Abu-Laban notes, Canada is widely seen around the world as a country where multiculturalism 'exists' (Abu-Laban 2002: 460)—where multiculturalism is a well-established practice, not just a rhetoric—and Canadian formulations are often studied as prototypes. For example, the way multiculturalism is linked to human rights in the preamble to the Canadian Multiculturalism Act is essentially duplicated in the UN's 1992 Declaration on the Rights of Minorities—both insist that the rights of minorities are founded on human rights norms, and so should be interpreted as further extending and implementing these norms.

In any event, Canada is far from unique in the way it ties multiculturalism to liberalism. We see a similar linkage in Australia, for example. According to James Jupp—who played a pivotal role in defining Australia's multiculturalism policy—multiculturalism in Australia:

is essentially a liberal ideology which operates within liberal institutions with the universal approval of liberal attitudes. It accepts that all humans should be treated

---

[21] For more on the fundamentally liberal inspiration for multiculturalism in Canada, see Forbes 1994: 94 ('Multiculturalism appeals to the common understanding of freedom as choice') and Lupul 2005, whose memoir gives ample evidence of the way civil rights liberalism provided the taken-for-granted background to the initial mobilization for Canadian multiculturalism.

as equals and that different cultures can co-exist if they accept liberal values. (Jupp 1995: 40)

As in Canada, multiculturalism was introduced in Australia by the same left-liberal or social-democratic political forces that were pushing for liberalization more generally, such as strengthened gender equality, non-discrimination, and gay rights.[22]

The same basic pattern can be found in other Western democracies that have moved in the direction of a more multicultural approach. As a general rule, multiculturalism has been adopted by social-democratic or left-liberal parties and coalitions that endorse liberalization more generally, and the resulting policies have been drafted in such a way that makes explicit their foundation in human rights norms.

To be sure, public confidence in this 'liberal expectancy' varies across time and across societies, and there have been times and places where people have become sceptical that multiculturalism can securely be rooted in liberal-democratic constitutionalism and human rights norms. And as we will see, this scepticism helps to explain some of the strong opposition to multiculturalism that has arisen recently, and some of the high-profile cases of a 'retreat from multiculturalism'. But these cases confirm the key point: namely, that wherever multiculturalism has been adopted and implemented within the West, it is a distinctly liberal model of multiculturalism, supported because and insofar as it is seen as consistent with, and indeed enhancing of, liberal-democratic values and human rights ideals. Where that link is not perceived, either in relation to multiculturalism generally or in relation to the claims of a particular minority group, public support for multiculturalism drops.

In short, we see varying levels of public belief in liberal multiculturalism across the West. What we don't see, however, is any other type of non-liberal multiculturalism, whether rooted in Herderian cultural conservatism or Nietzschean post-modernism. There are Herderian and Nietzschean multiculturalists in academia, particularly in some humanities departments, but it is not this sort of multiculturalism that has shaped public policy in the West. Really-existing multiculturalism in the West is liberal multiculturalism.

---

[22] While the current conservative government at the federal level in Australia has retreated from multiculturalism, some of the slack has been picked up by the Labour governments which dominate at the state level. For example, New South Wales recently adopted a new Multiculturalism Act.

Bringing Politics Back In

The narrative I've told so far of the rise of liberal multiculturalism as a stage in the evolution of human rights is an important part of the story, but not the whole story. I have started with it because, without understanding these links, the whole trend becomes inexplicable. For example, Brian Barry begins his influential critique of multiculturalism by saying that he's been baffled by the adoption of multicultural policies in the West (Barry 2001). His bewilderment is understandable, since he starts from the assumption that these policies are rooted in a relativist rejection of liberalism, and it would indeed be difficult to see why Western liberal democracies would abandon their constitutional rules and values to adopt such policies, or how such policies could emerge from the political process. However, if we are willing to contemplate the possibility of a multiculturalism that is rooted in human rights, and if we look for the legal, political, and conceptual links between the two, then the rise of liberal multiculturalism starts to become much more understandable.

However, this obviously is not the whole story. It attributes far too much to the 'power of ideas'. Multiculturalism may indeed be a plausible extension of the logic of human rights, leading from decolonization through racial desegregation to minority rights. But logic is not self-enacting, and ideas do not move of their own accord. The moral logic of multiculturalism needs to be articulated, mobilized, negotiated, and compromised within a larger field of power relations.[23] To imply that the rise of multiculturalism reflects the unfolding of the human rights revolution makes it sound as if public policies were formulated in academic political philosophy seminars in which participants attempt to dispassionately identify the logic of moral arguments. Political life is obviously not like that. To be sure, there is such a thing as 'the power of ideas'—ideas can inspire, inform, and persuade political actors. But this is one type of power amongst others, and often confronts the determined resistance of important actors whose interests or identities are potentially threatened by accepting new ideas.

In short, as an account of the fate of ethnic politics in the West, the story I've told so far is strangely devoid of actual politics. The normative logic behind multiculturalist claims is important, but we need a richer

---

[23] As Guilhot notes (2005), the literature on the diffusion of human rights and democracy often makes it sound as if these ideas travel on their own accord, ignoring the power relations that determine how these ideas are articulated and circulated, and by whom.

account of how these claims get deployed, contested, and negotiated in the messy real-world politics of contemporary Western democracies.

It would be impossible to give a comprehensive overview of how these political processes have played out across the Western democracies. The human rights revolution has created a conceptual opening for liberal multiculturalism to emerge in the West, but whether particular groups in particular countries are successful in pursuing it depends on complex political factors that are tied to specific national (or even local) contexts. To truly 'bring politics back in', we would need to engage in a high degree of 'methodological nationalism'—we would need to look at the details of the traditional political party structures and electoral systems of different countries, and the sorts of electoral incentives and alliances they make possible or preclude. We would also have to look at the way civil society is structured in different countries (e.g. corporatist versus liberal), and at the relative scope for different political tactics (e.g. litigation, media campaigns, civil disobedience, back-room lobbying).[24] Trying to summarize all of these factors would be an impossibly complex task.

We can however make a few more general observations about some of the political factors that have supported the trend towards multiculturalism, either by facilitating the political mobilization of minority groups, or by reducing political opposition to their claims.

The first condition that has enabled the effective mobilization of minorities is, of course, democracy itself. Democracy is relevant for many reasons. At the simplest level, the consolidation of democracy limits the ability of elites to crush ethnic political movements. In many countries around the world, elites ban political movements of ethnic groups, or pay thugs or paramilitaries to beat up or kill ethnic group leaders, or bribe police and judges to lock them up. The fear of this sort of repression often keeps non-dominant groups from voicing even the most moderate claims. Keeping quiet is the safest option for minorities in many countries.

In consolidated democracies, however, where democracy is the only game in town, there is no option but to allow ethnic groups to mobilize politically and advance their claims in public. As a result, members of ethnic groups are increasingly unafraid to speak out. They may not win the political debate, but they aren't afraid of being killed, jailed, or fired

---

[24] There have been a number of excellent studies that examine these political dynamics comparatively across the Western democracies. See, for example, Koopmans and Statham 1999, 2003 on the distinctive 'political opportunity structures' available to immigrants in different Western countries, and how this has affected the nature and outcome of their mobilization.

for trying. It is this loss of fear, combined with a new rights-consciousness deriving from the human rights revolution, which explains the remarkably vocal nature of ethnic politics in contemporary Western democracies.

Moreover, democracy involves the availability of multiple access points to decision-making. If a group is blocked at one level by an unsympathetic government, they can pursue their claims at another level. Even if an unsympathetic political party were to win power at the central level, and attempted to cut back on the rights of non-dominant groups, these groups could shift their focus to the regional level, or to the municipal level. And even if all of these levels were blocked, they could pursue their claims through the courts, or even through international pressure. This is what democracy is all about: multiple and shifting points of access to power.

A related factor is demographics. In the past, many governments had the hope or expectation that non-dominant ethnic groups would simply disappear, through dying out or assimilation or intermarriage. It is now clear that this is not going to happen. Due to high birth rates, indigenous peoples are the fastest-growing segment of the population in many of the countries where they are found. The percentage of immigrants in the population is growing steadily in most Western countries, and most commentators agree that even more immigrants will be needed in the future to offset declining birth rates and an ageing population. And sub-state national groups in the West are also growing in absolute numbers, even if they are staying the same or marginally declining as a percentage of the population. No one any-more can have the dream or delusion that minorities will disappear. The numbers count, particularly in a democracy, and the numbers are shifting in the direction of non-dominant groups.

These two factors of democracy and demography, taken together with the human rights revolution, help to explain the 'push' for policies of accommodation. Increasing rights-consciousness, increasing access to multiple arenas of safe political mobilization, and increasing numbers all help to explain the growing strength of political mobilization by ethnic groups in the West.

Principles and Geo-politics in the Human Rights Revolution

The more puzzling political question, perhaps, is why dominant groups have been willing to accept these demands. After all, most Western states have a dominant national group that forms a clear numerical majority, and in a democracy 'majority rules'. So why have majority groups become

111

more willing to respond to these demands, and to negotiate them? Why not use the power of the state to suppress these demands, with force if necessary, as was the case in the past? It would be nice to think that the powers of moral argument have been sufficient to overcome the long history of antagonisms and prejudice that have stained ethnic and racial relations in the West. But that doesn't seem likely. There must have been other more prudential or strategic factors underlying this change of heart.

Identifying these mixed motives for accepting multiculturalism is important, not only to better understand how multiculturalism emerged in the West, but also to better understand the prospects for promoting it around the globe. If we assume that multiculturalism arose in the West solely or primarily because of its powerful moral logic, then attempts to promote it abroad will largely consist in moral hectoring of other societies. As I noted in the Introduction, this indeed has been a tendency of many commentators, who bemoan the apparent inability of people in the post-communist or post-colonial world to understand the moral logic of tolerance and diversity, and who recommend (re-)educating the locals in the meaning of liberalism and human rights. In reality, however, the variable fate of liberal multiculturalism in different societies may have less to do with people's comprehension of the moral logic of human rights, and more to do with the larger framework of power relations into which these normative arguments are inserted.

One way to start uncovering these mixed motives for accepting multiculturalism is to return to the previous two stages of the human rights struggle against ethnic and racial hierarchy, and ask how they came about. Neither decolonization nor racial desegregation was solely the result of moral persuasion, and by identifying the other more strategic factors at work in those two cases we can better understand the contemporary politics of multiculturalism.

Consider the foundational commitment to racial equality, expressed in the 1948 UDHR. I said earlier that it was revulsion at Hitler's genocidal race hatred that motivated acceptance of the idea of racial equality. This is the usual account given by commentators. In Borstelmann's words, 'explicit racial domination lost its legitimacy in the gas chambers of the German holocaust' (Borstelmann 1993: 81). This catastrophe, it is said, 'shook the conscience of the world', and inspired the international community to recognize the sins of racialist ideologies, and to commit itself to the cause of racial equality.

In reality, however, the decision to base the post-war international order on racial equality was taken before the Holocaust was widely known, and indeed before the war was over (Wolton 2000: 2–3). And one important reason why the Allies agreed to this principle was precisely to help ensure that they would win the war. When the British and Americans first outlined their plans for the post-war order in the Atlantic Charter of August 1941, there was no specific reference to racial equality. Churchill felt that self-determination should be restored to the European peoples conquered and colonized by the Nazis, but he did not want this interpreted as a justification for granting self-determination to non-European peoples conquered and colonized by the British. And so the Atlantic Charter is carefully worded to say that 'sovereign rights and self-government be restored to those who have been forcibly deprived of them'. In other words, European peoples who possessed an internationally recognized sovereign state, like the Czechs and the Poles, would recover their 'sovereign' rights of self-determination, whereas non-European colonial populations that had never been recognized under international law as sovereign states would remain under the thumb of the British Empire. In case anyone misunderstood the subtlety of this wording, Churchill told the British House of Commons that 'at the Atlantic meeting, we had in mind, primarily, the restoration of the sovereignty, self-government and national life of the States and nations of Europe now under the Nazi yoke', which 'is quite a separate problem' from that of the rights of colonial populations who 'owe allegiance to the British Crown' (quoted in Borgwardt 2005: 30).

Churchill was indeed shocked by the Aryan supremacist ideology of the Nazis, but what shocked him (and many others) was the way the Nazis were treating other white Europeans as if they were no better than Africans and Asians. Nazi policy towards the Slavs was modelled directly on earlier German policies towards African colonial populations (Lindquist 1996; Ehmann 1998), and indeed Hitler said that 'Russia is our Africa and the Russians are our Negroes' (quoted in Lauren 1996: 136). While few Western powers had complained about German colonial practices of conquest, resettlement, and forced labour in Africa, even when it was known to lead to mass starvation and death, it was shocking to see the same practices applied within Europe itself. As St Clair Drake put it, 'exterminating Bushmen and Tasmanians was one thing: exterminating fellow Europeans "of a different race" was quite a different matter' (Drake 1951: 263, quoted in Layton 2000: 170 n. 3). Churchill's initial impulse, shared by most Allies, was to reiterate this traditional assumption that Europeans should be accorded a different and higher status than others. He wanted to criticize the Nazis, not for constructing racial hierarchies, but rather for misidentifying them, by ignoring the rules by which civilized European peoples should treat one an other.

And yet within a year of the Atlantic Charter, momentum had swung in favour of the idea that the new world order should be based on a principle of the equal rights of all peoples to self-determination. What changed? Part of the answer is military strategy. The British had been shocked by the fall of Singapore to the Japanese in February 1942, after the local population refused to fight for the British. The local Chinese, Malay, and Indian populations saw no reason to die fighting to save British imperialism. Why should they care whether they were ruled by British or Japanese overlords, particularly when the Japanese promised greater self-government? The 'disloyalty' of the local populations was also a factor in the rapid fall of Burma and Malaysia, devastating British morale and war planning. The British (pressed by their American allies) realized that if they hoped to have the support of their colonial populations in the war against the Japanese in Asia, or against the Germans and Italians in Africa, they must promise a post-war order in which the sins of white imperialism would be addressed. Thus the Americans pressed the British to promise to return Hong Kong to the Chinese and to grant India independence (and similarly pressed France to promise to relinquish Vietnam), so as to secure the cooperation (or at least neutrality) of the local populations in the war. As Sumner Welles, Roosevelt's chief foreign policy adviser, said in May 1942:

If this war is in fact a war for the liberation of peoples it must assure the sovereign equality of peoples throughout the world, as well as in the world of the Americas. Our victory must bring in its train the liberation of all peoples. Discrimination between peoples because of their race, creed or color must be abolished. The age of imperialism is ended.[25]

In August 1941, the British operated in the hope and expectation that British imperialism could continue unchanged after the war. After the fall of Singapore, they re-evaluated this assumption, and acquiesced in American claims that the war was a struggle against racial discrimination

---

[25] Quoted in Wolton 2000: 47. Wolton provides a fascinating account of the tense negotiations between the Americans and British over the issue of imperialism and its role in the war. The Americans of course changed their tune later in the war, after deciding that they wanted (in effect) to colonize various Japanese-controlled islands after the war, regardless of the will of the local populations. American enthusiasm for the principle of decolonization also waned as it became clear that some national liberation movements were controlled by Communists. There was, in short, very little principled commitment to decolonization on either side of the North Atlantic.

and imperialism. As Wolton puts it, 'the fall of Singapore had discredited what was seen as "white imperialism" ' (Wolton 2000: 152).

There is a salutary lesson here. The idea of racial equality is a powerful one, but its intrinsic persuasiveness was no greater in May 1942 than in August 1941, or in February 1919, when the Japanese unsuccessfully proposed a racial equality clause to the League of Nations.[26] What changed was the larger geo-political context that dramatically altered the costs and risks associated with accepting that idea.[27] As we will see, this has implications for how we understand the prospects for advancing minority rights.

A similar story can also be told about the impulse behind the second great stage of the human rights revolution—the African-American desegregation campaign. It is often said that the success of the civil rights movement reflected a growing public recognition that racial discrimination contradicted the founding ideals of human freedom and equality in the American Constitution. Desegregation, in other words, reflected a (long-overdue) working out of the inherent moral logic of American liberal and democratic principles.

But, here too, it would be a mistake to overemphasize the importance of moral persuasion. African-Americans had certainly been invoking that moral logic for many decades, but the sudden success of that argument in the 1950s had as much to do with foreign policy imperatives as with domestic moral persuasion.

---

[26] Of course, the Japanese demand for a racial equality clause was itself an exercise in *realpolitik*, not moral principle. As subsequent events made clear, the Japanese had their own ideology of racial supremacy (*shido minzoku*), which they viewed as giving them the right to rule over their inferior Asian neighbours (Lauren 1996: 140). The Japanese did not object to the Western belief in superior and inferior races—they simply objected to the way that the West refused to accept that the Japanese were one of the superior races, a refusal which (ironically) they ascribed to irrational racist prejudice. As this supremacist ideology become clear in the 1930s and 1940s, Japan's efforts to present itself as a leader in the struggle for racial equality were delegitimated, and after World War II, this leadership passed to India, which became the most vocal proponent of racial equality at the United Nations (Banton 2002).

[27] If this seems like an unduly cynical account of the West's conversion to the principle of racial equality, I should note that there are even more cynical accounts. Frank Füredi, for example, argues that the West endorsed the principle of racial equality, not to recognize the rights of non-European peoples, but rather to protect whites who might be subject to 'racial revenge' as the age of imperialism ended (Füredi 1998). White Europeans had in effect started a global race war, by asserting a right to colonize inferior non-European peoples, and were worried that the peoples of Asia and Africa would return the favour by construing decolonization as a global racial struggle, in which Asians and Africans should unite against white Europeans. According to Füredi, the West's new-found commitment to racial equality was an attempt to preclude or stigmatize any anti-European dimension to the decolonization struggle.

The United States emerged from World War II locked in a global struggle with the Soviet Union for influence and power. And in this contest, racial discrimination within the United States was a crippling liability. The Soviets ensured that news reports about the mistreatment of blacks in America were circulated widely in the Third World, and the State Department was receiving reports on a daily basis from its embassies overseas about the consequences this was having. One American ambassador noted 'the painful sensitivity of all Asian peoples on [racial discrimination] and the fantastic success which Communist propaganda has had in creating anti-American feeling...It is impossible to exaggerate' (Ambassador Chester Bowles, quoted in Layton 2000: 162 n. 78). Leading post-war American statesmen, such as John Foster Dulles and Dean Rusk, constantly reiterated that Jim Crow is 'ruining our foreign policy. The effect of this in Asia and Africa will be worse for us than Hungary for the Russians' (Dulles in Layton 2000: 131), or that 'The biggest single burden that we carry on our backs in our foreign relations...is the problem of racial discrimination' (Rusk in Lauren 1996: 244).

The foreign policy implications of domestic racial discrimination often had a tragic-comic element to it. Whenever African or Asian delegates to the United Nations in New York drove down to Washington to talk to American government officials, they passed into the land of Jim Crow, and were forced to use racially segregated restaurants and washrooms—an experience they found humiliating, to say the least. The American government set up a major fellowship programme to bring future leaders of Third World countries to study in the United States, in the hopes that this would encourage a positive view of America, but the first-hand experience of segregation often had the opposite effect. The American government hoped that many UN organizations would be headquartered in the United States, and offered to host the UN's Food and Agriculture Organization (FAO) in Baltimore, but the UN could hardly agree to locate its offices in segregationist Maryland. (The FAO ended up in Rome.) In all of these cases, the cost was not just a diminished international reputation for the United States, but a reinforcement of the Soviet claim to be the only true believer in racial equality, and the only true friend of the non-European peoples of the world.

Faced with these negative effects of racial discrimination on America's geo-political interests, President Truman eventually decided he had to act. As Lauren puts it, 'external pressure from the Cold War now began to play a monumental role in creating a new beginning for racial equality within the United States' (Lauren 1996: 201). After 1946, Truman instructed the

Justice and State Departments to submit amicus briefs supporting legal cases brought by African-American organizations, advising the courts that racial segregation was an obstacle to foreign policy, and a liability in the Cold War struggle with the Soviet Union. In the famous *Brown v Board of Education* case, for example, the federal government brief said 'It is in the context of the present world struggle between freedom and tyranny that the problem of racial discrimination in the US must be viewed' (quoted in Layton 2000: 27).

It is difficult to know how much weight should be given to these external geo-political factors in explaining the success of the African-American civil rights movement, as compared to domestic changes in political opinion about the morality of segregation. But it's worth noting that the initial push within the federal government for desegregation came from the Executive branch, and the State Department in particular, rather than from either the judiciary or the legislature. In fact, Truman's commitment to address racial discrimination was so out of line with public attitudes or judicial norms that he had to circumvent the other two branches, enforcing desegregation in federal institutions by Executive Order, rather than through legislation or judicial review. Without this foreign policy-inspired push from the Executive, it's not clear whether, or when, the moral logic of desegregation would have been accepted by either the white majority among the public at large or the courts.[28]

These accounts of the mixed motives underlying the first two stages of the human rights struggle against racial and ethnic hierarchy contain an important lesson—namely, that attitudes towards race and ethnicity are profoundly influenced by larger geo-political threats. The sorts of policies that are adopted are determined, at least in part, by perceptions of what will be a help or hindrance in the struggle with external enemies. Had it not been for the external threats posed by the Axis in World War II, or by the Soviets during the Cold War, the movement towards decolonization and desegregation might have been much slower, or even stopped in its tracks. Popular acceptance of the moral logic for these reforms was helped by the extra push that comes from concerns about geo-political security.[29]

[28] For detailed discussions of the Cold War impact on domestic race relations, see Borstelmann 2001; Layton 2000.

[29] I don't mean to suggest that the moral arguments and geo-political strategic reasons were entirely separate. Rather, we might say that the fear of losing World War II or the Cold War helped to concentrate people's minds on the issue of decolonization and desegregation, and provided a strong incentive to try to understand the feelings of indignity and humiliation generated by imperialism and discrimination. As Jackson (1993) notes, by the 1960s these new understandings of the injustice of colonialism had taken deeper root, and helped underpin the final decolonization push at the UN.

And this, I think, gives us an important clue to why Western democracies have adopted a new approach to minorities in the past forty years. For the first time in the twentieth century, and perhaps for the first time in several centuries, minorities in the West have not in fact been tools in a larger geo-political struggle. And this is crucial in explaining why states and dominant groups have been more willing to accept (however grudgingly and reluctantly) new models of multicultural accommodation. This is an important point that will resurface in later chapters, so let me explain it in some depth.

Geo-Political Security and the 'Desecuritization' of Ethnic Relations

Where states feel insecure in geo-political terms, fearful of neighbouring enemies, their treatment of minorities is heavily shaped by this sense of insecurity. In particular, states will never voluntarily accord rights and powers to minorities if they think this will increase the likelihood of minorities acting as potential collaborators with, or as a 'fifth column' for, a neighbouring enemy.

In the past, this has often been an issue in the West. For example, prior to World War II, Italy feared that the German-speaking minority in South Tyrol was more loyal to Austria or Germany than to Italy, and would therefore support any attempt by Germany/Austria to invade and annex South Tyrol. Similar fears were expressed about the German minorities in Belgium, Denmark, and the Baltics. These countries worried that Germany might invade in the name of 'liberating' their co-ethnic Germans, and that the German minorities would collaborate with such an invasion. These fears played a crucial role in shaping international responses to the 'minority problem' after both the world wars.

Today, however, this is essentially a non-issue throughout the established Western democracies with respect to national minorities and indigenous peoples. (The situation of some immigrant groups is more complex, as I discuss below.) It is difficult to think of a single Western democracy where the state fears that a national minority or indigenous group would collaborate with a neighbouring enemy and potential aggressor.[30] Part of the reason for this is that Western states do

[30] If we move beyond the established Western democracies, Cyprus is an obvious case: the Turkish-Cypriot minority is seen by the Greek-Cypriot-dominated state as likely to collaborate with aggression/intervention by Turkey.

not have neighbouring enemies who might invade them. NATO has been spectacularly successful in removing the possibility of one Western country invading its neighbours. As a result, the question of whether national minorities and indigenous peoples would be loyal in the event of invasion by a neighbouring state has been removed from the table.

Of course, Western democracies do have more long-distance potential enemies—such as Soviet Communism in the past, Islamic jihadism today, and perhaps China in some future scenario. But in relation to these long-distance threats, there is no question that national minorities and indigenous peoples are on the same side as the state. If Quebec gains increased powers, or even independence, no one in the rest of Canada worries that Quebec will start collaborating with Al Qaeda or China to overthrow the Canadian state.[31] Quebec nationalists may want to secede from Canada, but an independent Quebec would be an ally of Canada, not an enemy, and would cooperate together with Canada in NATO and other Western defence and security arrangements. Similarly, an independent Scotland would be an ally, not enemy of England; an independent Catalonia would be an ally of Spain, and so on.

This may seem obvious, but as we will see in Chapters 6 and 7, in most parts of the world minority groups are still seen as a fifth column, likely to be working for a neighbouring enemy. This is particularly a concern where the minority is related to a neighbouring state by ethnicity or religion, or where a minority is found on both sides of an international boundary, so that the neighbouring state claims the right to intervene to protect 'its' minority.

Under these conditions, we are likely to witness what political scientists call the 'securitization' of ethnic relations.[32] Relations between states and minorities are seen, not as a matter of normal democratic politics to be negotiated and debated, but as a matter of national security, in which the state has to limit the normal democratic process in order to protect its very existence. Under conditions of securitization, minority self-organization may be legally limited (e.g. minority political parties banned), minority leaders may be subject to secret police surveillance, the raising of particular sorts of demands may be illegal (e.g. laws against

---

[31] Well, almost no one. A recent column in a right-wing Canadian newspaper asked 'Would an independent Quebec be a friend to terrorists?' (Kay 2006).

[32] See Waever 1995 for a good discussion of the general phenomenon of 'securitization'. For a more extensive discussion of the securitization of ethnic relations, see Kymlicka and Opalski 2001: 66–8, 366 ff.

promoting secession), and so on. Even if minority demands can be voiced, they will be flatly rejected by the larger society and the state. After all, how can groups that are disloyal have any legitimate claims against the state? So the securitization of ethnic relations erodes both the democratic space to voice minority demands, and the likelihood that those demands will be accepted.

In most Western countries, however, ethnic politics have been almost entirely 'desecuritized'. Ethnic politics is just that—normal, day-to-day politics. Relations between the state and minority groups have been taken out of the 'security' box, and put in the 'democratic politics' box.

This desecuritization of ethnic relations, combined with the assurances provided by robust human rights protections, helps to explain why dominant groups in the West have accepted demands for multicultural reforms. Both of these factors dramatically reduce the risks to the members of dominant groups of adopting liberal multiculturalism. The former ensures that multiculturalism is not a threat to people's collective geo-political security, the latter ensures that multiculturalism is not a threat to their individual human security. Under these circumstances, multiculturalism is essentially a low-risk proposition, and dominant groups are more likely to acquiesce in it.

I use the term 'acquiesce', because it is important not to overstate or misinterpret the level of support for multiculturalism amongst members of dominant groups in most Western societies. The two factors I've just mentioned—the desecuritization of ethnic relations, and assurances of robust human rights protection—reduce the risks associated with multiculturalism, but do not provide any positive argument in favour of it. It's of course possible that some members of the dominant group have been persuaded by the arguments of minority leaders that multiculturalism is not just *consistent with*, but also *required by*, human rights norms, and is needed to ensure the full implementation of these norms. However, we shouldn't exaggerate the extent to which this moral argument has been accepted among the wider public. There's relatively little evidence that members of the dominant group have become 'true believers' in multiculturalism in that sense.[33]

What does appear to have happened, however, is that a sufficient number of citizens have become convinced that multiculturalism is consistent

---

[33] This is clear from the fact that support for multiculturalism as a way of accommodating already-present minorities often co-exists with opposition to admitting any new minorities, for example by tightening entry procedures, as has occurred in both Europe and North America (Rudge 1998).

with their country's basic liberal-democratic values (and its geo-political security), and hence is a *permissible* policy option. They may not be persuaded that multiculturalism is a particularly beneficial or virtuous policy, let alone a morally obligatory one, but so long as it respects human rights and state security, then it is an acceptable option, and not worth mobilizing against. In that sense, the attitude of most citizens towards multiculturalism is one of passive acquiescence, rather than active and wholehearted support. This is certainly what many polls have suggested.[34] But passive acquiescence can be enough. Democracy is often said to be a system of 'majority rule', but where majority groups are passive, and minorities are well-organized and motivated, minority views can be politically effective.[35]

The fact that liberal multiculturalism receives the passive acquiescence rather than active support of most members of dominant groups means that it is vulnerable to backlash and retreat, particularly if critics are able to raise fears that it may after all be a threat to human rights or state security.[36] And, as we'll see, this is precisely what has occurred in some high-profile cases of 'retreat from multiculturalism'.

[34] See, e.g., the polls reported in Evans 2006 and Crepaz 2006.

[35] We can formulate the political dynamics involved more specifically. As I noted earlier, liberal multiculturalism in the West has generally been adopted when left-liberal or social-democratic parties come to power. In most cases, the fact that these parties supported multiculturalism was not the reason why they came to power: most of their supporters were agnostic or even sceptical about the virtues of multiculturalism. However, where voters are confident that multiculturalism is consistent with liberal-democratic values and with geo-political security, they will not change their voting patterns simply to express their scepticism about its positive merits. If they have good reasons otherwise to support left-liberal or social-democratic parties, and if they believe that multiculturalism is low risk, they will continue to vote for those parties, even if they are not true believers in multiculturalism. For examples of this dynamic, see Evans 2006 and Crepaz 2006.

[36] It also means that there is a built-in asymmetry in majority and minority attitudes towards multiculturalism that can be a source of tension and misunderstanding. Since members of the majority typically believe that these policies are, at best, permissible but not required by liberal-democratic values and human rights norms, they believe that they have gone beyond the call of duty, and in that sense have been generous, and indeed virtuous, in adopting these policies. They expect minorities to be suitably grateful for this generosity, and to acknowledge their good fortune in living in a country with such a tolerant and well-meaning majority. Members of minority groups, on the other hand, typically think that the adoption of multiculturalism policies is the barest minimum required to acknowledge and remedy earlier injustices, and that no gratitude is owed for this modest step. From the minority perspective, the fact that members of the majority expect thanks and gratitude for adopting multiculturalism suggests that they haven't truly accepted the injustice of earlier forms of exclusion and assimilation, or fully abandoned their earlier claims to be exclusive owners of the state and of public space. This disjunction in attitudes can be an ongoing source of resentment and distrust, even when there is a (temporary) consensus on the details of a particular policy.

The Retreat from Multiculturalism?

So far in this chapter, I have looked at five key foundations of Western trends towards accommodating diversity. Increasing rights-consciousness, demographic changes, and multiple access points for safe political mobilization help to explain why non-dominant groups have become more assertive of multicultural claims; and the desecuritization of ethnic relations and a consensus on human rights help to reduce the risk to dominant groups of accepting these claims. When these five conditions are in place, the trend towards greater accommodation of ethnocultural diversity is likely to arise, regardless of the presence or absence of particular personalities, or particular political parties, or particular electoral systems.[37]

This analysis not only helps to explain the *rise* of multiculturalism in the West, it also helps, I believe, to explain the *retreat* from multiculturalism in some Western countries. Where one or more of these five conditions is absent, or put into question, public support for particular forms of multiculturalism can diminish. And indeed we can see clear cases of this, although the extent of the so-called 'retreat from multiculturalism' in the West has often been exaggerated, and misinterpreted.

Some commentators have argued that we are witnessing a general retreat from multiculturalism in the West, and a return to more traditional ideas of homogenous and unitary republican citizenship, in which ethnocultural diversity is banished from the public realm and relegated to the private sphere (e.g. Joppke 2004; Brubaker 2001; Entzinger 2003). This has led some critics to express the hope that multiculturalism will prove to have been a passing fad or fashion (Barry 2001).

In reality, however, the backlash against multiculturalism is quite localized, relevant only to the claims of certain minorities in certain countries. For example, it has not affected state policies towards national minorities. The trend I described in Chapter 3 towards greater recognition of substate national groups, often in the form of regional autonomy and official language status, remains untouched. There has been no backlash against the

---

[37] A certain level of economic prosperity may be another precondition. But if so, it is not because these policies of accommodation are themselves expensive. Federal or decentralized regimes can be just as efficient as unitary and centralized states, and even the costs of bilingualism are much lower than most people think (Grin 2004). In any event, it is clear that the resistance of states to these policies usually has nothing to do with their expense: nation-building states have often rejected cultural rights that have no financial cost at all (e.g. allowing privately funded minority schools). So if a certain level of economic prosperity is a precondition for the successful adoption of these models, it is not because the models themselves are expensive, but because one or more of the other conditions (e.g. democratic consolidation) may have economic prerequisites.

rights of national minorities within the Western democracies. There is no case in the West of a country retreating from any of the accommodations it has accorded to its substate national groups. On the contrary, as we will see in Chapter 6, this trend has been reaffirmed by the development of international norms, such as the Framework Convention for the Protection of National Minorities adopted by the Council of Europe.

Or consider the case of indigenous peoples. The trend towards greater recognition of indigenous rights, often in the form of land claims, recognition of customary law, and self-government rights, also remains fully in place in the West, without any measurable backlash or retreat. And it too has been reaffirmed by the development of international norms, such as the UN's Draft Declaration on the Rights of Indigenous Peoples, or comparable standards of indigenous rights by the Organization of American States, the International Labour Organization, or the World Bank, discussed in Chapter 7.

So there is no across-the-board retreat from multiculturalism. For both substate national groups and indigenous peoples, the trend towards the public recognition and accommodation of ethnocultural diversity remains intact, and indeed is now more firmly entrenched, not only rooted in domestic accommodations and negotiations, but also ratified and protected by international norms.

The retreat from multiculturalism, therefore, is largely restricted to one domain of ethnocultural diversity—namely, immigration. And, as we will see in Part III, unlike the case of national minorities and indigenous peoples, there has been no serious attempt to codify cultural rights for immigrants at the international level. The key question, therefore, is why immigrant multiculturalism in particular has come under such attack. We can begin by dismissing one popular explanation. As I noted earlier, various commentators have suggested that the retreat from immigrant multiculturalism reflects a return to the traditional liberal belief that ethnicity belongs in the private sphere, that the public sphere should be neutral, and that citizenship should be undifferentiated. On this view, the retreat from immigrant multiculturalism reflects a rejection of the whole idea of a liberal-democratic conception of multiculturalism.

But this cannot be the explanation. If Western democracies were rejecting the very idea of liberal multiculturalism, they would have rejected the claims of substate national groups and indigenous peoples as well as immigrants. After all, the claims of national groups and indigenous peoples typically involve a much more dramatic insertion of ethnocultural diversity into the public sphere, and a more dramatic degree of differentiated citizenship, than is demanded by immigrant groups. Whereas immigrants typically seek modest variations or exemptions in the operation of mainstream institutions, historic national minorities and indigenous peoples typically seek a much wider level of recognition and accommodation, including such things as land claims, self-government powers, language rights, separate educational systems, and even separate legal systems. These claims involve a much more serious challenge to ideas of undifferentiated citizenship and the privatization of ethnicity than is involved in accommodating immigrant groups. Yet Western democracies have not retreated at all from their commitment to accommodating these historic minorities.

Western democracies are, in fact, increasingly comfortable with claims to differentiated citizenship and the public recognition of difference, when these claims are advanced by historic minorities. For example, while the Netherlands is retreating from immigrant multiculturalism, it is strengthening the rights of its historic Frisian minority; Germany is retreating from immigrant multiculturalism, but is celebrating the 50th anniversary of the special status of its historic Danish minority; Britain is retreating from immigrant multiculturalism, but has accorded new self-government powers to its historic nations in Scotland and Wales; Australia is retreating from immigrant multiculturalism, but strengthening the institutionalization of Aboriginal rights; France is retreating from immigrant multiculturalism, but strengthening recognition of its historic minority languages; and so on. None of this makes sense if we explain the retreat from immigrant multiculturalism as a return of orthodox liberal ideas of undifferentiated citizenship and neutral public spheres.

So it is not the idea of liberal multiculturalism *per se* that has come under attack.[38] The backlash, rather, is largely restricted to immigration. And even within the sphere of immigration, the retreat from multiculturalism is far from uniform across countries: it is more pronounced in Western Europe than in North America, for example.

To understand this, we can return to our list of sources and preconditions. The two key factors that reduce majority opposition to multiculturalism have both been put in doubt in the context of Muslim immigration into Western Europe. Many people have questioned whether the liberal expectancy applies to Muslims in the same way it applied to earlier waves of immigrants. These fears extend back at least to the Rushdie affair, and

---

[38] Commentators who argue that Western democracies are rejecting liberal multiculturalism *per se* typically simply ignore the obvious counter-examples of national minorities and indigenous peoples—see, e.g., Joppke 2004.

have been reaffirmed by the Danish cartoon affair, as well as by persistent reports about coerced arranged marriages, honour killings, or female genital mutilation.[39] The optimistic assumption that human rights norms will inevitably strengthen and triumph within Muslim communities in the West has been placed in doubt.

The 9/11 attacks, and the subsequent Madrid and London bombings, have also led to the 'resecuritization' of state–Muslim relations, as fears have arisen that locally settled Muslims might collaborate with external enemies of the West, serving as a fifth column. As a result, a number of issues that used to be in the 'normal democratic politics' box have been put back into the 'state security' box. Debates about Muslim schools, for example, used to be discussed in terms of the relative merits of different models and mixes of public and private schooling, terms that are familiar from earlier debates about Christian and Jewish schools. But increasingly these debates have been influenced by concerns that Muslim schools, or other institutions set up to serve the Muslim community, might be captured by radicals, and used as a breeding ground for jihadists who are committed to attacking the West.[40]

Given that the public acceptance of multiculturalism in the West has depended on the perception that it is consistent with both the geopolitical security of the state and the personal security of individual citizens, support for a liberal multiculturalist approach to the integration of Muslim immigrants faces an uphill battle in Western Europe. Indeed, we have witnessed a partial backlash against liberal multiculturalism, particularly in countries where Muslims form a clear majority of the immigrant population and hence are the focus of debates around multiculturalism (Klausen 2005).[41] In most of Western Europe, the largest group

[39] Immigrants from many cultures bring with them practices that conflict with contemporary Western standards, but Muslims are often perceived as having a stronger *religious* commitment to maintaining these practices, and hence as more likely to invoke the ideology of multiculturalism to demand the right to maintain them. Also, it is widely believed that international Islamist movements are encouraging Muslim immigrants in the West to challenge the liberal boundaries of multiculturalism in the name of their religion, as part of a broader anti-Western struggle.

[40] Recall that the London bombers seem to have been recruited in a publicly funded community centre in Leeds that had been captured by jihadists.

[41] The size and proportion of immigrant groups is important here, and helps to explain the differences between Europe and North America. In both Canada and the United States, Muslims form a small percentage of the overall immigrant intake, dwarfed by Hispanics (in the United States) and East Asians (in Canada). As a result, policy debates about the integration of immigrants are rarely focused on Muslims. In North America, unlike much of Europe, no one equates the category of 'immigrant' with the category of 'Muslim'. This isn't to say that non-Muslim immigrant groups are warmly welcomed in North America or Europe, or that they do not face prejudice and discrimination. Within every country, there are

of non-European immigrants is Muslims—up to 80 per cent in countries like France, Spain, Italy, Germany, The Netherlands, etc., compared to 10 per cent or less in Canada and the United States—and so public discourse in Europe often simply equates the category of 'immigrant' with the category of 'Muslim'. Even in Britain, where the immigrant intake is more mixed in terms of religion, issues of Islam have come to dominate the debate. A recent article in the *Spectator* was titled 'How Islam Has Killed Multiculturalism' (Liddle 2004). The title and article are decidedly biased,[42] but it seems true that public support for multiculturalism has declined as Muslims have come to be seen as the main proponents or beneficiaries of the policy.

Of course, Islamophobia is not the only source of the recent backlash against immigrant multiculturalism in Europe. Indeed, some commentators argue that fears about Muslims are simply the most recent rationalization of a deeper and persisting free-floating anxiety about 'the other', and nostalgia for a time when everyone was assumed to share thick bonds of common history and identity. People dislike ethnic and racial diversity, but they do not want to appear as racists or xenophobes, so they look around for some more 'acceptable' reason to oppose immigrant multiculturalism, such as fears about illiberal practices or security threats (or crime, economic burdens, abuse of asylum procedures, etc.). If necessary, people invent or exaggerate these risks, even when there is little or no evidence for them, in order to hide the true nature of their opposition to immigrants. These fears are just the surface manifestations or rationalizations of deeper forms of public racism and xenophobia that are quite independent of contingent facts about the liberality or geo-political security impact of particular migrant groups. If racists and xenophobes couldn't invoke these specific fears, they would simply find some other rationalization for opposing immigration and multiculturalism.

This is undoubtedly part of the story, and it is surely true that multiculturalism will not gain wholehearted public acceptance unless or until the public's free-floating anxiety about diversity is reduced, and the

important variations in the attitude towards the claims of different immigrant groups. Public debates typically distinguish 'good' immigrant groups, who are seen as hard-working and law-abiding and hence deserving of reasonable multicultural accommodations, from 'bad' immigrant groups, who may be seen as illegal or lazy, or as prone to crime, religious fanaticism or political extremism. When the latter are seen as the prime beneficiaries of multiculturalism, public support for multiculturalism can dramatically diminish, leading to high-profile cases of retreat. For the importance of these perceptions in explaining support for multiculturalism, see Kymlicka 2004*a*.

[42] Note that Liddle says it is Islam, not Islamaphobia, which has killed multiculturalism.

racism and xenophobia that feed it are tackled. However, free-floating anxieties about newcomers, while strong, cannot explain the variation in support for immigration and multiculturalism between countries, or over time within countries. They cannot explain why some countries adopt multiculturalism policies while others do not, or why some countries start down the road of multiculturalism and then retreat. For example, multiculturalism was initially adopted in the Netherlands for their (predominantly Christian) ex-colonial immigrants (e.g. the South Moluccans, or the Antilleans), but it became much more controversial when Muslims from Turkey and Morocco became perceived as the main beneficiaries. A similar process occurred in Britain: multiculturalism was first demanded by (predominantly Christian) blacks from the Caribbean, and had significant levels of public support, but this support dropped when Muslim immigrants from Pakistan and Bangladesh became perceived as the main drivers of multiculturalism. In both cases, the perceived risks associated with the policy changed as the main target groups changed.[43] These variations suggest that in the enduring struggle between the public values of tolerance/non-discrimination and public fears about diversity, the outcome often depends on specific and contingent assessments of the risks involved. The varying fate of multiculturalism across the Western democracies suggests that many citizens are willing to accept multiculturalism policies when they are perceived as low risk, but oppose them when they are perceived as high risk.

This raises an obvious dilemma: it may well be that multiculturalism policies are most needed precisely when they are most high risk. Perhaps it is precisely when the members of a particular group are seen as a 'fifth column', or as a threat to the liberal-democratic consensus, that proactive efforts are needed to prevent the polarization of ethnic relations. Conversely, we might think that if there is little or no distrust between ethnic groups, then multiculturalism policies may be easier to sell but less necessary in practice. If so, multiculturalism might be most needed when it is least likely to be adopted, and most popular when it is least necessary. Jan Nederveen Pieterse suggests as much when he says that 'The core problem of liberal multiculturalism is that it provides a solution for which there is no problem and a remedy for which there is no ailment' (Pieterse

---

[43] A similar shift occurred briefly in the early 1990s in Canada, when, for the first time since the policy was adopted twenty years earlier, Muslim immigrants (primarily from Somalia) started to influence public debates around multiculturalism. This led to a brief drop in public support for multiculturalism, but since Muslims form just 10 per cent of the immigrant intake, they are not the main drivers of public opinion or public policy. See, on this, Kymlicka 2004a and Jedwab 2005.

2005: 1271). This is a paradox that arises in many post-communist and post-colonial contexts as well, and I will return to it in Part III. But the Western experience to date suggests that the public acceptance of multiculturalism depends on feelings of both basic individual and collective security, and when these feelings are eroded, multiculturalism will face a backlash and retreat.

But even as some states seek to curtail the perceived 'excesses' of multiculturalism in higher risk contexts, they typically emphasize that they are not reverting to older homogenizing and assimilationist models of immigration, and they continue to accept the need for public institutions like the schools, media, health care, and police to adapt to the realities of ethnic diversity. Immigrant groups are no longer expected to hide their ethnic identity in public life, and their claims for reasonable forms of recognition and accommodation in public institutions (e.g. in the common school curriculum) are acknowledged. In short, talk about a 'retreat from (immigrant) multiculturalism' typically obscures a more complex story in which a few multiculturalism policies are curtailed while others become more deeply institutionalized.[44] As with national minorities and indigenous peoples, a baseline level of 'recognition' and 'accommodation' for immigrants has increasingly been accepted as an inevitable and legitimate aspect of life in a liberal democracy.

So there is no single story of 'advance' or 'retreat' of multiculturalism in the West. There are different types of ethnocultural diversity, each raising its own distinctive sorts of multicultural claims, and each with its own trajectories of resistance, acceptance, and backlash. The five factors I have discussed in this chapter help, I believe, to explain these varying fortunes.

From Social Movement Multiculturalism to Corporate Multiculturalism

At this point, some readers may think that I have missed a crucial factor in explaining the emergence of multiculturalism—namely, global capitalism and the rise of neo-liberal economics. The emergence of multiculturalism in the past thirty to forty years more or less corresponds in time with the era of intense economic globalization, welfare state retrenchment, the privatization of public-owned companies and resources, and the deregulation of markets. And for some commentators, these two developments

[44] For examples of rhetorical shifts that obscure the persistence of multiculturalism policies in practice, see Hansen 2007; Schain 1999; Richardson 2004; and Entzinger 2006.

are clearly related—indeed, according to Slavoj Žižek, 'the ideal form of ideology of this global capitalism is multiculturalism' (1997: 44). On this view, multiculturalism somehow serves to facilitate or justify the extension of global capitalism and the 'Washington Consensus'.

I think this is a mistaken analysis—multiculturalism has quite different origins from neo-liberal economics—but it is true that multiculturalism has not been untouched by these larger changes in the global political economy. And it's important to figure out what these connections are.

The idea that multiculturalism emerged as a tool of global capitalism is simply not borne out by the facts. As I have repeatedly emphasized, multiculturalism was first introduced by left-liberal or social-democratic political parties, in response to popular mobilization by non-dominant groups. It was, in short, 'social movement multiculturalism'. At the beginning, the corporate sector and the political factions supporting neo-liberal economic restructuring—the Reaganites and Thatcherites—were opposed to multiculturalism, which they viewed as a classic example of how the state was being misused to subsidize 'special interests'.[45] Neo-liberal economic orthodoxy insisted that the state should not intervene in the 'cultural marketplace' by supporting minority languages or cultural activities.

So multiculturalism first emerged from popular mobilization in the face of resistance from business elites and neo-liberal ideologues. However, over time, it is fair to say that the corporate world has made its peace with multiculturalism, and indeed that a distinctive form of 'corporate multiculturalism' has emerged which interacts in complex ways with the earlier 'social movement multiculturalism'.[46]

Corporate multiculturalism and social movement multiculturalism have sometimes drawn on each other. The neo-liberal push for decentralization, for example, originally done in the name of economic efficiency, became more popular when it was linked to multiculturalist arguments about accommodating diversity. Conversely, social movement multiculturalists have sometimes needed the support of the corporate world. As we've seen, social movement multiculturalism was able to secure some important reforms, but these were fragile victories. Because multiculturalism is tolerated rather than actively supported by dominant groups, and hence is vulnerable to backlash and retreat, many supporters have

---

[45] For the pervasiveness of this critique of multiculturalism amongst the neo-liberal right in Canada, see Abu-Laban and Gabriel 2002.

[46] I take the terms 'social movement multiculturalism' and 'corporate multiculturalism' from James 2006 and Matustik 1998 respectively, although adapting them for my own purposes.

attempted to try to find more positive arguments in its favour that might be convincing to members of the dominant group. These include reaffirmations of the underlying moral argument that multiculturalism extends and furthers the logic of human rights, but defenders have also hoped to find other more strategic or self-interested reasons why members of the majority should support it. They want to show that 'multiculturalism pays', so that members of the dominant group can view multiculturalism as a benefit to themselves, and not just a moral obligation they owe to others.

And the most common strategy in this regard has been to emphasize the economic spin-offs from multiculturalism. Defenders have talked about 'productive diversity', citing evidence that firms with more diverse workforces tend to be more productive and innovative. Moreover, having employees with different cultural backgrounds and language skills is said to be an asset in an increasingly globalized economy. Only those with strong inter-cultural skills will be able to compete on the global stage. Chinese immigrants to North America, for example, should be encouraged to maintain their mother-tongue and cultural fluency, so as to serve as facilitators for global trade and investment. In short, 'multiculturalism means business', to cite a phrase that was popular in both Canada and Australia in the 1980s and 1990s.

A related argument appeals to the idea that multiculturalism makes a country more attractive for both tourists and potential highly skilled immigrants. Cities 'branded' themselves as multicultural, highlighting their ethnic neighbourhoods and ethnic restaurants, in order to attract visitors, elite immigrants, and foreign investment.[47]

These arguments have had some success in selling multiculturalism to members of dominant groups, but they also have an obvious downside. Taken on their own, they have the potential to reduce multiculturalism to a marketing ploy, as if the goal of multiculturalism is not to challenge inherited racial and ethnic hierarchies, but rather to repackage cultural differences as an economic asset in a global economy and/or as a commodity or lifestyle good that can be marketed and consumed. And indeed we see an ongoing battle by social movement multiculturalists in many

---

[47] Western countries have not generally competed to attract low-skilled immigrants, but there is a growing competition to attract elite immigrants—professionals and entrepreneurs—who are seen as contributing to a country's prosperity and vitality. And in this competition, it is widely, and I think correctly, assumed that multiculturalism provides a strategic advantage—see Shachar 2006.

countries to ensure that these marketing ploys supplement rather than displace the original emancipatory aims of multiculturalism.

This is hardly unique to multiculturalism. We see a similar dynamic with other movements for progressive social reform, including feminism and environmentalism. These movements initially emerged in the face of resistance from corporate elites and neo-liberal ideologues, but capitalism has attempted to recuperate these movements, and find ways to repackage them as brands and commodities. And so we see ongoing struggles by social movement activists to retain control over the agenda of these movements, to preserve their original reformist goals.

A number of terms have been developed to capture this phenomenon: critics have talked about 'corporate multiculturalism', 'consumerist multiculturalism', 'boutique multiculturalism', 'neo-liberal multiculturalism', or 'Benetton multiculturalism' (after one of the multinational corporations that most successfully branded itself as a purveyor of commodified cultural diversity).[48] The prevalence of this phenomenon has led some commentators to assume that this is the real source of the rise of multiculturalism in the West. But in fact, corporate multiculturalism has always followed social movement multiculturalism, and emerged in part as a way of building popular support for the latter. I'm not aware of any country in the West where multiculturalism was adopted primarily at the behest of corporate elites rather than social movement activists. Corporate elites have typically been latecomers to the multicultural bandwagon, and the first to jump off the wagon in periods of backlash and retreat against multiculturalism.[49]

In short, there is nothing in the logic of multinational capitalism that requires (or precludes) multiculturalism. In countries where social movement multiculturalism has achieved some success, corporate elites can

[48] For discussions, see Giroux 1994, chaps 1–2; Matustik 1998; Bonnett 2000; Mitchell 1993; Macdonald and Muldoon 2006; Hale 2002. Benetton's reputation for multicultural virtue was tarnished when it was discovered that Luciano Benetton himself was buying up huge chunks of land in Chile taken from the Mapuche Indians (Mascarenhas 2006).

[49] The relationship between social movement and corporate multiculturalisms is even more complicated outside the West. Within the West, corporate multiculturalism typically functions as a depoliticized and commodified form of social movement multiculturalism, invoking its tropes about the importance of equality, tolerance, and inclusion, but in non-threatening ways. Elsewhere, however, multinational corporations invoke multiculturalism in ways that completely contradict the goals of social movement multiculturalism. For example, in the name of 'respecting the different cultures we serve', companies such as Starbucks and McDonalds reportedly practice gender segregation and discrimination in Saudi Arabia, reproducing rather than challenging inherited patterns of hierarchy and exclusion, and violating rather than promoting universal human rights commitments to equality (Manning 2002; Johnston 2006).

seek to make money from it by marketing commodified forms of cultural difference as a consumer good. Where social movement multiculturalism is failing, corporate elites can happily distance themselves from it, as they traditionally have done.

In any event, recent events have revealed the essential superficiality of the ideology of corporate multiculturalism. After 9/11, Madrid, and the Danish cartoon affair, no one can plausibly think that multiculturalism should be endorsed or rejected on the basis of whether it increases global economic competitiveness or attracts tourism. These events have reminded us that the fundamental question is whether multiculturalism can serve as a means of citizenization: can multiculturalism help convert our inherited catalogue of uncivil ethnic and racial relations—including relations of conqueror and conquered; colonizer and colonized; settler and indigenous; racialized and unmarked; normalized and deviant; orthodox and heretic; civilized and backward; ally and enemy; master and slave—into relations of liberal-democratic citizenship?

The immediate reaction of many people, after 9/11, was to conclude that multiculturalism has failed in this regard, and has simply reproduced relations of enmity and hierarchy. However, as we will see in the next chapter, there is ample evidence that multiculturalism has in fact contributed to the construction of liberal-democratic citizenship. In any event, this is the right question to be asking. Earlier talk about 'productive diversity' and 'multiculturalism means business' can no longer distract us from addressing the more profound and important claims raised by the original movement for multiculturalism about the link between ethnocultural diversity, human rights, and liberal-democratic principles.

Conclusion

Any attempt to tell the story of the rise of multiculturalism in the West is inevitably partial and one-sided, and I do not claim to have provided a comprehensive account in this chapter. I have simply tried to identify some factors that I think have been of widespread and enduring importance across the Western democracies, and to cast doubt on some other explanations that have been offered.

Contrary to some commentators, I see little evidence that multiculturalism has emerged as a result of a revival of Herderian German romanticism or Nietzschean post-modernism or cultural conservatism, or of the resurgence of neo-liberal economic restructuring. Instead, I have focused on five other factors. On the one hand, increasing rights-consciousness due to the human rights revolution, demographic changes, and multiple access points for safe political mobilization help to explain why non-dominant groups have become more assertive of multicultural claims; on the other hand, the desecuritization of ethnic relations and a consensus on human rights help to reduce the risk to dominant groups of accepting these claims. These factors, taken together, help to explain both the breadth of the shift towards liberal multiculturalism in the West, but also its fragile nature, since they have typically generated only passive acquiescence rather than active support.

Of course, for the purposes of this book, the more important question is what light this analysis sheds on the prospects for the global diffusion of liberal multiculturalism. If these five conditions apply unevenly across the Western democracies, and are subject to ebbs and flows over time, this is even more true of other regions of the world. As we will see in Part III, it remains a rather rare occurrence for all five conditions of liberal multiculturalism to converge, and there is no general tendency for this constellation of factors to become more common around the world.

In fact, there seems to be a rather systematic imbalance in these trend-lines. To oversimplify, we could say that the conditions that help to generate greater demands for liberal multiculturalism are indeed becoming more common around the world. We can see the steady spread of a new discourse and consciousness of human and minority rights, as well as an (incomplete) process of democratization that is creating more spaces for safe political mobilization by minorities. But there seems to be no comparable trend regarding the conditions that enable and encourage states and dominant groups to accept these minority claims. In broad regions of the world the fears of dominant groups regarding their geo-political security or their individual security continue to paralyse efforts to adopt liberal multiculturalism. The predictable result is serious political turbulence, as the demand for liberal multiculturalism exceeds its supply.

This imbalance in the underlying conditions of liberal multiculturalism raises a number of profound challenges for international action in this field. There is an obvious danger that the efforts of the international community, whether by intergovernmental or non-governmental organizations, might unintentionally exacerbate this imbalance, inciting greater demands for liberal multiculturalism without strengthening the conditions that enable their acceptance. I think the international community has indeed ignored this danger in some cases, and in other cases over-reacted to it.

Before exploring this dilemma, however, we need to finish our exploration of liberal multiculturalism in the West by examining its track record in practice.

5

Evaluating Liberal Multiculturalism in Practice

In the previous chapter, I described the optimistic origins of liberal multiculturalism in the West, emerging as part and parcel of a larger human rights revolution, and committed to attacking inherited hierarchies and expanding individual freedom. But this story about the genealogy of liberal multiculturalism is primarily a story about beliefs, intentions, and aspirations, and doesn't tell us how things have worked out in practice. The key question, one might think, is not what were the naïve or pious hopes of the people who advocated or drafted these policies, but what have been their actual effects? We now have close to forty years experience with various forms of liberal multiculturalism. Are they working well? Are they a 'success' that warrants encouraging their global diffusion?

This is not an easy question to answer, given the many different forms of multiculturalism policies, and the many different goals they are intended to serve. There are a few things we can say with some confidence about the effects of multiculturalism in practice, but on many other important issues we simply lack the relevant evidence. In this chapter, I will survey what we know, and don't know, about the strengths and limitations of liberal multiculturalism in practice.

Let me start with one obvious but important point. At the most minimal level, it is clear that the adoption of liberal multiculturalism has not impaired what we might call the basic functioning of Western democracies, measured by such indicators as peace, democratic stability, the rule of law, or economic prosperity. None of the countries that have moved along the multiculturalist path in the West have subsequently descended into civil war or anarchy, or faced military coups, or suffered economic collapse. On the contrary, even a casual inspection of the list of countries which are 'strong' in their commitment to multiculturalism policies (see pp. 68–74 above) shows that they are amongst the most peaceful, stable, and prosperous societies on the planet.

This alone is sufficient to refute some of the more apocalyptic predictions that have been made about the destabilizing effects of multiculturalism. As Jacob Levy notes, critics of multiculturalism are fond of the 'reductio ad Hitlerum' argument (Levy 2004: 334),[1] treating the adoption of multiculturalism as the first step on a slippery slope towards racial and religious strife, the 'Balkanization' of society, the suppression of civil and political liberties, and the overthrow of the democratic constitutional order. With over forty years of experience to draw upon, it's clear that these predictions were off-target. As I discussed in Chapter 2, the experience of liberal multiculturalism in the West is a story about the progressive 'normalization' of ethnic politics, so that ethnic political mobilization becomes just one more form of everyday peaceful legal and democratic contestation.

We also have good reason to doubt many of the other pessimistic predictions about the effects of multiculturalism in practice. For example, some critics argue that the shift towards multiculturalism weakens the welfare state, by eroding the sense of pan-ethnic solidarity needed to sustain society-wide economic redistribution (Barry 2001; Michaels 2006). This is often called the 'recognition versus redistribution' trade-off—a politics of multicultural recognition is said to displace a politics of class-based redistribution. However, recent attempts to test this claim have failed to provide any support for it. Countries with strong multiculturalism policies have had no more difficulty sustaining their redistributive social policies than countries with modest or weak multiculturalism policies (Banting and Kymlicka 2006).

The fact that multiculturalism has proven to be consistent with the basic functioning of a liberal-democratic welfare state is enough to make it an attractive option for IOs to consider when dealing with multiethnic post-communist and post-colonial countries. In many of these countries, older models of a centralized and homogenizing nation-state have clearly failed, and new models are needed that can cope with the enduring reality of ethnic political mobilization. Since liberal multiculturalism is one such option, and has not jeopardized peace, democratic stability or prosperity in the West, it has been included in many of the IO-sponsored lists of 'best practices' or 'toolkits' for managing diversity.

---

[1] According to Irving Kristol, 'Multiculturalism is as much a "war against the West" as Nazism and Stalinism ever were' (Kristol 1991: 15).

But the mere fact that liberal multiculturalism hasn't led to the collapse of Western states doesn't really explain why IOs have attempted to promote this model around the world. In many contexts, IOs have treated liberal multiculturalism not simply as one legitimate option amongst others, but as a preferred option, even as the only legitimate option. The clearest example is the decision of the EU and NATO to insist on respect for minority rights as a condition of admission to these organizations. This preference for liberal multiculturalism cannot be explained solely by reference to the basic functioning of the state. After all, while it is clear that strong multiculturalism policies have proven to be consistent with peace, stability, and prosperity, it is equally obvious that such polices are not a precondition for the basic functioning of the state. Many Western countries with modest or weak multiculturalism polices are also stable, peaceful, and prosperous.

The justification for promoting liberal multiculturalism, therefore, lies elsewhere. There are many reasons why IOs have expressed a preference for multiculturalist models, which I will discuss in the next two chapters, but at least part of the explanation is that many people within these organizations share the optimistic view that multiculturalism advances a larger human rights agenda. This indeed is explicit in the preambles to the various international declarations and conventions on minority rights. Multiculturalism, on this optimistic view, not only preserves ethnic peace, but actually reduces inequalities and remedies injustices, enhances liberalization and democratization, and furthers the ideals of the human rights revolution and of civil rights liberalism. Is there any evidence for this optimistic view? We can safely conclude that the most pessimistic predictions about the destabilizing effects of multiculturalism have not come true, but have the optimistic claims made on its behalf been fulfilled?

This is a difficult question to answer, since it is not entirely clear how we would measure success in, say, 'enhancing liberalization and democratization', or 'advancing a larger human rights agenda'. These are diffuse and multidimensional goals, with implications for the social, economic, political, and cultural relationships and structures of a society. Any attempt to systematically measure success in reaching these goals would be an enormous undertaking.

For our purposes, however, we can focus our attention on two general areas. In previous work, I have said that the underlying principles of liberal multiculturalism can be captured in the twin ideas of 'equality between groups' and 'freedom within groups' (Kymlicka 1995), and I will use these two headings to frame my discussion in the rest of the chapter:

(i) Inter-group Equality Have multiculturalism policies succeeded in reducing inherited ethnic and racial hierarchies? Have they reduced the political marginalization, economic disadvantage, and cultural subordination of minorities? Some critics have argued that these policies have served to simply paper over the enduring reality of ethnic and racial hierarchies, substituting symbolic recognition for more substantive reforms. Others have argued that these policies may have actually reinforced hierarchies, by further stigmatizing 'the other' as different, dependent, and needy (e.g. Das Gupta 1999). Yet others argue that while diversity policies may indeed help remedy some inequalities, they do so in ways that are under- and over-inclusive, creating new and equally arbitrary forms of hierarchy in the process.

(ii) Individual Freedom Have multiculturalism policies succeeded in ensuring that the accommodation of ethnocultural diversity occurs within the boundaries of liberal values, consistent with human rights and civil liberties? As we've seen, these policies originated in civil rights liberalism, and were defended on the basis of enhancing the freedom of individuals 'to make the life that the individual is able and wishes to have', in the words of the Canadian Multiculturalism Act. This vision of a liberal multiculturalism in turn rested on confidence in the 'liberal expectancy', according to which the gravitational pull of liberal values will operate across ethnic and racial lines, and the legal system will provide robust protections against threats to those values. Have these intentions and expectations been fulfilled? Or, as some critics have argued, have multicultural policies inhibited the spread of liberal values within some minorities, strengthening the hands of conservative forces that seek to prevent liberal reforms, freezing identities and practices, imprisoning people in inherited cultural scripts, and thereby reducing people's freedom and jeopardizing their civil liberties and human rights?

Whenever multicultural policies have been adopted in the West, we have seen these duelling predictions of their likely effects on freedom and equality. Indeed, these divergent assumptions underpin most of the day-to-day debate around multiculturalism. With forty years of experience to draw upon, we should now be able to draw some conclusions about which of these hopes and fears have come true.

Unfortunately, there is far less evidence available than one might expect. Of the twenty-three policies I listed earlier as characteristic of the shift towards multiculturalism, very few have been systematically studied, a shortcoming that has often been lamented. A recent study for the World Bank attempted to compile the available evidence on the impact of multicultural reforms in the delivery of public services, particularly in the spheres of health care, education, and access to the law, and concluded that the evidence is too fragmentary and anecdotal to draw any firm conclusions (Marc 2005). Similarly, *The Economist* noted that 'astonishingly little is known' about the impact of affirmative action (*The Economist* 1995). The same could be said for most of the policies on my list.

This has left the field wide open for pundits to engage in armchair speculation, or to rush to premature judgement for or against multiculturalism. For example, some commentators note that racial prejudice has diminished in countries with multiculturalism policies, and conclude on this basis that multiculturalism is a success in reducing inter-group inequalities. But in fact racial prejudice has been declining across the Western democracies since the 1960s, whether or not they have multiculturalism policies, and indeed some people worry that multiculturalism policies can weaken or delay that trend by artificially reinforcing group boundaries and resentments (Harles 2004). We need to know more about what role, if any, multiculturalism policies in particular played in the trend towards declining prejudice, and whether or how that trend differs between countries with different forms or degrees of multiculturalism. To answer that question, however, requires the sort of large-scale cross-national and over-time data that hasn't been collected or analysed in relation to multiculturalism policies.

Conversely, critics note that in countries with multiculturalism policies, vulnerable members of some minorities continue to be the victims of illiberal treatment (such as coerced marriages) at the hands of their family or ethnic community, and conclude on that basis that multiculturalism is a failure in enhancing individual freedom (Wikan 2002). The multiculturalist's gamble on the liberal expectancy, it is said, has not worked—liberal norms are not being internalized within some minority groups, and liberal states have not been able or willing to protect the rights and freedoms of the vulnerable members of these groups.

But here again, illiberal practices persist in all Western democracies, whether or not they have multiculturalism policies, and some people argue that such policies provide the best tool for enhancing both the gravitational pull of liberal values and the capacity of state institutions to effectively protect these values within minority communities. Testing this hypothesis requires going beyond anecdotes to look at how different types of multiculturalism policy in different contexts shape

139

processes of political socialization within minority groups, and their relations with state institutions. And we simply don't have that sort of research.[2]

In fact, it is not easy to isolate the effect of multiculturalism policies from the other myriad factors that affect the status of minorities in multiethnic societies. If we could find two otherwise-identical societies that differ only in their commitment to multiculturalism policies, we might be able to draw some firm conclusions. But such 'natural experiments' do not exist in the field of ethnic relations, and efforts to build long-term cross-national databases that incorporate multiculturalism policies as a variable are only in their infancy.

For the foreseeable future, therefore, we have to acknowledge that we lack conclusive proof about the effects of multiculturalism policies. We are making political choices under uncertainty, and our judgements must therefore be tentative.

Nonetheless, there is some fragmentary evidence that is worth considering. In the rest of this chapter, I will examine the three basic forms of liberal multiculturalism relating to substate national groups, indigenous peoples, and immigrants. In each case, I will look at the evidence for the impact of liberal multiculturalism on both inter-group inequalities and on individual freedom.

Substate Nationalist Groups

As we saw in Chapter 3, there is an increasing tendency within the Western democracies to accommodate substate national groups such as the Québécois, Scots, Flemish, and Catalans through some form of federal or quasi-federal devolution of power. These reforms typically involve a combination of (a) territorial autonomy; and (b) recognition of a minority's language as an official language within the self-governing territory—a combination I have summarized under the label 'multination and multilingual federalism'.

These reforms have proven to be consistent with the basic functioning of a democratic state, but have they reduced inter-group inequalities and enhanced individual freedom? Let's start with the issue of inter-group

[2] An important first step to developing this comparative evaluation of different policy approaches towards multiculturalism and gender equality is the project on 'Gender Equality, Cultural Diversity: European Comparisons', coordinated by Anne Phillips and Sawitri Saharso. Having examined eight countries, their conclusion, in effect, is that we need more research.

equality. Critics of multiculturalism often object that it involves merely symbolic recognition of ethnocultural diversity, without substantive changes in the relative power and position of different groups. It is clear, I think, that this criticism is off-target in relation to multination federalism. To be sure, these reforms contain a strong symbolic component, and are centrally concerned to remedy the earlier exclusion of the minority's language and culture from public space and public institutions. Indeed, multilingual multination federalism gives a very high level of public recognition to the minority's culture, at least at the regional level. Its language is given official status; its history and literature are taught in schools; its arts are displayed in public museums; its legal traditions are maintained; its heroes are celebrated in public holidays and public statues; and so on. In fact, this model gives the national minority many of the same powers to express and diffuse its language and culture at the substate level that the majority group exercises through the central state. This is perhaps as close as one can get to equality or parity between majority and minority groups in the capacity to have one's culture affirmed in public space.

But multination federalism is not just about recognition. It also involves a substantial redistribution of political power, and hence increased opportunities for effective political participation by national minorities (Newman 1996), as well as a redistribution of economic opportunities. Consider, for example, the case of the French-Canadian minority in Canada. Prior to the 1960s, francophones were under-represented in the federal civil service, and were second-class citizens in their own province, relegated to the lower rungs of the economy, economically subordinate to the English elite that had been privileged under British rule. Since the mid-1960s, with the strengthening of both official bilingualism and provincial autonomy, francophone Quebecers have achieved a dramatic equalization with English Canadians along all dimensions, whether measured in terms of economic opportunities and standard of living, or in terms of effective political representation and voice, or in terms of the public status of language and culture. The historic patterns of economic disadvantage, political subordination, and cultural marginalization have essentially disappeared.[3]

---

[3] Indeed, we have reached the point where even some commentators who are sympathetic to Quebec nationalism have started to ask whether we have over-compensated for these historic inequalities, particularly in relation to political representation. See, for example, Resnick 1994 on the 'West Lothian' question: if Quebec achieves asymmetric provincial autonomy, should it give up some of its voice at the federal level in return?

Some critics acknowledge that multination federalism has helped reduce historic hierarchies, but worry that in the process it has just created new hierarchies. Has the historic privileging of English over French in Quebec simply been reversed, so that now the French are dominant over the English or other 'internal minorities', such as Aboriginal peoples or immigrants? There are certainly cases of such reversals around the world. Once Albanians in Kosovo acquired autonomy, they quickly turned on their former Serb oppressors. Similarly, commentators in Latin America speculate whether the empowerment of indigenous peoples will simply involve 'flipping the tortilla', turning the current *criollo* elite into a subordinated minority, while indigenous peoples become the new oppressors.

But there is little evidence for such a dynamic in the Western cases of multination federalism. The English minority in Quebec has stronger language rights than does the French minority in most other Canadian provinces, and remains economically prosperous. Similarly Quebec's policy towards Aboriginal land claims and self-government is more progressive than most other Canadian provinces (or indeed most other Western countries). And while Quebec's provincial 'interculturalism' policy towards immigrants may be less generous than the very strong multiculturalism policies adopted by the Canadian federal government, it is certainly stronger than those adopted in many other Western countries. Whether we look at the historically dominant English community, Aboriginals, or immigrants, the treatment of these internal minorities within Quebec meets or exceeds minimum standards and common practices of Western democracies.[4]

The same story can be told of internal minorities in other cases of multination federalism, such as the English in Scotland and Wales, or the Castilians in Catalonia, or the Italians in South Tyrol. These are hardly oppressed groups. They no longer disproportionately dominate the economy, political structures, or public culture, but they have not been reduced to second-class status in economic or political terms, in part because they remain the dominant group at the national level, which ensures protection of their rights and interests.[5]

[4] For a detailed evaluation of how Quebec meets these standards, see the edited collection *Is Quebec Nationalism Just?* (Carens 1995).

[5] I wish I could say that the absence of oppression reflects the fact that previously oppressed groups are more sensitive to the oppression of others. But a more plausible explanation is simply that territorial autonomy operates within a larger state structure, and remains constrained by the need to maintain the support of citizens and political elites across the country as a whole. Were a newly empowered national minority to start oppressing others, the existence of a consensus within the country on multinational federalism would vanish.

Others worry that the shift to multination federalism creates a new and invidious hierarchy within the substate national minority itself, between those inside and outside the self-governing territory. No matter how internal boundaries are drawn, there will be members of the national minority who live outside the self-governing territory. Wouldn't it be better, therefore, to find some non-territorial mechanism for protecting substate national minorities which would benefit its members wherever they live? This is a common objection to adopting multination federalism around the world. And indeed it's true that members of the minority living outside its self-governing territory often continue to face a stark choice between marginalization or assimilation. For example, the one million francophones in Canada who live outside Quebec continue to suffer from economic disadvantage and high rates of linguistic assimilation (Landry 2005).

However, the adoption of multination federalism can, and often does, go hand-in-hand with the recognition of non-territorial cultural and linguistic rights (e.g. to mother-tongue education) that apply throughout the country as a whole. So it is not an either-or choice between territorial autonomy or non-territorial rights. Various combinations are possible. Moreover, members of the minority who live outside the self-governing territory indirectly benefit from having a substate government that is committed to nurturing the minority's language and culture. This is perhaps one reason why members of the minority outside the self-governing territory generally are in favour of multination federalism: most francophones living in western Canada support Quebec's autonomy; most Catalans living in Madrid support autonomy for Catalonia; most Puerto Ricans living in New York support autonomy for Puerto Rico, most ethnic Welsh living in England support autonomy for Wales; and so on. Multination federalism is not a panacea for members of the minority living outside the self-governing territory, but nor is it a disadvantage or obstacle.

So we have some grounds for optimism that multination federalism can be an effective tool for reducing the inherited hierarchy between the dominant national majority and substate national minorities. But what about the second criterion of success—namely, individual freedom? Has multination federalism fulfilled the liberal expectancy? Has it operated within the constraints of liberal-democratic values and human rights, and helped to deepen a consensus across ethnic and racial lines on these values? Or has it strengthened the hand of traditionalists and cultural conservatives who seek to resist liberalization of their traditions and practices?

In general, it seems clear that multination federalism in the West fulfils the liberal expectancy. For one thing, all of these substate autonomies operate within the constraints of liberal-democratic constitutionalism, which firmly upholds individual rights. They are subject to the same constitutional constraints as the central government, and so have no capacity to restrict individual freedoms in the name of maintaining cultural authenticity or cultural purity. In fact, these substate autonomous governments typically show no wish to adopt such a conservative approach to their culture. Their members are as committed to liberal-democratic values as the majority group. Indeed, they are often hotbeds of social experimentation, adopting more progressive policies than those adopted at the central level. Policies on gender equality or gay rights, for example, are more progressive in Scotland than the rest of Britain; more progressive in Quebec than in other parts of Canada; and more progressive in Catalonia than other parts of Spain. Moreover, support for cosmopolitan values is also typically higher in these substate regions than in other parts of the country, including support for foreign aid, or for strengthening the role of the European Court of Human Rights, or other international human rights instruments.[6]

In all of these respects, multination federalism fulfils the liberal expectancy. This fact is sometimes obscured by the rhetoric of tradition adopted by some minority nationalist leaders. Claims to autonomy, for example, are often wrapped up in stirring historical narratives about the glories of the ancient traditions of self-government, and the need to return to them. Similarly, the maintenance of distinct legal traditions is sometimes described as a 'sacred duty', an essential part of the group's 'identity', which must therefore be preserved at all costs. And so on. And yet the very same leaders who invoke this rhetoric of tradition often support the dramatic revising of these traditions of self-government and law, so as to bring them in line with modern standards of human rights, and in accordance with modern aspirations for choice and freedom.

Consider the case of Catalonia. Virtually every commentator on the transition to democracy in Spain after the death of Franco in 1975 agrees that Catalan nationalism was a major force in supporting and guiding the democratization process, and that it remains a powerful locus of

---

[6] For some of the evidence, see Kymlicka 2001, chaps. 10–15; Grabb and Curtis 2005; Breuning 1999; Keating 2001.

liberalization within Spain, not just through its own internal policies, but also through Catalan support for liberal and democratic forces at the centre.[7] The construction of a democratic multination federal system in Spain out of the ashes of fascist dictatorship is surely one of the great success stories of the second half of the twentieth century, and Catalan nationalism was a vital part of that success. And yet the rhetoric of Catalan nationalists is often deeply draped in the language of tradition. Indeed, the Catalan struggle for regional autonomy was often described as a demand for the restoration or revival of their *'fueros'*—the system of local customary law that had been used in Catalonia before it was suppressed by the central Spanish state in 1716. While Catalan nationalists like to claim that their *fueros* were more democratic than the legal systems of other regions at the time (which may be true), the reality is that they were neither democratic nor liberal in any modern sense, and the contemporary exercise of autonomy in Catalonia has transformed the *fueros* beyond all recognition. The idea of 'tradition' was invoked by leaders to justify and inspire a profoundly modernizing project of regional autonomy.

This may seem like a paradox, but in fact is a ubiquitous feature of nationalist politics. As theorists of nationalism have long noted, nationalism is a 'Janus-faced' phenomenon: it invokes the glories of the past in order to mobilize people for projects of the modernization of society. It is an interesting question—beyond the scope of this book—why appeals to sacred traditions and glorious histories are often needed in order to mobilize support for modernizing reforms. But it is important to remember that states have typically justified stripping minorities of their traditional self-government by arguing that these minorities were 'backward' and that their traditions of government and law were 'uncivilized'. The first task of any nationalist movement, therefore, has been to contest these stereotypes, and to persuade others (and themselves) that they are *worthy* of self-government. When nationalist leaders say that their traditions of law and self-government should be respected, they are really saying that their nation is capable of exercising the right to decide on issues of law and government. They do not mean that they wish to exercise these national rights in an 'authentically traditional' way.

There is a related reason why modernizing nationalist elites emphasize cultural tradition. Ethnonational groups often demand self-government

---

[7] For a helpful overview, see McRoberts 2001; Requejo 2005.

on the grounds that it is needed to protect their cultural differences. Yet the causal relationship can go the other way. As Rainer Baubock puts it, 'Rather than self-government being a means to preserve cultural difference, this difference is more often preserved as a means to justify the claim to self-government' (Baubock 2000: 384, 2001: 332–5). For example, ethnonational minorities may claim that they need self-government in order to maintain their distinct legal traditions. In reality, the distinct legal tradition is often maintained in order to justify claims to self-government. After all, ethnonational minorities are continually required to explain why they deserve self-governing rights, and having a distinct legal tradition (or language) provides one possible answer.[8] This means that the maintenance of a distinct legal tradition does indeed become a kind of 'sacred' inheritance, but not in a conservative sense: it does not preclude dramatically reforming that distinct legal tradition so as to match international human rights standards, or to promote gender equality, as indeed has happened in these regional autonomies.

So I would argue that the model of multilingual, multination federalism emerging in the West is a promising example of a new approach that accommodates ethnocultural diversity in a way that deepens relations of liberal-democratic citizenship, reducing inter-group hierarchies while protecting freedom.[9] It is indeed the clearest example of success in this regard. One measure of this success is that, unlike the other two forms of liberal multiculturalism discussed below, there has been no significant movement in any of the Western democracies to roll back either the territorial autonomy or the official language rights granted to substate nationalist minorities.

In this context, then, the IO's commitment to support for liberal multiculturalism seems warranted. It is paradoxical, therefore, that this is the one model of liberal multiculturalism that IOs have been most ambivalent about, and indeed have recently backed away from diffusing internationally, for reasons discussed in Chapters 6 and 7.

---

[8] In the Canadian case, for example, the presence of the civil law tradition in Quebec not only provides an argument for Quebec's autonomy, but also provides an argument for why Quebec needs three of the nine seats on the Supreme Court (which sometimes has to rule on issues of civil law). If Quebecers gave up the civil law tradition, they would lose a central argument for autonomy and judicial representation. In this way, the civil law tradition becomes 'sacred', but not because of any conservative commitment to traditional values or lifestyles, and hence not in a way that precludes modernizing reform of the civil law tradition.

[9] For more detailed evaluations of these new models of multination states, and the sort of democratic citizenship they support, see Harty and Murphy 2005; Gagnon and Tully 2001; Norman 2006; Requejo 2005; Tierney 2004; Baubock 2006; Guibernau 1999.

Indigenous Peoples

Let me turn now to the second main form of liberal multiculturalism in the West, focusing on indigenous peoples. As we saw in Chapter 3, there has been a shift away from assimilationist policies towards models of internal decolonization based on a combination of land claims, self-government rights, and recognition of indigenous law.

How has this shift affected equality and freedom? Let me start with issues of inter-group equality: have these reforms simply provided symbolic recognition of indigenous difference, or have they effectively tackled underlying hierarchies? As in the case of substate national groups, there are many symbolic aspects to indigenous policies. For example, the public visibility of indigenous cultures has been dramatically enhanced within the larger society. Indigenous arts are now prominently displayed in museums and state institutions; indigenous leaders are recognized in state symbols (e.g. stamps); indigenous rituals are incorporated in state ceremonies (e.g. the presence of elders; indigenous prayers and phrases); indigenous history is included in school curricula; and various apologies have been made for historic wrongs. Indigenous languages and cultures are also naturally given symbolic recognition within indigenous peoples' own autonomous spaces and institutions. Within both indigenous communities themselves, and the larger society, there is now greater recognition and accommodation of indigenous culture.

But has this shift done anything to tackle the underlying political and economic inequalities between indigenous peoples and the settler societies that have historically dominated them? As with substate nationalist groups, there has been a clear enhancement in the political voice of indigenous communities, not just through increased self-government, but also through increased representation within the decision-making procedures of the larger society. As a result of various land claims, court cases, and treaty agreements, indigenous peoples are often guaranteed 'a seat at the table' on issues that affect their communities, and fairly robust duties of consultation are now recognized in most Western democracies.[10] So the opportunities for effective political participation by indigenous peoples have increased.

---

[10] For good examples of how these duties of consultation are interpreted, see the recent *Haida Nation* and *Taku River* cases in Canada (*Haida Nation v British Columbia (Minister of Forests)*, 2004 SCC 73; *Taku River Tlingit First Nation v British Columbia (Project Assessment Director)*, 2004 SCC 74). This duty of consultation is part of the World Bank's indigenous rights policy, as we will see in Chapter 7.

The impact of enhanced cultural recognition and political voice on the underlying economic inequalities is less clear. Whereas most sub-state national minorities in the West now share comparable standards of living to the dominant national group, indigenous peoples remain systematically disadvantaged on virtually all indicators (health, education, income, employment, suicide rates, incarceration rates, and so on). And debate persists about whether recent reforms are helping or harming efforts to address these forms of social and economic disadvantage, and hence whether progress in achieving equality depends on extending or dismantling new models of indigenous governance.[11] This disagreement is exacerbated by the fact that we have little reliable evidence one way or the other.

However, what evidence is available suggests that these decolonizing reforms are indeed a step in the right direction, and that further progress depends on building upon the emerging principles of targeted, group-differentiated indigenous rights. Cross-national studies of the comparative status of indigenous peoples in New World settler states suggest that inequalities are lower in countries with more robust indigenous rights policies (Kauffman 2004), and this result is confirmed by case studies from within individual countries, including the United States (Cornell and Kalt 1995, 1998, 2000), Canada (Chandler and Lalonde 1998), and New Zealand (Ringold 2005; May 1999). A recent international study by the ILO comes to a similar conclusion that poverty-reduction strategies work best when combined with respect for indigenous land claims and self-government rights (Tomei 2005).

It's important not to exaggerate the progress here. The negotiation of land claims and self-government agreements has been very slow and uneven. And there are doubts about whether the kinds of self-governing entities currently being created are capable of providing effective governance and economic opportunities. Many of them are too small and/or remote to provide the level of services and opportunities needed. Settler states have historically attempted to break up larger groups or coalitions of indigenous peoples into smaller groups, often no larger than an individual village or community. There are limits to the sort of self-government that such village-level units are capable of effectively exercising (Cairns 2000, 2005).

---

[11] For a recent example of scepticism about the trend towards models of internal decolonization and indigenous self-government, see Richards 2006.

Moreover, as with substate nationalist groups, there are questions about the status of indigenous people who live outside these self-governing territories. In many countries, over half of the indigenous population have moved from their traditional territories into urban areas. These groups have suffered just as much from the harms of colonialism, but in many respects fall between the cracks of the internal decolonization model.

One possible response to both of these problems is the idea of 'aggregation', in which some indigenous self-governing powers would be exercised at a regional level, rather than at a village or community level (IOG 2000). This would not only create larger and more viable units of self-government, but also make it easier to incorporate urban indigenous populations. This is a promising idea, but at the moment largely untested.[12]

In short, we have mixed results in relation to the reduction of intergroup hierarchies. Indigenous languages and cultures have a much higher public visibility and respect than thirty or forty years ago, and indigenous peoples have enhanced opportunities for effective political participation through both self-government and increased consultation in areas of shared government. But these changes have not substantially reduced the dramatic social and economic disadvantages facing indigenous peoples.

What about the second criterion of success: are these reforms fulfilling the liberal expectancy, accommodating diversity while still protecting human rights and diffusing liberal values? This too is a matter of considerable debate. Some commentators argue that indigenous rights are tied to ideas of cultural conservatism. Indeed, the claims of indigenous peoples are often cited as the paradigm example of claims rooted in ideas of tradition and cultural authenticity. Whereas substate national groups in the West are seen as sharing liberal values of individual freedom and human rights, indigenous peoples are often seen as rejecting these values in favour of communitarianism and traditionalism. Critics worry that granting multicultural rights, in this context, will lead to the limitation of individual freedom within the group.

There are some grounds for these worries. There are examples of indigenous groups seeking to engage in practices that many people would see as violating human rights, such as various forms of discrimination (against women, or religious minorities), or denials of due process (e.g. punishing alleged wrongdoers without fair trial), or the use of cruel and unusual punishments (e.g. spearing, banishments).[13] All of these practices have been

---

[12] See Green and Peach 2007 for discussion of one such model.

[13] For examples, see the discussion in Robinson 2003; Deveaux 2000; Speed and Collier 2000; Cowan 2007.

defended by some indigenous leaders (or their non-indigenous advocates) as 'traditional', and hence as worthy of protection under a conservative conception of multiculturalism.

At present, such practices are typically prohibited under the constitutional provisions of the larger state. However, (largely unsuccessful) attempts have been made by some indigenous leaders to gain exemptions from these constitutional requirements, and various critics have worried that this is evidence that the liberal expectancy is failing.[14] These worries have been reinforced by the experience of indigenous customary law in Latin America. Many Latin American countries have granted legal status to the 'uses and customs' of indigenous peoples. As a result, disputes and crimes within indigenous communities are often addressed through allegedly 'traditional' modes of conflict resolution and punishment, governed by 'traditional' elites. These are often described, by defenders, as 'authentic' practices, deeply rooted in the group's history, and hence essential to the group's identity. Careful studies of customary law in Guatemala, however, have shown that these claims are contestable. In fact, the three problems mentioned in Chapter 4 about cultural conservatism have all been found in studies of the operation of indigenous customary law. First, the legal practices that are said to be timeless and authentic are often in fact fairly recent, based on a pastiche of cultural influences (including both Spanish Catholicism and more recently evangelical Protestantism). Claims to cultural authenticity or purity hide the reality of cultural hybridity, and create false views about the 'unbridgeable gulf' between indigenous cultures and European cultures. Second, the claim that these practices are authentic, and essential to the group's identity, is often contested within the group. Local elites attempt to redefine these contested practices as 'sacred obligations' precisely in order to silence or delegitimize those group members who wish to challenge these practices. Third, the idea that there is a right to maintain such authentic traditions is invoked to justify discrimination against women or refugees, and other violations of human rights.[15]

These studies are looking at Latin America, not the consolidated Western democracies, and this is important to keep in mind. If the

---

[14] As I noted in Chapter 4, n. 4, a partial exception concerns American Indian tribes, who have a long-standing exemption from some provisions of the US Bill of Rights. However, it's worth noting that this exemption predates the post-war rise of liberal multiculturalism, and has been whittled away in the era of civil rights liberalism. Attempts to expand this exemption, or to introduce versions of it in other Western democracies, have failed.

[15] For a cataloguing of these problems in the case of Mayan customary law in Guatemala, see the work of Rachel Sieder (1997, 1999, 2001).

liberal expectancy is not working well in Guatemala—that is, if liberal-democratic structures are not exerting their predicted gravitational pull across ethnic and racial lines—it is surely at least partly due to the fact that there is little or no liberal democracy in Guatemala to begin with. The political structures of the larger society are known for their wide-spread human rights abuses, the lack of the rule of law, and entrenched patterns of discrimination. In this context, it would be a minor miracle if indigenous legal practices were somehow infused with the pristine spirit of liberal democracy.

The more relevant question for our purposes is whether the liberal expectancy is holding within the Western democracies themselves. And here we see a complex picture. On the one hand, as I noted earlier, some indigenous leaders assert that their self-governing decisions should not be subject to the constitutional provisions of the larger society, in the name of preserving their traditional legal systems. On the other hand, virtually all indigenous leaders accept the principle that indigenous laws should be consistent with international human rights norms, even though these may conflict with some aspects of their traditional practices.

This suggests that there are complicated legal and political strategies at work when indigenous leaders deny that they are subject to the larger society's constitution. In fact, we need to recognize that when indigenous peoples are told to comply with domestic constitutional norms, this actually involves two quite distinct demands that need to be kept separate. At one level, it demands that indigenous peoples adhere to a set of liberal-democratic norms or principles which are fairly common across the Western democracies, and now enshrined in international law. But at another level, it also demands that indigenous peoples accept the authority of a particular political entity and legal system—namely, that of the larger state established by the colonizing settlers. It is this second demand that is particularly offensive to many indigenous peoples. After all, in most cases, indigenous peoples did not consent to being ruled by this larger state, were not involved in formulating its constitution, and have never had any representation on the Supreme Courts that interpret these constitutions. Moreover, the legal system established by the colonial state has historically justified the conquest and dispossession of indigenous peoples, often on the basis of explicitly racist reasoning. Hence many indigenous peoples do not trust the legal system established by settler states, and do not believe that it ever acquired the legitimate right to rule over them. To ask indigenous peoples to uncritically accept the authority of the settler state's constitution and courts is, in effect, to ask them to accept the legitimacy of their colonization and conquest.

Under these circumstances, indigenous demands to be governed under their own 'customary' legal system, rather than being subject to the domestic constitution of the settler state, should not automatically be assumed to reflect an illiberal traditionalism or conservatism, or a defeat for the liberal expectancy. Like the Catalan demand for the restoration of their historic *fueros*, indigenous demands for the recognition of 'customary' law may be a modernizing project obscured by traditionalist rhetoric. Indeed, it may be that the liberal expectancy is best served by separating the two demands I mentioned earlier—that is, by finding a way of articulating and enforcing liberal-democratic norms that does not depend exclusively or primarily on the authority of the settler state's institutions. Perhaps the best way to promote a consensus on liberal-democratic values, and to securely protect individual rights, is to enable indigenous peoples to establish their own democratic constitutions and courts, subject to international human rights norms and/or to new rights-protection mechanisms in which indigenous peoples, domestic judges, and international monitors are all involved. This is precisely what some indigenous leaders have recommended as a more effective way of ensuring human rights protection than relying exclusively on the courts of the settler state.[16] The resulting legal system may be described as 'traditional' or 'customary', but in fact may have little to do with preserving 'tradition', and the members of the community may fully expect it to respect civil and political rights and to meet standards of democratic accountability. Indeed, this is what we see emerging in various Western countries: indigenous legal systems adapted to new circumstances and international norms, accountable to their members. And there is growing evidence that these members do in fact endorse liberal-democratic values, and expect their leaders to uphold them when exercising their law-making powers.[17]

In short, as with substate national minorities, there are strategic reasons for demanding respect for a distinct legal tradition: it serves as a marker of cultural difference, evidence of a worthy past, and a justification for a

[16] Some Aboriginal leaders in Canada have argued that imposing the Charter on Aboriginal governments without their consent is inconsistent with their inherent right to self-determination. There are indeed powerful legal arguments for this position, but these jurisprudential arguments do not necessarily reflect deep disagreements over political values (Schouls 2003; Kymlicka 2001, chap. 6; Carens 2000, chap. 8).

[17] See Tim Schouls's account of the depth of liberal-rights consciousness within Aboriginal communities, and the growing expectation amongst Aboriginal members that their leaders respect these values, enforced either through the Charter or some functionally equivalent rights-protecting mechanism (Schouls 2003: 93, 100–5, 167–71).

distinctive legal and political status. The problem facing many indigenous peoples, however, particularly in Latin America, is that unlike substate national minorities in the West, they have no self-governing power to amend their customary law. They have the right to follow indigenous law, but not to make indigenous law. They have the right to live according to their laws, but not the right to give themselves laws. Indigenous laws are recognized, but not indigenous law-makers (Levy 2000*a*).

The inevitable result of this stunted conception of legal pluralism is to trap indigenous peoples into a traditionalist framework. Since they have no power to democratically amend their traditional customary law, they must present these laws as 'authentic'. This suggests that the solution is not to abolish legal pluralism, but rather to strengthen it, by giving indigenous peoples the right to make indigenous law, as well as to follow it, and to ensure that this process of making indigenous law is publicly debated, and reflects the views of all members of the community, not just self-appointed guardians of 'tradition'. This indeed is what we increasingly see in the United States, Canada, and New Zealand.

Many states resist granting indigenous peoples law-making authority. Law-making authority is jealously preserved as the exclusive jurisdiction of the nation-state. Allowing indigenous peoples to follow customary law is not as threatening to the state as allowing indigenous peoples to make law. But as Speed and Collier note, it is rather hypocritical for states to then turn around and condemn indigenous peoples for the fact that their customary law may not be consistent with modern norms of human rights (Speed and Collier 2000).

Put another way, the recognition of customary law is important, not because it upholds authentic traditions, but because it implies recognition of the law-making capacity of indigenous peoples, and justifies their claim to exercise that capacity anew. As Rachel Sieder puts it, customary law should be understood as an oppositional project—attempting to wrest power from the central state—not as a project of cultural primordialism (Sieder 2001).

I think a similar story can be told about the role of treaty rights. Many indigenous groups demand that the provisions of centuries-old treaties be legally upheld. Some commentators take this demand as evidence of a conservative commitment to preserving authentic practices that date from the time of contact. I would argue, however, that treaties are often given a revered status in indigenous communities because they are tangible proof that indigenous peoples at the time of contact were regarded as possessing politically organized societies capable of entering into international agreements on a nation-to-nation basis. Treaties are signs of the historic political competence of indigenous peoples, and justification for reasserting that status, so that indigenous people can regain control over their destiny and adapt to new challenges. The revered status of customary law and treaty rights is evidence, not of cultural conservatism, but of the need to mobilize people for the project of indigenous self-government—a project that (like all nationalisms) is inherently culture-transforming. And within the Western democracies, this project is, by and large, conducted within the framework of liberal-democratic constitutional values, as the liberal expectancy would predict.

The picture that emerges from this discussion of the impact of indigenous rights on individual freedom is a complex one, not least because it is difficult to disentangle the rhetoric from the reality. On the one hand, we have many indigenous leaders who strongly affirm human rights values, although this may just be a rhetorical tool to hide a deeper commitment to cultural conservatism. On the other hand, we also have many indigenous leaders invoking a powerful rhetoric of traditionalism, although this may just be a rhetorical tool to justify projects of modernizing self-government. We need to look beyond the rhetoric to see what is actually happening on the ground, in the way indigenous peoples are exercising their rights and powers, and the way political values are being shaped within these communities. And here there are cautious grounds for optimism that the idea of a human rights-based model of indigenous governance is gradually taking root, both within indigenous communities and across the society as a whole.[18] And as we will see in Chapter 7, it is precisely such a model that is being diffused by the international community.

Immigrants

Finally, let me look at what is perhaps the most controversial form of liberal multiculturalism, adopted in relation to 'new' minorities formed through immigration. As we saw in Chapter 3, a shift has taken place within the traditional countries of immigration from older models of exclusion and assimilation to newer models of race-neutral admissions

---

[18] For more detailed evaluations of these new models of state-indigenous relations, and the sort of indigenous citizenship they support, see Havemann 1999; Ivison et al 2000; Borrows 2000.

and multicultural integration. How has this affected inter-group equality and individual freedom?

As with substate national groups and indigenous peoples, the most immediately apparent change concerns issues of the recognition of identity. In the past, it was often considered 'unpatriotic' (or 'unAmerican') for immigrants to visibly or proudly express their ethnic identity. Today, by contrast, it is considered normal and natural (at least within traditional immigration countries) for immigrants and their descendants to have an ethnic identity, to cherish it, to express it in public space, and to have it reflected and accommodated in public institutions. Immigrant ethnicity has become 'normalized'. It is now recognized that one of the many perfectly legitimate ways to be a good American (or Canadian, Australian, etc.) is to be a good Greek-American or Vietnamese-American. For most immigrant groups, ethnic identity is no longer a source of shame, or fear. And this is reflected in and reinforced by multiculturalism policies that impose a duty on public institutions like the schools or media to ensure that immigrant groups are visible in their programming, that traditional stereotyping is avoided, and that the contributions of immigrants to national history or world culture are recognized.

Of course, this process remains uneven. Since 9/11, immigrants from Arab or Muslim countries have faced pressure to hide their ethnic and religious identity. In the United States, people who too visibly or publicly identify themselves as Muslim today are suspected by some of being 'unAmerican'. As we saw in Chapter 4, two of the key pillars of liberal multiculturalism— the liberal expectancy and the desecuritization of ethnic relations—have been questioned in the case of Muslim immigrants. But I believe this is an exception (and hopefully a temporary one) to an otherwise powerful trend to normalize the presence of immigrant ethnic identities in public space.

For some critics, immigrant multiculturalism does not go beyond these forms of symbolic recognition to address underlying inequalities in access to political power or economic opportunities (e.g. Moodley 1992: 79). Defenders respond that the recognition of ethnic identities is just one dimension of a much broader multiculturalist policy framework that seeks to enhance the access and participation of immigrants in the economy and political life of the country. This is reflected in affirmative action policies, in the creation of mechanisms for political consultation, and in the commitment to identify and revise institutional rules that may (intentionally or unintentionally) disadvantage immigrants. For example, under the framework of multiculturalism, dress-codes, public holidays, naturalization rules, language requirements, even height and weight restrictions, have all been adapted to reduce their potential to create obstacles for certain immigrant groups. On this view, multiculturalism has significantly reduced many of the inherited obstacles, barriers, and stigmatizations that disadvantaged immigrant groups.

Here again, our ability to resolve this disagreement is hampered by the lack of any systematic cross-national data on the impact of multiculturalism policies on the status of immigrant ethnic groups. It is also made more difficult by the enormous variation in the economic and political status of different ethnic groups even within the same country. Some immigrant groups in the New World countries of immigration are better off than their native-born counterparts in terms of income or employment rates, others are worse off. It's entirely possible that the model of multicultural integration is working well for some ethnic groups, and not for others. We don't have the sort of fine-grained data needed to distinguish the differential impact of multiculturalism policies on various ethnic groups in the same country.

Studies suggest that states with liberal multiculturalism policies have lower levels of intolerance (Weldon 2006: 335), and better outcomes for immigrant youth (Berry et al 2006), and that the two countries with the strongest multiculturalism policies—Australia and Canada—also have the best track record in the economic and political integration of immigrants over the past thirty years (Kymlicka 1998). But that may be due in part to the fact that the immigration policies of these two countries focus heavily on selecting skilled immigrants, who arrive with greater levels of the human and social capital needed to integrate. Perhaps multiculturalism policies were not necessary for their successful integration, or were even a potential obstacle, by marking them out as 'different' and 'needy' (Das Gupta 1999).

In order to test the impact of multiculturalism policies, we would ideally like to find a 'natural experiment' where two sets of immigrants from the same country with the same background experiences and skills settle in different places, one of which has strong multiculturalism policies, the other not. As it happens, Irene Bloemraad has studied such a case: namely, Vietnamese immigrants in Boston and Toronto. There are virtually no relevant differences in the demographic characteristics of the Vietnamese immigrants who ended up in Toronto rather than Boston—they arrived with comparable levels of education, work experience, language fluency, and so on. Yet the Vietnamese in Toronto have integrated much better, and are more actively participating in Canadian public life. There are of course many possible explanations for this difference other than the presence of stronger multiculturalism policies (e.g. labour markets, political party structures, etc.), but Bloemraad systematically canvasses these alternative explanations, and concludes that multiculturalism policies were indeed a crucial part of the story. These policies encouraged and enabled the Vietnamese community to participate more quickly and more effectively in mainstream Canadian institutions. According to Bloemraad, the same pattern applies to Portuguese immigrants to Toronto and Boston as well—they arrived with similar demographic characteristics, but the Portuguese immigrants in Toronto have integrated better, due in part to Canadian multiculturalism (Bloemraad 2002, 2005, 2006).

This is just one case-study, and may not generalize. It obviously differs from the feeling in much of continental Europe, where it is widely believed that multiculturalism policies have failed, and inhibited the integration of immigrants. We would need to look carefully at why multiculturalism policies seem to have fared so differently in Europe compared to the New World. Part of the difference may lie in the characteristics of the immigrants (e.g. the relative balance of skilled and unskilled immigrants, or of legal versus illegal immigration), but much of it lies in the nature of the 'multiculturalism' that was adopted. As I noted in Chapter 3, most migrants in Europe were initially seen as temporary residents (e.g. guest-workers, temporary asylum-seekers), and hence the so-called 'multiculturalism' policies adopted for them were initially designed in the expectation that they and their children would return 'home'. This is the opposite of New World multiculturalism policies, which from the start were connected to ideas of integration and citizenship. While European expectations of return have gradually been abandoned, and multiculturalism policies revised accordingly, the policies in place in Europe have never fully corresponded with the sorts of multiculturalism policies in place in the New World, with their stronger emphasis on integration and citizenship.[19] Where the latter sort of multiculturalism

[19] As a result, when European countries add new policies designed to enhance immigrants' civic participation and citizenship identity, this is often described as a 'retreat from multiculturalism', even though the policies being introduced have always been part and parcel of New World conceptions of multicultural citizenship. For a recent example, see Hussain et al (2006), who recommend replacing 'multiculturalism' in Britain with 'interculturalism', the latter being distinguished by the former by its emphasis on (a) promoting interaction across ethnic lines; and (b) promoting a sense of national identity. This distinction makes no sense in the New World context, where 'multiculturalism' policies have always included an emphasis on inter-ethnic cooperation and the promotion of citizenship. For some reason, the term 'multiculturalism' has come to acquire a distinctive meaning in much of Europe such that any policies designed to promote integration are seen as a 'retreat' from multiculturalism.

polices are in place, it appears that they can positively assist in reducing the cultural, political, and economic inequalities facing immigrant ethnic groups.[20]

Even when these policies are successful in reducing inequality, they often suffer from a number of familiar problems. For example, the bureaucratic categories used to identify the beneficiaries of multiculturalism policies are often over-inclusive or under-inclusive, or reflect the logic of administrative convenience rather than the needs or aspirations of the intended beneficiaries. They may lump disparate groups into the same legal category, despite their different needs, or put similar groups into artificially distinct categories.[21] There is also the problem that within the

[20] A recent study of five European countries concludes that multiculturalism policies have a 'curvilinear' effect—that is, a modest level of such policies is beneficial for immigrant integration, but that strong multiculturalism policies are harmful (Koopmans et al 2005: 240). This conclusion is based on the interpretation of a single case: namely, the Netherlands. According to the authors, the Netherlands has done less well than other European countries such as the UK or Germany in integrating immigrants, and it has done so precisely *because* it has the strongest multiculturalism policies of the five countries. (For a similar argument, see Sniderman and Hagendoorn 2007). If this were correct, we would expect other countries with strong multiculturalism policies, such as Canada or Australia, to also fare badly in comparison with the UK or Germany. Yet the opposite is true: they do better. If we broaden the sample, the Netherlands appears to be an exception, not the rule, regarding the relative success of countries with strong multiculturalism policies. And there is an obvious explanation for the Dutch exception: as the authors themselves note, the original Dutch policy was not in fact designed to assist in immigrant integration and citizenship. Rather, it was initially designed to encourage immigrants to return home to their country of origin. As I noted in Chapter 3, this 'returnist' approach to immigrants is the very opposite of a liberal multiculturalism policy. And when the Dutch government did finally accept that immigrants were permanent residents and future citizens, it then simply slotted them into the existing 'pillarization' model designed originally to deal with religious divisions within the ethnic Dutch population (e.g. separate institutional 'pillars' for Protestants and Catholics). This pillarization model was not designed for, and does not address the needs of, ethnically and linguistically distinct newcomers. In short, the Netherlands started with a returnist approach and shifted to a pillarization model, neither of which is a model designed with the needs and aspirations of immigrant citizens in mind. Koopman and his colleagues note these 'paradoxes' of the Dutch approach to multiculturalism, but don't consider the implications of these facts for their general conclusion about the 'curvilinear' impact of multiculturalism policies. What distinguishes the Dutch case is not the strength of its multiculturalism policies—they are, if anything, weaker than in Canada and Australia—but the idiosyncratic form of these policies, rooted in returnism (designed for temporary migrants) and pillarization (designed for historic minorities). If we want to draw general conclusions about the impact of strong multiculturalism policies, and to determine whether the Dutch case is the exception or the rule for such countries, we need to broaden the sample, and look at other countries that have adopted strong multiculturalism policies designed for immigrant citizens, such as Australia and Canada. And, as I noted earlier, the few broad cross-national studies that we have do not support the curvilinear interpretation (see also Banting and Kymlicka 2006).

[21] For an example of the former, the (over)-use of the category of 'visible minority' in Canadian public policy arguably neglects the specificity of anti-black or anti-Islamic racism (Henry 1994; Commission on Systemic Racism in the Ontario Criminal Justice System 1995; Kymlicka 1998; Hum and Simpson 2007). A good example of the latter problem, found in relation to indigenous peoples, is the distinction between 'status' and 'non-status' Indians in

class of intended beneficiaries, it is often those who already have high levels of human capital that are most able to take advantage of these benefits, leaving fewer opportunities for truly disadvantaged members of the group. These objections have been raised, for example, in the context of affirmative action policies in both the United States and Canada.[22]

I call these 'familiar' problems because they in fact apply to all areas of social policy. Administrative categories are always over- or under-inclusive, distorted by the dictates of bureaucratic convenience or bureaucratic inertia; and public benefits are always captured disproportionately by those who are already well-off. This applies to policies targeted at poor neighbourhoods or regions, or at groups suffering from 'social exclusion', or at populations 'at risk'. Social policies based on class, age, gender, neighbourhood, region, or family status are all vulnerable to these problems. These are the familiar pathologies of public policy in a liberal democracy, and multiculturalism is not exempt from them. But there is no evidence that these pathologies are greater for multiculturalism than for other types of social policy, and within the limits set by these familiar problems, multiculturalism policies have had some modest successes in reducing inter-group inequality.

What about the second criterion of success: has immigrant multiculturalism fulfilled the liberal expectancy, giving members of minority groups more freedom 'to make the life that the individual is able and wishes to have', or has it instead imprisoned people in traditional roles and practices, and strengthened the hand of cultural traditionalists or religious fundamentalists who wish to limit liberal freedoms? This too is a hotly debated issue, since it is widely assumed that many immigrant groups, particularly non-European immigrants, bring with them illiberal political values and cultural practices, and will look for ways to maintain them, including through appeal to ideas of multiculturalism. As with indigenous peoples, and unlike substate national groups, non-European immigrants are widely seen as standing outside (or at least not fully integrated into) the liberal-democratic consensus.

This perception of non-European immigrants as prone to illiberal values and practices is often highly exaggerated. In fact, the evidence suggests that non-European immigrants today, at least in the New World countries

---

Canadian public policy, which is in many respects an artificial distinction. There are historical reasons in both cases for these categories, but they are increasingly out of touch with the realities they are trying to address.

[22] In India, this is called the problem of the 'creamy layer', skimming off benefits that were intended for the genuinely needy lower down.

of immigration, exhibit the same basic tendency to internalize liberal-democratic values that characterized previous waves of immigration from Europe. In Canada, for example, there are no statistically significant differences in political values between non-European immigrants who have lived in Canada for a long period and native-born Canadians of European descent (Soroka et al 2007; Frideres 1997). There is in fact a fairly deep consensus on human rights and liberal-democratic values across ethnic and racial lines (Howard-Hassman 2003), as the liberal expectancy would predict.

However, this trend towards convergence in political values is a long-term one. It doesn't take place overnight, and it doesn't take place without a struggle within immigrant communities themselves, as traditionalist leaders and/or political radicals battle against those who feel the gravitational pull of liberal-democratic values. This is an age-old phenomenon, found in every wave of immigration from every corner of the globe. There were similar struggles between traditionalists, liberals, and radicals amongst Irish Catholic immigrants to the New World in the nineteenth century, or amongst Eastern European immigrants in the first part of the twentieth century.

The question for us is how the presence today of liberal multiculturalism affects this age-old dynamic. Does the availability of multiculturalist programmes and institutions somehow strengthen the hand of traditionalists or radicals opposed to liberal values, and slow down the process of incorporating immigrants into a liberal-democratic consensus? Or does it strengthen the gravitational pull of liberal democracy?

We can expect that the different factions within immigrant groups will compete to control the institutions and programmes established under multiculturalism policies. And this raises the potential that the infrastructure of liberal multiculturalism will be captured and misused for illiberal or undemocratic purposes. Before examining whether this has in fact taken place, however, it's important to remember that this problem is not unique to multiculturalism. It is a systemic problem that arises from the very structure of liberal democracy. Liberal democracy gives the vote to Communists who want to abolish parliamentary democracy, just as it gives free speech to those who would refuse free speech to others. Similarly, policies intended to enhance local democracy are always subject to the risk that they will be captured by illiberal forces who wish to suppress the freedom of others. Consider the way that local hospital boards and school boards in North America have been captured by Christian conservatives who wish to stop abortion or sex education.

This 'paradox' has been a well-known feature of liberal-democratic theory and practice since its origins in the seventeenth century. As a result, there is a long history of discussion about how to prevent illiberal and undemocratic forces from abusing the rights and powers that liberal democracy extends. The solution, in all of these cases, is a combination of (a) civic education and political socialization, to help develop and sustain a broader political culture of human rights and civil rights liberalism; (b) mechanisms for identifying and publicizing actual or potential abuses—including freedom of speech; freedom of the press; freedom of information policies; and reporting, consultation, and accountability requirements—so as to bring issues into the court of public opinion, and to expose and marginalize illiberal tendencies; and (c) legal and constitutional safeguards that empower the state to prevent or remedy these abuses. These are the sorts of strategies used in all Western democracies to grapple with the problem of the illiberal and undemocratic abuse of liberal-democratic rights, and they apply as well to the case of multiculturalism policies.

Are these strategies working? I believe they are. The development of a human rights culture, combined with robust mechanisms of public exposure and legal safeguards, have ensured that the interpretation and implementation of immigrant multiculturalism policies remain within liberal channels.[23] This is true both at the level of formal legislation, and at the level of everyday policy implementation.

If we look first at formal laws and regulations, it is clear that multiculturalism policies are committed to upholding liberal values. Immigrant multiculturalism policies are intended to expand rather than restrict individual choice: they reduce the costs or stigmas individuals previously faced in expressing their ethnic identity, but do not provide any legal mandate or legal justification for abridging or violating individual rights.

---

[23] The recent debate in Ontario about allowing religious arbitration of family law disputes is an example of this. Some conservative Muslims ought to exploit an opening within the 1991 Arbitration Act to create private sharia-based arbitration for divorce disputes, and defended this proposal in the name of multiculturalism. The public exposure of potential abuses led to widespread public opposition, and a renewed commitment to ensure that norms of freedom and equality are respected. However, I should emphasize that the adoption of the 1991 Arbitration Act in Ontario, which created legal space for private family law arbitration, had nothing to do with Canada's official multiculturalism policy. It was essentially adopted as a cost-saving device, and to reduce strains on the over-burdened family law courts. Had the sharia proposal been pursued under the Multiculturalism Act, rather than the Arbitration Act, it is highly unlikely it would have been accepted, since the multiculturalism policy has stronger procedural and substantive safeguards. In short, it was a weakness in the Arbitration Act which Islamic traditionalists targeted, not any alleged vulnerability of multiculturalism to illiberal capture (Kymlicka 2005a).

No country, for example, has provided immigrant groups with an exemption from laws that prohibit forced marriages, female clitoridectomies, honour-killings, or the use of violent forms of discipline against children, no matter how 'traditional' such practices might be.

If we look at the realities on the ground, however, we know that illiberal practices do continue in some immigrant families (as they do in some non-immigrant families), often with the tacit knowledge of other members of the community. And we know that the state has sometimes proven unable or unwilling to defend vulnerable individuals from these violations of their rights and freedoms. Indeed, in virtually all Western democracies, there have been high-profile cases where the state has turned a blind eye to the mistreatment of individuals within some immigrant groups, ignoring reports of abuse, or refusing to intervene and/or prosecute.

Critics often assume that multiculturalism is somehow responsible for these failures. But as I just mentioned, cases of state failure to protect individuals from harm at the hands of their co-ethnics have been found in all Western democracies, whether or not they have multiculturalism policies. This problem has been observed in countries that have strongly embraced multiculturalism, such as Canada (Azmi 1999; Levine 1999), in countries that are moderate in their commitment to multiculturalism, such as Britain or the Netherlands (Phillips and Dustin 2004; Prins and Saharso 2006), in countries with only weak multiculturalism policies, such as Norway (Wikan 2002), and in countries that are resolutely opposed to multiculturalism, such as France (Dembour 2001).

Under these circumstances, disentangling the impact of multiculturalism policies is not easy. Do multiculturalism policies worsen the problem, either by encouraging immigrants to maintain their 'traditions' even when they are illiberal, or by discouraging state officials from intervening in the name of 'respect for diversity' and 'tolerance'? Or do multiculturalism policies reduce the problem, either by strengthening the gravitational pull of liberal democracy, or by providing state officials with more informed and effective guidelines for recognizing and responding to potential problems?

As always, we are hampered by the almost complete absence of any systematic studies of the issue. It is clear that multiculturalism policies in the West do not formally or publicly condone illiberal practices, and that any attempts by traditionalists to use the official rules and institutions of multiculturalism to gain public acceptance of illiberal practices have failed. We can imagine scenarios under which traditionalists within various immigrant groups might try to capture control over the infrastructure of official multiculturalism in order to defend these practices. For example, one could imagine that traditionalists from certain East African immigrant groups sitting on hospital advisory boards might demand that female genital mutilation be permitted in the hospital, or that traditionalists from South Asian groups sitting on police advisory boards might demand that the police not investigate or prosecute cases of family violence and forced marriages, or that traditionalists from the Middle East sitting on education advisory boards might demand that the schools teach students to condone honour-killings. However, if such attempts have been made, they have been entirely unsuccessful. So far as I am aware, no agency, board, or programme established or funded under multiculturalism policies in any Western democracy has endorsed any of these practices.[24] If traditionalists hoped to gain control over the institutions and funding programmes created under multiculturalism policies, they have more or less entirely failed. And this is what one would expect given the intentions of the policy. As we saw in Chapter 4, the philosophy underlying the policy is a philosophy of human rights and civil rights liberalism, and the policy is only intended to support organizations and activities which will advance that agenda.[25]

Indeed, immigrant groups are aware that any attempts to gain public sanction for illiberal practices are doomed to failure. For example, no South Asian ethnic leaders in Britain have asked that forced arranged marriages be legally recognized (Phillips and Dustin 2004), and no leaders of the relevant immigrant groups in Canada have asked that clitoridectomies be legally permitted (Government of Canada 1995; OHRC 1996). It is understood and accepted that immigrant multiculturalism, as a government policy, operates within the framework of the liberal-democratic constitutional order, and there is no realistic prospect of gaining public acceptance for illiberal practices.

There is, however, a more indirect worry about the impact of multiculturalism—namely, that the 'ethos' created by multiculturalism will paralyse the state officials who are charged with promoting liberal values and upholding individual rights. The teachers, doctors, social

[24] In the UK case, for example, public inquiries into failures to protect minority children have concluded that 'the legislative framework is sound' (Lamming 2003: 13), and that nothing in Britain's multiculturalism policies condoned these failures.

[25] This helps explain Bloemraad's finding that multiculturalism in Canada has encouraged or nurtured the development of a more gender-balanced and representative elite within ethnic communities than is traditionally found within such communities, or than is found in the United States (Bloemraad 2006).

service providers, child welfare officials, police, and prosecutors who are confronted with evidence of illiberal practices may turn a blind eye, rather than risk being accused of being ethnocentric or labelled a racist. Multiculturalism policies may affirm that the accommodation of diversity operates within liberal-democratic constraints, but the effect of these policies on the ground may be to encourage an uncritical cultural relativism, in which public officials presume that they shouldn't interfere with a group's 'culture' or 'traditions' (Wikan 2002).

An alternative view, however, is that the best way to support public officials charged with promoting liberal values and upholding individual rights is precisely by providing them with clear guidelines developed in cooperation with minority groups themselves, as part of a larger process of multicultural consultations and reforms. Perhaps it is where this process of multicultural reform has not taken place that members of ethnic groups are least likely to cooperate with state officials, and where state officials are most paralysed by fears of acting inappropriately.

So far as I know, no one has systematically studied these alternate hypotheses about the effects of multiculturalism on the persistence of illiberal values and practices, or the willingness of vulnerable members of immigrant groups to seek protection from the state, or the willingness of state officials to provide that protection. The little evidence we do have, examining the responses by doctors and social workers to cases of child abuse or spousal abuse in several Western countries, suggests that the presence or absence of official multiculturalism policies may actually make little difference one way or the other in terms of officials' willingness to intervene (Puri 2005; Williams and Soydan 2005). There is certainly no evidence that the presence of official multiculturalism policies makes things worse.

The reality is that all Western states are struggling with the issue of how best to deal with the challenge of protecting vulnerable members of immigrant communities. Countries are experimenting with a range of approaches, involving various combinations of education and deterrence, closed-door consultations and high-profile public campaigns and prosecutions. There are no easy answers to these complex problems, but it is clear that multiculturalism is neither the cause of these problems, which exist in countries without multiculturalism policies, nor a miracle cure for them.

In this respect the question of how to deal with illiberal cultural traditions is similar to the question of how to deal with political radicalism within immigrant communities. Some critics have said that the existence of 'home-grown' terrorist cells in countries with multiculturalism policies shows that these policies have failed to serve the goals of liberal-democratic citizenization. But of course home-grown terrorist cells have been identified in a wide range of Western countries, some with strong multiculturalism policies (Canada, Australia), some with modest multiculturalism policies (United States, United Kingdom), some with weak multiculturalism policies (Germany, Spain), and some ideologically opposed to multiculturalism (France). There is no evidence that multiculturalism policies exacerbate this problem, although nor do they guarantee that the problem won't arise.

Cases of illiberal cultural traditions and political radicalism within immigrant communities capture the headlines, for understandable reasons, since they challenge the most basic human rights principles of Western societies. But these problems shouldn't blind us to the broader trends. Within the traditional countries of immigration, the liberal expectancy is still holding for immigrants, as the gravitational pull of liberal-democracy operates over time. Pockets of illiberal traditionalism and radicalism exist in all Western democracies, but there is no evidence that multiculturalism policies exacerbate this problem, and some evidence that multiculturalism may in fact operate to strengthen the gravitational pull of liberal-democratic institutions, by encouraging and enabling immigrants to participate more comfortably and more effectively within them.

Conclusion

It should be clear, I hope, that we cannot simply declare multiculturalism to be either a 'success' or a 'failure' in the Western democracies. For one thing, we lack the systematic evidence that would allow us to distinguish the specific effects of multiculturalism policies from other factors that influence the status of ethnic minorities. And even if we had that evidence, it is unlikely that it would add up to a single overall judgement of success or failure. There are many different types of multiculturalism policies, and many different criteria for evaluating them, and the track record includes both successes and disappointments.

Having said that, we have enough experience with multiculturalism in practice to draw some provisional conclusions, and dispel some common misinterpretations. First, and most importantly, we have strong evidence that liberal multiculturalism is consistent with the pacification and domestication of ethnic politics. Where liberal multiculturalism is in place in the West, ethnic politics has become 'normal' politics, operating within peaceful and legal channels, in a way that doesn't threaten or impair the basic functioning of the state, in terms of peace, prosperity, the rule of law, or democratic stability. This by itself can be seen as a major accomplishment, given the way that ethnic politics in many parts of the world has destabilized and torn apart states, and inhibited democratization and development. As I said earlier, this fact alone would explain why so many IOs have expressed an interest in diffusing models of liberal multiculturalism.

Second, and more tentatively, we have some evidence that liberal multiculturalism is not just compatible with the basic functioning of a liberal-democratic state, but actually helps to deepen liberalization and democratization. It can challenge inherited ethnic and racial hierarchies, and reduce cultural stigmatization, political marginalization, and economic disadvantages. And it can do this in a way that enhances the opportunities for effective democratic participation and individual choice for members of minority groups.

It's important not to overstate this point. The evidence for these benefits is limited, and the observed benefits are often modest. In many cases, significant inequalities remain, as one would expect given the long duration of ethnic and racial hierarchies in the West, and how deeply they have become entrenched in society, even after explicitly racialist ideologies are officially disavowed. These inequalities can't be reversed by legislative fiat overnight, and much remains to be done to extend equality to all citizens. Similarly, multiculturalism has not provided a miracle cure for the challenges raised by illiberal traditions or political radicalism. Moreover, there is no guarantee that the infrastructure of multiculturalism will not be captured by illiberal forces intent on limiting civil liberties and individual autonomy, or on creating new forms of hierarchy and domination.

The best we can say, therefore, is that the trend towards multiculturalism has, in at least some cases, achieved some positive effects, exhibiting the same patterns of modest achievements that characterize most areas of social policy, subject to the same tendencies of political manipulation and bureaucratic ossification. This is hardly grounds for complacency or celebration, but it is grounds for cautious optimism, and there is no ground for thinking that further progress requires abolishing or retreating from the sorts of multiculturalism policies currently in place. Whether we are looking at language rights and regional autonomy for substate national groups, land claims and self-government rights for indigenous peoples, or multicultural accommodations for immigrant groups, we need to build on these policies, updating, extending and supplementing them with further policies that address the remaining forms of inequality, and that provide safeguards against illiberal pressures.

There is obviously much more that could be said about the effects of multiculturalism in practice, and more armchair speculations that need to be tested. Some of these claims about the (positive or negative) effects of multiculturalism are very difficult to measure, and there is large room for reasonable disagreement in the absence of reliable evidence.

However, for the purposes of this book, the key point is that various actors in the international community *believe* that liberal multiculturalism is a success in practice. At any rate, it is widely believed that there are several examples of multicultural 'best practices' in relation to immigrants, national minorities, and indigenous peoples that have managed to reconcile the accommodation of ethnocultural diversity with peace, democracy, human rights, and prosperity. This optimistic view may not be fully confirmed by the available evidence, but nor is it contradicted by that evidence. It is a reasonable interpretation of the Western experience, and helps to explain the efforts to globalize liberal multiculturalism which we will discuss in Part III.

Part III

Paradoxes in the Global Diffusion of Liberal Multiculturalism

Introduction to Part III

Inspired by the apparent success of liberal multiculturalism in the West, and alarmed by the prospects of escalating ethnic conflict in the post-communist and post-colonial world, the international community in the early 1990s embarked on a remarkable experiment in diffusing new ideas and norms about state–minority relations. There was a widespread consensus that the international community had to 'do something' to ensure that ethnic politics was not a threat to international peace and stability.

Not everyone agreed. Edward Luttwak famously suggested that we should 'give war a chance' (Luttwak 1999). Violent ethnic conflict is bad, he said, but it's important for both sides to learn the hard way that they can't defeat the other, and so accept the need to sit down and negotiate a compromise. Others would have given states a free hand to crush their minorities, by military force if necessary, turning a blind eye to whatever human rights violations occurred in the process, in the name of upholding the traditional doctrine of state sovereignty.

But in the heady days after the fall of the Berlin Wall, with its hope for the spread of peace and democracy, the clear consensus was to do something that manifested the new spirit of an international order founded on human rights rather than untrammelled state power. The goal was to address minority issues in a way that would strengthen the forces for democratization and the rule of law, rather than strengthen the hands of military authorities or police power. The old logic of allies and enemies, and winners and losers, was to be replaced with a new framework of democratic co-existence and cooperation within multiethnic states (Manas 1996). The goal, in short, was to promote something like liberal multiculturalism.

These intentions were clear enough, but what exactly can the international community do about state–minority relations? As I mentioned in Chapter 2, this question has arisen both at the regional level within Europe, as European organizations have confronted ethnic crises in the post-communist Balkans and Caucasus, and at the global level, as the United Nations and other international organizations have addressed the issue in the wider post-colonial context. In both cases, we can see anguished debates and paralysing uncertainties about how to articulate and promote new models of state–minority relations, and I will argue that many of the most crucial dilemmas remain far from resolved.

I will start in Chapter 6 with an overview of the European experience. The development of minority rights standards and mechanisms has gone further and faster in Europe than anywhere else. As a result, many of the paradoxes that are intrinsic to the process of internationalizing multiculturalism have first become clear in the European context.

In Chapter 7, I turn to the more global debates, and show how the difficulties that have arisen in the European case resurface, often in even more intractable forms, within international efforts dealing with the post-colonial world.

6

The European Experiment

The European story begins with the collapse of communism in Central and Eastern Europe in 1989, which was accompanied by a number of violent ethnic conflicts. In retrospect, these violent conflicts have largely been confined to the Caucasus and the Balkans. But this wasn't clear at the time. In the early 1990s, many commentators feared that ethnic tensions would spiral out of control in wide swaths of post-communist Europe. When the British magazine *New Statesman and Society* gave its June 1992 issue the headline 'Eurogeddon? The Coming Conflagration in East-Central Europe', it was reflecting a pervasive sentiment amongst European observers.

Faced with these potentially dire trends, the Western democracies in the early 1990s felt they had to do something. And they decided, in effect, to 'internationalize' the treatment of national minorities in post-communist Europe. They declared, in the words of the Organization for Security and Cooperation in Europe in 1990, that the status and treatment of national minorities 'are matters of legitimate international concern, and consequently do not constitute exclusively an internal affair of the respective State'.

It's an interesting question how and why this commitment emerged. After all, the EU had shown very little interest in the question of minority rights prior to 1989, and had deliberately avoided including any reference to minority rights in its own internal principles. Nor have Western countries traditionally shown much interest in protecting minorities elsewhere around the world. Western states have often propped up governments in Africa, Asia, or Latin America that were known to be oppressive to their minorities, even to the point of selling military equipment with the knowledge that it would be used against minority groups (e.g. selling arms to Indonesia to suppress minorities in Aceh and East Timor, or to

Guatemala to suppress the Maya). So why did the West suddenly become a champion of minorities in post-communist Europe?

As I suggested in Chapter 2, there were a number of reasons. One factor was humanitarian concern to stop the suffering of minorities facing persecution, mob violence, and ethnic cleansing. But humanitarian concern is rarely enough, on its own, to mobilize Western governments. A more self-interested reason was the belief that escalating ethnic violence would generate large-scale refugee movements into Western Europe, as indeed happened from Kosovo and Bosnia. Also, ethnic civil wars often create pockets of lawlessness which become havens for the smuggling of arms and drugs, or for other forms of criminality and extremism.

Another reason, more diffuse, was a belief in the West that the ability of post-communist countries to manage their ethnic diversity was a test of their overall political maturity, and hence of their readiness to 're-join Europe'. As the General Secretary of the Council of Europe put it, respect for minorities is a fundamental measure of a country's 'moral progress' (Burgess 1999).

In short, for a complex mixture of humanitarian, self-interested, and ideological reasons, minority rights have become internationalized in Europe. Meeting 'European standards' regarding the treatment of minorities has become a test of a country's readiness for Europe, evidence that a country has left behind its 'ancient ethnic hatreds' and 'tribal nationalisms', and is able to join a 'modern' liberal and cosmopolitan Europe.

Having decided that the treatment of minorities was a matter of legitimate international concern, European organizations then confronted the question of what, if anything, they could do to help improve state–minority relations in post-communist countries. They have largely proceeded along three tracks: publicizing best practices; formulating minimum standards; and case-specific interventions. All three strategies have been employed by European organizations since the early 1990s, and are intended to work together to create an effective and consistent regional approach towards minority issues. In reality, however, there are significant tensions amongst the three strategies which reflect a number of unresolved dilemmas in the very idea of internationalizing liberal multiculturalism.

In the rest of the chapter, I will look at these three strategies in turn, and consider the challenges each has faced. As we will see, there are multiple inconsistencies within and between these strategies, due mainly to the difficulty of integrating the optimistic pursuit of liberal multiculturalism with the more pessimistic fears of destabilizing ethnic conflict.

The 'Best Practices' Strategy

I will start with the most obvious and familiar strategy adopted by IOs—namely, to publicize 'best practices'. European organizations have attempted to identify examples of countries that have been particularly successful in managing the claims of their ethnic minorities, and to encourage other countries to learn from such successful models. This best practices strategy is found in virtually every context where IOs seek to influence domestic policies, from education and health care to the environment and financial reforms. And so over the past fifteen years we have witnessed a continuous stream of workshops and training sessions within Europe where examples of best practices are discussed, and reports and studies published, to familiarize people with them.

Some of these efforts have focused on a broad range of different types of minorities, including both 'old' historic minorities and 'new' immigrant minorities. But in the 1990s, the main focus was on the old minorities, which were seen as the most urgent issue for international monitoring. Not all types of ethnic diversity have the same potential for destabilization and violent conflict. For example, the presence of migrant workers is rarely a source of civil war or ethnic insurgencies. Even when migrant workers are mistreated and exploited, as they are in much of the world, they rarely take up arms, or seek to overthrow the state. As a result, the plight of migrant workers has been a matter of less urgency for the international community. There have been half-hearted attempts to publicize and promote best practices regarding the treatment of migrant workers, including recommendations that countries enable migrants to secure long-term residence and perhaps even citizenship, with the eventual goal of 'integration'.[1] But many countries in both the West and the developing world continue to view migrants as 'foreigners' who are 'temporary' residents, and the international community has been unable

---

[1] See, e.g., the report of the Global Commission on International Migration (2005), esp. chap. 4; the report of the Carnegie Endowment's Comparative Citizenship project (Aleinikoff and Klusmeyer 2002), esp. chap. 3; the UN's 2004 Human Development Report on 'Cultural Liberty in Today's Diverse World' (UNHDR 2004), esp. chap. 5, the UNESCO programme on 'International Migration and Multicultural Policies' (www.unesco.org/migration); or recent handbooks and guidelines of European organizations, including the OSCE (2006), the European Commission (2004), and the European Council (2004).

or unwilling to challenge that perception. As a result, international action on this issue has primarily been concerned to ensure that migrant workers have at least their basic human rights respected, rather than promoting a more robust idea of minority rights or 'multicultural citizenship' for migrants.[2]

The main concern of European organizations has been with a different type of ethnic diversity—namely, with non-immigrant groups that have been historically settled within a particular part of a country for a long period of time, and as a result of that historic settlement have come to see that part of the country as their historic 'homeland'. The minority's homeland is now incorporated within a larger state, or perhaps divided between two or more countries, but the minority still has a strong sense of attachment to this homeland, and often nurtures memories of an earlier time, prior to the origin of the modern state, when it had self-government over this territory. It is this sort of group—what we can call 'homeland minorities'—that has been involved in the violent civil wars in the Balkans and Caucasus, and which has been the focus of the initial European efforts in the field of minority issues.

And so the first strategy of European organizations was to catalogue and publicize best practices regarding the claims of homeland minorities. There are of course many examples around the world of relatively peaceful relations between states and homeland minorities, and in principle a catalogue of best practices might have drawn from a wide range of countries and continents. However, for obvious reasons, the first inclination of European organizations was to look for best practices within the Western democracies. Moreover, there was a desire to find examples that not only were peaceful, but also were consistent with international norms of human rights and democracy, and these considerations also privileged Western examples.

If we look for best practices in the West, a striking trend emerges— namely, the adoption of some form of territorial autonomy as a way of accommodating homeland minorities. As we saw in Chapter 3, there are

[2] For example, neither the 1977 European Convention on the Legal Status of Migrant Workers, nor the 1990 UN International Convention on the Protection of the Rights of all Migrant Workers and Members of their Families, seeks to promote any of the immigrant multiculturalism policies that I listed in Chapter 3. As Keller notes, the 'the cultural dimension of [immigrants'] lives is almost entirely neglected' in these Conventions (Keller 1998: 46). The one exception that proves the rule is Article 15 of the European Convention, which encourages 'special courses for the teaching of the migrant worker's mother tongue, to facilitate, inter alia, their return to their State of origin'. In other words, it encourages mother-tongue education, but only because it is assumed that migrants will return 'home'. There is no hint in these documents of a commitment to multicultural citizenship for migrants.

two different categories of homeland minorities in the West, and in both cases there has been a trend towards adopting territorial autonomy. The first category are indigenous peoples in the New World (United States, Canada, New Zealand, Australia) and in northern Europe (the Greenlanders in Denmark and Sami in Scandinavia). In all of these countries, particularly since the 1970s, there has been a shift towards recognizing some form of indigenous self-government over (what remains of) their traditional territory. This is reflected in a wide range of land claims settlements and self-government agreements, and in some cases a degree of legal pluralism (e.g. recognizing customary law).

The second category of homeland minority are substate national minorities, including the Scots and Welsh in the United Kingdom; the Catalans and Basques in Spain; the Flemish in Belgium; the Québécois in Canada; the Puerto Ricans in the United States; the Corsicans in France; the German minority in South Tyrol in Italy; the Swedes in Finland; and the French and Italian minorities in Switzerland. In all of these countries, substate national groups have been offered a significant degree of territorial autonomy, usually through some form of federal or quasi-federal devolution of power, as well as some form of official language status.

In the case of both indigenous peoples and national minorities in the West, therefore, we see a trend towards the granting of territorial autonomy. These autonomy regimes work in conjunction with other minority rights, such as land claims and legal pluralism for indigenous peoples, official language status for national minorities, and various non-territorial forms of cultural autonomy for those members of the homeland minority who have moved elsewhere in the country. These are obviously very strong forms of multiculturalism, involving a substantial restructuring of the state and redistribution of political power. As a result, the changes were initially very controversial in most Western democracies. And yet, today, the basic idea of territorial autonomy for homeland minorities is widely accepted. It is inconceivable that Spain or Belgium, for example, could revert to a unitary and monolingual state. And no one is campaigning for such a reversal. Indeed, no Western democracy that has adopted territorial autonomy for its homeland minorities has reversed this decision.

For the reasons discussed in Chapter 5, this model is widely seen as successful. It has enabled countries to deal with a difficult and potentially explosive issue—namely, the existence of a substate group that perceives itself as a distinct people or nation with the right to govern its historic territory—in a way that is consistent with peace and democracy, firm respect for individual civil and political rights, and economic prosperity.

It is not surprising, therefore, that several European organizations have presented territorial autonomy as a best practice to be publicized and encouraged for the accommodation of homeland minorities. Indeed, the very first statement by a European organization on minority rights after the collapse of Communism—the initial 1990 OSCE Copenhagen Declaration—went out of its way to endorse territorial autonomy. Article 35 of the Declaration states:

The participating States note the efforts undertaken to protect and create conditions for the promotion of the ethnic, cultural, linguistic and religious identity of certain national minorities by establishing, as one of the possible means to achieve these aims, appropriate local or autonomous administrations corresponding to the specific historical and territorial circumstances of such minorities and in accordance with the policies of the State concerned.

Similarly, the Parliamentary Assembly of the Council of Europe has also passed numerous declarations on 'Positive experiences of autonomous regions as a source of inspiration for conflict resolution in Europe'.[3]

European organizations have not only publicized these examples, but have also attempted to 'normalize' them. As I noted in Chapter 2, in the past examples of substate autonomy were seen as 'exceptions' or 'deviations' from what a 'normal' state looks like, the norm being a highly centralized state like France, with an undifferentiated conception of republican citizenship and a single official language. But this model of a centralized, unitary, and homogenous state is increasingly described by IOs as an anachronism, whereas pluralistic, multilingual, and multilevel states are presented as the more truly 'modern' approach. In this way, specific examples of autonomy are situated within a broader discourse of modernity in which a more fragmented, diffuse, and multilevel conception of statehood and sovereignty has become the norm. By normalizing this new conception of state–minority relations, the international community hopes to encourage states to consider in a more open-minded way the virtues of liberal multiculturalism.

This, then, was the first strategy—to publicize and normalize ideas of territorial autonomy as a best practice for accommodating homeland minorities. However, it was more or less a complete failure, at least with respect to post-communist countries in the early 1990s. Policy-makers

---

[3] See Parliamentary Assembly's Recommendation 1609 (2003).

from post-communist countries were happy to join study tours of, say, Catalonia or South Tyrol and spend a few days on the Mediterranean or in the Alps at European Union expense. And they were politic enough to say how much they learned from these sessions about the values of tolerance and diversity. But then they would go back home and continue to support policies that (depending on the country) abolished pre-existing minority autonomies, reduced minority-language rights, closed minority-language schools, fired minorities from public service, and in some cases stripped minorities of their citizenship.

Even when such explicitly anti-minority policies were not adopted, there was no move in any post-communist country to seriously consider adopting territorial autonomy. No country set up a parliamentary commission to study the prospects for democratic multination federalism, or for adopting some scheme of official bilingualism. In short, there is no evidence that exposure to these best practices inspired any significant change in government policies. Indeed, in several post-communist countries, it remained illegal for political parties to even include claims to territorial autonomy in their political platforms. The whole issue remained a taboo in most post-communist countries, and the very idea of autonomy was often dismissed as an aberration that did not belong in a normal state.[4]

The only exception occurred in cases where minorities had already seized part of the territory of the state, and set up some scheme of autonomy (or even self-declared independence) in contravention of the constitution. At this point, in order to regain control of the lost territory, some states were willing to discuss the merits of federalism, particularly if they were unable to recapture the territory militarily. For example, the government of Georgia, after losing control over secessionist regions in Abkhazia and South Ossetia, has expressed an interest in federalism as a way of reintegrating these regions; the government of Moldova, after losing control over the secessionist region of Transnistria, has discussed various plans for federalization as a way of reuniting the country; Azerbaijan, after losing control over the secessionist region of Ngorno-Karabakh to ethnic Armenians, has offered autonomy as a way of reintegrating the lost territory; Bosnia adopted a scheme of cantonization in order to reintegrate territories controlled by ethnic Serbs and Croats; Serbia offered autonomy in the hope of reintegrating Kosovo, now controlled by ethnic Albanians under an international protectorate; and Cyprus has offered federalism as a way of restoring its northern region, now controlled by

---

[4] For examples, see Kymlicka and Opalski 2001: 384.

ethnic Turks.[5] In all of these cases, states that have lost control over territory to rebellious minorities have been willing to discuss various models of autonomy or federalism, when that was seen as the only alternative to accepting secession.

But there are no cases where post-communist states in control of their territory decided, of their own accord, to debate the merits of adopting some scheme of federal or quasi-federal autonomy for their national minorities, as part of a larger process of democratization.[6] The publicizing and normalizing of Western best practices for homeland minorities fell on deaf ears.

The Missing Sources and Preconditions of Liberal Multiculturalism

Confronted with this intense resistance to accommodating homeland minorities, various commentators and international actors have blamed it on the pre-modern attitudes of the peoples and cultures of the region. One popular explanation, particularly amongst journalists, is that whereas nationalism in the West is 'civic' nationalism, based on shared loyalty

[5] Croatia also briefly offered autonomy to the secessionist region of Krajina when it was controlled by ethnic Serbs. When the Serbs didn't accept, the Croatian army invaded, recaptured the territory, and promptly expelled the Serbs, to make sure there would be no chance of Serbian autonomy in the future. Other countries also tried the military option in dealing with secessionist regions. Georgia, Moldova, and Azerbaijan all attempted to militarily regain control over their secessionist regions, but lost the resulting wars, and so are now negotiating autonomy for Abkhazia and Ossetia, Transnistria, and Ngorno-Karabakh. The initial position of the Bosnian government of Alija Izetbegovic was also for a centralized unitary state, with no provisions for minority autonomy, and the current cantonal arrangements are the result of an inconclusive civil war. Negotiating autonomy, in all of these cases, is truly a last resort, adopted only after minorities have seized territory, and military attempts to reconquer the territory have failed. The case of Crimea in Ukraine is a partial exception to this generalization. While the ethnic Russian minority in Crimea did not literally take up arms and seize military control over the region, it did exercise *de facto* control over the territory, and threatened to unilaterally (and unconstitutionally) declare independence or to rejoin Russia. In response, Ukraine eventually negotiated a form of special autonomy for the region, rather than face civil war (Marples and Duke 1995), although it had earlier threatened that the declaration of Russian autonomy in Crimea would lead to war (Laitin 1998: 100).

[6] A possible exception is Russia itself, which had a federal constitution when it was part of the Soviet Union, and retained a federal form as it seceded from the USSR. But this is only a partial exception, since the central Russian state was not in fact in control of all of its territory during the breakdown of the USSR, as several minority regions had seized control and declared various degrees of autonomy/sovereignty. Moreover, it's important to note that multination federalism is contested in Russia. Many Russian leaders and intellectuals do not like what they call 'ethnic federalism', and would prefer to replace it with a German-style form of administrative federalism, in which national minorities do not exercise territorial self-government (Vasilyeva 1995; Opalski 2001). Their acceptance of the existing system is almost entirely strategic and transitional. So Russia is not as different from other post-communist countries as it first appears.

to common principles, and hence more accommodating of minorities, nationalism in post-communist Europe is 'ethnic' nationalism, based on ancestry and blood, and hence more hostile or aggressive towards minorities (e.g. Ignatieff 1993). On the basis of such explanations, various programmes have been adopted to teach more 'modern' attitudes towards diversity and tolerance, through inter-cultural exchanges and inter-faith dialogue.

I do not think this is a helpful answer. Attempts to test empirically the proposition that nationalism in post-communist Europe is more 'ethnic' than in the West haven't come up with much supporting evidence (Kuzio 2001). In any event, the civic/ethnic distinction doesn't explain how states respond to minority nationalism. So-called 'civic' nations, such as France, have historically been reluctant to accord territorial autonomy to national minorities, and there is nothing in the logic of civic nationalism that requires national minorities to be accorded self-government. Indeed, many defenders of civic nationalism oppose self-government claims precisely on the grounds that minority nationalism is 'ethnic' nationalism, and hence has no place in a civic nation. Conversely, there is nothing in the logic of 'ethnic' nationalism that precludes according self-government to other ethnic nations, and there are many historic examples of two or more 'ethnic' nations sharing power in a single state.[7]

We need to look elsewhere for an explanation of opposition to self-government for substate national groups. And one place to look is to re-examine the conditions that have enabled the adoption of such robust forms of minority rights in the West. The reality is that several of the sources and preconditions of liberal multiculturalism in the West were either weak or absent in most post-communist countries (and, as we will see in Chapter 7, in most of the world).

In Chapter 4, I divided these facilitating conditions into two categories: factors that encouraged minorities to mobilize for greater rights, and factors that encouraged majority groups and states to be willing to accept these claims. There were important differences between the West and post-communist Europe in relation to both categories.

In terms of minority mobilization, a crucial enabling condition in the West was democratic consolidation: it provided guarantees of safe political mobilization, ensuring that minorities would not be jailed, attacked, or persecuted for airing their aspirations and claims. In post-communist

---

[7] On the multiple confusions involved in standard discussions of civic/ethnic nationalism, see Kymlicka 2001, chaps. 12–15.

Europe in the early 1990s, these guarantees were not present. Minorities lacked firm confidence that they could safely mobilize. Indeed, in many cases ethnic political mobilization remained illegal, or subject to police harassment, long after the fall of Communist dictatorships. The safest option was to lie low, in part because the police, courts, and army were clearly in the hands of the dominant group (often after having been purged of their minorities).

Despite this fear, many minorities in the region did mobilize for autonomy and language rights, in part because new constitutions were being drafted in all post-communist countries, and these constitutions were setting the political ground rules for the future. It was important for minorities, therefore, to at least try to voice their concerns. Groups demanding some form of territorial autonomy included the ethnic Hungarians and Albanians in Serbia; the ethnic Abkhaz and Ossetians in Georgia; the ethnic Armenians in Azerbaijan; the ethnic Hungarians in Romania; the ethnic Russians in the Narva region of Estonia, and in the north of Kazakhstan; ethnic Romanians in Ukraine; ethnic Poles in Lithuania; ethnic Albanians in western Macedonia; amongst others.

The real difference with the West, therefore, was not in the extent of minority mobilization, but rather in the strength of the state's resistance to minority claims. In the West, these claims have been debated seriously, and in many cases accepted, at least in part. In post-communist Europe, they have run into a brick wall.

Why? The two key preconditions in the West that lowered the risk to states and dominant national groups of accepting minority claims were (a) the existence of reliable human rights protections; and (b) the desecuritization of ethnic relations. Neither was present in post-communist Europe in the early 1990s.

For majorities in the West, the consolidation of robust legal mechanisms for protecting human rights, and the more general development of a human rights culture, provided guarantees that accommodating minority claims to self-government would not lead to islands of tyranny in which the basic security or citizenship rights of individuals would be in jeopardy. These guarantees dramatically lowered the stakes involved in debates about minority rights. In post-communist Europe in the early 1990s, however, these guarantees were absent. Dominant groups lacked confidence that they would be fairly treated within self-governing minority regions. Indeed, in those cases where minorities seized territory and established their own autonomous governments, the results were often various forms of discrimination and harassment against anyone who

182

didn't belong to the minority, if not outright ethnic cleansing. Ethnic Georgians were pushed out of the Abkhazia region of Georgia when it declared autonomy/sovereignty; ethnic Croats were pushed out of the Serb-dominated region of Slavonia when it declared autonomy; ethnic Serbs were pushed out of Albanian-dominated Kosovo when it achieved autonomy, and so on. Neither side could rely on effective legal institutions and an impartial police to ensure that human rights were respected.

These fears about individual security were compounded by geo-political fears about the security of the state. A crucial precondition for the adoption of multination federalism in the West was the 'desecuritization' of state–minority relations. With respect to both national minorities and indigenous peoples in the West, there is no longer any fear that they will collaborate with enemies of the state, and this allows claims for self-government to be treated as 'normal' democratic politics. In post-communist Europe, however, the perception of homeland minorities as a potential fifth column who are likely to collaborate with neighbouring enemies remains pervasive, and so ethnic relations remain highly securitized.

In order to understand this perception, we need to recall the history of the region. The current configuration of states in Central and Eastern Europe is the result of the breakdown of three empires after World War I—the Russian Romanov empire, the Austro-Hungarian Habsburg empire, and the Turkish Ottoman empire—and the more recent collapse of the Soviet empire in 1989. Each of these empires encompassed the homelands of several national groups, many of whom acquired independent states in the ashes of the former empires (e.g. Poles, Romanians, Czechs, and Slovaks, Bulgarians, Serbs, Latvians, etc.).

This process of state formation in the shadow of imperial breakdown created several distinctive security problems relating to homeland minorities. First, the boundaries of these newly independent states typically (and inevitably) left some members of the national group on the 'wrong' side of a new international border. When the border between Germany and Poland was drawn, there were many ethnic Germans on the Polish side of the border. Similarly, there were large numbers of ethnic Hungarians on the Romanian side of the border with Hungary, or ethnic Russians on the Latvian side of the border with Russia, or ethnic Turks on the Bulgarian side of the border with Turkey, or ethnic Albanians on the Macedonian side of the border. These are often called 'kin-state minorities', because their ethnic kin dominate a neighbouring state, and they are assumed to have a higher loyalty to this kin-state than to the state they live in. As a result, it is often assumed that such minorities are irredentist—that is, they wish to redraw international boundaries so that the territory they live on is (re)-joined to their kin-state. Indeed, it is often assumed that they would willingly collaborate with their kin-state if it militarily invaded the country in order to claim this territory, as indeed some have done at various points in the twentieth century. No state is likely to voluntarily accord self-governing powers to a minority under these circumstances.

Where homeland minorities take the form of irredentist kin-state minorities, there is a much higher likelihood that ethnic relations will be perceived as a threat to state security.[8] But this is not inevitable. There are factors that can either alleviate or exacerbate the problem. One factor that alleviates the problem is if the neighbouring states are close allies, integrated into larger regional economic and security organizations, such that the kin-state has no interest in destabilizing its neighbour. This is precisely what has defused the problem of kin-state minorities in Western Europe. In the past, Belgium, Denmark, and Italy resisted according strong rights to their ethnic German minorities because they were perceived as kin-state minorities with a primary loyalty to Germany.[9] But once Germany became a close ally rather than a potential enemy as a result of the EU and NATO, the trans-border affiliations of ethnic German minorities became unimportant (and indeed became viewed as a potential asset in ongoing processes of regional integration).[10] In the post-communist

---

[8] For the centrality of this 'triadic relationship' between states, minorities, and kin-states in post-communist Europe, see Brubaker 1996. By contrast, many of the paradigmatic examples of national minorities in the West do not have a kin-state (e.g. Catalans and Basques; Scots and Welsh; Québécois; Puerto Ricans). Even the French and Italians in Switzerland are not, strictly speaking, appropriately viewed as kin-state minorities. As Grin notes, the task of maintaining unity in Switzerland is made easier because the French-speaking part of Switzerland 'has never, at any point of its history (bar a few years of Napoleonic rule with partial annexation) been part of France; the French-speaking Swiss are in no way descendants or cousins of the French... Similarly, German-speaking Switzerland has never been part of Germany, and Italian-speaking Switzerland has never been part of Italy' (Grin 1999: 5).

[9] Indeed, the whole minority rights movement in inter-war Europe and the League of Nations was often perceived as a German plot to use ethnic German minorities as a tool to destabilize neighbouring states. The main pan-European organization of national minorities in the inter-war period—the Congress of European Nationalities, established in 1925—included many non-German minorities, but was primarily organized by ethnic Germans from the Baltics, and primarily funded by the German Foreign Office, both during the Weimar republic and then under the Nazis. That the Nazis used the Congress, and the minority issue generally, as a tool to destabilize neighbouring states is clear enough. There is more debate about the intentions of the original organizers of the Congress in the 1920s. For the argument that many of the key figures were genuinely committed to a liberal model of minority rights, rather than German irredentism or supremacism, see Housden 2006.

[10] The same applies to other potential 'kin-state minorities' in the West that are linked by ethnicity to a neighbouring state. The French in Switzerland or Belgium are not seen as a fifth

countries in the 1990s, however, there was no equivalent of the EU and NATO to turn potential enemies into allies. In the absence of regional security arrangements, post-communist countries were in a Hobbesian state of nature, distrustful of all their neighbours. And in this context, the presumed disloyalty of kin-state minorities was quickly perceived as a security threat.

Another factor that can either alleviate or exacerbate the problem of kin-state minorities is the balance of power between a state, its minorities, and the neighbouring kin-state. The perceived threat to state security is obviously reduced if the state feels itself to be a strong state confronting weak enemies, whether these are internal irredentist minorities or their kin-states across the border. Unfortunately, in the post-communist world, the balance of power tended to exacerbate rather than alleviate the problem. In many cases, the national groups that acquired independence after imperial collapse view themselves as the historically weak parties, confronted with minorities and kin-states that have been historically dominant. The result is the phenomenon known as 'minoritized majorities'—majorities which continue to think and act as if they are weak and victimized minorities, and which therefore continue to live in existential fear for their existence.[11]

This is a phenomenon that is pervasive in the post-communist world, but virtually unknown in the West, and so needs to be explained. If one simply looks at the numbers, and ignores the historical background, it may appear that kin-state minorities in most post-communist countries are fairly small and weak. Ethnic Hungarians in Slovakia, for example, are around 15 per cent of the population, and hence are relatively powerless in relation to the overwhelming ethnic Slovak majority in the country. Historically, however, the Hungarians were members of the privileged and dominant group within the larger Habsburg empire, and were active collaborators in Habsburg policies to create Hungarian hegemony in the region. The ethnic Slovaks, by contrast, were a subordinated group, subject to coercive 'Magyarization' campaigns. After independence, this

column for France; the Flemish are not seen as a fifth column for the Netherlands; the Swedes in Finland are not seen as a fifth column for Sweden, and so on. This is testament to the extraordinary success of the EU and NATO in 'desecuritizing' national minority politics in Western Europe. Memories die hard, however: see Hillard 2002 for the claim that the post-1990 movement to develop European norms of minority rights and regional autonomy is a German plot to destabilize its neighbours, reviving the same strategies used earlier by the Nazis, the Weimar Republic, and the Kaiser. (An excerpt in English of his febrile speculations was published in *Geostrategies*, No. 4, posted at: <http://www.strategicsinternational.com/4enhilard.htm>.)

[11] The phrase was coined, I believe, by Tove Skutnabb-Kangas. For an application to the Baltics, see Druviete 1997.

hierarchy has of course been reversed: Slovaks are now the dominant group, and Hungarians are the threatened minority subject to Slovak nation-building policies. But the memory remains: Slovaks view ethnic Hungarians not just as a potentially irredentist group that is loyal to their kin-state, but as a historically powerful and privileged group that collaborated with a hegemonic imperial power to oppress the Slovak language and culture. And, in the absence of effective regional security arrangements, the fear persists that this could happen again—that the Hungarian minority could collaborate with the Hungarian kin-state to once again subordinate Slovaks and crush their national independence.

We see the same phenomenon in Poland regarding the German minority; in Romania and Serbia regarding the Hungarian minority; in the Baltics, Ukraine, and Moldova regarding the Russian minority; in Croatia and Bosnia regarding the Serbian minority;[12] in Bulgaria regarding the Turkish minority, to name a few. In all of these cases, minorities are seen (rightly or wrongly) as allies or collaborators with external powers that have historically oppressed the majority group, and the majority group in turn acts as a 'minoritized majority'.[13]

In short, several factors operated to exacerbate the securitization of ethnic relations in post-communist Europe. The phenomenon of home-land minorities seeking self-government raises difficulties at the best of times, since it challenges the state's claim to represent a single people and to derive its legitimacy from an undivided popular sovereignty. But this challenge becomes much greater, and more likely to be secu-ritized, when (a) the homeland minorities are potentially irredentist minorities with loyalty to a neighbouring kin-state, and (b) these neigh-bouring kin-states are former imperial powers which have historically

[12] Yugoslavia was not an 'empire' in the way that the Soviet Union was, and so Serbia was not an 'imperial power' in the way that Russia was. But it was the dominant group within Yugoslavia, and nationalist leaders amongst the Bosnians and Croats were constantly battling against what they perceived as attempts to turn (parts of) Yugoslavia into a 'Greater Serbia', using Serbian minorities in other republics as a tool.

[13] This analysis differs from Arjun Appadurai's view, which claims that violence is more likely when minorities are smaller, a phenomenon he calls the 'anxiety of small numbers' (2006: 8). According to Appadurai, smaller minorities seem like a 'tiny obstacle' to the achievement of the majority's fantasy of national purity, and the smaller the size of the minority, 'the deeper the rage' that majorities feel at their inability to achieve this fantasy (2006: 53). But the example he most commonly cites of violence against minorities concerns the 100-million strong Muslim minority in India, which is in fact the largest minority in the world! And, as he elsewhere notes, Hindu anxieties about this (not-so-tiny) obstacle are intimately linked up with larger geo-political fears that the Muslim minority will collaborate with India's neighbouring Muslim states. His own example, therefore, suggests that it is the strength of minorities in combination with their potential regional allies that generates fear, not their smallness.

subordinated the national groups which now form a majority in neighbouring states; and (c) there are no regional security arrangements to guarantee non-aggression. Where these factors are present, as they are in post-communist Europe, the likely result is a pervasive securitization of ethnic relations.

This securitization is reflected in three assumptions that dominate public debate on minorities in the region: (a) that minorities are disloyal, not just in the sense that they lack loyalty to the state (that is equally true of secessionists in Quebec or Scotland), but in the stronger sense that they have collaborated with former oppressors, and continue to collaborate with current enemies or potential enemies;[14] therefore, (b) a strong and stable state requires weak and disempowered minorities. Put another way, ethnic relations are seen as a zero-sum game: anything that benefits the minority is seen as a threat to the majority; and therefore (c) the treatment of minorities is above all a question of national security.[15]

So both of the main factors that enabled dominant groups in the West to accept liberal multiculturalism—namely, human rights guarantees and desecuritization—were absent, or only weakly present, in post-communist Europe in the early 1990s. Given this fact, it is hardly surprising that attempts to publicize and normalize best practices of liberal multiculturalism fell on deaf ears in post-communist Europe.[16] The homeland

[14] This pervasive rhetoric of loyalty/disloyalty is exacerbated in some countries by a local version of Huntington's 'clash of civilizations' thesis (Huntington 1996). On this view, the world is divided into distinct 'civilizations', grounded essentially in religion, that are in more or less inherent conflict. So the conflict between the Serbs and Albanians over Kosovo is not just a conflict between languages, cultures, or nations, but also between civilizations—an Orthodox Christian civilization and a Muslim civilization. Two civilizations cannot co-exist as equal partners in a single state. One civilization must be dominant, and the other subordinate (and hence prone to disloyalty). This clash of civilizations view is also invoked, not only in conflicts between Christians and Muslims, but also between Orthodox and Catholics (e.g. in Romania), or between Protestants and Orthodox (e.g. in Estonia). Where people accept this premise about the clash of civilizations, there is no room for questions about fairness or justice to minorities. Relations between conflicting civilizations are a matter of power and security, not justice.

[15] For discussions of this disloyalty/security/fifth-column view, see Andreescu 1997 (re Hungarians in Romania); Mihalikova 1998: 154–7 (re Hungarians in Slovakia); Nelson 1998; Solchanyk 1994 and Jaworsky 1998 (re Russians in Ukraine); Offe 1993: 23–4; Strazzari 1998 (re Albanians in Macedonia); Pettai 1998 (re Russians in the Baltics).

[16] Opposition to territorial autonomy in post-communist Europe is often said to be the result, not only or primarily of security fears, but of other factors, such as the way ethnic groups are inter-mixed rather than territorially concentrated, or fears of 'escalation' and 'proliferation' (Offe 1998, 2001). Escalation is the fear that groups granted internal self-determination will then escalate their demands into full-blown secession. Proliferation is the fear that if internal self-determination is offered to one highly vocal or mobilized group, then other groups, previously quiescent, will come out of the woodwork and demand their

minorities seeking self-government were often perceived as a geo-political threat to the security of the state, and a threat to the individual human rights of people living in the potentially self-governing territory. Under these circumstances, it would have been surprising indeed if there had been much genuine interest in Western models of multination federalism. Instead, most post-communist states clung firmly to the goal of turning themselves into centralized, unitary, and monolingual nation-states, premised on a singular and undifferentiated conception of popular sovereignty, no matter how much the West described this model as *passé.*[17]

The distinctive history of imperialism and collaboration in the region also creates another important obstacle to the adoption of Western models—namely, perceptions of historic injustice. In many post-communist countries, there is a strong sense that historical wrongs have not yet been acknowledged or remedied. Some people say that this focus on historical rights and wrongs is unique to Eastern Europe, and that Western democracies have managed to get beyond this 'backward-looking' obsession with history and to focus instead on 'forward-looking' co-existence. It is certainly true that feelings about historic injustice run deep in many post-communist countries. (It is a cliché, but partly true, that if you ask a Serb about the rights of the Albanians in Kosovo, he/she is likely to say 'you need to understand what happened in 1389'.) But I think the same is true in many Western countries as well. Appeals to historical injustice are increasingly common in the West. Consider the recent explosion of writing on the issue of reparations to African-Americans for the historic wrongs of slavery and segregation (Robinson 2000; Brooks 2004). Claims for the rectification of historic injustice are also a vital part of contemporary mobilization by indigenous peoples in New Zealand, Australia, and Canada, and even of some immigrant groups—for

own autonomy. However, the same two fears of escalation and proliferation were present in the West as well, and yet Western states have nonetheless proceeded with internal autonomy. Fears of escalation and proliferation have turned out to be exaggerated, at least in the Western context. Similarly, the level of territorial concentration of minorities in post-communist countries is not substantially different from those in the West. (I criticize Offe's claims about territorial concentration, escalation, and proliferation in Kymlicka 2002.) If we want to understand why opposition to territorial autonomy is so much stronger in post-communist Europe than in Western Europe, we need to understand the underlying factors that make issues of escalation and proliferation so threatening—and these, I would argue, relate to the complex of securitization, historic hierarchies, and lack of confidence in the mechanisms for rights-protection.

[17] This is particularly true of those countries, like Romania or Turkey, influenced by the French Jacobin tradition. For the strength of this ideology in post-communist Europe, see Liebich 2004.

example, Japanese-Americans and Japanese-Canadians seeking apologies and compensation for their detention in World War II (James 1999).[18] Indeed, as I argued in Chapter 4, the rise of liberal multiculturalism in the West is intimately tied up with the recognition and acknowledgement of the injustice of historic ethnic and racial hierarchies.

As we've just seen, however, there is an important difference in the nature of the historic hierarchies in the West and in post-communist Europe. In the West, it is almost always a *minority* that is seeking apology and compensation from the state that has historically mistreated it. Hence the argument from historic injustice operates to strengthen minority rights claims, and to buttress the argument for greater equality between majority and minority. It is invoked to pressure the majority to say 'never again we will try to expel, subordinate or oppress you'.

In post-communist countries, however, it is typically the *majority* that feels that it has been the victim of oppression, often at the hands of minorities acting in collaboration with foreign enemies. Hence the majority wants the minority to express guilt, and to offer an apology, as a way of saying that never again will the minority be disloyal to the state. We see this in the Czech Republic regarding the German minority; in Slovakia regarding the Hungarian minority; and in the Baltics regarding the Russian minority; amongst others.

In short, the sort of historic injustice that is central to post-communist debates, unlike in the West, is the historical oppression of the majority group by its minorities in collaboration with a kin-state or foreign power. This, I think, truly distinguishes Eastern Europe from the Western experience (except perhaps in Cyprus), although as we'll see in Chapter 7 there are comparable examples from Africa and Asia as well.

In this context, arguments about historic injustice work *against* minority rights claims. In the West, homeland minorities typically would have been stronger than they now are were it not for historic injustices perpetrated by the larger state—for example, there would have been more people speaking the minority's language and practising its culture, over a wider area. Minority rights can be seen, in part, as a way of acknowledging and remedying that harm. In post-communist countries, however, historic injustice is often seen as having expanded the scope and prestige of the minority's language and culture at the expense of the majority. Indeed, taken to their logical conclusion, arguments of historic injustice

---

[18] There is now an enormous literature on the strength of movements in the West for reparations and redress for historic wrongs—e.g. Barkan 2000; Torpey 2006; Weiner 2005.

may suggest that minorities have no right to exist on the territory of the state, if their very presence is related to such an historic injustice. Were it not for unjust Russian and Soviet imperialism, there would be few Russians in the Baltics. Were it not for unjust Ottoman imperialism, there would be few Turks in Bulgaria. If the goal is to remedy the wrongs created by these historic injustices, why not try to undo the Russification of the Baltics, either by expelling the Russians or by insisting that they assimilate to Estonian and Latvian culture? Why not try to undo the Turkification of Bulgaria under the Ottomans, either by expelling the Turks or by insisting they assimilate to Bulgarian culture?[19]

In short, whereas arguments about rectifying historic injustice in the West operate to strengthen the minority's claim for a more equal distribution of rights and resources between majority and minority, in post-communist countries they can be invoked to weaken the minority's claims, and indeed to question the very legitimacy of the minority's existence.

These profound differences in human rights protection, geo-political security, and historic injustices create obvious grounds for opposition to the adoption of Western models of multination federalism. Of course, in all of these cases, it's important to distinguish objective facts about security threats and historic wrongs from the way these facts are perceived and discussed. Political actors make choices about whether or when to highlight (or exaggerate) these factors in public debate. The perception of kin-state minorities as a security threat, and as collaborators in historic injustices against the majority, is something that is deliberately inculcated and reproduced by certain political elites, for their own self-interested reasons.

This indeed is central to understanding the process of securitization. Strictly speaking, an issue only becomes 'securitized' if certain political actors decide to describe it in these terms—as an existential threat to the state and its dominant national group—and succeed in persuading enough others of this description. In some cases, this may reflect a sincere belief about the objective threats, but in other cases, it represents a conscious choice and political strategy. Why would political elites adopt this strategy? Securitizing an issue has two important implications. First,

---

[19] This is precisely what Bulgaria tried to do in the 1980s, for example by forcing all the Turks to adopt ethnic Bulgarian names. The Communist Bulgarian government at the time argued that the coerced assimilation of the Turks was simply reversing the unjust pressure that the Ottomans put on Slavs to convert to Islam and to assimilate to Turkish culture (Tomova 1998).

since securitized issues are said to have the potential to undercut the state, they trump normal democratic processes of debate and negotiation. After all, the first task of the state is to secure its existence, and only then can it afford to discuss and negotiate. As Waever puts, by securitizing issues, political leaders claim that these issues

> must be addressed prior to all others because, if they are not, the state will cease to exist as a sovereign unit and all other questions will become irrelevant.... Operationally, however, this means: *In naming a certain development as a security problem, the 'state' can claim a special right*... By uttering 'security', a state-representative moves a particular development into a specific area, and thereby claims a special right to use whatever means are necessary to block it. (Waever 1995: 54–5, emphasis in original)

Second, securitizing an issue also trumps issues of justice. The whole question of what justice requires between majority and minority is submerged, since national security takes precedence over justice, and since disloyal minorities have no legitimate claims anyway. This helps to explain why there is little scholarly or public debate in post-communist countries about the principles of justice that should regulate the accommodation of ethnocultural diversity. In the fervid debate over the Albanian-language university in Macedonia, for example, it is difficult to find anyone asking what fairness requires in the sphere of higher education in multinational and multilingual states, or how mother-tongue higher education relates to liberal principles of freedom and equality. Security trumps justice, and disloyal minorities forfeit any claims of justice.

The only exception to this filtering out of justice arguments relates to the historic injustices that the *majority* has suffered, and for which the minority is perceived to be responsible. This sort of justice claim passes through the securitization filter, since it provides the historical evidence to support the securitization of the issue in the first place. So the historic injustice and securitization arguments feed off each other, and both operate to exclude any claims of justice that the minority might advance. Under conditions of securitization, 'justice' means that the majority should be compensated for the historic wrongs it has suffered from its disloyal minorities; it does not mean that minorities have any claim to a fairer or more equal distribution of power, rights, and resources.[20]

---

[20] For example, the 'Justification' section of the 1995 Law on the State Language in Slovakia consists mainly in recounting various Habsburg laws and policies from the nineteenth century that suppressed the use of Slovak and promoted Magyarization. There is no attempt to discuss what would be a fair accommodation in the current situation of the diverse interests

In short, when minority issues are securitized, the space for moral argument and democratic debate drastically shrinks. I believe that this displacement of justice by security is what most clearly distinguishes the debate on national minorities in post-communist Europe from the West.[21] Indeed, the low level of securitization of national minority issues in the West is, on reflection, quite remarkable. After all, several countries in the West contain active secessionist movements—in Quebec, Flanders, Scotland, Puerto Rico, and Catalonia. In all of these cases, there are political parties that contest the very existence of the state, and so threaten the security of the state. And in some cases, these secessionist parties have even come to power at a regional level, or shared power in coalitions. Yet in all of these cases, Western political actors have not securitized issues of minority nationalism. As we saw in Chapter 4, there has been a (re)-securitization of some issues relating to immigrant groups in the West, particularly Muslim immigrants after 9/11. But this has not yet had a spillover effect on debates about national minorities. The claims of these movements continue to be addressed through a discourse of liberal-democratic justice—that is, in terms of freedom, equality, and solidarity. And they are resolved through normal democratic procedures and negotiations. In other words, secessionist politics in the West is normal politics. It is seen as normal and natural that secessionist politicians are speaking on television, sitting on parliamentary committees, and campaigning in the streets. No one thinks that the active participation of secessionist politicians is a reason for suspending normal democratic procedures or debates, or for trumping claims of justice.[22]

In post-communist countries, by contrast, even the most modest demands by national minorities can be subject to securitization. The opening of private universities, the use of bilingual street signs, the choice of alphabets, even the naming of children, have all been securitized in various post-communist countries. The government of Macedonia, for example, declared that it would be a threat to the very existence of the state if the Albanian minority in Macedonia were to have a university

of the majority and minorities. (The Justification is reproduced and discussed in Minority Protection Association 1995.)

[21] Except again for Northern Ireland and Cyprus, which have historically been highly 'securitized'.

[22] In the past in the West, secessionist parties were banned or kept under secret police surveillance; secessionist professors were sometimes fired from their jobs, and so on. But today, secessionist politics is normal politics.

operating in their own language (and hence bulldozed the buildings of the private University of Tetovo, killing two people in the process).[23] Independent observers have difficulty seeing how a privately funded Albanian-language university can threaten the existence of a state, but Macedonian political elites insist that this is indeed a matter of national security, rather than one of culture or education or economics. To take another example, when the self-governing region of Tatarstan in Russia decided to stop using the Cyrillic alphabet for the Tatar language—an alphabet that had been imposed on them during Soviet Communism—Russian parliamentarians declared this to be a threat to national security (Cashaback 2005).

This sort of omnipresent securitization is clearly not inevitable. It reflects a deliberate decision by political elites to play the 'security card', often in a reckless and irresponsible fashion that damages the prospects of improved ethnic relations. The willingness to play this card, and its success as a political strategy, is one of the factors which distinguishes debates about homeland minorities in the East and West.[24] The success of multination federalism in the West is linked to a cross-party consensus not to 'play the security card' when dealing with minority nationalist issues. The health of a democracy depends on the self-restraint of political leaders in playing this card, and the scepticism of citizens when elites do try to play it. In post-communist countries, however, there are many political elites who are willing to play it, and it has proven to be an effective strategy for gaining electoral support.

One way to think of this process is to say that there is a threshold at which the security card gets played. In order to avoid state repression, national minorities need to keep their demands below this threshold, while simultaneously trying to negotiate that threshold upwards.[25] But

---

[23] For the unhappy story of the Albanian university in Tetovo, see Pritchard 2000.

[24] I used to think that the most important distinguishing fact about post-communist countries is precisely that they are post-communist—i.e. they are undergoing economic and political transition. I now think that the most distinctive factor is that they are post-imperial (post-Ottoman, post-Habsburg, or post-Soviet)—i.e. that majority–minority relations are operating in a context of 'minoritized majorities' who have historically been oppressed by their own minorities or the allies of these minorities.

[25] As Waever puts is, the task for minority leaders is 'to turn threats into challenges: to move developments from the sphere of existential fear to one where they could be handled by ordinary means, as politics, economy, culture, and so on' (Waever 1995: 55). In short, the goal is to negotiate limitations on the use of the security card. Or in Waever's terms, the motto for defenders of democracy should be 'less security, more politics!' (56).

where is this threshold? We can list some typical national minority demands in descending order of strength:

1. secessionist violence/terrorism
2. democratic secessionist mobilization
3. territorial autonomy
4. minority-language higher education
5. veto rights
6. collective rights
7. official language status
8. minority-language elementary schools
9. minority-language street signs

In the West, the threshold today is very high—in-between 1 and 2. In effect, minority nationalism only becomes securitized when it involves terrorism, as in Northern Ireland or the Basque Country. So long as it remains peaceful and democratic, then minority nationalism is not securitized, even if it is explicitly aimed at secession. In post-communist countries, by contrast, the threshold today is very low—between 7 and 8. Any claim for territorial autonomy, minority language higher education, collective rights, or official language status triggers the security card. Only very weak claims, such as mother-tongue elementary schools, can safely be left to the normal processes of democratic politics.

This securitization of minority nationalism relates to, and exacerbates, the first problem I mentioned of the weakness of liberal-democratic institutions. Securitization is not only harmful to minorities, but to democracy itself, and to the existence of a peaceful civil society. There seems to be a negative correlation between democratization and minority nationalism. Those post-communist countries without significant minority nationalisms have democratized successfully (Czech Republic, Hungary, Slovenia, Poland); those countries with powerful minority nationalisms are having a more difficult time (Slovakia, Ukraine, Romania, Serbia, Macedonia, Georgia). The minority issue is not the only factor here, but I believe it is an important one.

In an essay first published in 1946, Istvan Bibo provided a thoughtful analysis of this problem. He argued that the experience of nineteenth-century Hungary taught state elites that their minorities might use their democratic freedom to secede. Ever since, states in Eastern and Central Europe have feared the exercise of democratic freedoms by minorities. As a result, they have consistently tried to suppress, dilute, or contain these democratic freedoms, sometimes by embracing fascism or other forms of authoritarianism (i.e. by suppressing everyone's freedom), sometimes by disempowering minorities (i.e. by suppressing the minority's freedom). But in either case, the result is a stunted and fearful form of democracy. As he puts it,

In a paralyzing state of fear which asserts that freedom's progress endangers the interests of the nation, one cannot take full advantage of the benefits offered by democracy. Being a democrat means, primarily, not to be afraid: not to be afraid of those who have different opinions, speak different languages, or belong to other races. The countries of Central and Eastern Europe were afraid because they were not fully developed mature democracies, and they could not become fully developed mature democracies because they were afraid. (Bibo 1991: 42)

I believe that this remains true today. Many post-communist states with minority nationalisms have the shell of liberal democracy, but remain afraid of the full and free exercise of democratic freedoms.

In this respect, the refusal of post-communist countries to make room for an open and democratic debate on the merits of Western best practices is not just the predictable or inevitable result of differences in historical and geo-political circumstances between West and East. It is also due in part to deliberate strategies by political elites to (over)-emphasize the security risks involved, precisely in order to suppress such debates. And it is possible that the best practices strategy would have had more success if post-communist elites had been more cautious in playing the security card. But it would be a mistake to treat the security-based objections to adopting Western best practices of multination federalism as wholly invented by self-interested elites. Multination federalism really does pose greater risks in Eastern Europe than in the West. There are objective differences in the level of human rights protection, in the potential irredentism of homeland minorities, in the presence or absence of regional security organizations, and in the nature of the historic hierarchies and injustices at work. Post-communist political elites may often exaggerate these risks, but the strategy of IOs of publicizing best practices routinely neglects these risks. Publicizing best practices may help diffuse awareness of the logic of liberal multiculturalism, but it is naïve to hope that this logic will be persuasive in contexts where there are credible grounds for viewing ethnic politics as a potential threat to individual and collective security. Given the profound differences in circumstances and history, efforts at publicizing Western best practices without addressing these underlying risk factors were doomed to failure.

From 'Best Practices' to 'Norms' and 'Standards'

It quickly became clear that the strategy of publicizing best practices was not going to be sufficient on its own. Left to their own devices, post-communist states were unlikely to pick up on Western models, and indeed, in many cases, were moving farther away from them, restricting rather than advancing minority rights guarantees.

If European organizations were to make a difference, they needed another strategy with more teeth. Rather than simply offering a set of good practices for post-communist countries to adopt or not as they saw fit, this second strategy involved setting explicit legal or quasi-legal norms and standards that post-communist countries were expected to meet. Adherence to these norms and standards would be monitored by various international bodies, with a range of incentives for those who complied and sanctions for those who did not.

The most important and tangible example of these incentives and sanctions was the decision by the European Union and NATO to make minority rights protection one of the criteria that candidate countries had to meet in order to become members of these organizations.[26] Since most post-communist countries viewed membership in the EU and NATO as pivotal to their future prosperity and security, any recommendations that the West might make regarding minority rights were taken very seriously. As a result, minority rights moved to the centre of post-communist political life, a core component of the process of 're-joining Europe'.

Having made this decision, the next step was to create institutional mechanisms that could monitor how post-communist countries were treating their minorities. Since 1991, various international bodies have been created with the mandate of monitoring the treatment of minorities, and of recommending changes needed to live up to European standards of minority rights. A crucial step here was the formation of the Office

---

[26] Minority rights were included in the so-called 'Copenhagen Criteria' adopted in 1993 for countries wishing to join the EU. See European Council, 'Conclusions of the Presidency, Copenhagen', 21–2 June 1993, DOC SN 180/93, para. 7, available at: <http://www.europa.eu.int/comm/enlargement/intro/criteria.htm>. Minority rights were also included in the criteria the European Commission adopted for the recognition of new states during the breakdown of Yugoslavia (Caplan 2005).

of the High Commission on National Minorities of the Organization for Security and Cooperation in Europe (OSCE-HCNM) in 1993, linked to OSCE mission offices in several post-communist countries. Another important step occurred at the Council of Europe, which set up a number of advisory bodies and reporting mechanisms as part of its Framework Convention on the Protection of National Minorities (FCNM) in 1995.[27] The European Union and NATO did not themselves create new monitoring bodies specifically focused on minority rights,[28] but they have made clear that they support the work of the OSCE-HCNM and the Council of Europe, and expect post-communist countries to cooperate with them, as a condition of accession.

Between 1991 and 1995, then, a rapid consensus developed amongst all the major European organizations that the best approach to influencing the treatment of national minorities in post-communist countries was to establish minimum norms and standards, along with international mechanisms to monitor a country's compliance with them. This compliance would then be one of the bases for decisions about whether a particular country was able to 're-join Europe'.

It was hoped and expected that this approach would be more effective than simply publicizing best practices. But it raises an obvious question: what are these European standards of minority rights? We can identify certain general trends regarding national minorities over the past forty years, of the sort discussed in Chapter 3, and European organizations had their lists of best practices, from consociational power-sharing in Switzerland to bilingualism in Finland to federalization in Spain to special autonomy in South Tyrol or the Aland Islands. But general trends and lists of best practices are not the same as formal standards or agreed-upon principles. European organizations did not yet have any general norms of the form 'all national minorities have the right to X . . . '.

Indeed, one of the most striking aspects of the European experiment with minority rights is that the decision to establish norms and standards was made in 1991 without any clear idea amongst the main actors about what these standards should be, or even how to go about formulating them. Western states differ significantly in the rights they accord to

---

[27] These include the Committee of Experts on Issues Relating to the Protection of National Minorities; the Parliamentary Sub-Committee on the Rights of Minorities; and the Advisory Committee on the Framework Convention for the Protection of National Minorities.

[28] The EU did set up the European Monitoring Centre on Racism and Xenophobia in 1997, but it has focused primarily on immigrant groups (rather than national minorities), and primarily on member-states in the West, not candidate countries in post-communist Europe.

various minorities, in the terms they use to describe different types of minorities, and indeed whether they even acknowledge the existence of 'minorities'. Where then does one look to formulate 'European standards' of minority rights?

Observers with a long memory recalled that this question had been tackled earlier, at the last major period of imperial breakdowns after World War 1, resulting in the minority protection scheme of the League of Nations. A mini-industry has arisen examining that older scheme, and trying to learn lessons from its successes and failures for contemporary European debates (e.g. Kovacs 2003; Cornwall 1996; Sharp 1996; Burns 1996; Fink 2004). However, as we saw in Chapter 2, the minority protection scheme of the League of Nations was ad hoc and particularistic. It involved drafting treaties on a country-specific basis, but only for some countries (usually the defeated countries, or newly independent countries), and only for some minorities in those countries (usually those with a powerful kin-state), while leaving many other minorities in other countries unprotected. It did not attempt to articulate general standards or international norms that all countries would be expected to meet, or that all national minorities would be able to claim, and hence was widely perceived as unprincipled. That indeed was one reason why the idea of minority rights fell out of favour and largely disappeared from the post-war international law context.

As we will see later in the chapter, European organizations have not been able to avoid engaging in their own version of this country-specific ad hoc intervention in defence of particular minorities in particular countries. But in the early 1990s, there was a strong desire to formulate a more principled approach, in the form of pan-European standards. The people charged with drafting these European standards wanted to find a conception of minority rights that expressed the liberal-democratic values that the West hoped and expected post-communist countries to adopt, and that articulated their implications for issues of state–minority relations. These standards were intended to identify what is expected of a 'modern' and 'decent' liberal democracy. However, the drafters also had to ensure that these norms were in fact realistic and achievable in the relatively inauspicious circumstances of many post-communist countries. The whole point, after all, was to 'do something' about the imminent dangers of ethnic conflict in the region.

It was obviously an immense challenge to formulate a set of norms that would simultaneously embody the optimistic hopes and expectations for diffusing a liberal-democratic approach to ethnic diversity while also addressing the pressing fears of destabilizing ethnic violence. Moreover, given the perceived urgency of the situation, the drafters were expected to do this quickly, without time to conduct extensive grass-roots consultation with the various stakeholders, or to conduct systematic social science research into the effectiveness of different types of state–minority policies.

Given the difficulty of the task, and the short time-frame, it is hardly surprising that the resulting norms suffer from serious limitations. Indeed, I believe that the strategy of formulating pan-European legal norms has essentially failed, at least in terms of its original goals. It has failed to coherently combine the long-term goal of diffusing liberal multiculturalism with the short-term need to prevent and resolve potentially destabilizing ethnic conflicts, and ends up serving neither goal well. Whereas the best practices strategy naïvely promoted liberal multiculturalism without attention to the immediate risk factors, the legal norms strategy suffers in some ways from the opposite problem of sacrificing long-term goals on the altar of short-term expediency.

Formulating European Minority Rights Norms: Generic or Targeted?

This fundamental tension between long-term goals and short-term exigencies surfaces throughout the current framework of European norms on minority rights, but one of the clearest examples concerns the question of categories. In any attempt to formulate international norms of minority rights, the first, and in many ways most fateful, step concerns the choice of categories: what kinds of minorities are we trying to protect? The sorts of rights that seem realistic and defensible will largely be determined by the prior question of which types of minorities we have in mind as the intended beneficiaries. And answering this question, it turns out, is much more difficult than one might expect, in part because long-term goals and short-term pressures point in different directions.

As I mentioned in Chapter 1, there are two general strategies for categorizing minority rights. We can formulate 'generic minority rights' that are intended to apply to all ethnocultural minorities, or we can formulate 'targeted minority rights' that are intended to apply to particular types of minorities, such as indigenous peoples, national minorities, immigrants, the Roma/gypsies, and so on.

A clear example of the generic minority rights strategy can be found in the United Nations. As we saw in Chapter 2, the idea of minority rights, while generally rejected after World War II, retained a foothold in the famous 'minorities clause' of Article 27 of the UN's 1966 International Covenant on Civil and Political Rights (ICCPR), which states that:

In those States in which ethnic, religious or linguistic minorities exist, persons belonging to such minorities shall not be denied the right, in community with the other members of their group, to enjoy their own culture, to profess and practise their own religion, or to use their own language.

The generic nature of this clause has only emerged over time. When first adopted in 1966, it was left deliberately unclear whether this Article was truly a generic minority rights provision intended to apply to all ethno-cultural minorities. Various New World countries, for example, insisted that immigrant groups do not count as 'ethnic, religious or linguistic minorities', and hence that the provision only applied to historic minorities in Old World countries created as a result of population transfers or the moving of international boundaries. The Brazilian representative, for example, stated that they 'did not recognise the existence of minorities on the American continent', since 'the mere coexistence of different groups in a territory under the jurisdiction of a single State did not make them minorities in the legal sense. A minority resulted from conflict of some length between nations, or from the transfer of a territory from the jurisdiction of one State to that of another' (quoted in Thornberry 1991: 154). Similarly, many African states involved in the drafting of Article 27, such as Liberia, Guinea, Mali, Ghana, insisted that the provision didn't apply to them either. On this view, the concept of 'minorities' only applies to European-style 'national minorities', and not to either New World or Third World states. And indeed the main push for Article 27 came from various European states who retained their long-standing concern about the 'minority issue' in Europe, and who wanted to resurrect some version of the old League of Nations minority protection scheme.[29] In 1966, therefore, the range of groups covered by Article 27 was unclear, to say the least.

---

[29] Even today, many African countries deny that they contain 'minorities'. In Senegal's report to the UN under the ICCPR, for example, it claims: 'On account of the cultural and social intermingling which is a feature of the national community, there are no minorities in Senegal' (UN Doc. CCPR/C/103/Add.1, 22 November 1996, para. 12). See also Zambia's report (UN Doc. CRC/C/11/Add.25, 19 November 2002, para. 470), and the discussion in Lennox 2006.

But, over time, the Article has been interpreted by the UN's Human Rights Committee as applying to all ethnocultural minorities, no matter how large or small, recent or historic, territorially concentrated or dispersed. Indeed, the Committee has recently declared that Article 27 applies even to visitors within a country![30] Article 27, in other words, can be seen as a truly *universal* cultural right—a right that can be claimed by any individual, and carried with her as she moves around the world.

But just for this reason, it suffers from inevitable limitations. If we try to identify specific cultural rights that apply to all groups, no matter how large or small, new or old, concentrated or dispersed, it is difficult to think of many substantive examples. And indeed, for a long period of time, the Article 27 'right to enjoy one's culture' was understood primarily as a guarantee of negative rights of non-interference, rather than positive rights to assistance, funding, autonomy, or official language status. In effect, it simply reaffirmed that members of minorities must be free to exercise their standard civil liberties—i.e. rights of freedom of speech, association, assembly, and conscience.

Understood in this way, the generic rights approach reflected in Article 27 was widely seen as insufficient to deal with the challenges of ethnic conflict in post-communist Europe. The minimal guarantees of civil liberties, while vital, are inadequate to address the issues underlying the potentially violent and destabilizing ethnic conflicts in post-communist Europe. These conflicts centre on various positive claims, such as the right to use a minority language in courts or local administration; the funding of minority schools, universities, and media; the extent of local or regional autonomy; the guaranteeing of political representation for minorities; or the prohibition on settlement policies designed to swamp minorities in their historic homelands with settlers from the dominant group. Article 27 has nothing to say about such claims.[31] It protects certain civil rights relating to cultural expression, but it does not prohibit states from rescinding funding to minority-language schools and universities, abolishing local autonomy, gerrymandering electoral rules or constituency boundaries, or encouraging settlers to swamp minority

---

[30] Human Rights Committee, General Comment No. 23, 'Rights of Minorities (Article 27)', adopted 8 April 1994, para. 5.1 and 5.2 ('Thus migrant workers or even visitors in a State party constituting such minorities are entitled not to be denied the exercise of these rights'). See also Bengoa 2000.

[31] Over the years since 1966, the UN Human Rights Committee has attempted to reinterpret the Article so as to include certain positive rights, particularly for indigenous peoples, but it has not been reinterpreted in a way that addresses the positive claims underlying the conflicts in post-communist Europe.

homelands. None of these policies, which can be catastrophic for national minorities, and which often lead to violent conflict, violate the rights to cultural expression and association protected in Article 27.[32] If European standards were to be useful in resolving such conflicts, they would have to address claims for positive minority rights.

The problem here is not simply the particular wording of Article 27; it is inherent in the very strategy of relying exclusively on generic minority rights. The commitment to identifying generic cultural rights limits the sorts of minority rights that can be recognized. In particular, it precludes claims that flow from facts of historic settlement or territorial concentration. Since Article 27 articulates a universal and portable cultural right that applies to all individuals, even migrants and visitors, it does not articulate rights that are tied to the fact that a group is living in (what it views as) its historic homeland. Yet it is precisely claims relating to residence in a historic homeland that are at stake in all of the violent ethnic conflicts in post-communist Europe—for example, in Bosnia, Kosovo, Macedonia, Georgia, Chechnya, Ngorno-Karabakh. Indeed, homeland claims are at the heart of most violent ethnic conflicts in the West as well (e.g. the Basque Country, Cyprus, Corsica, Northern Ireland). In all of these cases, minorities claim the right to govern themselves in what they view as their historic homeland, including the right to use their language in public institutions within their traditional territory, and to have their language, history, and culture celebrated in the public sphere (e.g. in the naming of streets, the choice of holidays, and state symbols). None of these claims can plausibly be seen as universal or portable—they only apply to particular sorts of minorities with a particular sort of history and territory. In short, these are all cases of ethno*national* (or ethnonationalist) conflict, revolving around competing claims to nationhood and national territory.

If European standards were to be useful in resolving the pressing conflicts in post-communist Europe, they would need to go beyond generic minority rights and articulate *targeted* minority rights, focused on the specific types of ethnonational groups involved in these conflicts. Moreover, moving towards a more targeted approach could also help clarify and diffuse the logic of liberal multiculturalism. As we saw in Chapter 3, liberal multiculturalism in the West operates in a group-differentiated way: immigrants, national minorities, and indigenous peoples have all been

---

[32] For a more detailed elaboration of the way that traditional civil rights principles fail to protect national minorities from grave injustice, see Kymlicka 2001, chap. 4.

moving along different paths in terms of their minority rights. Insofar as European norms were intended to help diffuse the logic or ethos of liberal multiculturalism, shifting to a more targeted approach would help signal the legitimacy of such group-differentiated minority rights.

As a result, the new European norms that have emerged since 1990 are all examples of targeted minority rights—in particular, they are targeted at so-called 'national' minorities. Whereas Article 27 lumps together 'national, ethnic, religious and linguistic' minorities, the Council of Europe's Framework Convention refers only to 'national minorities'. Similarly, the OSCE's office is called the High Commissioner on National Minorities. While there is no universally agreed-upon definition of 'national minorities', the term has a long history in European diplomacy, where it has referred to what I have been calling substate national groups. These historically settled homeland groups are, in effect, the losers in the process of European state formation, either because they ended up without a state of their own ('stateless nations' such as the Basques or Chechens), or ended up on the wrong side of the border, cut off from their co-ethnics in a neighbouring kin-state ('kin-state minorities' such as the ethnic Germans in Italy, or ethnic Hungarians in Romania).

As we've seen, these are the sorts of groups involved in the violent and destabilizing ethnic conflicts that generated the call for European norms in the first place, and it was appropriate therefore to focus on them in the first instance when formulating targeted norms. Most European countries have explicitly stated that immigrant groups are not national minorities, and some have also excluded the Roma from the category of national minority, on the grounds that they are a non-territorial minority.[33] These exclusions are increasingly contested, for reasons I explain below, with the result that the traditional understanding of national minority co-exists in European debates alongside newer and broader definitions that are less tied to history and territory. But originally at least, European organizations were targeting their efforts at historically settled substate national minorities.[34]

---

[33] These limitations are listed in the reservations that countries file when ratifying the Convention. A full list can be found in Council of Europe 2005: 77–82.

[34] This is clear from the 'Explanatory Note' accompanying the Framework Convention which states that the 'decisive step' toward the Convention was taken at the 1993 Vienna Summit where 'it was agreed that the national minorities which the upheavals of history have established in Europe had to be protected and respected as a contribution to peace and stability' (para. 5). However, as the Explanatory Note goes on to explain, it was not possible to build this understanding into the definition of the term national minority: 'it was decided to adopt a pragmatic approach, based on the recognition that at this stage, it is impossible

This commitment to developing targeted norms for national minorities was courageous. No other international body has attempted to formulate such norms. Several international organizations have developed targeted rights for other types of minority groups. For example, the United Nations, the International Labour Organization, and the Organization of American States have all developed targeted norms regarding indigenous peoples, as we will see in Chapter 7. Some of these organizations have also formulated norms targeted at migrants.[35] However, no one had previously attempted to formulate international norms directed at national minorities.

This gap is puzzling. If one thinks about the sorts of state–minority relations with the greatest potential for large-scale harm, injustice, and violence, one could argue that they typically involve national minorities. While both indigenous peoples and migrants are vulnerable groups in need of international protection, most of the violent and destabilizing ethnic conflict around the world involves conflicts between states and homeland ethnonationalist groups. This is true not just of Western and Eastern Europe, as we've seen, but also of Asia, the Middle East, and Africa (e.g. Kashmir, Tamil Eelam, Aceh, Kurdistan, Tigray, Oromo, Ogoni, etc.). As Walker Connor notes, the phenomenon of minority nationalism is a truly universal one. The countries affected by it

are to be found in Africa (for example, Ethiopia), Asia (Sri Lanka), Eastern Europe (Romania), Western Europe (France), North America (Guatemala), South America (Guyana), and Oceania (New Zealand). The list includes countries that are old (United Kingdom) as well as new (Bangladesh), large (Indonesia) as well as small (Fiji), rich (Canada) as well as poor (Pakistan), authoritarian (Sudan) as well as democratic (Belgium), Marxist-Leninist (China) as well as militantly anti-Marxist (Turkey). The list also includes countries which are Buddhist (Burma), Christian (Spain), Moslem (Iran), Hindu (India), and Judaic (Israel). (Connor 1999: 163–4).

In this light, developing international norms that address the difficult challenges raised by such ethnonational groups is a central task for the theory and practice of minority rights around the world. The European experiment in defining these norms, therefore, is of pivotal significance. And the difficulties this experiment has encountered contain important lessons for the more general project of developing international norms.

to arrive at a definition [of national minorities] capable of mustering general support of all Council of Europe member States'. (para 12). See also Klebes 1995.

[35] e.g. the UN's Convention on the Protection of the Rights of All Migrant Workers, 1990, or the 1977 European Convention on the Legal Status of Migrant Workers.

Formulating the Rights of 'National Minorities'

The challenge facing European organizations, then, was to formulate norms that can provide a principled basis for responding to the claims of ethnonational groups, in a way that both reflects distinctively liberal-democratic values and that provides effective guidance for dealing with the risks of destabilizing ethnic conflict.

Given the relatively successful experience of Western democracies with multination federalism, and the various examples of best practices involving territorial autonomy and official language status, the initial impulse of many commentators was to try to formulate a principle of *self-government* for national minorities. As we've seen, if there is such a thing as a 'European standard' for dealing with mobilized national minorities in the West, some form of internal autonomy would appear to be it.

Attempting to formulate such a norm would obviously go well beyond the meagre provisions of Article 27, but it would not be entirely unprecedented in international law. There is a long-standing principle in international law that all 'peoples' have a right to 'self-determination', and a right to internal autonomy could be seen as an extension or application of this principle. The principle of self-determination is affirmed in the founding Charter of the United Nations, and is reaffirmed in Article 1 of the 1966 International Covenant on Civil and Political Rights.[36] It is therefore a long-standing norm within international law, although it has not traditionally been applied to national minorities. According to some commentators, however, a suitably revised interpretation of the principle of self-determination could and should be applied to national minorities, and would provide a principled basis for addressing their claims.

It is generally accepted that the right to self-determination in Article 1 cannot simply be extended in an unqualified form to national minorities, since it is typically understood to include the right to form one's own state. Precisely for this reason, its scope has been drastically restricted in international law. It has been limited by what is called

[36] Article 1: 'All peoples have the right of self-determination. By virtue of that right they freely determine their political status and freely pursue their economic, social and cultural development.' Originally, the UN Charter only referred to a 'principle' of self-determination, not a 'right'. The transformation into a right occurred in Resolution 1514 (XV) of 1960, and Resolution 2625 (XXV) of 1970. There is a huge literature on the interpretation of the right of self-determination in international law, including Bayefsky 2000; Castellino 2000; Knop 2002; Alston 2001; Brölmann et al 1993; Cassese 1995; Danspeckgruber and Watts 1997; Crawford 1988; McCorquodale 2000; Musgrave 1997; Tierney 2000; Tomuschat 1993; Ghanea and Xanthaki 2005—to mention just book-length treatments.

the 'salt-water thesis'. Although the Article says that *'all* peoples' have the right of self-determination, in fact the only 'peoples' who have been able to assert this right are those subject to colonization from overseas. National minorities within a territorially contiguous state have not been recognized as separate 'peoples' with their own right of self-determination, no matter how culturally or historically distinct they have been. Groups like the Scots or Kurds may think of themselves as distinct 'peoples', and most historians and social scientists may accept this label, but the international community has not recognized them as such, for fear that this would entail granting them a right to form an independent state.

However, if we adopt a more modest interpretation of the right to self-determination, one that is consistent with the territorial integrity of states, it may be possible to extend its scope to include national minorities. This is the goal of various models of 'internal self-determination'. According to these models, national minorities, as distinct 'peoples' or 'nations' living in their historic homelands, have the right to some form of self-determination within the boundaries of the larger state, typically through some form of territorial autonomy. Many commentators have argued that it is morally arbitrary to accord self-determination to overseas peoples while denying it to internal peoples. Both have a sense of distinct nationhood and a desire for self-government, and both have typically been subject to conquest, involuntary incorporation, and historic discrimination. A morally consistent approach to self-determination would, therefore, recognize its applicability to internal national minorities (and indigenous peoples), at least in the form of a right to territorial autonomy (e.g. Moore 2001).

This approach not only has the virtue of promoting greater moral consistency in international law, but also reflects the actual practice of most Western democracies. Throughout the early 1990s, therefore, many intellectuals and political organizations representing national minorities pushed for international recognition of a right to internal self-determination. And, for a brief period from 1990 to 1993, there was some indication that this campaign might be successful. As we saw earlier, the very first statement by a European organization on minority rights after the collapse of Communism—the OSCE Copenhagen Declaration of 1990—explicitly endorsed territorial autonomy. An even stronger endorsement of territorial autonomy came in 1991, when the European Commission declared that Yugoslav republics seeking independence must establish a 'special status' for regions where national minorities form a local majority, modeled on the South Tyrol example.[37] This was, in part, an attempt to find a satisfactory resolution to the specific challenges raised by the Serbian minority in Croatia, but it is significant that the European Commission formulated its response in the form of a more general principle endorsing territorial autonomy for national minorities in new states seeking recognition by the EU.

This principle was re-affirmed and generalized even further in 1993 in Recommendation 1201 of the Council of Europe's Parliamentary Assembly. It contains a clause (Article 11) stating that

In the regions where they are a majority, the persons belonging to a national minority shall have the right to have at their disposal appropriate local or autonomous authorities or to have a special status, matching this specific historical and territorial situation and in accordance with the domestic legislation of the State.

Unlike the 1990 OSCE Copenhagen declaration, this 1993 Parliamentary Recommendation recognizes territorial autonomy as a 'right', not just as a good practice, and unlike the 1991 European Commission guidelines, applies it to European states generally, not just to new states seeking recognition.

In short, between 1990 and 1993, the three main European organizations had all endorsed territorial autonomy, either as a best practice (OSCE in 1990), as a condition for recognizing the independence of new states (European Commission in 1991), or as a proposed right under international law (Council of Europe Parliamentary Assembly in 1993).

Many national minority organizations in post-communist Europe viewed these developments as a great victory. Ethnic Hungarian organizations in particular viewed it as evidence that Europe would support their claims for territorial autonomy in Slovakia, Romania, and Serbia. They assumed that Recommendation 1201 would play a central role in the Council of Europe's Framework Convention for the Protection of National Minorities which was being drafted at the same time, and that complying with this Recommendation would be required for candidate countries to join the EU.

This expectation was bolstered by developments at the United Nations, where there was also talk about enshrining a right to self-government.

---

[37] For a detailed discussion of these standards, and their ultimate demise, see Caplan 2005, Libal 1997. The guidelines were rendered obsolete when Germany unilaterally recognized Croatia and Slovenia before the standards were met

In 1994, for example, Liechtenstein submitted to the UN's General Assembly a 'Draft Convention on Self-Determination through Self-Administration', which recognized a right of internal autonomy for all 'peoples', where peoples were explicitly defined to include substate homeland minorities.[38] Article 2 of this Draft Convention, for example, states

All peoples have the right of self-determination. Within the framework of that right, each State party to the present Convention shall respect the aspirations of all communities within its territory to an appropriate degree of self-administration and shall secure that degree of self-administration to them.

The Liechtenstein Draft Convention did not advance very far at the UN, but it is evidence of how widespread ideas of internal self-determination were at the time. Moreover, these ideas were also appearing in another closely related context of international law: namely, the rights of indigenous peoples. As we'll see in the next chapter, the UN's 1993 Draft Declaration on the Rights of Indigenous Peoples has several articles affirming the principle of internal self-determination. The most explicit is Article 3, which states that 'Indigenous peoples have the right of self-determination. By virtue of that right, they freely determine their political status and freely pursue their economic, social and cultural development'. This Draft Declaration is still a draft, and hence not yet international law. But the basic idea that indigenous peoples have a right to internal self-determination is now widely endorsed throughout the international community, and is reflected in other recent international declarations on indigenous rights, including by the Organization of American States and the International Labour Organization.[39]

This shows that there is no inherent reason why international law cannot accept the idea of internal self-determination. The status of national minorities in post-communist Europe is not identical to that of indigenous peoples in the Americas or Asia. But there are some important similarities in both history and aspirations, and many of the

[38] For the draft resolution submitted to the General Assembly, see UN A/C.3/48/L.17. The Draft Convention itself is reprinted as an appendix in Danspeckgruber 2002: 382–93, together with legal commentaries. See also the discussion in Welhengama 1998. When the Draft Convention was rebuffed at the UN, the Prince of Liechtenstein set up the Liechtenstein Institute on Self-Determination at Princeton University, in the hope that it would generate greater public debate and academic analysis of the issues involved. See <http://www.princeton.edu/lisd/>.

[39] See the discussion in Chapter 2, n. 7, regarding the explicit or implicit recognition of a right of self-determination for indigenous peoples by various UN bodies, including HRC, UNESCO, CERD, UNDP, etc.

standard arguments for recognizing a right of internal self-determination for indigenous peoples also apply to national minorities.[40] (I will return to the similarities and differences between national minorities and indigenous peoples in the next chapter.)

So there were several reasons why national minorities in post-communist states could reasonably hope that some form of internal self-government would be codified as part of the 'European standards' for the treatment of national minorities. Internal self-government is in fact the standard practice within Western Europe today; it has been recognized as a valid principle in international law with respect to indigenous peoples; it can be seen as a more consistent application of the idea of the self-determination of peoples, avoiding the arbitrariness of the traditional 'salt-water' interpretation; and it was endorsed in important statements by European organizations, including the OSCE in 1990, the European Commission in 1991, and the Council of Europe Parliamentary Assembly in 1993. There was much talk of an 'emerging right to autonomy', in both Europe and the UN. Indeed, many academic commentators argued that formulating such a right would only make explicit what was already implicit or emerging in international law.[41]

However, as it turns out, the Parliamentary Assembly's Recommendation 1201 reflects the high-water mark of support for territorial autonomy within European organizations. Since then, there has been a marked movement away from it. The Framework Convention, adopted just two years after Recommendation 1201, decisively rejected the Parliamentary Assembly's advice, and avoided any reference to territorial autonomy. Not only is territorial autonomy not recognized as a 'right', it is not even mentioned as a recommended practice. Nor does territorial autonomy appear in any subsequent declaration or recommendation of European organizations, such as the series of Hague, Oslo, and Lund Recommendations

[40] Aukerman 2000. Indeed, the most influential text on the international law on indigenous rights accepts that other national groups should also be able to claim rights to internal self-determination (see Anaya 1996, and the discussion in Kymlicka 2001, chap. 6). It's worth noting that organizations representing one national minority in Eastern Europe—namely, the Crimean Tatars—have explicitly defined themselves as an 'indigenous people' for the purposes of international law.

[41] On the idea of an emerging right of autonomy, see Eide 1993; Welhengama 1998, 2000; Hannum 1990; Sisk 1996; Lewis-Anthony 1998; Hannikainen 1998; Heintz 1998; and the various essays in Skurbaty 2005 and Suksi 1998. In the words of Patrick Thornberry, 'a preliminary rush to judgement suggests that autonomy is hardly there in the minority rights text, but close examination discovers strands and whispers of autonomy or something like it' (Thornberry 1998: 123; cf. Thornberry 1995: 42–3).

adopted by the OSCE from 1996 to 1999,[42] or the new constitution of the European Union.[43] And the European Commission for Democracy through Law has ruled that national minorities do not have rights of self-determination, even in the form of internal self-determination (European Commission for Democracy through Law 1996). For all intents and purposes, ideas of internal self-determination have disappeared from the debate about 'European standards' on minority rights (Cilevics 2005).

There are a number of reasons for this. For one thing, there was strong opposition to the idea of entrenching a right to territorial autonomy for national minorities *in the West*, and to the idea that there would be international monitoring of how Western states treated their minorities. France, Greece, and Turkey have traditionally opposed the very idea of self-government rights for national minorities, and indeed deny the very existence of national minorities (Dimitras 2004). And even those Western countries that accord autonomy to their substate national groups do not necessarily want *their* laws and policies regarding national minorities subject to international monitoring. This is true, for example, of Switzerland and the United States (Chandler 1999: 66–8; Ford 1999: 49). The treatment of national minorities in various Western countries remains a politically sensitive topic, and many countries do not want their majority–minority settlements, often the result of long and painful negotiation processes, re-opened by international monitoring agencies. In short, while they were willing to insist that post-communist states be monitored for their treatment of minorities, Western democracies did not want their own treatment of national minorities examined.[44]

This resistance from within the West might have been sufficient to scupper any attempt to formulate a right to self-government for national minorities. But the more immediate difficulty was the growing

---

[42] Hague Recommendations on Education Rights of National Minorities (1996); Oslo Recommendations on Linguistic Rights of National Minorities (1998); Lund Recommendations on Effective Participation of National Minorities (1999).

[43] The European Free Alliance, a coalition of minority nationalist parties from various regions of Western Europe (e.g. Catalonia, Scotland, Flanders, South Tyrol), proposed that the EU Constitution contain a clause that recognized 'the right of self-government of all those territorial entities in the Union whose citizens have a strong and shared sense of national, linguistic or regional identity'. The proposal was never seriously debated (<http://www.greens-efa.org>). For the failed efforts to strengthen the recognition of 'stateless nations' in the European Constitution, see McCormick 2004.

[44] This is reflected in the fact that while countries seeking accession to the EU are expected to ratify the Framework Convention, and hence open up their minority policies to international monitoring and evaluation, those countries that are already member-states of the EU are not required to do so. Needless to say, this double-standard is a source of great resentment amongst post-communist countries.

recognition by European organizations that it was unrealistic to impose such a norm of self-government in the post-communist region. Any idea of minority self-government was bitterly opposed by post-communist countries as a threat to their very existence. As a result, there was virtually no chance of gaining a domestic consensus within post-communist countries in favour of autonomy for substate national groups, even if adopting it had been made a precondition for 're-joining Europe'. Even the powerful incentive of joining the EU and NATO would not have been sufficient to generate popular support for a model that was widely seen as a threat to both geo-political security and to individual security, and a perpetuation of historic wrongs. Any attempt by Western organizations to push such models would have required maximum pressure, and would have made relations between East and West much more conflictual and costly. Indeed, any attempt to impose territorial autonomy might well have generated a backlash against pro-European reform forces and played into the hands of authoritarian forces who were resisting democratization and liberalization. To have insisted that robust minority rights are an inherent part of the process of democratization and European integration might have simply eroded popular support for that process.

Given these obstacles, it is not surprising that efforts to codify a right to autonomy or internal self-determination for national minorities have failed. While the international community has shown some willingness to consider this idea in the case of indigenous peoples, for reasons discussed in the next chapter, internal self-determination has proven too controversial in the case of European national minorities. As the OSCE High Commissioner on National Minorities noted, claims to territorial autonomy meet 'maximal resistance' on the part of states in the post-communist region. Hence, in the High Commissioner's judgement, it was more 'pragmatic' to focus on modest forms of minority rights (van der Stoel 1999: 111; cf. Klebes 1995).

Not everyone agreed with this hasty retreat from the commitment to self-government. Some commentators viewed it as premature, and as pandering to post-communist elites who were inventing or exaggerating security fears for their own self-interested reasons. Insofar as there were legitimate concerns about autonomy, it was argued, they could be addressed. For example, if there were legitimate worries about human rights, they could be addressed by entrenching stronger human rights mechanisms into any agreement for autonomy, including appeal to the European Court of Human Rights. And if there were legitimate worries about the potentially destabilizing links between irredentist minorities and their kin-states, these could be addressed by building guarantees of the territorial integrity of states into any agreement on autonomy, and by insisting that both minorities and kin-states renounce any irredentist ambitions. There was talk, for example, of including a loyalty clause in minority rights provisions, in which minorities affirmed their loyalty to their own state over any kin-state. There was also the suggestion that any outstanding territorial disputes with neighbouring kin-states should be resolved before autonomy regimes were introduced.[45] The prospect of eventual inclusion in the EU or NATO was yet another factor that could be invoked to reduce security fears. In this way, it was hoped that any legitimate fears about human rights and geo-political security could be addressed, and that any remaining opposition to autonomy from scare-mongering political elites could be ignored or marginalized.

In the turbulent conditions of the transition from Communism in the 1990s, however, most people recognized that these 'paper guarantees' of human rights and territorial integrity were essentially unenforceable. The international community's bitter experience in Bosnia and Kosovo showed that even when European organizations were present in force on the ground, they were often unable to effectively protect human rights, or to prevent groups from seizing control over territory. Nor had the international community been able to prevent some states from deliberately encouraging rebellion in other states. (It was widely believed, for example, that Russia was supporting secessionist or irredentist movements in Georgia and Moldova.)

While European organizations were often exasperated by the tendency of post-communist elites to continually play the security card in relation to all minority rights issues, there was a broad consensus that these security fears were sometimes justified. European organizations came to accept that some of the key facilitating conditions for adopting liberal multiculturalism were absent, and the resistance to autonomy in post-communist states wasn't just a matter of pre-modern prejudice or intolerance, but was rooted in difficult geo-political conditions. This view was strengthened by a series of academic writings that expressed scepticism about the appropriateness of adopting Western models of

---

[45] Indeed, the EU did make the resolving of all border disputes a condition of accession, as a way of trying to reduce irredentist worries. The EU also encouraged states to sign bilateral friendship and cooperation treaties with all of their neighbouring states acknowledging the mutual acceptance of borders. On the role of bilateral treaties as a tool of minority protection, see Bloed and van Dijk 1999; Gal 1999.

multination federalism in post-communist Europe (e.g. Snyder 2000; Brubaker 1996; Wimmer 2003; Liebich 1995; Dorff 1994; Offe 1993, 1998; Roeder 2004; Leff 1999; Bunce 1999; Kolsto 2001; Cornell 2002; Deets and Stroschein 2005).

Insofar as European organizations could not provide effective guarantees against these security risks, it was difficult to justify the claim that adopting autonomy for national minorities should be seen as part and parcel of democratization, or as a precondition of rejoining Europe. Indeed, there were credible fears that enshrining a right to autonomy would be positively harmful to democratic prospects in the region, encouraging minorities and kin-states to bypass democratic procedures. Armed with such an internationally recognized right, national minorities might not only redouble their peaceful struggles for autonomy, but might be emboldened to simply seize territory in the name of claiming their 'rights'. And kin-states might be more likely to intervene in neighbouring states in the name of upholding 'European standards'.

As a result, European organizations have not only backed away from formulating territorial autonomy as a legal norm, they have also, in many cases, stopped recommending it as a best practice. The OSCE High Commissioner, in particular, has said that territorial autonomy should be viewed not as a best practice but as a last resort, and has discouraged various minorities from advancing autonomy demands on the grounds that such demands are destabilizing under existing conditions of geo-political insecurity. Far from imposing self-government on post-communist Europe, some European organizations are now actively discouraging it.[46]

Not surprisingly, then, when European standards of minority rights were finally codified, they dropped all reference to self-government or autonomy, and reverted to a much weaker set of norms. Indeed, the Council of Europe's Framework Convention and the OSCE's Recommendations are essentially updated versions of the old 'right to enjoy one's culture' approach. They do move beyond Article 27 by explicitly including certain modest positive rights, such as the right to spell one's surname in accordance with one's own language, and the right to submit documents to public authorities in a minority language. These changes are significant, but they remain essentially variations on the idea of a 'right to enjoy one's culture'.

[46] This is particularly true in relation to the Hungarian minorities in Romania and Slovakia, who were subject to international pressure to abandon claims for autonomy (Schwellnus 2005: 15; Bessenyey-Williams 2002).

As such, they do not articulate any principles or models for how liberal democracies should deal with the distinctive characteristics and aspirations of national minorities—that is, their sense of nationhood and claims to a national homeland. As we've seen, what such groups typically seek is not just the right as individuals to join with other individuals in enacting particular cultural practices, but the right as a national community to govern themselves in their homeland, and to use their self-government powers to express and celebrate their language, history, and culture in public space and public institutions. Both the Framework Convention and the OSCE Recommendations are silent on how such claims should be addressed. They do not discuss how to resolve (often-competing) claims relating to territory and self-government, or how to assign official language status. They neither endorse the models of multination federalism developed in the West, nor offer any alternative to these models. They simply sidestep any attempt to formulate principles for resolving these conflicts. Not surprisingly, they are widely criticized by minority leaders and commentators as 'paternalism and tokenism' (Wheatley 1997: 40).[47]

In the end, then, the long-term goal of promoting and diffusing a distinctly liberal-democratic model of multiculturalism for national minorities was abandoned in response to the short-term exigencies of maintaining stability in the process of democratic transition in post-communist countries. This retreat from a right to autonomy was understandable under the circumstances, and probably even inevitable.[48] It has, however, generated a number of dilemmas. The existing framework of minority rights norms in Europe is both politically ineffective and conceptually

[47] For example, these norms often allow minorities to submit documents to public authorities in their language, but don't require that they get an answer in their own language. More generally, they do not prevent states from centralizing power in such a way that all decisions are made in forums controlled by the dominant national group. States can continue to organize higher education, professional accreditation, and political offices so that members of minorities must either linguistically assimilate in order to achieve professional success and political power, or migrate to their kin-state. (This is often referred to as the 'decapitation' of minority groups: forcing potential elites from minority communities to leave their community to achieve higher education or professional success.)

[48] I say 'probably' inevitable, because in principle one could have imagined a more complex and creative form of legal drafting that attempted to distinguish long-term goals from short-term requirements, and maintained autonomy as a long-term goal. One could even imagine a model of international minority rights norms that involved a sequenced set of rights, in which minorities can only claim autonomy after they have first shown that they can exercise weaker minority rights in a responsible way. This indeed is the way the Liechtenstein Draft Convention discussed earlier is formulated: minorities start with Article 27-type rights to enjoy their culture, then move on to non-territorial forms of autonomy, and then to territorial autonomy, but only if they meet various benchmarks of democracy and human rights along the way.

unstable, and there are hard choices to be made about where to go from here.

The existing norms are ineffective because they do not solve the problems they were intended to address. Recall that the original point of developing these norms was to deal with violent ethnic conflicts in post-communist Europe, such as in Kosovo, Bosnia, Croatia, Macedonia, Georgia, Azerbaijan, Moldova, and Chechnya. None of these conflicts revolved around the right of individuals to join with others to enjoy their culture. The violation of such rights was not the cause of violent conflict, and respect for such rights would not resolve the conflicts. The same is true about the other major cases where European organizations feared potential violence, such as the Hungarian minorities in Romania and Slovakia, or the Russian minorities in former Soviet republics.

In all of these cases, the issues in dispute are not covered by the FCNM or the OSCE Recommendations. The conflicts in these cases involve large, territorially concentrated groups who have manifested the capacity and the aspiration to govern themselves and to administer their own public institutions in their own language, and who typically have possessed some form of self-government and official language status in the past. They have mobilized for territorial autonomy, official language status, minority-language universities, and consociational power-sharing. None of these groups is satisfied with the meagre rights guaranteed by the FCNM and OSCE Recommendations.[49]

The fact that national minorities in post-communist countries are not satisfied with the rights provided under existing European norms is sometimes taken as evidence of the illiberalism of their political culture, or the radicalism of their leadership. But it's worth noting that no sizeable politically mobilized national minority in the West would be satisfied either. No one can seriously suppose that national minorities in Catalonia, Flanders, Quebec, Berne, South Tyrol, Aland Islands, or Puerto Rico would be satisfied with minority elementary schools but not mother-tongue universities, or bilingual street signs but not official language status, or local administration but not regional autonomy.

This isn't to say that there are no contexts in post-communist Europe where current FCNM or OSCE norms provide a realistic basis for state–minority relations. I think they work well in those countries which

---

[49] Some commentators have hoped that the FCNM can indirectly be used to support stronger claims to autonomy or power-sharing, through its commitment to 'effective participation'. I discuss this argument below.

are essentially ethnically homogenous—for example, where the dominant group forms 90 to 95 per cent of the population—and where the remaining ethnic groups are small, dispersed, and already on the road to assimilation. This is the situation, for example, in the Czech Republic, Slovenia, and Hungary. None of the minorities in these countries is capable of exercising regional autonomy, or of sustaining a high degree of institutional completeness (e.g. of sustaining their own universities), and most already show high levels of linguistic assimilation. For these groups, the FCNM/OSCE norms provide all that they could ask for. They allow such small and half-assimilated minorities to negotiate their integration into the dominant society with a certain amount of dignity and security. Similarly, the FCNM/OSCE norms will likely be satisfactory to small, dispersed, and partly assimilated minorities in other post-communist countries, such as the Vlach in Macedonia, or the Armenians in Romania.

The problem is that these minorities were not (and are not) the ones involved in serious ethnic conflict. The problem of ethnic violence and potentially destabilizing ethnic conflict in post-communist Europe is almost exclusively confined to groups that are capable of exercising self-government and of sustaining their own public institutions, and which therefore contest with the state for control over public institutions.[50] And for these groups, the FCNM and OSCE norms are largely irrelevant. If the goal is to effectively deal with the problem of potentially destabilizing ethnic conflict, then we need norms that actually address the source of these conflicts. And any norms that start from an Article 27-style 'right to enjoy one's culture' are unlikely to do that.[51]

As I said earlier, this ineffectiveness may be inevitable. The question of how to deal with destabilizing ethnonationalist conflicts may simply be too tough a nut to crack in terms of legal principles. Perhaps the only realistic approach to these conflicts is through ad hoc

[50] One possible exception to this generalization is the Roma. Some commentators speculate that issues relating to the Roma could become sources of violence and instability, even though the Roma have not shown an interest in territorial autonomy or in creating their own separate public institutions. I will return to the Roma case below.

[51] There is no conceptual or philosophical reason why a right to enjoy one's culture can't be interpreted in such a robust way as to support claims to territorial autonomy or official language status. Indeed, this is precisely what various 'liberal nationalist' political theorists have done in their writings. The idea of a right to culture is invoked by writers like Yael Tamir and Joseph Raz as the basis for their defence of a right to national self-determination (Tamir 1993; Margalit and Raz 1990). But, politically speaking, there is no chance that such a 'nationalist' reading of a right to culture will be adopted in international law. On the contrary, the Article 27 right to enjoy one's culture has always been understand precisely as an alternative to the Article 1 right of self-determination.

case-specific interventions, rather than through attempting to formulate general norms. And indeed, as I will discuss below, this is precisely what European organizations have ended up relying on in several cases.

However, even if we abandon the goal of formulating effective legal norms for ethnonationalist conflicts, there is another, deeper, problem with the current system of European minority rights norms—namely, they are conceptually unstable. There is a mismatch between the targeted form of the rights and their generic content. Existing norms target the category of national minorities, but then recognize only generic minority rights of the sort recognized in the universal Article 27. Why should generic minority rights to enjoy one's culture only be guaranteed to one type of group? The initial goal was to identify principles for dealing with a particular type of homeland group characterized by its historic settlement and territorial concentration. But since the actual rights that were codified in the FCNM and OSCE Recommendations do not recognize any rights arising from historic settlement and territorial concentration,[52] there is no obvious reason why they shouldn't apply to non-territorial groups like the Roma, or indeed to immigrant groups as well. Surely generic minority rights should be protected generically?

And indeed we can see a movement within both the Council of Europe and the OSCE to enable a wider range of groups to benefit from existing standards. The main strategy for broadening the class of eligible groups is to simply redefine the term 'national minorities' so that it becomes essentially an umbrella term for all ethnocultural groups, regardless of their historic presence in a state or degree of territorial concentration. The older understanding of 'national minorities' as one type of group amongst others, distinct from indigenous peoples, the Roma, and immigrant groups, is being replaced with a much broader understanding of national minorities which encompasses all of these different types of ethnocultural groups.

For example, the Advisory Committee that monitors the Framework Convention has criticized Denmark's claim that indigenous peoples fall

---

[52] There are three places in the FCNM where reference is made to historic settlement. Articles 10(2), 11(3) and 14(2) refer to 'areas traditionally inhabited by substantial numbers of persons belonging to national minorities'. However, none of these clauses actually generates any clear positive rights. They simply encourage states to contemplate the possibility of, for example, using bilingual road signs. The Explanatory Report accompanying the FCNM specifically denies that these clauses include any right to official language status or self-government (Council of Europe 2005: 17–35). The idea that national minorities should have guarantees regarding participation in decisions affecting 'regions where they live' was part of the original text of Article 15 of the FCNM, but was deleted from the final text, to avoid any hint of territoriality.

under a different category of international law than national minorities. It has also criticized claims by Albania that the Roma do not fall under the category of national minorities, and claims by Estonia that the ethnic Russians who entered the country during the period of Soviet occupation do not qualify as national minorities. More generally, it has encouraged all countries to apply an 'inclusive' understanding of national minorities, one that does not require minorities to have a historic presence in the country, or even to be citizens of the country.[53] In short, in the Committee's usage, the term 'national minorities' is no longer one type of group amongst others in a taxonomy of minorities, but rather is becoming the umbrella term used to encompass all ethnocultural groups.[54]

This push to redefine 'national minorities' as an umbrella term is still contested. Despite admonishment from the Advisory Committee, several states continue to cling to their original understanding that the Convention is targeted at a particular type of group defined by its historic presence in the state. This is of course paradoxical, in one sense, since these very same states have gutted the Convention of any substantive norms that actually address the distinctive needs of traditional national minorities. But even as they have weakened the content of the Convention's norms, many of these states still want to preserve it as a targeted document, so as not to acquire any new legal obligations in relation to other minority groups, such as immigrants. Indeed, any attempt to formally amend the Convention to explicitly include immigrants would almost certainly fail, due to opposition from most states, both in the West and East. But many people—including virtually all of the prominent scholars and advocacy organizations in the field—are supporting the call for a more inclusive definition of national minorities.[55]

If this inclusive redefinition of national minorities is adopted more generally by European organizations, it would essentially complete the retreat from the original goal of developing targeted norms that address

---

[53] For a good overview of the Committee's opinions on how countries should understand the category of national minorities, see Wheatley 2005: 48–56; Hoffman 2002. On whether citizenship is a precondition for recognition as a national minority, see Thiele 2005. For the Danish case, see Opinion on Denmark ACFC/INF/OPI(2001)005, para. 16.

[54] As Wheatley puts it, the Committee has 'rejected the idea that there can be a strict taxonomy of the ethno-cultural groups recognized in international legal instruments' (Wheatley 2005: 49).

[55] This is a clear example of the point discussed in Chapter 1 about the 'relative autonomy' of IOs. The main push to expand the definition of national minorities does not come from powerful states, or from governments at all. It is emerging from the 'global policy networks' of academics, advocacy groups, philanthropic foundations, and bureaucrats that work below the radar screen to interpret and implement international norms. One of the few commentators to defend the more restrictive definition is Malloy 2005.

the distinctive issues raised by homeland ethnonational minorities. At present, the FCNM is targeted in form but generic in the substance of its rights provisions. If the Advisory Committee is successful, the FCNM will become generic in both form and substance. The FCNM would no longer be an important experiment in developing targeted minority rights: it would revert to the original Article 27 approach that articulates generic cultural rights applicable to all minorities, new or old, large or small, dispersed or concentrated.

The question of how to define national minorities for the purposes of the FCNM may seem like a technical legal question. But I believe it is a pivotal decision, one that raises profound dilemmas for the future development of international norms of minority rights. There are powerful moral and prudential arguments for abandoning the targeted character of the FCNM and shifting to a more generic minority rights strategy. But there are also costs associated with this shift, costs that have not been adequately acknowledged in the debate so far. The shift has potential implications not just for the fate of the particular legal text at hand, but for the broader project of diffusing liberal multiculturalism around the world.

There are several arguments for including all ethnocultural groups as national minorities under the FCNM. One is a simple matter of consistency: since the rights identified in the Convention are not grounded in facts of history or territory, it seems arbitrary to limit its scope to historic or territorial minorities. But there is another, more important, reason—namely, that many of the groups excluded by the more restrictive definition of national minorities are desperately in need of international protection from potentially hostile states and dominant groups, and have no other means of legal protection than the FCNM.

Consider the Roma. Because the Roma do not have a kin-state or a historic homeland in Europe, they do not raise the same sorts of irredentist or secessionist security issues as traditional national minorities. As a result, the initial flurry of efforts to formulate and monitor European norms of minority protection largely ignored the Roma. Recall that the initial justification for saying that minority issues are a matter of 'legitimate international concern' was the fear of regional instability—that is, the fear that ethnic conflict within one country could have international repercussions on the peace and stability of other countries. It's doubtful that the plight of the Roma raises this sort of threat to international peace and stability. And indeed the OSCE's High Commissioner on National Minorities has explicitly said that because the Roma do not pose a threat of inter-state violence or instability, issues regarding the Roma are better addressed within human rights organizations than within the High Commissioner's security-based mandate (Guglielmo and Waters 2005: 766–9).

From a humanitarian point of view, however, the Roma are, if anything, even more in need of international protection than traditional kin-state or substate national minorities. They are often the most disadvantaged members of society, facing the most pervasive and entrenched forms of discrimination, harassment, and racial prejudice, often at the hands of state officials, as well as suffering from political marginalization, residential segregation, and poverty.

Indeed, concerns about the Roma have begun to eclipse earlier concerns about kin-state minorities. As fears of escalating ethnic civil wars involving kin-state minorities in Eastern Europe have faded, the plight of the Roma has become more central to public debates about the 'minority problem' in post-communist Europe. For example, when the EU assesses how well countries seeking accession are fulfilling the minority rights criterion, their focus since 1998 has been on the treatment of the Roma more than on the treatment of kin-state minorities (Hughes and Sasse 2003).

The EU's attention to the Roma is not solely, or even primarily, a result of humanitarian concern. After all, the EU has shown little concern for the plight of the Roma in the EU's own member-states like Spain, Italy, or Greece, even though they often face the same sort of discrimination and disadvantage as the Roma in post-communist countries (Johns 2003: 694–6). The EU's concern, rather, is that if the Roma continue to be treated as pariahs in post-communist countries, they will emigrate *en masse* to the West, either as refugee claimants, illegal migrants, or (once post-communist countries join the EU) under the EU's own freedom of mobility rules. The unwelcome prospect of large numbers of Roma migrants from the East arriving in the West has motivated the EU to focus on improving the treatment of the Roma in post-communist countries (Schwellnus 2005; Guglielmo and Waters 2005). The EU therefore needed to find a legal basis and institutional mechanism for monitoring state policies towards the Roma, and the most obvious option was to expand the definition of 'national minority' to include the Roma, whose treatment would then be subject to the FCNM and its reporting procedures.[56]

---

[56] See, e.g., Recommendation 1557 (2002) of the Parliamentary Assembly on 'Legal Situation of the Roma in Europe', which recommended that they be recognized as 'an ethnic or national minority group' in every state.

As I will discuss below, it's not clear that the substantive provisions of the FCNM are all that relevant or helpful to the Roma, but at least it provides them with a form of legal recognition and access to international monitoring. (This has indeed generally taken place—most countries now include the Roma in their lists of national minorities.)

The Roma are just one example of a minority group that is of particular concern to the EU, but which does not match the traditional definition of a national minority. Another example is the ethnic Russian minority in the former Soviet republic of Latvia. Most of these Russians moved to Latvia after World War II (when Latvia was illegally incorporated into the Soviet Union), in some cases as part of a deliberate strategy of 'Russification' of the Baltics. As a result, they are relatively recent newcomers, lacking a historic presence or homeland in Latvia, and on this basis, Latvia refuses to recognize them as a national minority for the purposes of the FCNM, and indeed has made it difficult for ethnic Russians to acquire citizenship.[57] But while the Russian minority differs in important respects from prototypical kin-state national minorities, it raises many of the same security fears as traditional national minorities, including the fear that Russia might use them as a fifth column to destabilize Latvia. Given this perceived threat to regional security, the EU wanted a way of monitoring the treatment of the ethnic Russians. The simplest option was to expand the definition of 'national minority' to include them, regardless of their relatively recent settlement and lack of citizenship status, so that they would be subject to the FCNM. (This is still resisted by both Estonia and Latvia.)

The largest group not covered by the traditional understanding of national minority is the millions of post-war immigrants into Western Europe, particularly Muslims from North Africa, Turkey, or South Asia. Like the Roma, they have often been subject to discrimination, harassment, and marginalization, and in many countries are the most disadvantaged in terms of income, education, and employment. For many minority rights advocates, it is crucially important to find some way of ensuring international monitoring of their treatment, and the simplest option is to define them as national minorities for the purposes of the FCNM. Here again, it's not clear that the substantive provisions of the FCNM really address the distinctive needs of immigrants, but its monitoring

[57] There was a small ethnic Russian community in Latvia prior to the Soviet era, and their descendants are recognized as a national minority. The situation is similar in Estonia, although in this case there is a longer history and higher degree of territorial concentration of ethnic Russians in the north-east of Estonia.

function would at least provide a degree of international supervision that is currently absent. (This call to include immigrants under the rubric of national minorities is still resisted by most states.)

Given the pressing needs of these minority groups, and their vulnerability to hostile publics and states, it seems perverse to exclude them from protection under the FCNM on the grounds that they aren't national minorities according to traditional usage or dictionary definition. Surely they are as much in need of international protection, if not more so, than historic homeland groups? It is the urgent need to extend international protection to these vulnerable groups, and not the simple argument of consistency, which explains why so many commentators and advocates take it as self-evident that Europe should adopt a more inclusive definition of national minority.

However, there is an alternative way of protecting these groups. Rather than turning the FCNM into a generic minority rights document that covers all groups, one could instead supplement the FCNM with additional targeted norms, formulated specifically for other types of groups that are currently unprotected. Indeed this is precisely what has been suggested by various European organizations. For example, the Parliamentary Assembly of the Council of Europe recommended that a minority rights document be drafted that is targeted specifically for immigrants. In its Recommendation 1492, the Assembly said that it 'recognizes that immigrant populations whose members are citizens of the state in which they reside constitute special categories of minorities, and recommends that a specific Council of Europe instrument should be applied to them'. Similarly, the OSCE has discussed the proposal for a 'Charter of Romani Rights', advanced by the Roma National Congress, premised on the idea that the Roma are a 'transnational minority' rather than a 'national minority'.[58] The Council of Europe's 'European Roma and Travellers Forum' has also recently endorsed the idea of a Charter of Romani Rights.

As these proposals show, one possible response to the fact that some vulnerable minorities are not covered by existing targeted norms is not to abandon the idea of targeted norms and shift to a generic strategy,

[58] See 'Report on the Condition of Roma in the OSCE Region' (Kawczynski 2000). The proposed Charter includes the right to send voting representatives to the European Parliament, Council of Europe, and United Nations; the right to veto measures that concern the fate of the Roma; the right to receive native language instruction, and the right to run an autonomous school system. For a detailed discussion of various proposals for Roma-specific targeted norms and bodies at the European or UN level, see Klimová-Alexander 2005; Goodwin 2004; Rooker 2002; Cocen Group 2002.

but rather to fill the gaps by creating a multi-targeted framework of minority rights. This is obviously a more complicated approach, but in some respects is potentially a preferable approach. After all, it's far from clear that the Roma or immigrants would actually benefit that much from being covered by the FCNM. The FCNM was not drafted with their needs or circumstances in mind, and doesn't address any of their specific issues (such as residency rules or naturalization requirements for immigrants, or the issue of segregated schooling for the Roma).[59] In a paradoxical way, extending the FCNM to these groups may actually make it less likely that effective international norms will be drafted to deal with their concerns— it pre-empts or short-circuits proposals to develop more effective targeted norms.

The inadequacy of the FCNM to address their needs is made clear by the fact that, at the level of programmes and policies, European organizations continue to treat the Roma and migrants separately from national minorities. The Council of Europe, OSCE, and EU all have their own Roma-specific bureaucracies, such as the Coordinator for Roma Issues, Specialist Group on Roma, Gypsies and Travellers, and European Roma and Travellers Forum (Council of Europe), the Contact Point for Roma and Sinti Issues (OSCE), and the inter-departmental commission and steering group on Roma (EU). Why are these bodies necessary, given that the Roma are now covered by the institutional structures that monitor and make recommendations regarding the treatment of national minorities? The answer, I think, is that the European norms established for national minorities are at best insufficient, and at worst largely irrelevant, for the Roma. Extending the FCNM to the Roma may seem like a good way to help protect a vulnerable group, but since the generic norms in the FCNM do not address the specific vulnerabilities facing the Roma, it doesn't provide effective guidance. At present, the real work on Roma issues at the pan-European level is often done, not through the generic FCNM, but through a myriad network of Roma-specific bodies.

A similar situation applies to the case of immigrants. Although some advocates would like them to be included under the umbrella of 'national minorities', the reality is that their needs are not addressed by the FCNM, and instead are being dealt with through immigrant-specific bodies, such as the Council of Europe's European Committee on Migration and

---

[59] 'Traditional minority protection policies were not designed with Roma in mind, and the benefits Roma derived were peripheral to those policies' purposes' (Guglielmo and Waters 2005: 765).

Migration and Roma Department. Similarly, the European bureaucratic structures dealing with immigrant languages are separate from those dealing with the 'historic' or 'traditional' minority languages.[60]

In short, even as European organizations shift towards a more generic formulation of minority rights, downplaying the distinction between different categories of minorities, they continue in practice to engage in targeted policies and programmes in recognition of the profound differences in needs and aspirations of these different types of groups. European organizations are driven by practical necessity to engage in targeted programmes, but seem unwilling or unable to acknowledge the need for targeting at the level of legal norms or political principles. The result is a series of mixed messages: on the one hand, European organizations criticize countries for continuing to distinguish traditional national minorities from other ethnocultural groups; on the other hand, European organizations themselves draw this distinction in their own bureaucratic structures and programmes.

Insofar as our goal is to articulate and diffuse the logic of liberal multiculturalism in a clear and consistent way, the shift to generic minority rights is a mixed blessing. Arguably, a better way to ensure that all vulnerable minority groups are protected is not to turn the FCNM into a generic document that covers all forms of diversity, but rather to supplement the FCNM with other targeted minority rights documents, tailored to meet the distinctive needs and aspirations of each type of group.

Unfortunately, this is probably not a realistic option in the European context. It is extremely unlikely that EU states today would adopt a progressive declaration on the rights of immigrants, given that Europe is in the midst of a populist backlash against both immigrants and multiculturalism policies. Any new declaration on the legal status of immigrants is more likely to embody old-fashioned ideas of assimilation and exclusion than newer models of multicultural citizenship. (It's worth noting, in this respect, that no EU state has ratified the UN's 1990 Convention on the rights of migrant workers.) There are also political difficulties confronting the proposal to draft a Roma Charter of Rights.[61]

---

[60] The Council of Europe's Charter for Regional or Minority Languages explicitly excludes immigrant languages from its coverage, as does the European Bureau of Lesser-Used Languages (EBLUL). As we've seen, there are also targeted policies for indigenous peoples at the EU, both for the Sami in Europe and in relation to overseas development assistance.

[61] Including disagreements within Roma groups themselves about the sort of group-differentiated rights they might want. As Peter Vermeersch notes, Roma leaders 'rarely made unambiguous statements about whether they were in favour of group-specific measures, such as affirmative action, desegregation, education in the Romani language, or the recognition of

As a result, it seems that the only feasible way to extend international protection to the Roma or immigrants is through the back door—that is, by fitting them into the pre-existing scheme of minority protection in Europe, targeted originally at the category of national minorities. Since it is unrealistic to expect any new minority rights provisions to be adopted in the foreseeable future, and since the only existing pan-European framework of minority rights targets national minorities, any group that wants to be protected has to find a way to qualify as a national minority. It is often said that for those who only possess a hammer, everything starts to look like a nail. Similarly, if the only tool of minority protection in Europe targets national minorities, then every minority starts to look like a national minority.

Under these circumstances, the decision to convert the FCNM into a generic minority rights document is understandable, and perhaps inevitable. It may be the only way to extend recognition and monitoring to vulnerable groups that would not otherwise be covered by international minority rights norms. But if this is indeed the path that Europe takes, we need to realize that it comes at a price. The first casualty is the original and courageous goal of developing minority rights norms that grapple with the distinctive claims of ethnonationalist groups. The bold experiment of articulating international norms targeted at such groups, and capable of resolving potentially violent ethnonationalist conflict, has been abandoned. As I mentioned earlier, developing such norms would have been an enormous contribution to the theory and practice of minority rights, not just for Europe, but for the world generally, given the pervasiveness of ethnonationalist conflicts.

But it is not just traditional national minorities that will pay the price. As one of the first experiments in developing targeted norms, the FCNM could have served as a springboard for the development of other targeted norms in Europe, such as for the Roma or immigrants, and encouraged attempts to formulate targeted norms in other regions of the world. It could have established a precedent for the viability and legitimacy of the targeted strategy at the international level, and also thereby helped diffuse the group-differentiated logic of liberal multiculturalism more generally.

I do not know whether this sort of 'multi-targeting' for national minorities, the Roma, and immigrants is (or was) a realistic option for

the Romani language as a minority language' (Vermeersch 2005: 462 cf. Koulish 2005). They have been encouraged to adopt an identity as 'national minorities', and have achieved a seat at the table as a result, but are uncertain about the implications of this label or identity.

Europe. To be viable, it would have required a more systematic effort to coordinate the different proposals for developing targeting norms. At present, proposals for targeted norms have arisen in an ad hoc way, in different European bodies, at different times, often in response to particular crises. There has been no attempt to bring these different proposals together, and then step back and ask what it would mean to adopt a multi-targeted strategy, and how the different forms of targeting would work together as part of a larger framework of European standards. Perhaps the political circumstances were simply not present for such an exercise.

But it is surprising how quickly advocates and experts in the European minority rights policy network have abandoned the project of developing targeted norms, whether for national minorities, Roma, or immigrant minorities.[62] Indeed, far from defending the legitimacy and necessity of targeted norms, many of these experts and advocates have defended the shift to a generic approach by implying that it is inherently 'arbitrary' to insist that groups meet some test of historic presence or territorial settlement in order to qualify as 'national minorities', and by implying that a more 'inclusive' definition is inherently more fair or legitimate.

From my perspective, this is a grave mistake. As we've seen in Chapter 3, the logic of liberal multiculturalism does attach importance to facts of history and territory. Across the Western democracies, the policies adopted for 'old' homeland minorities across the West differ from those adopted for 'new' immigrant minorities. As Perry Keller notes, 'distinctions between the rights of traditional and immigrant minorities are found in the laws and policies of almost every European State' (Keller 1998: 43), and the FCNM's original emphasis on traditional national minorities was simply following this well-established practice of the Western democracies.

It may be that, under current political conditions, it is expedient to abandon that original goal of developing targeted norms, and instead focus on strengthening a generic rights strategy. But if so, it's important to be clear that this is indeed a matter of political expediency, and not a repudiation of the legitimacy of targeted norms. Shifting to a generic strategy may be the most expedient way of extending coverage to otherwise unprotected groups, but it should not be misinterpreted

---

[62] There is still some support for the project of developing targeted norms in the case of indigenous peoples, which I will discuss in the next chapter, but as we will see, ambivalence about the general idea of targeting is affecting the indigenous rights movement as well.

as a judgement that there is anything arbitrary about targeting *per se*. On the contrary, it is important to insist that the logic of liberal multiculturalism requires group-differentiated rights, even if the current framework of European norms, for contingent political reasons, does not reflect that fact. Otherwise, the FCNM could be invoked by political actors in some countries as grounds for rejecting any and all minority claims based on history and territory, and thereby become an obstacle to, rather than vehicle for, the diffusion of the group-differentiated logic of liberal multiculturalism. Indeed, we can already see examples of this misinterpretation.[63]

I think that European organizations, and their policy networks, have laid themselves open to this potential misinterpretation. I say 'misinterpretation', because I believe that the shift from a targeted to a generic approach is mainly being done for reasons of expediency, not out of a principled opposition to targeting *per se*, and that most experts and advocates have not intended to dispute the legitimacy of targeted norms. But I should acknowledge that there are some influential actors within these policy networks who really do reject the legitimacy of targeted rights on principle, or at least reject the legitimacy of targeted rights based on claims of history and territory. Indeed, some argue that the underlying cause of ethnic conflicts in the post-communist region is precisely the fact that ethnic identities are linked to territory through ideas of a group's 'homeland' or 'traditional territory'. Such 'blood and soil' identities are said to be at the root of the violent conflicts in the Balkans and Caucasus. The problem is not that states have mismanaged competing claims to territory, but the very fact that ethnic groups have formulated their identities and claims in terms of history and territory. The goal of European efforts, on this view, should be to break this link, by promoting generic minority rights that do not make any reference to history or territory, such as various non-territorial models of minority rights and multicultural citizenship. Put another way, European norms should uphold generic minority rights, but should resist any concessions to minority nationalism, by recognizing only de-territorialized and de-nationalized minority claims (e.g. Nimni 2005).[64]

---

[63] See, e.g., the claim by the Romanian parliament that the proposal for Szekler autonomy in Transylvania contradicted 'European standards'. According to the Parliament, the autonomy proposal does not simply go beyond what is required by FCNM and OSCE Recommendations, but actually violates these norms, precisely because it relies on claims of historic settlement. (Opinion of the Chamber of Deputies 102/2004.03.11)

[64] For a discussion of these efforts to de-territorialize minority rights, see Kymlicka 2005*b*; Baubock 2004.

For such actors, the shift from targeted national minority rights to a generic strategy isn't just a tactical retreat or an expedient response to political contingencies, but is a matter of principle. Indeed, some of these commentators would have preferred to eliminate the category of 'national minorities' altogether from European legal instruments, given that the term has traditionally been associated with ideas of historic settlement and territory.[65] But since it would now be difficult to remove the term national minority from European usage, the next best option is to redefine the term to reduce any implication that history and territory matter. For some people, this indeed is one of the motivations for expanding the category of national minority to include all ethno-cultural groups, including immigrant groups. This extension is motivated not only by the humanitarian goal of extending protection to vulnerable groups, but also by the ideological goal of undermining the very idea of 'national(ist)' minority rights rooted in history and territory.

There are in fact different versions of this argument. For some people, this need to break away from territorial approaches is specific to the post-communist region, given its unique history of empires and border-changes, and doesn't apply to existing models of territorial autonomy for national minorities in the West, or for indigenous peoples around the world. But for others, the idea of separating ethnicity from territory is presented as a general ideal, indeed as the only truly liberal and democratic approach, and as the only approach consistent with (post-)modern ideas of mobility, globalization, and multiple, fluid, and hybrid identities. The implication, although this is rarely made explicit, is that national minorities in the West are backward insofar as they continue to tie the accommodation of their identity to projects of territorial self-government, that Western democracies are retrograde in accepting such ethnonationalist demands, and that European organizations should pressure Western

---

[65] Even if the existing Framework Convention does not endorse claims to territorial autonomy, the very fact that it targets 'national minorities' implicitly reinforces the idea that 'national' groups have different legal claims from dispersed minorities (like the Roma) or new minorities (immigrants), and it's difficult to see what those claims could be based on other than territoriality. If one's aim is to de-territorialize minority identities, then it makes sense to stop using the category of national minority, except as an umbrella term that encompasses all groups. And this is increasingly what some European commentators argue. The idea of targeting minority rights at 'national minorities', understood as historic/territorial minorities, is questioned on the grounds that the very category implies that facts of historic settlement and territorial concentration have moral and legal significance, regardless of what substantive rights are accorded to such groups.

democracies to abandon these forms of territorial autonomy in favour of non-territorial approaches.

This idea that we should seek to de-territorialize and de-nationalize the identities and claims of substate national groups is a familiar one in academic and public debates over minority rights, advanced by statists, republicans, and liberal cosmopolitans alike, but I think it is entirely unrealistic. As we saw in Chapter 3, this is precisely what Western democracies attempted and failed to do in the past. The shift to multinational federalism emerged only when Western states abandoned these quests to de-territorialize and de-nationalize their substate minorities, and accepted the durability and legitimacy of minority nationalist aspirations linked to history and territory. This is a pivotal part of the evolution of the logic of liberal multiculturalism.

In any event, this ideological opposition to minority nationalist claims obviously does not represent the dominant view within European organizations, since as we've seen, the initial impulse of these organizations was to promote Western models of territorial autonomy as a best practice. And as we'll see shortly, these organizations continue to promote such models in many of their case-specific interventions in post-communist countries. Moreover, no one to my knowledge has seriously proposed that European organizations should seek to discredit existing forms of multination federalism within the West, even though they are clearly rooted in nationalist ideologies based on claims of historic settlement and traditional territory. So there is no evidence that European organizations, in shifting from a targeted to generic strategy, intended to be advancing a principled opposition to the idea of group-differentiated claims based on history and territory.

However, the strong presence of this anti-targeting voice within European organizations has created considerable confusion about what exactly these organizations are doing, and why. A strong consensus has emerged that it is unrealistic to expect post-communist states to adopt Western models of multination federalism, and that European norms should only mandate weaker and non-territorial models of minority rights, such as those in the FCNM. However, this apparent consensus obscures considerable differences in underlying reasoning. For some people, this decision is a regrettable necessity, rejecting or deferring the most progressive forms of minority rights developed in the West in order to accommodate the same fears about 'national security' and 'disloyal minorities' that dominated nineteenth-century debates. And for them, it is important to keep alive ideas of autonomy in the post-communist region, if only as a long-term goal, and to defend the legitimacy of targeted norms based on history and territory.[66] Others, however, wishing to make a virtue out of necessity, argue that this decision to shift to generic non-territorial minority rights is progressive, reflecting a twenty-first century willingness to move beyond the intellectual strait-jacket imposed by nineteenth-century nationalist ideologies of the link between ethnicity and territory. For them, the time has come to bury regressive ideas of territorial autonomy and of targeted national minority rights once and for all.

Whatever the underlying reasons, the undisputed effect has been a dramatic shift in the nature and purpose of European norms of minority rights. On the fifth anniversary of the coming into force of the Framework Convention, the Council of Europe organized a conference entitled 'Filling the Frame', celebrating how minority rights norms have been progressively elaborated over the life of the Convention (Weller 2003). My own view, by contrast, is that the original goals of the Convention have essentially been abandoned. The resulting norms are neither effective in resolving the pressing issues of destabilizing ethnic conflict, nor do they help in articulating the long-term logic of liberal multiculturalism.

As I've said repeatedly, the decisions made by European organizations about how to formulate and interpret the Convention have been understandable, pragmatic, and perhaps even inevitable. But the result is that the bold experiment in developing targeted minority rights norms is on the brink of collapse. Indeed, we have come almost full circle in the European experiment in formulating minority rights. European efforts at establishing minority rights norms started from the assumption that the generic minority rights approach of Article 27 was too weak to address the sorts of issues underlying ethnopolitical conflict in post-communist Europe, in part because it only identified minority rights that are common to all groups, no matter how large or small, old or new, concentrated or dispersed. After a fascinating if flawed fifteen-year experiment in

---

[66] See, e.g., the Parliamentary Assembly's Recommendation 1609 (2003) on Positive Experiences of Autonomous Regions as a Source of Inspiration for Conflict Resolution in Europe, or the Congress of Local and Regional Authorities of Europe's Recommendation 43 (1998) on Territorial Autonomy and National Minorities, or the Parliamentary Assembly's Recommendation 1735 (2006) on 'The Concept of "Nation"', which refers to 'traditional national minorities', and which states that national minorities 'are often created by changes in state borders' and 'represent a constitutive part and a co-founding entity of the nation-state' (para. 9). These are all rearguard actions to try to keep international focus on the sorts of groups originally envisaged by the term national minority, and to maintain international support for the model of territorial autonomy at least as a long-term targeted goal for such groups.

developing targeted minority rights, we seem to be returning to where we started.

From 'Norms' and 'Standards' to Conflict Prevention/Resolution

It seems then that neither of the two strategies I have looked at so far has effectively addressed the problem that originally inspired European action on minority issues—namely, fears about the destabilizing effects of ethnic conflict in post-communist countries. The strategy of publicizing Western best practices naïvely ignored the fact that the underlying conditions needed for those practices to be adopted are missing in much of the region; and the strategy of formulating legal norms did not address the actual issues at stake in the conflicts.

So what then have European organizations done to prevent and contain destabilizing ethnonationalist conflicts? As I noted earlier, ethnonationalist conflicts in the post-1989 era threatened to undermine regional peace and stability, with spillover effects on neighbouring countries. The international community's decision to 'do something' about minority issues was premised on the need, and indeed the duty, to protect Europe against such potentially destabilizing ethnic conflicts. If the first two strategies failed in this regard, what then has been done?

The answer, as I've already hinted at, has been to engage in ad hoc, country-specific interventions. In several countries experiencing violent ethnic conflict, or where such conflict seemed imminent, European organizations have been actively involved in mediating negotiations between governments and minority leaders, and in making proposals for how their disputes should be resolved. Indeed, in some cases, European organizations have essentially drawn up the terms of a possible resolution, and then pressured both states and minority leaders to accept these Western-drafted agreements.[67]

For example, European organizations played a key role in drafting the terms of the Ohrid Agreement in Macedonia, granting official language status and greater local powers to the restive Albanian minority, and then pressured the government to accept it (which it did, in order to maintain

[67] For discussions of the European Union's efforts at case-specific conflict resolution, see Keating and McGarry 2001; Toggenberg 2004; Coppieters 2004; McGarry and Keating 2006.

NATO military support).[68] Western organizations also helped draft the Dayton Agreement in Bosnia, creating a structure of regional autonomy and consociational power-sharing for the Bosnian Muslims, Serbs, and Croats, and then pressured the parties to accept it (which they did, in order to avoid NATO military sanction). Another example, although not from a post-communist country, is in Cyprus, where the UN essentially drafted a new constitution (the Annan Plan), in cooperation with European organizations, proposing federalization and consociational power-sharing as a means to overcome the long-standing conflict between the Greek majority and Turkish minority. (Despite enormous pressure from the EU, this draft was rejected by the Greek majority in a referendum.)

In all of these cases, European organizations were actively involved in drafting agreements to resolve past violent conflicts (Cyprus), ongoing violent conflicts (Bosnia), or prospective violent conflicts (Macedonia). And in each case, quite substantial minority rights guarantees were included, going far beyond the minimal provisions of pan-European legal standards on minority rights such as the Framework Convention. But precisely because these minority rights provisions are case-specific, and not based on pan-European standards, there is no consistency in approach across different countries. These country-specific interventions are not derived from any common set of standards. There are no clear criteria for explaining why European organizations endorse official language status for some groups but not others, or support territorial autonomy in some countries but not others.

Not surprisingly, European organizations have been criticized for the seemingly arbitrary, unprincipled, and inconsistent nature of their recommendations. As critics have noted, the EU's country-specific recommendations have 'not produced any coherent minority rights standard' (Schwellnus 2005: 23), and indeed 'have demonstrated their preparedness to follow virtually any policy measure to create stability' (Johnson 2006: 51).

I think this appearance of arbitrariness and inconsistency is potentially misleading. There is a kind of logic which has consistently guided these case-specific interventions. Unfortunately, it is not the logic of liberal

---

[68] Macedonia was worried that, without NATO support, it would not be able to defeat the sizeable Albanian minority in a civil war, especially since the latter were supported by the well-armed and experienced Albanian rebels in neighbouring Kosovo. When NATO made clear that its continuing support for Macedonia depended on cooperating in the Ohrid Agreement, the government had little choice but to accept, although it still faced a difficult time selling the agreement to the general Macedonian population.

multiculturalism, but of security. And as we'll see, the logic of security generates its own set of dilemmas.

In fact, European organizations have systematically been monitoring post-communist countries along two parallel tracks, one concerning international norms, and one concerning regional security. As we've seen in the previous section, European organizations have set up a number of bodies to monitor whether post-communist countries are complying with international minority rights norms. But they have also, simultaneously, been monitoring these countries to assess whether they pose a threat to regional peace and security, and in particular trying to identify those cases in which the status and treatment of minorities might lead to destabilizing spillover effects. This parallel process of security monitoring has largely been organized through the OSCE, including the office of the High Commissioner on National Minorities. Indeed, the High Commissioner's mandate is explicitly defined as part of the OSCE's 'security' basket, with the task of providing early warnings about potential threats to regional security, and making recommendations that would defuse these threats (Estebanez 1997; van der Stoel 1999; Neukirch et al 2004). And behind the OSCE lies NATO, with its security mandate, and its power to intervene militarily if necessary, as we saw in Bosnia and Kosovo.

In short, we have two parallel processes of 'internationalizing' state–minority relations in Europe: one process monitors post-communist states for their compliance with norms of minority rights (what we can call the 'legal rights track'); and a second process monitors post-communist states for their potential threats to regional stability (the 'security track').[69]

In fact, the security track has always been more important than the legal rights track in determining actual interventions in post-communist states. The most important and well-known cases of Western interventions on minority issues in post-communist states have been based on calculations about how to restore security, not on how to uphold generic norms such as the FCNM.[70]

Consider the way Western organizations have intervened in the major cases of ethnic violence in post-communist Europe: for example, in Moldova, Georgia, Azerbaijan, Kosovo, Bosnia, and Macedonia. In each

---

[69] For a more detailed discussion of these two tracks, see Kymlicka and Opalski 2001: 369–86.

[70] As Johnson notes, 'the second [security] approach, dealing with diplomacy to diffuse situations of conflict, has been far more evident in Eastern Europe to date, and we can expect this to continue into the future' (Johnson 2006: 50).

of these cases, Western organizations have pushed post-communist states to go far beyond the requirements of the FCNM. They have pushed states to accept either some form of territorial autonomy (in Moldova, Georgia, Azerbaijan, Kosovo) and/or some form of consociational power-sharing and official language status (in Macedonia and Bosnia).

In short, in the contexts where destabilizing ethnic conflicts have actually arisen, Western organizations have recognized that the FCNM is of little use in resolving the conflicts, and that some form of power-sharing was required. The precise form of this power-sharing has been determined by a range of contextual factors, not least the actual military balance of power amongst the contending factions. Given that the West's motivation is to protect regional security, their intervention requires accurately assessing the threat potential raised by the various actors, and then calibrating their recommendations accordingly. Intervention grounded in *realpolitik*, in other words, not any principled conception of state–minority relations.

The security track has a number of attractions as a vehicle for dealing with the issue of ethnic diversity. It allows for a high degree of flexibility and sensitivity to context when making recommendations to individual countries. This may appear to some critics as evidence of arbitrariness or inconsistency, but can instead be seen as a healthy and indeed inevitable recognition of complexity. In some cases, this flexibility may be employed to demand reforms that go beyond the FCNM, as in the cases I've just mentioned. But it also allows the possibility that European organizations might exempt particular countries from some of the FCNM's requirements, if that would enhance security. In the case of Bulgaria, for example, the current (French-style) constitution is almost certainly in violation of the FCNM, since it denies the existence of minorities and forbids ethnic political parties. But the Turkish minority in Bulgaria has not shown any signs of restiveness, in part because these constitutional provisions are not rigorously enforced, and indeed Bulgaria is often cited as one of the few positive examples of non-conflictual ethnic relations in the Balkans.[71] Under these circumstances, European organizations operating within the security track have decided, in effect, to let sleeping dogs lie, and not to pressure Bulgaria to reform its constitution in line with the FCNM.

---

[71] The Bulgarian case is fascinating in the disjunction between legal forms and actual practices. While the constitution forbids ethnic parties, there is in fact a strong ethnic Turkish party, and indeed it has been included in governing coalitions, resulting in a *de facto* form of ethnic power-sharing (Brusis 2003). The EU has judged that *de facto* ethnic cooperation is more important than formal compliance with international norms (Schwellnus 2005).

Given its flexibility and adaptability, some commentators view the security track as preferable to relying on the legal rights track. Indeed, some people would argue that the legal rights track should be abandoned, particularly given the conceptual and political difficulties encountered in formulating legal rights. If there is no feasible way to ground effective international norms of minority rights on either a generic right to enjoy one's culture or a targeted right to internal self-determination, why not just give up on the idea of a legal rights track, while preserving the capacity to intervene in post-communist Europe based on considerations of security?

I suspect that there are some leaders of Western organizations who regret having established the legal rights track in the early 1990s, and who might now wish to retreat from it. After all, the EU and NATO survived and flourished for many years without paying any attention to minority rights.[72] Why not reconsider the decision to make minority rights one of the foundational values of the European order? Moreover, as we've seen, the original decision in the early 1990s to develop legal norms was based on a mistaken prediction about the likelihood that ethnic conflict would spiral out of control. It has since become clear that ethnic violence is a localized phenomenon in post-communist Europe, and that the prospects for violence in countries like Slovakia or Estonia are virtually nil for the foreseeable future. So perhaps it is unnecessary to monitor whether these countries are treating their minorities in accordance with (so-called) European norms.[73]

To be sure, Western observers might not approve of some of the policies that these countries would adopt if left to their own devices. But it is unlikely that their adoption would lead to violence and regional instability. Some post-communist countries might experiment with heavy-handed assimilationist policies, but if so, these policies would almost certainly fail, and in the end a domestic consensus would emerge on a more liberal policy. This is what happened in the West, and there's no reason to assume it wouldn't or couldn't happen in the East. Moreover,

---

[72] Recall that, prior to 1989, the EU tacitly allowed Greece to persecute its national minorities, and NATO allowed Turkey to persecute its national minorities (Batt and Amato 1998; DeWitte 1993, 2002), and neither organization showed interest in the plight of the Roma in member-states like Spain or Italy (Simhandi 2006).

[73] It's interesting to note that the first draft of the EU Constitution incorporated all of the 'Copenhagen criteria' except for minority rights. This was a tacit recognition, I suspect, that the original decision to make minority rights a condition of EU membership was based on a (mis-)reading of the security situation in the early 1990s, not any genuine normative commitment. A weakened version of the minority rights norm was re-inserted in the final text of the Constitution (Drzewicki 2005).

liberal policies are more likely to be perceived as legitimate, and hence to be stable, if they emerge from these sorts of domestic processes, rather than being imposed from without.

For these reasons, some commentators have suggested that we stop pressuring post-communist countries to comply with international norms on minority rights.[74] However, I doubt such a retreat is possible. As I mentioned earlier, ideas of minority rights have now become institutionalized at several different levels in Europe, and would be difficult to dislodge.

Moreover, the security track, on its own, generates a number of perverse incentives and unintended consequences. In particular, the security track has a perverse tendency to reward state intransigence and minority belligerence. It gives the state an incentive to invent or exaggerate rumours of kin-state manipulation of the minority, so as to reinforce the claim that the minority is disloyal and that extending minority rights would jeopardize the security of the state. It also gives the minority an incentive to threaten violence or simply to seize power, since this is the only way its grievances will reach the attention of the international organizations monitoring security threats. Merely being treated unjustly is not enough to attract Western attention within the security track, unless it is backed up with a credible threat to be able to destabilize governments and regions.[75]

For example, consider the OSCE's approach to territorial autonomy. As we've seen, after its initial recommendation of territorial autonomy in 1990, the OSCE has shifted towards discouraging territorial autonomy, and has actively counselled various minorities to give up their autonomy claims, including the Hungarians in Slovakia. But the OSCE has supported autonomy in several other countries, including Ukraine (for Crimea), Moldova (for Gaugazia and Transnistria), Georgia (for Abkhazia and Ossetia), Azerbaijan (for Ngorno-Karabakh), and Serbia (for Kosovo). What explains this variation? The OSCE says that the latter cases are 'exceptional' or 'atypical' (Zaagman 1997: 253 n. 84; Thio 2003: 132),

---

[74] See, for example, Burgess 1999, who argues in effect that we should give assimilation a chance. Assimilationist policies in post-communist Europe might be unpleasant, and might fail, but it's important for states (and dominant groups) to learn the limits of their capacities, and the strength of minority resistance, and so accept the necessity of coming to some settlement with their minorities.

[75] 'Minorities should not be confronted with the situation that the international community will only respond to their concerns if there is a conflict. Such an approach could easily backfire and generate more conflicts than it resolves. An objective, impartial and non-selective approach to minorities, involving the application of minority standards across the board, must therefore remain" (Alfredsson and Turk 1993: 176–7; cf. Chandler 1999: 68).

but so far as I can tell, the only way in which they are exceptional is that minorities seized power illegally and extraconstitutionally, without the consent of the state.[76] Where minorities have seized power in this way, the state can only revoke autonomy by sending in the army and starting a civil war. For obvious reasons, the OSCE discourages this military option, and recommends instead that states should negotiate autonomy with the minority, and accept some form of federalism or consociationalism that provides after-the-fact legal recognition for the reality on the ground. Hence the OSCE's High Commissioner on National Minorities recommended that it would be dangerous for Ukraine to try to abolish the autonomy ethnic Russians established (illegally) in Crimea (van der Stoel 1999: 26).

By contrast, wherever a minority has pursued territorial autonomy through peaceful and democratic means, within the rule of law, the OSCE has opposed it, on the grounds that it would increase tensions. According to the OSCE's High Commissioner, given the pervasive fears in post-communist Europe about minority disloyalty and secession, any talk about creating new territorial autonomy arrangements is bound to increase tensions, particularly if the minority claiming territorial autonomy borders on a kin-state. Hence the High Commissioner's recommendation that Hungarians in Slovakia not push for territorial autonomy, given Slovak fears about irredentism (van der Stoel 1999: 25).

In short, the security approach rewards intransigence on both sides. If a minority seizes power, the OSCE rewards it by putting pressure on the state to accept an 'exceptional' form of autonomy; if the majority refuses to even discuss autonomy proposals from a peaceful and law-abiding minority, the OSCE rewards it by putting pressure on minorities to be more 'pragmatic'. This is perverse from the point of view of justice, but it seems to be the inevitable logic of the security-based approach. From a security perspective, it may indeed be correct that granting territorial autonomy to a law-abiding minority increases tensions; while supporting territorial autonomy after it has been seized by a belligerent minority decreases tensions.

Insofar as this is the logic of the security approach, it has the paradoxical effect of undermining security. Long-term security requires that

---

[76] In all of these cases except Crimea, the minority seized power through an armed uprising. In the case of Crimea, the Ukrainian state barely existed on Crimean territory, and so the Russians did not have to take up arms to overthrow the existing state structure. They simply held an (illegal) referendum on autonomy and then started governing themselves.

both states and minorities moderate their claims, accept democratic nego-tiations, and seek fair accommodations. It requires that state–minority relations be guided by some conception of justice and rights, not just by power politics. And this, of course, is what the legal rights track was supposed to be promoting, and why it must supplement the case-specific security track.

The problem is how to get the two parallel tracks of security and legal norms working together, rather than at cross-purposes. We need to find a way of formulating legal norms that helps to illuminate why country-specific proposals for official language status and regional autonomy can be permissible and legitimate extensions of these norms, and not just concessions to belligerence. Conversely, we need to find a way of for-mulating case-specific security recommendations that shows how those recommendations emerge out of more general principles and values about the accommodation of diversity. To date, this sort of coherence is lacking.

Some of the key actors involved in the European debates are keenly aware of this problem. During his long tenure in office (1993–2001), the former High Commissioner on National Minorities, Max van der Stoel, was preoccupied with the need to link legal norms of minor-ity rights with his country-specific security recommendations.[77] Where existing legal norms were inadequate to make these links, he pushed for the formulation of new norms, such as the OSCE's Recommenda-tions on the education, language, and participation rights of national minorities.[78]

However, even with these OSCE Recommendations, the problem per-sists. Indeed, it is unsolvable so long as the legal norms are formulated solely as generic minority rights. There is simply too vast a gulf between the generic minority rights formulated in the FCNM and OSCE Recom-mendations and the sorts of policies and institutions needed to resolve or prevent serious ethnopolitical conflicts. Despite van der Stoel's best efforts, the country-specific proposals adopted by European organiza-tions on issues of official language status, consocational power-sharing, or territorial autonomy clearly reflect the logic of security, rewarding minorities that have seized power or threatened violence, while dis-couraging minorities that have played by the democratic rules of the game.

---

[77] See his thoughtful discussion of the problem in his speech on 'Peace and Justice, Power and Principle', reprinted in van der Stoel 1999: 111–22.

[78] For the High Commissioner's role in initiating new norms, see Ratner 2000; Neukirch et al 2004; Wilkinson 2005.

The Right to Effective Participation

We can see the dilemmas here by exploring one of the main approaches the HCNM (and others) has used to link the legal norms and security tracks—namely, to emphasize the idea that members of national minorities have a 'right to effective participation' in public affairs, particularly in matters affecting them. This approach is seen as offering sufficient flexibility to accommodate short-term security concerns, while still providing a clear, rights-based normative framework.

This idea of effective participation is not new—it was already present in the OSCE's original 1990 Copenhagen Declaration. Indeed it was on the basis of this principle that the Declaration recommended TA. Minority autonomy was advocated as a good vehicle for achieving effective participation. More recent declarations, such as the 1995 FCNM, have dropped the reference to internal autonomy, but retain the commitment to effective participation (in Article 15). Indeed, references to effective participation are becoming more prominent. For example, it is the central topic of a recent set of OSCE Recommendations (the Lund Recommendations on Effective Participation of National Minorities, adopted in 1999).

This idea of a right to effective participation is attractive for a number of reasons, but in the end I believe it reproduces rather than resolves the problems confronting the current European framework of minority rights. One reason it is attractive is that it sounds admirably democratic. Moreover, it avoids the tokenist connotations of a right to 'enjoy one's culture'. It recognizes that minorities want not only to speak their languages or profess their religions in private life, but also want to participate as equals in public life. A right to effective participation recognizes this political dimension of minority aspirations, while avoiding the 'dangerous' and 'radical' ideas of national self-determination (Kemp 2002).

From the perspective of normative theory, this approach has the added advantage of avoiding the danger of 'essentializing' groups. Both the 'right to enjoy one's culture' and the 'right to internal self-determination' seem to rest on assumptions about the inherent character of national minorities: the former implies that such groups have a shared and distinctive 'culture' that they seek to preserve, the latter implies that they have a shared and distinctive 'national identity' that they seek to advance through self-government. Yet we know that such groups are not internally homogenous. Members of the group are likely to disagree over the sorts of cultural traditions they wish to maintain, and the extent to which they wish to remain culturally distinct from the larger society. Similarly, they are likely to disagree over the nature of their national identity, or the sort of self-government needed to protect it. For the international community to endorse a right to culture or a right to self-determination appears to prejudge these internal debates, siding with those who argue for greater cultural distinctiveness and/or greater national autonomy, as if 'culture' or 'nationhood' were somehow essential and indisputable characteristics of these groups, rather than contested claims.

This sort of concern has been invoked by postmodernists and critical theorists as a grounds for rejecting the constitutionalization of substantive minority rights, and endorsing instead purely procedural minority rights, such as guarantees of participation and consultation (e.g. Benhabib 2002; Fraser 2003: 82). These procedural rights avoid making substantive assumptions about the distinctiveness of a group's culture or the boundedness of its identity. A right to effective participation allows members of a group to advance claims of culture and nationhood, but requires that these claims be vindicated through deliberative democratic processes, rather than pre-approved by constitutional norms or international law (Laitin and Reich 2003; Williams 1995; Jung 2007).

The main reason why effective participation has become so popular, however, is that it is vague, subject to multiple and conflicting interpretations, and so can be endorsed by people with very different conceptions of state–minority relations. In this sense, the apparent consensus on the importance of effective participation hides, or postpones, deep disagreements on what this actually means.

On the most minimal reading, the right to effective participation simply means that the members of national minorities should not face discrimination in the exercise of their standard political rights to vote, engage in advocacy, and run for office. This minimalist reading is invoked to push Estonia and Latvia to grant citizenship to their ethnic Russians, and to enable them to vote and run for office even if they lack full fluency in the titular language.

On a somewhat more robust reading, effective participation requires not just that members of minorities can vote or run for office, but that they actually achieve some degree of *representation* in the legislature. This may not require that minorities be represented precisely in proportion to their share of the overall population, but serious under-representation would be viewed as a concern. This reading is invoked to prohibit attempts by states to gerrymander the boundaries of electoral districts so as to make it more difficult to elect minority representatives. It can also be invoked to prohibit attempts by states to revise the threshold needed for minority political parties to gain seats in PR electoral systems.

In Poland, for example, the German minority regularly elects deputies to parliament because it is exempted from the usual 5 per cent threshold rule. A similar policy benefits the Danish minority party in Germany. By contrast, Greece raised its electoral threshold precisely to prevent the possibility of Turkish MPs being elected (MRG 1997: 157). This sort of manipulation might well be prohibited in the future.

But neither of these two readings—focusing on the non-discriminatory exercise of political rights and equitable representation—gets us to the heart of the problem in most cases of serious ethnic conflict. Even when minorities are able to participate without discrimination, and even when they are represented in rough proportion to their population, they may still be permanent losers in the democratic process. This is particularly true in contexts where the dominant group views the minority as potentially disloyal, and so votes as a bloc against any policies that empower minorities. (Consider the nearly universal opposition within Slovakia to autonomy for the Hungarian-dominant regions, or the opposition within Macedonia to recognizing Albanian as an official language.) In these contexts, it may not matter whether minorities exercise their vote, or elect MPs in accordance with their numbers: they will still be outvoted by members of the dominant group. The eventual decision will be the same whether minorities participate in the decision or not.

Taken literally, the term effective participation would seem to preclude this situation of national minorities being permanent political minorities. After all, 'effective' participation implies that participation should have an effect—i.e. that participation changes the outcome. The only way to ensure that participation by minorities is effective in this sense within divided societies is to adopt counter-majoritarian rules that require some form of power-sharing. This may take the form of internal autonomy or of consociational guarantees of a coalition government.

We can call this the maximalist reading of a right to effective participation—one that requires counter-majoritarian forms of federal or consociational power-sharing. This is obviously the interpretation that many minority organizations endorse. But it is strongly resisted by most states, East and West, for precisely the same reason that earlier references to internal self-determination were resisted (fears of disloyalty, irredentism, etc.). Having successfully blocked the move to codify a right to internal autonomy, states are not going to accept an interpretation of effective participation that provides a back-door for autonomy. Agreement on a right to effective participation has been possible precisely because it has been seen as an alternative to, not a vehicle for, minority self-government. The interpretation of effective participation is therefore likely to remain focused at the level of non-discrimination and equitable representation— i.e. at a level which does not address the actual sources of destabilizing ethnic conflict.

There is one potential exception to this generalization. European organizations may adopt a maximalist interpretation of effective participation *where forms of power-sharing already exist.* It is widely recognized that attempts by states to abolish pre-existing forms of minority autonomy are a recipe for disaster (e.g. Kosovo, Ngorno-Karabakh, Ossetia, etc.). European organizations would therefore like to find a basis in international law to prevent states from revoking pre-existing forms of minority autonomy. The norm of effective participation is a plausible candidate: attempts to revoke pre-existing autonomy regimes can be seen as a deliberate attempt to disempower minorities, and hence a denial of their right to effective participation.

This idea that effective participation protects *pre-existing* forms of autonomy and power-sharing has been developed by some commentators,[79] and has implicitly been invoked by the OSCE itself, when justifying its recommendations for TA and consociationalism in countries like Georgia and Moldova. I said earlier that these power-sharing recommendations emerged out of the security track, rather than from any reading of international legal norms. But Western organizations have been keen to show that these recommendations were not just a case of rewarding belligerent minorities, and that there is a normative basis for their recommendations. The claim that abolishing pre-existing forms of power-sharing erodes effective participation provides a principled basis for their recommendations.

The difficulty, of course, is to explain why it is only *pre-existing* forms of TA that protect effective participation. If TA is needed to ensure the effective participation of Abkhazians in Georgia, or Armenians in Azerbaijan, why isn't it also needed for Hungarians in Slovakia or Albanians in

---

[79] Annelies Verstichel argues that the Advisory Committee examining conformity with the FCNM has implicitly adopted a non-retrogression clause regarding autonomy (Verstichel 2004). Similarly, Lewis-Anthony argues that the jurisprudence regarding Article 3 of the First Protocol of the European Charter of Human Rights can be extrapolated to protect existing forms of autonomy (Lewis-Anthony 1998). At a more philosophical level, Allen Buchanan argues that there should be international protections for existing forms of TA, but denies that there should be norms supporting claims for TA by groups that do not yet have it (Buchanan 2004).

Macedonia? If abolishing pre-existing autonomy disempowers minorities, why aren't minorities whose claims to autonomy were never accepted also disempowered? (Conversely, if power-sharing institutions are not needed to ensure the effective participation of the Hungarians in Slovakia, why are they needed for Armenians in Ngorno-Karabakh, or Russians in Crimea?)

There seems to be no principled basis for privileging those minorities that happen to have acquired or seized autonomy at some point in the past. The differential treatment of minority claims to autonomy can only be explained as a concession to realpolitik. From a prudential point of view, it is simply much more dangerous to take away pre-existing autonomies from minorities who have fought in the past to acquire it than to refuse to grant new autonomies to minorities who have not shown the willingness to use violence in their pursuit of autonomy.

In short, interpretations of effective participation that privilege pre-existing autonomy suffer from the same flaw as the security track: i.e. they reward belligerent minorities while penalizing peaceful and law-abiding minorities. Like the security track, the effective participation approach, as it is currently being developed, is calibrated to match the threat potential of the contending parties. Those minorities with a capacity and willingness to destabilize governments and regions can acquire and maintain serious forms of power-sharing in the name of effective participation; those minorities who have renounced threats of violence do not.

This suggests that the effective participation approach replicates rather than resolves the problems we identified with the other approaches.[80] If effective participation is interpreted maximally to entail power-sharing,

[80] Some commentators have suggested that the Advisory Committee which monitors compliance with the FCNM can and should adopt a norm of 'progressive implementation'. According to this norm, countries would be expected and required to fulfil progressively stronger interpretations of the various FCNM provisions. What counts as adequately fulfilling the FCNM's norms regarding language rights or effective participation today will not be sufficient five years from now. Each time a state submits a report to the Committee, it will be asked 'what have you done for minorities *lately*?'. The idea is not simply to prevent countries from back-sliding (the non-retrogression clause I mentioned earlier), but also to progressively raise the bar in terms of what is required to meet the FCNM norms (see, e.g., Verstichel 2004; Weller 2003). There is no doubt that the Advisory Committee has done some innovative thinking along these lines, aided by the fact that it is composed of independent experts rather than state representatives (Hoffman 2002). If my analysis is correct, however, there are likely to be limits on the extent to which the independent experts on the Advisory Committee will be able to ratchet up the requirements of the FCNM. In particular, I doubt that official language status or TA will come to be seen as requirements of the FCNM, except where minorities have shown a willingness and capacity to undermine stability and security. At the end of the day, the Advisory Committee is only advisory: its recommendations must be approved by states. I suspect that any attempt at raising the bar to include TA and official language status will be rejected by states for the same reason that previous attempts to codify such rights have failed.

then it is too strong to be acceptable to states, and will be rejected for the same reason that the targeted internal self-determination approach was rejected. If effective interpretation is interpreted minimally to cover only non-discrimination and equitable representation, then it is too weak to resolve serious cases of ethnic conflict, and will be ineffective for the same reasons that the generic right to culture approach was ineffective. And if we examine how the idea of effective participation has actually been invoked in cases of conflict, we will see that, like the security track, it is based on power politics, not general principles.[81] Effective participation is becoming a new and important site for the playing out of tensions between short-term security and long-term justice, but it does not, by itself, provide a formula for resolving those tensions.

[81] Put another way, when we talk about effective participation, we need to ask 'participation in what'? From the point of view of post-communist states, the members of national minorities should be able to participate in the institutions of a unitary nation-state with a single official language. From the point of view of many minority organizations, the members of national minorities should be able to effectively participate in the institutions of a multi-lingual, multination federal state. These different conceptions of the state generate different conceptions of what is required for effective participation within it. Commentators often write as if the principle of effective participation can be invoked to resolve these conflicts over the nature of the state, but in fact we need first to resolve these conflicts before we can apply the principle. And to date, that basic conflict over the nature of the state has been resolved in post-communist Europe by force, not principles. Where minorities have seized autonomy, effective participation is interpreted as supporting federal and/or consociational power-sharing within a multilingual, multination state. Where minorities have not used force, effective participation is interpreted as requiring only non-discriminatory participation and equitable representation within a unitary, monolingual state. Advocates of the idea of effective participation suggest that it can provide a principled formula for resolving deep conflicts over the nature of the state. It seems to me, however, that the idea of effective participation presupposes that this issue has already been resolved, and is therefore either too strong (if it presupposes that states have accepted the idea of internal self-government within a multination state) or too weak (if it presupposes that national minorities have accepted the idea of a unitary and monolingual state). This puts a different light on claims about the 'essentializing' character of minority rights. I noted earlier that many postmodernists and critical theorists have rejected the idea of substantive minority rights to culture or self-determination on the grounds that they prejudge and falsely homogenize the character of the group. Yet in rejecting such claims, they did not intend to be supporting essentializing accounts of the nation-state as a unitary and monolingual state composed of a single people. They hoped that the idea of effective participation could be neutral in the struggle between minority nationalists and nationalizing states, and could be implemented without prejudging whether it is a multilingual, multination state or a monolingual, unitary nation-state. Yet it is not clear that the idea of effective participation can be implemented without taking a stand on this question. If so, the risk of essentialism arises equally whether we accept or reject claims to internal self-determination. Accepting such claims runs the risk of essentializing our conception of the national minority; rejecting them runs the risk of essentializing our conception of the state. Whichever choice we make, we must therefore put in place safeguards that allow citizens to continually challenge oppressive essentialisms, whether minoritarian or majoritarian. This is a central element of a genuinely *liberal* conception of minority rights.

Conclusion

Inspired by a desire both to promote a more liberal and democratic model of diversity, and to prevent harmful and destabilizing ethnic conflict, European organizations have adopted a wide range of approaches to help reshape state–minority relations in post-communist Europe. In this chapter, I've surveyed three types of approaches: publicizing best practices; formulating legal norms; and case-specific interventions.

The overall results of these efforts can best be described as confusing, almost schizophrenic. Each of these three sets of activities has its own difficulties in formulating a clear and consistent message, but if we put them all together, the confusions multiply.

The 'publicizing best practices' approach involves disseminating information about the most advanced forms of Western liberal multiculturalism, often in a naïve way, without attention to the preconditions that enabled these practices to be adopted in the first place. The result is at best ineffective, and at worst potentially destabilizing, if it encourages minorities in post-communist countries to make claims that states lack the capacity to meet.

The 'formulating legal norms' approach is caught in a deep bind. It initially adopted a 'targeted' approach to legal norms, aiming not to identify generic minority rights norms, but rather to focus on particular types of 'national minority' groups and their distinctive claims. This decision reflects both the logic of liberal multiculturalism in the West, which involves group-differentiated claims, and the logic of ethnic conflict in post-communist Europe, which is intimately tied up with issues related to the history and territory of 'homeland' groups. However, the very fear of ethnic conflict that inspired these efforts at formulating targeted norms has also paralysed these efforts. European organizations have rejected Western models for addressing the claims of homeland groups, on the grounds that they are likely to be dangerous and destabilizing in the context of post-communist transitions, without offering any plausible alternative in their place. As a result, the current norms simply do not address the issues at stake. Moreover, some actors are now questioning the desirability or even legitimacy of separating out homeland groups as a target of minority rights norms. There is an awareness that, sociologically, homeland groups generate distinct forms of ethnopolitical mobilization, rooted in claims of history and territory, but there is radical uncertainty about whether or how international law should recognize the moral and legal legitimacy of such claims. As such, the whole legal norms approach remains suspended in mid-air, politically ineffective, and conceptually unstable. Formally speaking, it remains targeted, but in a way that tracks neither the logic of ethnic conflict in post-communist countries nor the logic of liberal multiculturalism in the West, and so faces pressure to shift back to a more generic approach.

The 'case-specific intervention' approach offers yet another set of messages. Almost invariably, these interventions involve pushing states to go beyond the minimal requirements established in the legal norms approach, often advocating fairly strong forms of territorial autonomy, official language status, or consociational power-sharing. The difficulty, however, is that these interventions and recommendations are only made in cases where minorities have been able to pose a credible threat of destabilizing the state. As a result, the recommendations are widely perceived, not as the expression of a principled commitment to advanced minority rights norms, but as an unprincipled pay-off to belligerent minorities.

There is a perverse irony here. Case-specific interventions often involve versions of the models of multination federalism affirmed in the best practices approach, and thereby offer much stronger minority protection than anything endorsed under the legal norms approach. But their piecemeal promotion, responding to security threats rather than principled arguments, generates cynicism about the entire minority rights project.

If we put these three tracks together, the result is a mixed message, to put it charitably. European organizations became involved in this field in the hope of shaping state–minority relations in a more constructive direction, but it is often very difficult to tell what message they are actually trying to convey to either states or minorities. European efforts simultaneously encourage and discourage ethnopolitical mobilization by homeland minorities; they simultaneously endorse and dispute the value of Western models of multination federalism; they simultaneously affirm and reject the legitimacy of targeted minority rights.

As we will see in the next chapter, these ambiguities are not uniquely European: they characterize the more general global debates over liberal multiculturalism as well. The same basic dilemmas—the naïvety of the 'best practices' discourse; the tension between generic and targeted legal norms; and the perverse effects of case-specific interventions—are equally found in global efforts at diffusing liberal multiculturalism.

7

The Global Challenge

The post-1990 European experiment with minority rights is, in many ways, a distinctive story. It is a new chapter in a very old story about the role of 'national minorities' in the construction of the system of European 'nation-states'. But the challenges encountered in this experiment are not uniquely European. Global international organizations have adopted many of the same basic strategies as European organizations for diffusing liberal multiculturalism, and have run into many of the same dilemmas. In this chapter, I will look at the activities of international organizations along the same three tracks—namely, (i) publicizing best practices/models; (ii) formulating legal norms; and (iii) case-specific conflict resolution interventions. In each case, the difficulties we saw in the European context resurface, often in even more intractable forms.

The Limits of Best Practices

As I noted in Chapter 2, the 'minority problem' jumped to the top of the political agenda in 1989–90, both within Europe and at the UN, as intra-state ethnic conflict replaced superpower rivalry as the main threat to peace, stability, development, and human rights. In response, the UN engaged in extensive efforts to identify and publicize best practices. In 1990, for example, the UN Research Institute for Social Development (UNRISD) initiated a three-year project on 'Ethnic Conflict and Development', followed in 1993 by a further project on 'Ethnic Diversity and Public Policy', and the creation of a permanent 'Initiative on Conflict Resolution and Ethnicity' (INCORE) at the United Nations University. In each case, the goal was, in large part, to compile a catalogue of best practices, which were then publicized through academic publications and public reports, as well as associated workshops and training sessions.[1]

The goal was not just to publicize these best practices but also to normalize them. It was important to present these best practices not as regrettable exceptions or aberrations needed to pacify belligerent or bothersome minorities, but rather as the natural and desirable evolution in ideas of what constitutes a 'normal' state. These best practices were situated in the context of a historical shift away from highly centralized and homogenizing ideas of a unitary nation-state towards a more fluid and multilevel conception of sovereignty, and a more diversity-friendly conception of citizenship. This evolution was presented, not as a concession to demands rooted in pre-modern forms of tribalism and ethnic nationalism, but rather as a progressive response to the challenges raised by distinctly modern forms of ethnic identity and ethnic politics. This attempt to normalize multicultural best practices is clear, for example, in the 2004 UN Human Development Report, entitled *Cultural Liberty in Today's Diverse World*.[2]

These efforts have produced a global network of activists, academics, intellectuals, and policy-makers who are intimately familiar with the discourses and practices of liberal multiculturalism. A dense web of research projects and training and advocacy activities link UN officials with sympathetic partners in the NGO community (such as Minority Rights Group), philanthropic organizations (such as the Rockefeller Foundation or George Soros's Open Society Institute), quasi-academic institutions (such as the International Centre for Ethnic Studies or the International Peace Academy), often with funding from 'like-minded' member-states (such as Norway or Canada).

At one level, the creation of such a global network is a remarkable achievement in a relatively short period of time. And, as we saw in Chapter 2, the basic ideas being promoted by this network have had a demonstrable impact throughout the various branches of the UN and affiliated IOs, including those dedicated to development, human rights, and peace and security. At a rhetorical level, at least, it is difficult to find any global intergovernmental organization today that is not invoking the discourse of liberal multiculturalism.

Yet this apparent success hides a deeper failure. Attempts to promote liberal multiculturalism beyond this relatively narrow circle of cosmopolitan

---

[1] The academic outputs of the UNRISD projects include Stavenhagen 1996; Young 1998, 1999.

[2] In the interests of full disclosure, I should mention that I was an advisor to this Report.

elites have failed throughout most of the post-colonial world. This is particularly true of any model of liberal multiculturalism that involves ideas of minority self-government. Ideas of territorial autonomy are intensely resisted in most post-colonial states, as they are in most post-communist states. As Ashis Nandy puts it, 'Any proposal to decentralise or to reconceptualize the state as a truly federal polity goes against the grain of most postcolonial states in the third world' (Nandy 1992: 39 cf. Mozaffar and Scarritt 2000). Indeed, in many countries ideas of minority self-government are a taboo topic, and in some countries there are laws that prohibit the voicing of such demands.

There are exceptions to this generalization. The most prominent is Latin America, which has proven to be a receptive ground for ideas of multiculturalism (or 'interculturalism', as is more common in the Spanish-language debates), particularly in relation to indigenous peoples. A commitment to targeted rights for indigenous peoples has become a well-established component of the idiom of democratization in the region, not just amongst Western-trained elites, but in civil society more generally. This is reflected in the dramatic rise of what Donna Lee Van Cott calls 'multicultural constitutionalism' throughout Latin America (Van Cott 2000, chap. 9). The shift from military dictatorships to democracy has been accompanied by constitutional recognition of the distinct legal status of indigenous groups, including rights to self-government, land claims, and recognition of customary law in many countries.

Moreover, IOs have clearly played a vital role in enabling and encouraging this shift towards the recognition of indigenous rights in Latin America, through their support for indigenous advocacy groups, and their diffusion of best practices and standards. Alison Brysk's book *From Tribal Village to Global Village* (Brysk 2000) traces the dense web of connections linking local struggles for indigenous rights with IOs and their affiliated 'global policy networks', and many other commentators have also highlighted the crucial role that IOs and international NGOs have played.[3]

Latin America, therefore, represents the clearest case where international efforts to diffuse liberal multiculturalism have had local resonance, and led to domestic reforms. Indeed, these ideas have taken root to such an extent that Latin American countries as a group have become more

---

[3] According to Van Cott, the impact of ILO Convention 169 on domestic developments in Latin America 'cannot be overstated' (Van Cott 2000: 262). See also Yashar 2005; Sieder 2002; Postero and Zamosc 2004; Tilley 2002; Diaz Polanco 1997; Rodriguez-Pinero 2005.

vocal and active proponents of international norms of indigenous rights than the Western democracies.[4]

As in the consolidated Western democracies, there are vibrant and unresolved debates in Latin America about how well these models of multiculturalism are actually working in practice to empower indigenous peoples and to diminish inherited status hierarchies. Some critics argue that they involve merely symbolic changes. Indeed some argue that these policies were designed by neo-liberal elites precisely to deflect political attention away from underlying power structures (Hale 2002), a concern that has been reinforced by the fact that indigenous political movements sometimes enter into tactical alliances with neo-liberal political parties (Albo 1994). Others argue that while perhaps providing tangible benefits to indigenous peoples, multicultural reforms are creating new ethnic hierarchies in the process—for example, by excluding Black (Afro-Latino) groups who are not typically considered as 'indigenous peoples' (Hooker 2005). Yet others argue that they are imprisoning people in cultural scripts, and jeopardizing individual freedom. In order to qualify for new targeted rights, members of indigenous communities are expected to 'act Indian' (Tilley 2002)—that is, to follow 'authentic' cultural practices— an expectation that strengthens the hand of conservative or patriarchal leaders within the community who assert the authority to determine what is 'authentic' (Sieder 2001).

As in the West, there are few systematic studies that would enable us to evaluate these claims. But there is strong prima-facie evidence that multiculturalist reforms in Latin America have in fact provided a foothold for indigenous peoples to demand and achieve substantive redistributions of powers and resources, not just symbolic recognition.[5] Moreover, far from rendering invisible the claims of Afro-Latinos, the successful mobilization of indigenous peoples has often helped to raise the visibility of Afro-Latinos, and to legitimize their claims to a seat at the table, as part of a broader movement towards multicultural constitutionalism.[6] And if the models of indigenous self-governance and customary law do not fully conform to international human rights norms, that is also true of state legal and political structures, which are plagued with problems such as

[4] For example, when the UN's Draft Declaration on indigenous rights was put up for a vote at the UN's Human Rights Council in 2006, the main opposition came from British settler states (Canada, United States, Australia), not from Latin American states.

[5] For a preliminary attempt to test the competing hypotheses about the link between multiculturalism and neo-liberalism in Latin America, see Van Cott 2006. See also Gustafson 2002; Albo 1994; de la Pena 2002; Bonnett 2006.

[6] For the cooperation between indigenous and Afro-Latino movements, see Van Cott 2000.

the unstable rule of law, discrimination, and human rights abuses (Speed and Collier 2000).

Most commentators, therefore, have viewed the shift to multicultural constitutionalism in Latin America as a positive force, helping to enhance democratic participation amongst previously excluded groups, to reduce the danger of a return to authoritarian rule, to build legitimacy for the process of democratic consolidation, and indeed to serve as a laboratory for innovative experiments in democratic citizenship (Yashar 2005).

In all of these respects, however, Latin America remains the exception. In Africa, Asia and the Middle East, the general trends are quite different. Far from moving in the direction of a more 'multicultural' or 'multination' conception of the state, many countries in these regions cling to the project of building centralized and homogenized nation-states. Claims for minority autonomy remain firmly off-limits. Any forms of minority autonomy that predated independence have typically been abolished, and any promises to establish autonomies that were made in the process of achieving independence have often been broken.[7] In those few states where some form of territorial autonomy now exists (or is under negotiation), this has typically been the outcome of violent struggle and civil war, and has often been adopted under international pressure (e.g. in Sudan, Indonesia, Sri Lanka, Burma, Philippines, Ethiopia, Iraq, etc). India is perhaps the only state in Asia, Africa, or the Middle East to have voluntarily and peacefully adopted forms of territorial autonomy for its homeland minorities.[8]

Attempts by the international community to challenge this taboo, and to encourage a more open-minded consideration of autonomy, have largely fallen on deaf ears. As I noted in Chapter 1, even democratic reformers who might be expected to sympathize with ideas of liberal multiculturalism are often resistant to it. The assumption that robust ideas of minority rights should be seen as part and parcel of the process

---

[7] For example, promises of autonomy made to Baluchistan in Pakistan, Arakan and Kachin-land in Burma/Myanmar, South Moluccas in Indonesia, East Turkestan in China, Bougainville in Papua-New Guinea, Eritrea in Ethiopia, Bioko in Equatorial Guinea, Nkole, Bunyoro, and Buganda in Uganda, Ashanti in Ghana, Bamileke in Cameroon, the Druze in Syria, the Berbers in Morocco (Riffians), and Algeria (Kabyles).

[8] I say 'perhaps' because the initial design of federalism in India was not intended primarily to enable homeland minorities to exercise self-government. The restructuring of Indian federalism to accommodate homeland groups only really started in 1956, after a series of uprisings, and it remains the case that homeland groups in India often need to take up arms in order to get their claims for autonomy heard (Patil 1998; Mukarji and Arora 1992). Much the same applies to the restructuring of Nigerian federalism to accommodate its homeland minorities, which again was largely prompted by violence.

of democratization is disputed in much of Africa, Asia and the Middle East.

For the sake of convenience, it would be helpful to have a single term to cover the countries in Africa, Asia, and the Middle East. In the rest of this chapter, I will call them 'post-colonial states', to distinguish them from the post-communist states of Eastern Europe, the consolidated democracies of Western Europe, and the New World European settler states of the Americas and Australasia. This is obviously an inexact label. Some states in Africa, Asia, or the Middle East were never officially colonized (e.g. Ethiopia, Thailand, China), and hence are not technically 'post-colonial' states. However, these states are the exception to the general rule of European colonization of Africa, Asia, and the Middle East, and in any event they were typically considered as falling under one or other European power's zone of influence, and hence exhibit many of the same legacies as their neighbouring post-colonial states.

The term 'post-colonial' is misleading in another way, since New World settler states like the United States, Australia, or Mexico were also once colonies, and hence could technically be considered 'post-colonial'. But in these cases, it was the European settler populations, not the groups which existed on the territory before colonialism, who demanded independence. It was the colonizers themselves who decided to break their links with the imperial power. The countries in Asia, Africa, and the Middle East, by contrast, are 'post-colonial' in a very different sense: the historic populations of these societies have regained self-rule by overthrowing the European colonizers, who typically then returned to their imperial metropole.

Despite its imprecision, therefore, I think the term 'post-colonial' is helpful in capturing some key characteristics of these three regions. But for those readers who find it misleading, feel free to simply replace 'post-colonial states' with 'states in Asia, Africa, and the Middle East'.

Assessing the Sources and Preconditions

The key question, then, is why liberal multiculturalism has faced such resistance in post-colonial states. There are a number of ways of explaining this resistance. As in post-communist Europe, some commentators invoke the alleged prevalence of pre-modern forms of tribalism or ethnic nationalism, and the absence of more modern understandings of civility and tolerance. A more sophisticated version of this argument appeals to different 'civilizational values'. Liberal multiculturalism, it is said, represents a distinctly Western conception of the relationship between the individual and his or her culture, or between individuals and the community more generally. Other civilizations have other values, and hence other ways of dealing with issues of minorities. Asian societies, for example, are said to be based on a more 'communitarian' conception of society, which emphasizes harmony and deference, rather than the assertion of liberal rights (e.g. He 1998, 2004). Similar claims have been raised about Islamic approaches to minorities (e.g. Yousif 2000).

The idea that we can draw a clear and sharp distinction between 'Western values' and 'Asian values' or 'Islamic values' will be familiar to those who have followed debates about the universality of human rights (e.g. An'Na'im 1992; Bauer and Bell 1999; D. Bell 1999, 2004; Taylor 1996; Ghai 1999). I won't rehearse these long-standing debates, except to note that even if it made sense to distinguish a Western 'individualist' approach and an Asian/Islamic 'communitarian' approach—which is doubtful—this would not shed light on the issue we are discussing. Claims for minority autonomy are often defended precisely in the name of protecting communities, so as to enable group members to maintain their languages and cultural traditions, honour their gods, respect their elders and ancestors, and so on. One would expect that any communitarian who claims to believe in the importance of such values would support, not oppose, minority autonomies. The attempt by post-colonial states to impose highly centralizing and homogenizing nation-building policies on their ethnoculturally diverse populations is as antithetical to any plausible conception of communitarianism as it is to liberal multiculturalism.[9]

Moreover, these homogenizing policies of post-colonial states, far from reflecting the underlying values of historic civilizations, are clearly inconsistent with the historical traditions of the peoples and cultures of Asia, Africa, or the Middle East. Most of the political systems that predated European colonization had complex systems of inter-ethnic tolerance and co-existence. As has often been pointed out, the Ottoman empire was much more tolerant of its internal diversity than were any of the European empires at the time. The pursuit of ethnocultural homogenization is a post-colonial project, not a pre-modern tradition or civilizational value.[10]

---

[9] I develop this argument in more depth in Kymlicka 2004b.

[10] Indeed, Shatzmiller says that the exclusion of minorities in post-colonial Muslim-majority nation-states is a 'complete reversal of the Islamic traditions of political inclusion' (Shatzmiller 2005: 285).

Trying to explain the fate of ethnocultural minorities in post-colonial states by reference to pre-modern attitudes or civilizational values is a non-starter. We need to look elsewhere, and one place to start is by recalling the sources and preconditions of liberal multiculturalism in the West. The reality is that these conditions are found very unevenly in the post-colonial world. Let me focus on five issues, some of which overlap with the situation in post-communist Europe, some of which are distinctive to Asia, Africa, and the Middle East.

I will start with the two key factors that facilitated the acceptance of liberal multiculturalism by states and dominant groups in the West: namely, human rights guarantees and desecuritization. In the post-colonial world, as in post-communist Europe, there are difficulties with both.

(1) Human Rights Guarantees The perceived risk associated with adopting liberal multiculturalism depends, in part, on the sequencing of minority rights in relation to broader issues of state consolidation and democratization. In the West, with the important exception of Spain, the restructuring of the state to accommodate homeland minorities occurred after the development of reasonably well-functioning state institutions, with well-established traditions of constitutional limitations on government, the rule of law, an independent judiciary, a professional bureaucracy and police, a democratic political culture, and a prosperous market economy. As I noted in Chapter 4, the existence of such well-rooted traditions of liberal constitutionalism was crucial to the sort of liberal multiculturalism that emerged in the West. Liberal norms both inspire and constrain contemporary forms of ethnopolitics in the West, and this has provided a sense of security to all citizens that, however struggles over multiculturalism are resolved, the results will operate within well-defined parameters of democracy and human rights.

In the post-colonial world, however, as in post-communist states, claims by homeland minorities to pluralize the state are often occurring prior to the consolidation of well-functioning state institutions, and prior to the emergence of a democratic political culture. And this dramatically increases the risks associated with adopting territorial autonomy. There are fewer guarantees that minorities who receive autonomy will exercise their powers in a way that respects human rights. They may instead use their powers to create islands of local tyranny, establishing authoritarian regimes based on religious fundamentalism or ethnic intolerance. This can be a threat to the human rights of individuals both inside and outside the minority group. In relation to non-members, homeland minorities may attempt to attack the rights and property of 'outsiders' who have moved (perhaps several generations ago) into the minority's territory, including members of the dominant group in the state as a whole (e.g. Javanese who migrated into minority lands in the rest of Indonesia). In the absence of an effective human rights framework and political culture, such outsiders may be dispossessed of their property, fired from their jobs, stripped of their residency rights, or even expelled or killed. In short, the operation of autonomy can literally be a matter of life and death.[11]

In relation to the group's own members, the devolution of self-governing powers can lead to human rights abuses within the group—for example, in relation to gender equality. Indeed, Gurpreet Mahajan argues that the fundamental difference between the minority rights debate in India and in the West concerns the protection of individual rights within groups. I earlier stated that the goal of liberal multiculturalism can be summarized as 'equality between groups, and freedom within groups'. In India, she argues, issues of inter-group inequality came to the fore before adequate protections existed for individual rights within groups. In the West, by contrast, the issue of redressing inter-group inequalities only arose after firm protections of individual rights were already in place (Mahajan 1998: 152–5; cf. Jain 2005; Nanda 2003).

(2) Regional Insecurity A second factor concerns geo-political security. Most post-colonial states have one or more enemies on their borders. These neighbouring enemies would like to destabilize the state, and one familiar tactic for doing so is to recruit minorities within the state, and to encourage them to engage in destabilizing protest, even armed insurrection. In such a context of regional insecurity, minorities are perceived as potential fifth-columnists or collaborators with neighbouring enemies, and autonomy for such minorities is perceived as a threat to national security.

[11] For the Indonesian case, see Bell 2001; for India, see Weiner 1998; Srinivasavaradan 1992; for Nigeria, see Ejobowah 1998; Bach 1997; Lemarchand 1997; for Ethiopia, see Alemante 2003; Tronvoll 2000; for Cameroon, see Eyoh 2004. For Africa more generally, see Geschiere 2005; Ceuppens and Geschiere 2005. It's important to emphasize that the presence or absence of particular national-level legal and political institutions is not sufficient to explain violence. The resort to violence is always strongly mediated by local factors. Studies in India, for example, have shown that variations in the local organization of civil society help to explain why some cities or regions are more prone to violence than others, even when they are governed by the same macro-level institutions. In particular, an ethnically-integrated civil society can act as a bulwark of peace even when effective macro-level institutional guarantees of human rights are lacking (Varshney 2002). But clearly the absence of macro-level institutional guarantees creates risks that would not otherwise exist. Indeed, in the West, we can see the reverse effect: the presence of robust macro-level human rights protections helps to ensure peace even when civil society is not well integrated, as in Belgium or Canada, where civil society organizations are often organized into 'parallel societies' along linguistic lines.

As I noted earlier, this dynamic no longer applies to national minorities in the West, due mainly to the protective regional security umbrella created by NATO, and this has played a crucial role in enabling the adoption of multination federalism. In most of the post-colonial world, however, state–minority relations remain highly securitized. In several cases, security fears arise from the belief that the minority's main loyalty is to a (potentially hostile) neighbouring kin-state with whom it may collaborate. We see this in India regarding the Kashmiri minority (and the Muslim minority more generally); in Sri Lanka regarding the Tamil minority; in Afghanistan regarding the Uzbek minority; in Cambodia regarding the Vietnamese minority; in Pakistan and Bangladesh regarding the Hindu minority; in Bangladesh regarding the Biharis; in Thailand regarding the ethnic Malays; in Vietnam regarding the Chinese minority; in Iran and Israel regarding the Arab minority; in Ethiopia regarding the Somali minority; and so on. In several of these cases, there have even been policies to encourage or force the allegedly disloyal minority to 'return' to their 'home' country.

A related problem arises when a particular national group is found in two or more countries, divided by modern international boundaries, and who may have dreams of forming (or regaining) a common state. The classic case in the Middle East is the Kurds, divided between Iran, Iraq, Turkey, and Syria, who have longed to create an independent Kurdistan. A comparable situation in Asia concerns the Baluchis, spread across Afghanistan, Iran, and Pakistan, who have sometimes expressed the desire for an independent state. The Pashtuns (Pathans) who are divided by the Afghan/Pakistan border have also periodically expressed a desire to be unified in a single state. And there are of course countless ethnic groups in Africa divided by modern international boundaries, many of whom have expressed a desire to form a single state, such as the Ewe (divided between Ghana, Togo, and Benin), or the Tuareg (divided between Mali, Niger, and Algeria).[12]

In both of these contexts, the state fears that the minority will collaborate with its kin across the border—whether it be a neighbouring kin-state or just a neighbouring kin-group. But there are other ways in which minorities can be suspected of collaborating with hostile external powers who threaten the state. In some cases, these external powers are former imperial powers (as with the South Moluccans in Indonesia, who are seen as collaborators with the Dutch; or the Montagnards in Vietnam,

---

[12] On the multiplicity of such cases of 'partitioned Africans', see Asiwaju 1985.

who are seen as collaborators with the French and Americans). In other cases, minorities are seen as collaborating with international movements that threaten the state. In the past, this often involved the fear that minorities were part of an international Communist conspiracy set upon overthrowing capitalist countries.[13] More recently, this has been replaced by the fear that minorities are part of an international movement of radical Islamists to overthrow secular states. For example, Muslim minorities in India (Kashmir), Indonesia (Aceh), Philippines (Mindanao), or Ethiopia (Somaliland) are said to have links with international networks of Islamic militants. In other cases, the concern is that minorities are serving as agents of foreign capital, fomenting rebellion to gain preferential access to natural resources: this is sometimes said to underlie the problems in West Papua.

In all of these cases, minorities are seen (rightly or wrongly) as allies or collaborators with external powers that threaten the larger state.[14] To an outside observer, these minority groups might appear to be weak and marginalized, with little power and few resources to challenge the state. But from the state's point of view, these minorities are the local agents for larger regional or international powers or networks that are very strong, and pose a credible threat to the state.[15] This dynamic is likely to arise wherever states are weak, and regional security organizations do not exist, or are ineffective.

(3) Distrust of the International Community These first two factors—the fear that robust minority rights may be a threat to the personal security of individuals and to state security—are also found in post-communist Europe. But the prospects for liberal multiculturalism are significantly complicated in post-colonial states by a third factor that is not found in post-communist Europe—namely, distrust of the international organizations

---

[13] Several minorities in Indonesia were suppressed on the grounds that they collaborated with China in the 1965 Communist coup. In some cases, assumptions about ethnic kinship and ideological kinship reinforce each other: for example, Chinese minorities in several Asian countries have been assumed to have both ethnic and ideological reasons for collaborating with China.

[14] For discussions of this fifth-column view of minorities in Asia, see Ho 2000 (re Chinese minorities throughout the region), Ganguly 1997: 266 (re Chinese minorities throughout the region), 269–70 (re Malays in Singapore); ICES 1995: 17–25 (re Vietnamese in Cambodia); Anderson 2004 (re Papuans in Indonesia); Krishna 1999, chap. 3; Shastri 1997: 155; Dharmadase 1992: 141, 230, 295–6; Nissan 1996: 34 (re the Tamils in Sri Lanka); MRG 1997: 579 (re the Hindu minorities in Pakistan and Bangladesh); Grare 2006 (re the Baluchis).

[15] A particularly depressing example is the Horn of Africa, where each of the countries in the region has actively supported rebel minorities in nearby countries as a tool for destabilizing their neighbours. I discuss the challenges this raises for current efforts at federalizing Ethiopia in Kymlicka 2006*b*.

that are promoting minority rights. Many people in the post-colonial world have doubts not only about the message of liberal multiculturalism, but also about the messenger.

To be sure, post-communist countries often resent the paternalism, condescension, and double-standards exhibited by Western organizations that insist on minority rights as a condition of 're-joining Europe'. But they do not doubt that, in the end, these organizations are committed to protecting the stability and territorial integrity of their member-states, including the candidate countries seeking accession. Indeed, post-communist countries seek admission to the EU and NATO precisely as a way of guaranteeing their own stability and territory.

In much of the post-colonial world, however, there is little confidence that the 'international community' is committed to protecting the stability and territory of non-Western states. On the contrary, there is a widespread perception that IOs are internationalizing minority rights precisely in order to destabilize certain countries. In particular, it is widely believed in many post-colonial states that the international sponsorship of minority rights is simply a plot or conspiracy by the West, and particularly the United States, to weaken and divide post-colonial states, especially those that might pose a challenge to American hegemony. Many Chinese intellectuals, for example, have argued that the international discourse of minority rights is a plot by the CIA to incite secessionist movements amongst their two most important ethnonationalist groups—Tibetans in the south-west and the Muslim Uighurs in the north-west—so as to break up China. A similar conspiracy theory is pervasive in the Arab and Muslim worlds, where it is assumed that the international discourse of minority rights is intended to weaken countries like Iraq, Iran, Egypt, Syria, Pakistan, and Indonesia by inciting rebellion and/or secession amongst their various minorities.[16]

---

[16] Bourdieu and Wacquant offer a (slightly) more subtle version of the argument that the global diffusion of minority rights discourse is part of 'the cunning of imperial reason'. They argue that Americans are engaged in the 'world-wide export of US scholarly categories', and are thereby imposing their own particular 'folk-concepts' as 'the universal standard for the struggle of all groups oppressed on grounds of colour (or caste)', and thereby implicitly establishing the United States as the model modern society to which all other societies must conform (Bourdieu and Wacquant 1999: 48, 44). One can indeed find examples where American officials imply that multiculturalism and minority rights are an American invention. For example, Strobe Talbot, Deputy Secretary of State under President Clinton, once said that 'If there is to be a post-Cold War peace in Europe...it must be based on the principle of multiethnic democracy...The United States is one of the first and greatest examples of that principle...[so] it is in our interest that multiethnic democracy ultimately prevails' (quoted in Chandler 2000: 66; cf. Atanasoski 2006; Anderson 1992). But in fact, the specific models of multiculturalism and minority rights being advanced by IOs, whether in post-communist Europe or the post-colonial world, are not drawn primarily from the American

This sort of conspiracy theory is clearly incorrect as an account of the origins of the current wave of international norms on minority rights. As I mentioned earlier, the post-1990 trend to internationalize state–minority relations arose out of fears of the destabilizing consequences of ethnic civil wars in the Balkans and the Caucasus, and was reinforced by the horrors of state collapse in places like Rwanda and Somalia. The push to identify international norms and best practices of multiculturalism came largely from people within the West who had supported these reforms within their own countries, and who sincerely believed that they were a (modest) success. Their goal was not to weaken and destabilize post-colonial states, but precisely to help make them stable and successful, by diffusing models of state–minority relations that had worked in the West.

Nonetheless, these conspiracy theories remain powerful in the post-colonial world, and have been exacerbated by the double standards that Western powers have adopted when applying minority rights norms. The United States, for example, strongly condemned Iraq under Saddam Hussein for its mistreatment of the Kurds, yet turned a blind eye to the mistreatment of the Kurds in Turkey. The obvious explanation for this double-standard is that Iraq was an enemy of the United States, while Turkey was a military ally and member of NATO. In such cases, references to minority rights have become instrumentalized as a tool of superpower politics, and do not reflect any sincere concern for the rights of minorities.

Similarly, there is a widespread perception in the Muslim world that Western concern with liberating (Christian) East Timor from its forced annexation into (Muslim) Indonesia is hypocritical, given the lack of concern with liberating Muslim minorities that have been incorporated into other states in violation of international law, as in Kashmir or Palestine.

---

experience, and do not rely on American 'folk-concepts'. The concept of 'national minorities', for example, has no roots in the American historical experience or in American scholarship. Indeed, when the OSCE asked its member-states to identify legislation bearing on the rights of national minorities, the US State Department responded 'It is unclear that the concept of "national minorities" as understood in a European context applies to conditions in the United States' (OSCE 1997, Annex). Similarly, international debates about the rights of 'indigenous peoples' are not dominated by American models or scholars. As Alistair Bonnett notes, none of the approaches being promoted by IOs in Latin America 'is designed to disseminate or reproduce American models, and none can be said to have successfully implanted anything approaching a replica American racial society in any "developing" society' (Bonnett 2006: 1094). This is not to say, of course, that the American government does not monitor developments regarding international minority rights norms with an eye to their geo-political interests, as I will discuss. But the United States is not the main source of the models or concepts being used in contemporary international debates on minority and indigenous rights.

The Western preoccupation with the suffering of Christian minorities in (Muslim-majority) Sudan contrasts with Western indifference to the suffering of Muslim minorities in (Christian-majority) Philippines or Russia. The academic and popular literature on minority issues in the post-colonial world is rife with such examples of perceived double-standards and inconsistencies, with the result that Western support for minority rights is seen as having no moral sincerity or legitimacy.

Put another way, post-colonial states not only fear that neighbouring enemies will use international norms of minority rights as a tool of desta-bilization, but also fear that the international community itself will use them in this way whenever a country dares to threaten American/Western hegemony. Post-communist states in Europe share the former fear, but since they hope and expect to become part of the hegemonic Western power, they do not share the latter fear.

A major challenge, then, is how to deal with the widespread perception that international support for minority rights is simply a tool of geo-politics. This is not a problem unique to the issue of minority rights. Similar complaints have been raised about Western double-standards regarding traditional human rights, or democracy. But in these cases, IOs and their affiliated policy networks have been able to persuade broad segments of the elites and general public around the world that the underlying ideals of human rights and democracy have intrinsic worth, even if those ideals are sometimes invoked insincerely and hypocritically by particular political actors. And so the response to the instrumental-ization of human rights by superpowers is not to weaken international protection, but rather to try to strengthen it—that is, to develop more consistent and impartial procedures for monitoring and assessing human rights protection.

In the case of minority rights, however, efforts to persuade people in post-colonial states of the intrinsic merits of the ideals of liberal multi-culturalism have been less successful. As a result, in response to existing inconsistencies and double standards, there is greater disagreement about whether to strengthen or to dilute the international monitoring of minor-ity rights. If the American government has applied double standards to Turkey and Iraq regarding the Kurds, should the response be to weaken international support for the autonomy-aspirations of the Iraqi Kurds, or to strengthen international support for the Kurds in Turkey? If there have been double-standards in the international response to the mistreatment of minorities in Sudan and the Philippines, should the response be to reduce international support for the autonomy of Christian minorities in Sudan, or to strengthen international support for the autonomy of Muslim minorities in the Philippines?

Many minority rights advocates assume that the goal should be to level up, not level down. This is what I referred to in Chapter 1 as 'filling the frame' of international minority rights norms. But in the absence of a consensus on the intrinsic merits of liberal multiculturalism, and given fear of its use as a tool of geo-politics, the more likely response is to level down. While many post-colonial states are offended by the perceived double-standards in the application of norms of minority rights, most would prefer to deal with this by weakening international support for minority rights, not strengthening it. They would prefer to empty the frame of international minority rights, not fill it.

These first three factors explain a great deal of the resistance to liberal models of multiculturalism amongst state elites and dominant groups in the post-colonial world. Even if they were attracted to the principles of liberal multiculturalism, and accepted the philosophical legitimacy of certain minority claims, they might still firmly resist it on the grounds that it is too risky in their circumstances. In a condition of regional insecurity surrounded by neighbouring enemies and hostile international powers, autonomy arrangements can be a threat to the very security of the state. And in the absence of democratic consolidation, autonomy arrangements can be a threat to the very life and liberty of individual citizens who belong to the 'wrong' group. Under these circumstances, the intended goal of multiculturalism—namely, replacing uncivil relations of enmity and exclusion with more equitable relations of liberal-democratic citizenship—may be subverted. Institutions and policies designed to promote 'citizenization' in multiethnic states may be captured by internal and external actors who seek to perpetuate and exacerbate relations of enmity and exclusion.

However, the opposition to liberal multiculturalism does not simply derive from these contingent risks to state security and individual rights. There are other factors as well in the post-colonial world that put into question the underlying normative justification for liberal multiculturalism. The reality is that some of the factors that legitimate the claims of minorities in the West do not apply with the same force in other parts of the world.

(4) Colonial Legacies of Ethnic Hierarchies A fourth important factor affecting the post-colonial world is precisely the legacy of colonialism on interethnic relations. Colonial rulers were naturally fearful of the numerically

largest groups within their colonies, who posed the greatest threat to their rule. As a result, they often chose to privilege minorities within each colony, and to recruit them disproportionately into the colonial education system, military, and civil service. It was assumed that such privileged minorities would be more loyal to the colonial rulers, in part because they too might have had their own fears about the larger groups. A classic case concerns the Tamil minority in Sri Lanka, who were privileged by the British over the Sinhalese majority.

As a result, when independence was granted, the larger groups in many post-colonial states felt that it was they who had been the victims of historic injustice, and that minorities had been the beneficiaries of this injustice. Justice, therefore, required not the strengthening of minority rights, but rather their curtailment.[17] And indeed one of the first acts of the independent Sri Lankan state was to retrench the minority rights of the Tamils, leading eventually to civil war.

As we saw in Chapter 6, a similar phenomenon exists in many post-communist states, where the majorities within newly independent states feel themselves to be the victims of historic injustice at the hands of their minorities. In the West, by contrast, the homeland minorities demanding minority rights have almost universally been the victims of historic injustice at the hands of the majority groups. Their languages have historically been suppressed by the majority group, their natural resources exploited, their traditional forms of self-government suppressed, and so on. Their contemporary claim for autonomy, therefore, is buttressed by the fact that they have been the victims of historic injustice at the hands of the dominant majority. In this context, claims to multiculturalism can be seen as 'righting a historic wrong'. Claims for autonomy by certain minorities in post-colonial states, however, are often seen by the majority group as perpetuating an historic wrong, reinforcing a colonial-era injustice originally adopted precisely in order to suppress the majority group.[18] Just as claims for 'minority rights' by white South Africans have little popular

---

[17] Indeed, in many cases it is widely believed that colonial powers actually *created* the perception that there were distinct ethnic groups within the colony, artificially turning what had been a fluid and overlapping set of identities into distinct 'tribes' or 'peoples', as part of their 'divide and rule' strategies. Under these circumstances, suppressing minority identities is sometimes justified on the grounds that these identities are the inauthentic results of external manipulation, and that assimilationist policies are simply reversing this historic injustice.

[18] This phenomenon is exacerbated in those countries where minorities maintained power even after independence, due to the lack of democracy—as in Syria, pre-civil war Lebanon, Rwanda, apartheid South Africa, or Iraq under Hussein. In such countries, talk of 'minority rights' is seen as justifying the undemocratic retention of power by a privileged minority.

resonance, so too claims by other historically privileged minorities fall on deaf ears.

(5) Demography A related factor concerns the demography of ethnic diversity in Western states compared to many post-colonial states. In virtually every Western democracy, there is a clearly dominant majority group that has controlled the state, and used that control to diffuse its language, culture, and identity. Indeed, the state is typically named after this dominant group—it literally has a state to call its own. Minority rights, in this context, are understood as a means of protecting minorities against the clear and present danger that a dominant majority will use its control of the state to assimilate or exclude minorities. And autonomy is clearly one effective tool for protecting minorities in this regard.

In many post-colonial states, however, there is no majority group. In many African countries, for example, no single ethnic group makes up more than 20 or 30 per cent of the population. In this context, it is less clear what types of minority rights are required. To be sure, the members of different ethnic groups have a legitimate interest in receiving their fair share of state benefits and resources, but there may be no comparable fear of being subject to the assimilationist projects of a dominant national group. If no single group is capable of capturing the state and using it as a tool for diffusing its particular language, culture, and identity, then minorities do not need protection against that particular danger. And in that sense, there may be less basis for claiming that autonomy is needed to protect minorities from a culturally alien central state dominated by another ethnonational group.[19]

If we put all of these factors together, it should not be surprising that attempts to promote the best practices of Western multiculturalism have largely failed. The Western discourse assumes that homeland minorities have historically been subordinated by a dominant majority group that controls the state. Liberal multiculturalism is a way of remedying that historic wrong, and ensuring that it doesn't occur again. The Western discourse also assumes that this issue can be negotiated as an issue of domestic social policy, independently of regional state security, and that the outcomes of these domestic negotiations can reliably be expected to operate within the framework of liberal-democratic constitutionalism, thereby contributing to the process of citizenization.

---

[19] For further discussion of the relevance of this factor in Africa, see Kymlicka 2006*b*.

These assumptions rarely apply outside the consolidated Western democracies. Latin America comes closest to matching the Western pattern. As with minorities in the West, indigenous peoples in Latin America have clearly been subordinated by a historically dominant group that controls the state, and multiculturalism can be seen as a way of remedying this injustice. Moreover, because indigenous peoples do not have kin-states or irredentist ambitions, multicultural reforms can be adopted as a matter of domestic policy, without raising fears of geo-political security. And there is greater trust that IOs are not out to destabilize these countries. It is not surprising, therefore, that the diffusion of liberal multiculturalism has some prospect of success in this region.[20]

In most of Asia, Africa, and the Middle East, however, the circumstances are very different. In many post-colonial states, there is no dominant majority group that controls the state, and even if there is, it often sees itself as the victim of historic injustice at the hands of privileged minorities acting in collaboration with colonial powers. Talk of minority rights is seen as perpetuating that historic wrong. Moreover, in conditions of regional insecurity and weak state institutions, minority rights are seen as posing threats to both state security and individual rights, undercutting attempts to construct bonds of citizenship. And the attempt by the international community to promote minority rights is often seen as a tool of geo-politics to bolster Western hegemony and to weaken any states that challenge it.

From Best Practices to Norms and Standards

Given these circumstances, it is not surprising that efforts by international organizations to publicize best practices of liberal multiculturalism have had as little success in post-colonial states as they had in post-communist states. If anything, the conditions in Africa, Asia, and the Middle East are

[20] The underdeveloped nature of the rule of law in Latin America means that there is no guarantee against the possibility that indigenous self-government will create islands of local tyranny. However, since indigenous self-government in Latin America has tended to be village-level, rather than regional, few non-indigenous peoples have ended up under indigenous governments. So the fear that members of the dominant group will be persecuted by indigenous governments has been rare. That leaves the fear that indigenous governments will oppress some of their own members, such as women, and this has indeed been the official basis on which some Latin American countries have resisted indigenous self-government. Whether this is their real motivation has been questioned by many commentators (Speed and Collier 2000).

even less propitious for the voluntary adoption of liberal multiculturalist models than they are in Central and Eastern Europe.

International organizations seeking to influence state–minority relations have therefore attempted to supplement the best practices approach with other, more effective, strategies. In particular, like European organizations, they have embarked on the project of formulating legal or quasi-legal norms and standards that all countries are expected to meet.

As we saw in the European context, any attempt to formulate norms and standards immediately confronts the question of categories. Is the goal to formulate generic minority rights, applying to all ethnocultural minorities, or to formulate targeted minority rights, applying to particular types of minorities, such as indigenous peoples, national minorities, immigrants, pastoralists, and so on?

The initial foray into this area by the UN reflects the generic strategy. As we've seen, Article 27 of the 1966 International Covenant on Civil and Political Rights has been interpreted to cover all ethnocultural minorities, whether new or old, large or small, territorially concentrated or dispersed. Precisely for this reason, however, it proved unable to deal with the distinctive claims raised by historic homeland minorities, whose aspirations are rooted in the facts of historic settlement and territorial concentration. It was in response to this problem that European organizations decided instead in the early 1990s to adopt a targeted approach focusing on the issues raised by national minorities.

The UN has adopted a different response to the limitations of Article 27. On the one hand, it has attempted to resuscitate the generic strategy, by trying to strengthen the generic 'right to enjoy one's culture' so as to include some positive minority rights. This was the goal of the UN Declaration on the Rights of Persons Belonging to National, Ethnic, Religious and Linguistic Minorities, adopted by the General Assembly in 1992, and of the UN Human Rights Committee's 'General Comment on Article 27' in 1994.

However, these reaffirmations and expansions of the generic approach involve only mild changes to the basic principles of Article 27, and remain silent on the distinctive issues raised by homeland minorities, with their claims rooted in history and territory.

And so the UN has also embarked on its own version of the targeted rights approach, alongside its ongoing generic rights strategy. The UN, however, has chosen to target a different category of homeland minority. Whereas European norms are targeted at national minorities, the UN norms are targeted at indigenous peoples. This is an important difference, with profound implications for the global diffusion of liberal multiculturalism, and we need to understand why these different targets have been chosen.

The first step is to clarify the terms. What precisely is the difference between 'national minorities' and 'indigenous peoples'? Like most terms used to categorize ethnocultural groups, the terms indigenous peoples and national minorities have contested definitions and unclear boundaries. There is a relatively clear and uncontroversial core to each category—what we might consider the paradigm examples of each type of group—and then a more fuzzy periphery, where attempts to apply the term become increasingly contested.

If we focus on their respective core examples, the terms indigenous peoples and national minorities designate quite different types of homeland minorities. To oversimplify, the term indigenous peoples arose primarily in the context of New World settler states, and refers to the descendents of the original non-European inhabitants of lands colonized and settled by European powers. Most of the early work on indigenous issues at the ILO and UN, for example, focused on the 'Indian' populations in Latin America. National minorities, by contrast, is a term invented in Europe to refer to European groups that lost out in the rough and tumble process of European state formation over the past five centuries, and whose homelands ended up being incorporated (in whole or in part) into larger states dominated by a neighbouring European people. National minorities were active players in the process by which the early-modern welter of empires, kingdoms, and principalities in Europe was turned into the modern system of nation-states, but they either ended up without a state of their own ('stateless nations', like the Scots or Chechens), or ended up on the wrong side of the border, cut off from their co-ethnics in a neighbouring kin-state ('kin-state minorities', like the ethnic Germans in Italy, or ethnic Hungarians in Romania).

These are the core cases for the two categories. A preliminary and crude way of distinguishing them is to say that national minorities have been incorporated into a larger state dominated by a neighbouring European people, whereas indigenous peoples have been colonized and settled by a distant colonial European power. But there are other ways of marking the distinction between the two types of groups that supervene on this basic historical difference. It is widely accepted, for example, that the subjugation and incorporation of indigenous peoples by European colonizers was a more brutal and disruptive process than the subjugation and incorporation of national minorities by neighbouring societies, and that this has left indigenous peoples weaker and more vulnerable. It is also often assumed that there is a 'civilizational' difference between indigenous peoples and national minorities. Whereas national minorities typically share the same modern (urbanized, industrialized) economic and socio-political structures as their neighbouring European peoples, indigenous peoples are often assumed to have retained pre-modern modes of economic production, engaged primarily in subsistence agriculture or a hunting/gathering lifestyle. And, as a result of large-scale colonizing settlement, it is also often assumed that indigenous peoples have been relegated to isolated and remote areas, unlike national minorities.

In their core cases, therefore, and in everyday usage, the two terms refer to quite different types of groups, rooted in fundamentally different historical processes, and differing in their contemporary characteristics, including their vulnerabilities, mode of production, and habitat.

So understood, both terms have their origins in distinctively Western historical processes. National minorities are contenders but losers in the slow process of state formation within continental Europe itself; indigenous peoples are the victims of the construction of European settler states in the New World. As such, it's not immediately clear whether either term can usefully be applied outside Europe and the New World. And indeed various African and Asian countries have insisted that neither category applies to them.[21]

However, if we focus on the sorts of contemporary characteristics that typify these two types of groups, then we can find analogous types of groups in other contexts. For example, we can find groups in Asia or Africa that share the cultural vulnerability, pre-modern economies, and remoteness of some indigenous peoples in the New World, even if they are not the subjects of a European settler state. Such groups include various 'hill tribes', 'forest peoples', and 'pastoralists'.

Similarly, we can find groups in many post-colonial states that are similar to European national minorities in being active players, but eventual losers, in the process of decolonization and post-colonial state formation. These would include groups like the Tamils in Sri Lanka, Tibetans in China, Kurds in Iraq, Acehnese in Indonesia, Oromos and Tigrayans in Ethiopia, or the Palestinians in Israel. Like national minorities in Europe, they may have hoped to form their own state in the process of

---

[21] For example, the government of Zambia claims that 'Zambia does not have the classifications of indigenous populations and minority communities as defined by the United Nations Organization' (UN Doc. CRC/C/11/Add.25, 19 November 2002, para. 470), quoted in Lennox 2006.

decolonization, or at least to have secured a degree of autonomy, and indeed may have been promised autonomy to secure their cooperation in the decolonization struggle, but ended up being subordinated to a more powerful group within a larger state, or divided between two or more post-colonial states.

So while the distinction between indigenous peoples and national minorities as two different kinds of homeland minorities has its origins in Europe and European settler states, there are plausible ways of extending its application to the larger world.

Having outlined the distinction between the two types of groups, we can now return to the question of why European organizations have targeted national minorities while the UN has targeted indigenous peoples. In the former case, the answer, as we saw in the last chapter, is that European organizations saw national minorities in post-communist Europe as posing a profound threat to international peace and security, with risks not only of intra-state violence, but also of spillover effects that could destabilize the entire region. It was on this basis that European organizations declared that the treatment of national minorities was a matter of legitimate international concern.

At the UN, however, we see a different rationale for developing targeted rights.[22] There was no comparable fear that indigenous people form a threat to international peace and security. This is partly because indigenous peoples do not have nearby kin-states that might call upon them to serve as a fifth column, and partly because they are generally seen as falling outside the main battle-lines of inter-state rivalries and regional geo-politics. In any event, they are often too small or remote to pose an effective challenge to state power. Just as it is part of the everyday image of national minorities that they are potential players or pawns in regional

---

[22] There was not only a different rationale for targeted norms at the UN, but also, and relatedly, a different process. In the case of the OSCE and Council of Europe, the decision to develop targeted norms for national minorities was taken at the highest levels of these organizations, as a response to urgent threats to peace and security, prior to any significant degree of lobbying by national minorities themselves. Indeed, minority organizations did not play any meaningful role in the initial process of formulating these European norms from 1990 to 1995. At the UN, by contrast, the decision to develop targeted norms for indigenous peoples emerged more slowly, and through a bottom-up process, as a result of massive mobilization and lobbying by indigenous peoples themselves, with the support of independent experts associated with the Sub-Commission on Human Rights. While indigenous peoples and their advocates have been able to move their agenda upwards and outwards, beyond its initial home in the Sub-Commission, this has often been in the face of the relative indifference of the highest organs of the UN, such as the Security Council, or indeed the General Assembly.

geo-politics, it is part of the everyday image of indigenous peoples that they are isolated from regional geo-politics.[23]

The explanation for targeting indigenous peoples, therefore, was not geo-political security threats, but a more humanitarian concern to protect a particularly vulnerable group. As we saw in Chapter 2, the initial expression of this humanitarian concern, reflected in the 1957 ILO Convention, was profoundly paternalistic, based on the assumption that indigenous peoples were too 'backward' to be able to know how to deal with the challenges of the larger world. It was a humanitarian concern laced with cultural contempt. But the more multiculturalist models of indigenous rights that have emerged in the 1980s and 1990s reject this paternalist approach, while still emphasizing the distinctive vulnerability of indigenous peoples to state-imposed projects of assimilation and development. The explanation for this distinct vulnerability is no longer located in the alleged deficiencies or idiosyncracies of indigenous cultures, but rather in the brutal way that European settler states have colonized and settled indigenous lands. The way that indigenous peoples have been dispossessed, resettled, and dispersed in the name of 'national development' became a major embarrassment not only to their states, but also to the international organizations that had been promoting these development projects.[24]

As I noted in Chapter 4, we need to understand these newer ideas of indigenous rights as a third stage in the post-war human rights struggle against ethnic and racial hierarchy, building upon earlier struggles for overseas decolonization and racial desegregation. The ideas advanced by the 'Red Power' movement that arose in the United States in the 1960s (and comparable indigenous movements in other New World countries) were clearly modelled on and inspired by both of these earlier struggles, drawing on the discourse of both decolonization and anti-racism. When the international community first endorsed the principle of decolonization, it only applied this principle to overseas colonies, not to the

---

[23] Nietschmann (1987) talks of a 'Fourth World War' between states and indigenous peoples, but this is a reference to the global prevalence of local conflicts between states and indigenous peoples, not a prediction that local conflicts could become enmeshed in larger regional or global geo-political struggles.

[24] The concern amongst organizations like the World Bank to show that they had learned from high-profile scandals involving the mistreatment of indigenous peoples was grounded as much in a self-interested desire to preserve their public legitimacy as a humanitarian concern for indigenous peoples. But the reason why these had become high-profile scandals in the first place was the humanitarian concern amongst the wider Western and international public. Transnational advocacy networks in support of indigenous peoples were able to tap into this humanitarian public sentiment, and use it to put pressure on IOs like the World Bank.

indigenous peoples colonized by European settler states in the New World. But from a moral perspective, this is clearly inconsistent. Indeed, given that indigenous peoples were subject not only to imperial conquest (as with colonies in Africa or Asia), but also to colonizing settlement, one could argue that they suffered an even greater injustice from colonialism than overseas colonies. In any event, once the international community had accepted principles of overseas decolonization and racial desegregation, it was difficult to deny indigenous claims of historic injustice, or to deny the appropriateness of some form of (internal) decolonization.

International concern and support for indigenous rights, therefore, reflect a mixture of motivations, drawing on powerful moral arguments about the injustice of colonization and racial discrimination, combined with lingering paternalistic ideas about the distinctive vulnerability of 'backward' cultures. But whatever the precise mixture of reasons, it is clearly a different motivation from that which underpinned the targeting of national minorities in Europe. National minorities were targeted for reasons of geo-political security; indigenous peoples were targeted for moral and humanitarian reasons of historic injustice and protection of the vulnerable.[25]

Both of these are perfectly legitimate reasons for embarking on the project of developing targeted rights. But they both have limitations that we need to be conscious of. The fact that UN norms of indigenous rights are based on humanitarian concerns rather than geo-political security is a source of both strength and weakness. On the positive side, the absence (or at least relative mildness) of geo-political security issues has made it easier to make serious progress in developing robust minority rights norms.[26] As we saw in Chapter 6, such progress has proven impossible in the context of European national minorities. The very geo-political security fears that led European organizations to target national minorities have also prevented these organizations from actually addressing any of the distinctive issues raised by national minorities, particularly their claims relating to history and territory. As a result, the evolving European norms are targeted in form but generic in content, and because of this

---

[25] In this sense, the indigenous rights track fits the pattern discussed by Keck and Sikkink in which perceptions of 'innocence' and 'vulnerability' are central in determining which causes are picked up within international human rights networks (Keck and Sikkink 1999: 204).

[26] Security issues are not entirely absent in relation to indigenous peoples—see Van Cott 1996 and Toyota 2005 on the securitization of indigenous issues in Latin America and South-East Asia respectively. Since indigenous peoples often inhabit border areas, their land claims and self-government rights are sometimes seen as raising security issues, even if they are not suspected of collaborating with neighbouring states. And indigenous peoples were an important element in some rebel movements in Latin America (e.g. in Guatemala).

inconsistency, the very project of developing targeted rights for national minorities as a supplement to generic minority rights is in danger of collapsing.

The UN norms on indigenous rights, by contrast, clearly do address the specific needs and challenges of indigenous peoples. They are targeted in both form and content. They focus precisely on the distinctive issues raised by the fact that indigenous peoples define themselves in relation to their historic homelands, and express a strong desire to retain or regain political control over themselves, their institutions, and their territories. Indeed, virtually all of the international instruments relating to indigenous peoples reiterate the intention to respect and honour this connection between indigenous peoples and their historic territories.

At their most ambitious, these evolving international norms and standards of indigenous rights are very powerful indeed. Whereas the European norms on national minorities start from the Article 27 right to enjoy one's culture, the UN's norms on indigenous rights start from a modified version of the Article 1 right to self-determination. The 1993 UN Draft Declaration on the Rights of Indigenous Peoples, for example, includes the following articles:

Article 3: Indigenous peoples have the right of self-determination. By virtue of that right, they freely determine their political status and freely pursue their economic, social and cultural development.

Article 15: [Indigenous peoples] have the right to establish and control their educational systems and institutions providing education in their own languages, in a manner appropriate to their cultural methods of teaching and learning.

Article 26: Indigenous peoples have the right to own, develop, control and use the lands and territories...which they have traditionally owned or otherwise occupied or used. This includes the right to the full recognition of their laws, traditions and customs, land-tenure systems and institutions for the development and management of resources...

Article 31: Indigenous peoples, as a specific form of exercising their right to self-determination, have the right to autonomy or self-government in matters relating to their internal affairs...

Article 33: Indigenous peoples have the right to promote, develop and maintain their institutional structures and their distinctive juridical customs, traditions, procedures and practices, in accordance with internationally recognized human rights standards.[27]

[27] Quoted from the version adopted by the Working Group on Indigenous Populations in 1993, and the Sub-Commission on Prevention of Discrimination and Protection of Minorities in 1994 (E/CN.4/Sub.2/1994/56). After more than a decade of meetings of debates, a

In short, the Draft Declaration recognizes indigenous rights over territory and resources, as well as rights to autonomous legal, political, and cultural institutions. Although these articles are being proposed as minimum standards that all countries would have a responsibility to meet, they are in fact very close to the best practices of Western democracies in relation to indigenous peoples.

This Draft Declaration is still just a draft, but as I noted earlier, its core ideas have been picked up by various organs within the UN system, and similar ideas have been articulated by the ILO, and in the Draft Declaration on Indigenous Rights in the Organization of American States.[28] So these ideas are circulating widely throughout IOs and their associated global policy networks, and as we've seen, they have had demonstrable effects, especially in Latin America.[29]

In this way, the UN's targeted norms for indigenous peoples can be seen as a genuine success. They address the distinctive needs of indigenous peoples in a way that European targeted norms for national minorities do not, and thereby provide evidence that the very strategy of developing targeted norms is a legitimate and potentially effective one. Indeed, many commentators point to the emergence of international indigenous rights as one of the few truly successful examples of how international law can be used as a tool of 'counter-hegemonic globalization' (e.g. Falk 1999, 2000).

The fact that the targeted indigenous track is based on humanitarian motivations, not security issues, has made this remarkable progress possible. However, the decision to shift from a security-inspired focus on national minorities to a humanitarian focus on indigenous peoples also has its limitations. One obvious limitation is that it leaves us with no global legal norms addressed to the distinctive needs and challenges raised by national minorities in the post-colonial world. Yet it is precisely conflicts involving such (ethno-)national or minority nationalist groups that pose the greatest threat to peace, security, human rights, and development in much of the post-colonial world. It is the ethnopolitical struggles of groups like the Tamils, Kurds, Kashmiris, and Oromos that have posed

slightly modified version was adopted by the Human Rights Council in 2006, see UN Doc. A/HRC/1/L.3, Annex (23 June 2006).

[28] See pp. 33–4 above.

[29] For helpful studies of the international indigenous rights movement, and its successes and failures in influencing the UN and other IOs, see Tennant 1994; Barsh 1994; Passy 1999; Feldman 2002; Muehlebach 2003.

a potential threat to regional peace and stability, not the struggles of pastoralists or forest dwellers.

One potential response to this gap would be to supplement the existing UN norms on indigenous peoples with another set of targeted norms directed at national minorities—that is, to formulate a global version of the Council of Europe's Framework Convention for the Protection of National Minorities. As we've seen in Chapter 3, this sort of 'multi-targeting' would reflect the logic of liberal multiculturalism, which involves a range of group-differentiated legal tracks, including distinctive tracks for national minorities and indigenous peoples.

Unfortunately, that is, at best, a very long-term goal. The prospects for developing global norms on national minorities are non-existent in the foreseeable future, for all the reasons we've discussed earlier. The West has backed away from formulating such norms in the European context, and there is no support at the UN or in any other regional organization for even embarking on such a project. The only attempt that I'm aware of to formulate such norms at the global level—namely, the Draft Convention on Self-Determination through Self-Administration submitted by Liechtenstein to the UN General Assembly in 1994—was never seriously considered or debated.[30] So the current UN framework which adopts targeted norms for indigenous peoples but not for national minorities is unlikely to change.

For some commentators, the absence of targeted protection for national minorities is simply a regrettable gap in the UN's current approach, but doesn't put into question the validity of the targeted indigenous norms. We should make progress where we can, and if the current circumstances only allow for progress on the indigenous track, then we should move forward there, and not wait until we can move forward on all the possible targeted tracks simultaneously.

In my view, however, the matter is more complicated. The sharp distinction in legal status between indigenous peoples and national minorities is creating a number of paradoxes and perverse effects that may ultimately destabilize the indigenous track itself. It may be that the only way to sustain a system of targeted indigenous rights is also to find a way to develop targeted norms for national minorities.

In order to understand the problem here, we need to recall how the category of indigenous peoples fits into the broader patterns of liberal multiculturalism in the West. As I noted earlier, both indigenous peoples

---

[30] See the discussion on p. 208 above.

and national minorities are recognized and treated as homeland minorities in most Western democracies. There are important sociological and historical differences between the two types of homeland minorities, and these carry with them legal implications in most Western countries, but it is important not to lose sight of their commonalities. Both types of groups are treated as homeland minorities, and both have been accorded territorial autonomy within Western liberal democracies. In this respect, they are distinguished from 'new' minorities composed of immigrants, guest-workers, and refugees. From the perspective of the theory and practice of liberal multiculturalism in the West, indigenous peoples and national minorities belong together as self-governing homeland minorities, in a different category from new minorities.

In the emerging international discourse, however, the important commonalities between indigenous peoples and national minorities have been obscured, and instead an artificial chasm has been created between the rights of indigenous peoples and other homeland minorities. There was, at first, an understandable moral justification for this trend. As we've seen, the subjugation of indigenous peoples by European colonizers was typically a more brutal and disruptive process than the subjugation of national minorities by neighbouring European societies, and this has left indigenous peoples more vulnerable, and hence in more urgent need of international protection. As a result, there was a plausible moral argument for giving priority to indigenous peoples over national minorities in the codification of rights to self-government in international law, even if the basic normative arguments for self-government apply to both.[31]

However, what began as a difference in relative priority and urgency between the claims of indigenous peoples and national minorities has developed into an almost total rupture between the two at the level of international law. Across a wide range of international documents and declarations, indigenous peoples have been separated out from other homeland minorities, and claims to territory and self-government have been restricted to the former. National minorities, by contrast, are lumped together with new minorities and accorded only generic minority rights, ignoring their distinctive needs and aspirations relating to historic

---

[31] According to James Anaya, the foremost expert on indigenous rights in international law, all substate nations or peoples have the same substantive rights to internal self-determination as indigenous peoples. The rationale for having international norms targeted specifically at indigenous peoples, on his view, is purely a remedial one: indigenous peoples are more likely to have had their substantive rights violated in the past (Anaya 1996). Unfortunately, the current international discourse obscures, rather than illuminates, the common substantive rights of different homeland groups.

settlement and territorial concentration. As a result, the distinction between indigenous peoples and other homeland minorities has acquired a significance and rigidity within international law that is entirely missing in the theory and practice of liberal multiculturalism.

This attempt to draw a sharp distinction between indigenous peoples and national minorities in international law raises a number of difficult questions. It creates (i) moral inconsistencies, (ii) conceptual confusion, and (iii) unstable political dynamics. Let me explain each of these points.

The sharp distinction in rights between the two types of groups is morally inconsistent, because whatever arguments exist for recognizing rights of self-government for indigenous peoples also apply to the claims of self-government for other vulnerable and historically disadvantaged homeland groups. In an interesting paper, Miriam Aukerman compared the claims of indigenous peoples with those of national minorities in post-communist countries, and noted the strong similarities in underlying goals and justifications. As she puts it, 'Indigenous peoples and Central-East European [national] minorities share the goal of preserving their distinctive cultures, and justify their claims to group-differentiated rights with similar appeals to self-determination, equality, cultural diversity, history and vulnerability' (Aukerman 2000: 1045).

Indeed, this is clear from the UN's own explanations and justifications for the targeted indigenous track. The Chair of the UN's Working Group on Minorities (Asbjorn Eide) and the Chair of the UN Working Group on Indigenous Populations (Erica-Irene Daes) were both asked to write a note on their understanding of the distinction between indigenous peoples and minorities (Eide and Daes 2000). In trying to explain why indigenous peoples are entitled to targeted rights beyond those available to all minorities under the generic Article 27, the two Chairs identified three key differences: (a) whereas minorities seek institutional integration, indigenous peoples seek to preserve a degree of institutional separateness; (b) whereas minorities seek individual rights, indigenous peoples seek collectively exercised rights; (c) whereas minorities seek non-discrimination, indigenous peoples seek self-government. These are all relevant differences between indigenous peoples and non-homeland groups, such as immigrants, but they do not distinguish indigenous peoples from national minorities. On all three points national minorities fall on the same side of the equation as indigenous peoples.

In an earlier document prepared for the Working Group on Indigenous Populations, Daes offered a somewhat different account (Daes 1996). She stated that the crucial distinguishing feature of indigenous peoples, compared to minorities in general, is that they have a strong attachment to a traditional territory which they view as their historic homeland. As she puts it, 'attachment to a homeland is nonetheless definitive of the identity and integrity of the [indigenous] group, socially and culturally. This may suggest a very narrow but precise definition of "indigenous", sufficient to be applied to any situation where the problem is one of distinguishing an indigenous people [from] the larger class of minorities' (Daes 1996, para. 39). But this criterion—'attachment to a homeland'— obviously picks out homeland minorities in general, including national minorities, not indigenous peoples in particular.

As these quotes show, discussions within the UN of the distinction between indigenous peoples and minorities systematically ignore the existence of national minorities. Daes claims, for example, that it is 'possible to identify at least two factors [in the case of indigenous peoples] which have never been associated with the concept of "minorities": priority in time and attachment to a particular territory' (Daes 1996: para. 60). But of course these ideas have always been associated with the concept of a national minority.

Or consider Daes's concluding summary of the fundamental distinction between minorities and indigenous peoples:

Bearing the conceptual problem [of distinguishing indigenous peoples from minorities] in mind, I should like to suggest that the ideal type of an 'indigenous people' is a group that is aboriginal (autochthonous) to the territory where it resides today and chooses to perpetuate a distinct cultural identity and distinct collective social and political organization within the territory. The ideal type of a 'minority' is a group that has experienced exclusion or discrimination by the State or its citizens because of its ethnic, national, racial, religious or linguistic characteristics or ancestry. From a purposive perspective, then, the ideal type of 'minority' focuses on the group's experience of discrimination because the intent of existing international standards has been to combat discrimination, against the group as a whole as well as its individual members, and to provide for them the opportunity to integrate themselves freely into national life to the degree they choose. Likewise, the ideal type of 'indigenous peoples' focuses on aboriginality, territoriality, and the desire to remain collectively distinct, all elements which are tied logically to the exercise of the right to internal self-determination, self-government, or autonomy. (Eide and Daes 2000, paras 48–9)

This is a fine summary of the distinction between two ideal types of groups, but it provides no explanation or justification for distinguishing indigenous peoples from other homeland minorities. On all of Daes's criteria, national minorities and indigenous peoples fit into the same ideal type based on territory and autonomy, while new and dispersed minorities fall into the other.

Daes is not unaware of this problem, and acknowledges that it may be difficult to find a principled basis for distinguishing the claims of indigenous peoples from other homeland minorities. Nonetheless, she insists that *in practice* the two types of groups make different claims: 'The facts remain that indigenous peoples and minorities organize themselves separately and tend to assert different objectives, even in those countries where they appear to differ very little in "objective" characteristics' (Eide and Daes 2000, para. 41). Steven Wheatley makes a similar claim: 'There is no objective distinction that can be made between groups recognized as minorities, national minorities, indigenous peoples and peoples. What distinguishes these groups is the nature of their political demands: simply put, minorities and national minorities demand cultural security; peoples demand recognition of their right to self-determination, or self-government' (Wheatley 2005: 124).

These are extraordinary claims. As we've seen, the whole history of European debates on 'the minority problem' has been shaped precisely by the fact that national minorities *do* make claims to self-government and not just to cultural security.[32] And not just in Europe. As we saw in Chapter 2, the flurry of international norm-setting in relation to minority rights in the early 1990s was driven by the fear of a global proliferation of ethnic civil wars between states and their substate national groups. While the UN's concern with indigenous peoples dates back to the 1970s and 1980s, the sudden explosion of interest given to 'minorities' at the UN dates from the end of the Cold War, and the ethnic conflicts it unleashed. The fear of 'ethnic pandemonium' rested precisely on the fact that struggles for self-government are found, not just amongst indigenous peoples, but also amongst many substate ethnonational groups around the world. And yet the current debate on minority rights within the UN seems to operate on the premise that the phenomenon of minority nationalism

---

[32] It may be the case that in post-colonial states, indigenous peoples today are more likely to demand self-government than national minorities, although I'm not at all sure this generalization is true. But even if so, Daes and Wheatley are surely reversing cause and effect. They imply that international law recognizes rights of self-government for indigenous peoples and not for national minorities because the former are more likely to demand such rights. I would argue the reverse: insofar as indigenous peoples today are more likely to demand such rights, it is because international law supports such claims, while offering no support to similar claims by national minorities. Indeed, most states around the world oppose codifying a norm of self-government for national minorities precisely because they know that national minorities do want self-government, and states do not want these substate nationalist projects to receive any international support or encouragement.

does not exist: minorities, by definition, do not seek self-government. The very problem that helped generate the post-Cold War international concern for minority rights in the first place is defined out of existence.

If we refuse to close our eyes to the phenomenon of national minorities, then the moral inconsistencies in the current UN framework become very noticeable. Virtually all of the moral principles and arguments advanced within the UN for targeted indigenous rights also apply to national minorities, and the sharp gulf in legal status between the two types of groups lacks any clear moral justification. For *realpolitik* reasons, it may be impossible to extend international norms of self-government to national minorities. As we've seen, states are less willing to contemplate demands for self-government by groups that pose a credible threat to the state, and these groups tend to be national minorities rather than indigenous peoples. But we shouldn't dress up this *realpolitik* consideration in the language of moral principle, or ignore the moral inconsistencies it generates.

The attempt to draw a sharp distinction in legal status between national minorities and indigenous peoples is not only morally problematic, it is also conceptually unstable. The problem is not simply how to justify the sharp difference in legal rights between national minorities and indigenous peoples, but how to identify the two types of groups in the first place. The very distinction between indigenous peoples and other homeland minorities is difficult to draw outside the original core cases of Europe and European settler states.

In the West, as we've seen, there is a relatively clear distinction to be drawn between European national minorities and New World indigenous peoples. Both are homeland groups, but the former have been incorporated into a larger state dominated by a neighbouring people, whereas the latter have been colonized and settled by a distant colonial power. It is far less clear how we can draw this distinction in Africa, Asia, or the Middle East, or whether the categories even make sense. Depending on how we define the terms, we could say that none of the homeland groups in these regions are 'indigenous', or that all of them are.

In one familiar sense, no groups in Africa, Asia, or the Middle East fit the traditional profile of 'indigenous peoples'. All homeland minorities in these regions have been incorporated into larger states dominated by neighbouring groups, rather than being incorporated into settler states dominated by European settlers.[33] In that sense, they are all closer to the

---

[33] Some commentators argue that Israel should be included as a European settler state, and hence that Palestinians fit the traditional definition of an indigenous people (Jabareen 2002, 2005; Jamal 2005).

profile of European national minorities than to New World indigenous peoples. And, for this reason, several Asian and African countries insist that none of their minorities should be designated as 'indigenous peoples'.

In another sense, however, we could say that all homeland groups in these regions (including the dominant majority group) are 'indigenous'. During the era of colonial rule, all historically settled groups, majority and minority alike, were designated as 'natives' or 'indigenous' in relation to the colonial rulers. In this sense, all homeland groups in post-colonial states (including the dominant group) are equally 'indigenous'. And indeed the governments of several Asian and African countries declare that *all* their groups, majority and minority, should be considered 'indigenous'.[34]

These two approaches yield diametrically opposed results, but whether we say that all groups are indigenous or that no groups are indigenous, the upshot in either case is to undermine the possibility of using the category of 'indigenous peoples' as a basis for targeted norms within post-colonial states. For this reason, some commentators have argued that the legal category of indigenous people is misleading, and should not be applied, in Africa and Asia (e.g. Béteille 2000). However, the result of this approach would leave some of the most vulnerable homeland minorities in the world without any meaningful form of international protection. If targeted indigenous norms do not apply in Asia or Africa, that leaves only the (very weak) generic minority rights under Article 27, and these provide no protection for homeland-related interests.

In order to take advantage of the protections of international law, therefore, various IOs and their affiliated global policy networks have attempted to re-conceptualize the category of indigenous peoples so that it covers at least some homeland minorities in post-colonial states. On this view, we shouldn't focus on whether homeland minorities are dominated by settlers from a distant colonial power or by neighbouring peoples. What matters is simply the facts of domination and vulnerability, and finding appropriate means to remedy them.[35] If homeland groups suffer

---

[34] This label was not extended to ethnic groups brought by the colonizers, such as the Indians recruited by the British to work throughout the Empire. They were (and in some cases still are) viewed as 'foreigners' or 'immigrants'. Under colonialism, they were privileged in relation to the 'indigenous' natives; since independence, they have often been subordinated to them. For the difficulties this has caused in the African context, see Mamdani 1996.

[35] According to Daes, attempts to distinguish long-distance colonizing settlement from incorporation into states dominated by neighbouring societies rest on an 'unjustified distinction' (Daes 1996, para. 63). Similarly, the African Commission's Working Group on Indigenous Populations/Communities stated that 'Domination and colonisation has not

from domination and vulnerability, we should use the indigenous track to protect them, even if their oppressors are their historic neighbours and not long-distance colonizing settlers. Hence various IOs have encouraged groups in Africa and Asia to identify themselves as indigenous peoples in order to gain greater international visibility and protection.[36]

This push to extend the category of indigenous peoples beyond its core case in the New World is fully understandable. It is a logical, perhaps even inevitable, result of the humanitarian motivation that led to the targeting of indigenous peoples in the first place. Insofar as the motivation for targeting this category of group was the distinctive vulnerability of indigenous peoples in New World settler states, it was natural to expand the category to include groups elsewhere in the world that share similar vulnerabilities, even if they were not subject to settler colonialism.

The difficult question this raises, however, is how to identify *which* homeland groups in Africa or Asia should be designated as indigenous peoples for the purposes of international law, and on what basis. This is not a new question. There is a long history of efforts to compare or equate the legal status of New World indigenous peoples with that of other groups in other regions of the world. It has been common, for example, to equate the status of indigenous peoples with that of so-called 'tribals' or 'hill tribes' in South Asia or to the 'nomadic tribes' of the Middle East and North Africa. Indeed, the first international declaration on indigenous rights—ILO Convention 107 of 1957—specifically links the status of 'tribals' in Asia or Africa with that of indigenous peoples in the New World. This Convention was entitled 'On the Protection and Integration of Indigenous *and Tribal* Populations' (my emphasis). As the title suggests, and the text of the Convention makes clear, the ILO at the time viewed 'indigenous' and 'tribal' as two distinct types of groups, albeit with related interests. Both are described as 'less advanced' in their social and economic conditions, and as culturally vulnerable, but they differ in their relationship to colonialism: 'indigenous' groups in the New World are characterized as the descendents of the societies that existed 'at

exclusively been practised by white settlers and colonialists. In Africa, dominant groups have also after independence suppressed maginalized groups, and it is this sort of present-day internal suppression within African states that the contemporary African indigenous movement seeks to address...' (*Report of the African Commission's Working Group on Indigenous Populations/Communities*, African Commission on Human and Peoples' Rights, 2005: 92).

[36] See, e.g., the Danish government's project to encourage countries in South-East Asia to ratify ILO 169 (the 'Pro-169 project'), the IWGIA efforts to promote the use of the indigenous category in Africa, and the long-standing practice in the UN of financing African groups to attend the Working Group on Indigenous Peoples (Lennox 2006).

the time of conquest and colonization', whereas 'tribal' groups in Asia, Africa, and the Middle East were not characterized in terms of conquest or colonization.

While the ILO noted the distinction between these two types of groups, it treated them together under the 1957 Convention because it viewed both as 'backward', incapable of dealing with the challenges of modernity, and hence in need of special protection. According to the ILO's views at the time, this paternalistic justification for targeted rights applied equally to New World indigenous peoples and Third World tribal groups. And many states in Africa, Asia, and the Middle East accepted this argument. Indeed, the 1957 ILO Convention was signed not only by various New World countries, but also by eleven states in Africa and Asia, who accepted the obligation to protect their 'tribals' (Rodriguez-Pinero 2005: 234–42).

However, this earlier attempt by the ILO to link New World 'indigenous' groups and Asian/African 'tribal' groups rested on a common cultural contempt for their 'backwardness'. Once we set aside this paternalistic and condescending attitude, it's less clear whether it makes sense to treat the two types of groups together under international law. As I noted earlier, the more recent notions of indigenous rights are not based on paternalism, but rather on the discourse of internal decolonization, drawing on the logic and tactics of the struggle for overseas decolonization and racial desegregation. These newer conceptions of indigenous rights appeal to the injustices involved in the process of colonizing settlement, and invoke rights to internal self-determination as a way of remedying this historic injustice. Given this shift to a decolonization-based model of indigenous rights, it is no longer clear whether or how 'tribals' fit into this new conceptual framework of indigenous rights. It made sense to link indigenous peoples and tribal groups when the underlying justification was paternalistic protection for 'backward' cultures. But if the underlying justification is decolonization, it is unclear why tribals should continue to be covered by indigenous rights norms, given that on the ILO's own definition tribals are not characterized by a history of conquest or colonization.

Not surprisingly, therefore, when the ILO abandoned its earlier paternalistic approach and shifted to a new decolonization-based model of indigenous rights in its 1989 Convention, many countries in Africa, Asia, and the Middle East dropped out. They assumed that the new decolonization-based Convention only applied to indigenous peoples in New World settler states, and did not apply to tribals in post-colonial states. Whereas eleven states in Africa, Asia, and the Middle East had signed the 1957 Convention to protect vulnerable tribals, not a single state in these regions, has signed the 1989 Convention to decolonize indigenous peoples. Since these states do not think of themselves as having 'colonized' or 'conquered' the tribal populations that are located within the state's boundaries (boundaries often established by European imperial rulers), they do not view themselves as having a moral or legal obligation to 'decolonize' these groups. These states argue that the relationship between post-colonial states and their tribal populations is fundamentally different, historically and morally, from the relationship between European settler states and indigenous peoples.

This loss of support for the new ILO Convention within Africa and Asia can be seen as a logical corollary of the new emphasis on a model of internal decolonization. Most IOs, however, are resisting the conclusion that the new ILO Convention should only apply to the New World. They are pressuring states in Africa and Asia to sign the new ILO Convention, and to accept that some of their homeland minorities should be designated as indigenous peoples. But the question remains: how do we determine which minorities in Asia and Africa qualify as indigenous, and which do not? Once we start down the road of applying the category of indigenous peoples beyond the core case of New World settler states, there is no obvious stopping point. Indeed, there are significant disagreements within various IOs about how widely to apply the category of indigenous peoples to homeland minorities in post-colonial states. Some would limit it to particularly geographically isolated peoples, such as hill tribes or forest peoples in South-East Asia, or to pastoralists in Africa. Others would limit it to groups that fall outside the market economy—that is, to those groups living as hunter-gatherers or subsistence cultivators, but not involved in either trade or the labour market. (This seems to be one of the World Bank's criteria, invoked to deny indigenous status to the Berbers in Algeria.)

These narrow definitions of indigenous people are obviously inconsistent with the way the term is used in the New World. In Latin America, for example, the term indigenous peoples applies not only to isolated forest peoples in the Amazon, such as the Yanomami, but also to peasants in the highlands who have been in intensive contact and trade with the larger settler society for 500 years, such as the Maya, Aymaras, or Quechuas. Similarly many indigenous peoples in North America, such as the Mohawks, have been involved in either settled agriculture and/or the labour market for generations. To limit the category of indigenous peoples to groups that are geographically isolated or not involved in trade or the labour market would be to exclude some of the largest and most politically influential indigenous groups in the New World.

And so other commentators would extend the category of 'indigenous peoples' in post-colonial states much more widely to encompass all historically subordinated homeland minorities that suffer from some combination of political exclusion, poverty or cultural vulnerability. (This seems to be the recent approach of the ILO, at least in South-East Asia, where the term 'indigenous people' is often used as a synonym for 'ethnic minority'.)[37] On this view, the label 'indigenous peoples' would become virtually synonymous with 'homeland minority', rather than a subcategory of homeland minority. The difference between the narrower and broader conceptions of indigenous peoples is potentially enormous— estimates of the number of people who would qualify as indigenous peoples in Indonesia range from 2 to 60 per cent of the population, depending on whether a narrower or broader definition is used (Evers 1995).

There is an enormous literature on this question of how to apply the category of indigenous peoples in Africa and Asia, and on the relative merits of broader and narrow definitions.[38] This is a matter on ongoing debate within various IOs, each of which has adopted different definitions, to the consternation of many commentators who wish that a single definition would be adopted across the international community.

From my perspective, however, the fact that different definitions are being used by different IOs is not the only, or even the primary, problem. The more serious problem is that all of these proposed approaches, whether narrow or broad, invoke criteria that clearly are a matter of degree. Homeland minorities in post-colonial states fall on a continuum in terms of their cultural vulnerability, geographical isolation, level of integration into the market, and political exclusion. We can, if we like, set a threshold somewhere along this continuum in order to determine which of these groups are called 'indigenous peoples' and which are 'national minorities', but any such threshold is likely to appear rather arbitrary, and incapable of bearing the weight that international law currently requires of it. International law treats the distinction between indigenous peoples and national minorities as a categorical one, with enormous implications for the legal rights each type of group can claim. In the post-colonial

---

[37] See, e.g., the ILO's 'ethnic audit', conducted under the auspices of the 'indigenous' policy (Tomei 2005).

[38] See Kingsbury 1995, 1998, 1999a; Scheinin 2005; Barnes 1995; Bowen 2000; MRG 1999; World Bank 2005; and the voluminous debate triggered by Adam Kuper's 2003 article in *Current Anthropology* (Kuper 2003), with commentaries and responses in *Current Anthropology* (vol. 45/2; vol. 47/1), *Anthropology Today* (vol. 20/2), and the *New Humanist* (vol. 118/3).

world, however, any attempt to distinguish indigenous peoples from national minorities on the basis of their relative levels of vulnerability or exclusion can only track differences of degree, not the difference in kind implied by international law.[39]

The attempt to preserve such a sharp distinction is not only morally and conceptually unstable, it is also, I suspect, politically unsustainable. The problem here is not simply that the category of indigenous peoples has grey areas and fuzzy boundaries, with the potential for being over- or under-inclusive. That is true of all targeted categories, and there are well-established techniques of democratic deliberation and legal interpretation for dealing with such boundary disputes. The problem, rather, is that too much depends on which side of the line groups fall, and as a result, there is intense political pressure to change where the line is drawn, in ways that are politically unsustainable.

As should be clear by now, the current UN framework provides no incentive for any homeland minority to identify itself as a national minority, since this category provides no rights that are not available to any other ethnocultural group. Instead, all homeland minorities have an overwhelming incentive to (re-)define themselves as indigenous peoples. If they come to the international community under the heading of 'national minority', they get nothing other than generic Article 27 rights; if they come instead as 'indigenous peoples', they have the promise of rights to land, control over natural resources, political self-government, language rights, and legal pluralism.

Not surprisingly, we see an increasing tendency for homeland groups in Africa, Asia, and the Middle East to adopt the label of indigenous peoples. An interesting case is the Arab-speaking minority in the Ahwaz region of Iran, whose homeland has been subject to repeated state policies of Persianization, including the suppression of Arab language rights, renaming towns and villages to erase evidence of their Arab history, and settlement policies that attempt to swamp the Ahwaz with Persian settlers. In the past, Ahwaz leaders have gone to the UN Working Group on Minorities to complain that their rights as a national minority are not respected. But since the UN does not recognize national minorities as having any distinctive rights, the Ahwaz have run into a dead end. And so they

---

[39] See the frank admission of the Chair of the UN's Working Group on Minorities: 'The usefulness of a clear-cut distinction between minorities and indigenous peoples is debatable. The Sub-Commission, including the two authors of this paper, have played a major role in separating the two tracks. The time may have come for the Sub-Commission to review the issue again... The distinction is probably much less useful for standard-setting concerning groups accommodation in Asia and Africa.' (Eide and Daes 2000, para. 25; see also Eide 2004).

have re-labelled themselves from a national minority to an indigenous people, and have attended the UN Working Group on Indigenous Populations instead! Similarly, various homeland minorities in Africa that once attended the Working Group on Minorities have now started re-branding themselves as indigenous peoples, and attending the Working Group on Indigenous Populations, primarily in order to gain protection for their land rights (Lennox 2006: 18).

This is just the tip of the iceberg. Any number of minorities are now debating whether to adopt the label of indigenous peoples, including the Crimean Tatars (Dorowszewska 2001), the Roma (Banach 2002; Klimová-Alexander 2006), or Afro-Latin Americans (Lennox 2006). Even the Kurds—the textbook example of a stateless national minority—are debating whether to redefine themselves as an indigenous people, so as to gain international protection. So too with the Palestinians in Israel (Jamal 2005; Jabareen 2005), the Abkhaz in Georgia or Chechens in Russia (Aukerman 2000), and the Tibetans in China.[40]

In all of these cases, minorities are responding to the fact that generic minority rights are 'regarded as fatally weak' (Barsh 1994: 81), and as 'completely inadequate . . . to their needs' (Aukerman 2000: 1030), since generic rights do not protect any claims based on historic settlement or territorial attachments. Given international law as it stands, recognition as an 'indigenous people' is the only route to secure protection for these interests. Perhaps, in time, the Scots and Basques will also claim this status (Barsh 1994: 81). After all, what homeland minority wouldn't want the rights currently being formulated for indigenous peoples?[41]

This trend for substate nationalist groups to redefine themselves as indigenous peoples should not surprise us, since it is in effect simply the flip-side of an earlier trend by which indigenous peoples adopted the label and rhetoric of substate nationalism. Throughout much of the nineteenth and twentieth centuries, the principle of 'national self-determination' was

---

[40] Another interesting case is the lower-caste Dalits in India, who have sometimes come to the UN as a 'minority' at the Working Group on Minorities, but who are pursuing other options, including the possibility of being treated as an 'indigenous people', or alternatively as a 'racial' group under the Convention Against Racial Discrimination. Neither label really fits, but both are seen as offering more effective protection than the 'minority' label.

[41] Such groups are sometimes criticized for invoking the indigenous label 'strategically', in a way that doesn't reflect their 'authentic' identity. But there are no such things as 'authentic' categories of ethnocultural groups. Such categories are devised for legal and political purposes, and are to be evaluated for how well they serve those purposes. In this case, my concern is not that the current UN framework encourages the strategic use of the indigenous category for the purpose of claims-making, but rather that it encourages forms of claims-making that may undermine the indigenous category itself.

the most powerful rhetorical tool available to homeland minority groups seeking self-government. As we've seen, this was not a *legal* tool that homeland minorities could invoke—international law never recognized minorities as eligible to claim the right of national self-determination. But it was nonetheless a powerful *political* tool, useful both in mobilizing members of the minority and in defending claims to substate self-government. However, many indigenous groups had difficulty appealing to this principle because they were not seen as 'nations', unlike substate national minorities like the Scots, Québécois, or Basques. They were labelled as indigenous 'groups', 'communities', or 'populations', but not as 'nations', and hence not entitled to self-determination. And so one of the first tasks indigenous leaders faced as they attempted to rebuild an indigenous rights movement in the 1960s and 1970s was to redefine themselves as 'nations', and to adopt the rhetoric of substate nationalism. In the Canadian case, for example, virtually all of the indigenous communities recognized by the federal Indian Act petitioned to change their official name to 'First Nations'.[42] Indigenous peoples in other New World countries similarly adopted the rhetoric of being 'nations within', and of seeking a 'nation-to-nation' relationship with the state (e.g. Fleras and Elliot 1992).

Today, however, it is indigeneity, not nationhood, that provides the stronger political and legal claim to self-determination, at least at the UN. If in the 1970s and 1980s it was politically advantageous for indigenous peoples to adopt the label and rhetoric of substate nationalist groups, as a way of getting states and dominant groups to take seriously their aspirations to self-government, today it is politically advantageous for substate nationalist groups to adopt the label and rhetoric of indigenous peoples. This reciprocal borrowing of tactics and discourses between national minorities and indigenous peoples shows the strong continuity in their basic claims and justifications, and the futility of attempts to create a legal firewall between the two.

This back-door route for national minorities to gain significant targeted rights through adopting the label of indigenous peoples may seem like a good thing. After all, from the point of view of the theory and practice of liberal multiculturalism, the underlying moral logic should be to acknowledge the legitimate interests relating to historic settlement and territory shared by all vulnerable homeland minorities, and expanding

---

[42] On the adoption of the rhetoric of nationhood by indigenous peoples, see Papillon 1999; Alfred 1995; Chartrand 1995.

the category of 'indigenous people' to cover all homeland minorities is one possible way to do this. It may indeed seem a serendipitous way of short-circuiting the hostility to targeted national minority rights in the international community.

Unfortunately, this is not a sustainable approach. The tendency of national minorities to adopt the label of indigenous peoples, if it continues, may well lead to the total collapse of the international system of indigenous rights. As we've seen, IOs have repeatedly and explicitly rejected attempts to codify rights of self-government for powerful substate national groups, in part because of their geo-political security implications. They are not going to allow such groups to gain rights of self-government through the back-door, by simply redefining themselves as indigenous peoples.

If more and more homeland groups start to adopt the indigenous label, as I suspect they will, the likely result is that the international community will start to retreat from the targeted indigenous rights track. Indeed, the first signs of such a retreat are already visible. There are a number of ways this retreat could take place. The most obvious is that member-states may bring negotiations on the UN and OAS Draft Declarations to a halt.[43] Or they may gut these declarations of their substantive content—for example, by removing rights to land or self-government, and limiting their focus to issues of cultural recognition. Or they may attempt to sharply limit the scope of application of these declarations—for example, by limiting them to 'remote' groups who do not participate in the wage economy, such as forest dwellers. Whatever the technique, the result of such a retreat would be to undermine the major progress that has occurred to date in the indigenous track.[44]

---

[43] These negotiations have already slowed to a crawl, a delay that is usually ascribed to the reluctance of states to accept a principle of internal self-determination for indigenous peoples. But I suspect that the delay is at least partly due to the fear that there are insufficient safeguards to prevent the category of indigenous peoples expanding to include some national minorities.

[44] For various expressions of this worry, see Aukerman 2000: 1017 ('The very success of the indigenous peoples movement in developing an ambitious rights framework and in gaining an institutionalized presence at the United Nations through the working group threatens to undermine the fragile, unspoken standards of inclusion which have characterized the movement up until now'); Kingsbury 1998: 419 ('There is an appreciable risk for the indigenous peoples' movement that the existing and highly functional international political distinction between indigenous peoples and ethnic and other minorities will erode, galvanizing opposition to claims of indigenous peoples'); and Barsh 1994: 81–2 ('Indigenous organizations will have to choose between excluding these [national minority] groups from the movement and attracting the hostility of many states that have previously taken no interest in indigenous issues').

This suggests that the long-term future of the targeted indigenous track at the UN and other IOs is not yet clear. The targeted indigenous track is often cited as the clearest success in the development of international minority rights, but this judgement may be premature. It has indeed been a success, but it is in danger of becoming a victim of its success. The achievements of the targeted indigenous track in the New World, particularly in empowering indigenous peoples in Latin America, is encouraging IOs to redefine and extend the category in ways that are morally inconsistent, conceptually unstable, and politically unsustainable.[45]

It is not obvious how we can overcome this instability. As we've seen, the dilemma has arisen as a combined result of two key decisions about how to develop targeted norms at the global level, both of which were pragmatic, understandable, and perhaps even inevitable. First, a decision was made to create a sharp gulf in legal status between indigenous peoples and national minorities, highlighting the former as a beneficiary of strong targeted rights, while ascribing only generic minority rights to the latter. In principle, one could imagine an alternative approach in which IOs would adopt a strategy of dual-targeting (or multi-targeting), developing separate legal tracks for both indigenous peoples and national minorities. But as we've seen, the attempt to develop targeted norms for national minorities in Europe failed, and the prospects for success at the global level are even worse. As a result, the decision to create a legal firewall between the two types of groups was clearly a pragmatic decision, even if it introduced an element of moral inconsistency into the UN framework.

The second decision was to extend the category of indigenous peoples beyond its original context of New World settler states to Asia, Africa, and the Middle East. Here again, one could imagine in principle an alternate approach in which IOs would acknowledge that the category of 'indigenous peoples' (and perhaps also 'national minorities') is essentially rooted in the history of Europe and European settler states, and would therefore attempt to develop an entirely different framework of targeted

---

[45] All of these definitions also run the risk of creating a mismatch between the form and content of indigenous rights. As we've seen, the content of indigenous rights is increasingly based on a model of internal decolonization, premised on the claim that it is arbitrary to endorse decolonization for the overseas colonies of European empires but not for internally colonized indigenous peoples within European settler states. Indigenous rights, on this view, are a more consistent working out of the logic of decolonization. Yet these rights are being accorded to groups in Asia and Africa, not based on the criteria of internal colonization, but on the basis of some combination or threshold of economic marginalization, political exclusion, and cultural vulnerability. It's obviously desirable to protect minorities who suffer from these conditions, but it's not clear why decolonization-based models are the right remedy.

categories for minorities in other parts of the world. But we have no concrete proposals or examples of what these alternate categories might be, and (as we will see in the next chapter) countries in Asia, Africa, and the Middle East have shown no interest in developing their own region-specific forms of targeted rights. The only realistic way to extend any level of international protection to minorities in post-colonial states, beyond the generic Article 27 rights, was to extend the category of indigenous peoples. Since the only tool of international protection that was available was targeted at indigenous peoples, it was understandable and pragmatic to redefine minorities in need of protection as indigenous peoples.

The combined result of these two pragmatic decisions, however, is instability. The second decision to globalize the category of indigenous peoples makes it increasingly difficult—morally, conceptually, and politically—to sustain the legal firewall between indigenous peoples and other homeland minorities required by the first decision.

Globalizing the category of indigenous peoples, therefore, yields short-term pragmatic benefits, but also raises long-term risks. Perhaps the benefits clearly outweigh the risks. But it is surprising how quickly actors within the relevant global policy networks have accepted that this is the right way to proceed. There is virtual unanimity amongst professional advocacy groups, and their academic advisors and philanthropic funders, that the category of indigenous peoples should be globalized.[46] As we've

---

[46] The main exception is the 1999 report by Miguel Alfonso Martinez, the UN's Special Rapporteur on the rights of indigenous peoples. In his study on the use of treaties to establish constructive arrangements between states and indigenous peoples, Alfonso Martinez insisted that it is 'necessary to re-establish a clear-cut distinction between indigenous peoples and national or ethnic minorities', and that the only way to do so is by limiting the former category to New World settler states 'in which the "indigenous peoples" category is already established beyond any doubt from a historical and modern-day point of view' (Alfonso Martinez 1999, paras 68–9). He argued that the situation of indigenous peoples in New World settler states is qualitatively different, historically and morally, from that of tribals or other oppressed minorities in Asia or Africa:

These dissimilarities hinge on a number of historical factors that call for a clear distinction to be made between the phenomenon of the territorial expansion by indigenous nations into adjacent areas and that of the organized colonization, by European powers, of peoples inhabiting, since time immemorial, territories on other continents. . . . The overseas colonial undertaking differed completely from the very common phenomenon of expansion into adjacent territories (at the expense of their neighbours) practiced by the peoples in those 'new' territories before the arrival of the European colonizer. The inherent nature of the colonial undertaking, the exploitative, discriminatory and dominating character of its 'philosophy' as a system, the methods employed and the final results it had on very dissimilar societies mark the difference (paras 73, 175)

This was a lone voice in the wilderness within the global policy network on indigenous rights, however, and virtually all other actors within these networks repudiate his position.

seen, this strategy is still being resisted by some post-colonial states, and is disputed by some outside academics (e.g. Béteille 2000; Bowen 2000), but within the policy networks that are affiliated with the UN indigenous track, there has been little dispute about the appropriateness of this strategy. It is often just taken for granted that developing a more 'inclusive' definition of indigenous peoples is preferable, and that there is no need to develop new legal categories that are more appropriate for the context of post-colonial states.

Perhaps this is indeed the best or only strategy. But if so, we should be conscious of the risks involved, and we should start to think creatively about how we will deal with the instabilities that will inevitably arise. It is interesting, in this respect, to compare the global debates on indigenous rights with the European debates on national minority rights. In both cases, we see instability in the efforts to create targeted rights. And in both cases, the underlying problem is the same—namely, the paralysing impact of geo-political security fears regarding substate national(ist) minorities. In the European context, these fears led IOs to abandon their attempts to formulate norms that dealt with substantive issues of territory and self-government, and to retreat to a set of generic minority rights. In the global case, the UN focused on the category of indigenous peoples precisely to avoid such paralysing fears, and as a result was able to formulate targeted norms that do in fact address substantive issues regarding land and political autonomy. But this very success is creating strong pressure to extend indigenous norms to other homeland minorities who also have legitimate interests in land and self-government, and this is re-opening the security fears.[47] Attempts by the UN to maintain a legal firewall between the two types of homeland minorities will be difficult to sustain in the face of intense but contradictory pressures to expand and contract the category of indigenous peoples. The international community is committed to expanding the category of indigenous peoples beyond the core case of

---

[47] Kingsbury notes that if more and more homeland groups re-identify themselves as indigenous peoples, 'There is an appreciable risk for the indigenous peoples' movement that the existing and highly functional international political distinction between indigenous peoples and ethnic and other minorities will erode, galvanizing opposition to claims of indigenous peoples' (Kingsbury 1998: 419). But of course (as he notes) this distinction is not 'highly functional' for everyone. On the contrary, it is highly dysfunctional for most homeland minorities, who are relegated to the category of generic minority rights. This distinction has been highly functional for indigenous peoples, who have been able to make progress by separating their claims from the more controversial and securitized claims of national minorities. But the result is that international law is 'fatally weak' for national minorities (Barsh 1994), and it is this fatal weakness which explains why the distinction is being challenged.

New World settler states, but this expansion makes it more difficult to sustain the firewall, morally and conceptually, and indeed increases the incentive for more and more homeland minorities in post-colonial states to claim the status of indigenous peoples in a way that is politically unsustainable, and that will likely lead to a retrenchment of the indigenous track.

The long-term success of the indigenous track may depend, therefore, on developing a more coherent account of the relationship between indigenous peoples and other homeland minorities. The international community has systematically avoided addressing this question to date, but it cannot be postponed forever. The firewall strategy was important to get the indigenous track off the ground, but it cannot provide a stable long-term foundation.

From Norms/Standards to Case-Specific Conflict Resolution

Even if there is some way to preserve a sharp distinction between indigenous peoples and other homeland minorities, this still leaves us with the question of what the international community should do about substate national(ist) minorities in the post-colonial world, such as the Kurds, Tamils, Palestinians, Chechens, Oromos, Tibetans, and so on. Their claims are more likely to be at the root of violent and destabilizing ethnic conflict than those of indigenous peoples, and hence cannot simply be ignored by the international community. Yet the two strategies we've discussed so far—publicizing best practices and formulating legal norms—have not addressed their claims. The best practices approach to such cases is unrealistic, and neither the generic minority rights track nor the targeted indigenous rights track addresses them.

And so global international organizations have had to adopt yet another strategy for trying to influence state–minority relations. The obvious alternative is to adopt a case-specific security approach, focused not on formulating norms and standards, but on conflict prevention and conflict resolution in particular countries. As we saw in Chapter 6, this third 'security track' was also adopted in Europe, given the limitations of their best practices and legal norms strategies, and indeed has turned out to be the most important approach in actually dealing with issues of ethnic conflict in post-communist countries.

And if we examine how the international community has responded when called upon to help resolve conflicts and rebuild states, we see a striking trend. Where the UN has become actively involved in serious conflicts between states and national minorities, it has typically promoted some form of autonomy, as in Cyprus, Sudan, Iraq, Indonesia, Sri Lanka, and Burma. This of course repeats the experience within post-communist Europe. As we saw in Chapter 6, when serious ethnic conflict between states and homeland minorities has arisen in post-communist Europe, European organizations have typically pushed for the adoption of some form of federal or quasi-federal territorial autonomy—for example, in Kosovo, Bosnia, Macedonia, Ukraine, Moldova, Georgia, and Azerbaijan.

The paradoxical result is that the UN, despite its clear hostility to ideas of a principled right to self-government for substate national groups, has in fact ended up promoting Western-style models of multination federalism in several high-profile cases. In many of these cases, the international community's main goal has been simply to secure peace. But its encouragement of models of autonomy for homeland minorities is also based on the hope and expectation, derived from Western experiences, that these models can serve as a vehicle for consolidating relations of liberal-democratic citizenship, respecting human rights, and enabling economic development. And these liberal multiculturalist assumptions are indeed part of the official international rhetoric surrounding the signing of these peace deals. Yet because these endorsements have only occurred in the context of resolving violent conflicts, rather than as part of a more general principled commitment to minority autonomy, they are widely perceived as pay-offs to belligerent minorities. Rather than serving as opportunities for the promotion of an ethos of liberal multiculturalism, they instead send the message that violence pays.

Conclusion

The history of UN efforts in the field of minority rights is, in many ways, very different from that of European organizations. And yet, I have argued, we see the same failed strategies, the same unresolved dilemmas, and the same mixed messages. We see a strategy of promoting best practices that is naïve and potentially dangerous; we see a legal norms strategy that seeks to combine generic minority rights with targeted minority rights, but does so on the basis of categories that are unstable; and we see a case-specific conflict resolution strategy that rewards belligerence. Taken together, these various strategies send different, and often contradictory, messages about what kinds of ethnopolitical mobilizations are seen as legitimate by the international community.

In the final chapter, I will consider whether there is any way forward that can avoid, or at least reduce, these endemic dilemmas of the global diffusion of liberal multiculturalism.

8

Conclusion: The Way Forward?

Over the past fifteen years, international organizations have embarked on a bold experiment in promoting ideals of liberal multiculturalism and in formulating international norms of minority rights, but this experiment is facing an uncertain future. There are multiple instabilities in the way IOs have framed their discourses and norms, which inhibit their effective diffusion and implementation. Moreover, the initial sense of urgency about this issue has largely faded, and questions of minority rights have dropped down the list of international priorities. Without renewed attention and commitment, the likely outcome is a gradual retreat from the more progressive dimensions of this experiment.

What then is to be done? Where do we go from here? To oversimplify, we can imagine two options. One would be to abandon the project of internationalizing multiculturalism, and to turn back the clock to the era before 1990, when state–minority relations were not a priority issue for the international community.

In my view, this would be highly undesirable. The international community has a legitimate, and indeed essential, role to play in assisting both states and minorities. Minorities around the world are demanding greater respect and recognition, and there is no reason to expect that such demands will diminish in the foreseeable future. Contemporary struggles for multiculturalism have emerged out of earlier human rights struggles against ethnic and racial hierarchies, and appeal to some of the most powerful moral ideals of the modern world. Minorities are unlikely to back away from such claims. Yet many post-communist and post-colonial states have difficulty responding to these claims, which threaten not only their traditional self-understandings as unitary and homogenous nation-states, but also pose potential threats to security, human rights and development. Even within Western states, liberal multiculturalism has proven vulnerable to backlash and retreat. State–minority relations are continually in danger of reverting to older patterns of illiberal and undemocratic relations—including relations of conqueror and conquered; colonizer and colonized; racialized and unmarked; normalized and deviant; orthodox and heretic; civilized and backward; ally and enemy.

If we are to break out of these patterns, and replace them with relations of democratic citizenship, the international community must be an active participant. It's worth remembering that international pressure played an important and beneficial role in the development of minority rights in several Western states, although this is often forgotten. For example, the autonomy arrangement for the Åland Islands was an externally determined solution under the League of Nations, which has worked very well. Germany's accession to NATO in 1955 was conditional on its working out a reciprocal minority rights agreement with Denmark, an agreement which is now seen as a model of how kin-states can work constructively through bilateral relations to help minorities in neighbouring states. There was strong international pressure on Italy to accord autonomy to South Tyrol in 1972, which today is seen as a exemplar of successful accommodation. In all of these cases, a degree of international pressure was needed to initiate settlements, although they have become domestically self-sustaining, and indeed have often been enhanced or expanded as a result of domestic procedures. Given this history, it seems naïve to assume that countries in the post-communist or post-colonial world will inevitably and peacefully move towards significant minority rights through their own domestic democratic processes, without some degree of international support or even pressure.

IOs have a responsibility both to protect vulnerable minorities from serious injustice, and to enable states to meet these obligations of justice. To abandon this task would be a betrayal of the founding ideals of the international community.

In any event, a full-scale retreat from minority rights is not a realistic option. The commitment to multiculturalism and minority rights, while relatively recent, is now deeply institutionalized within the international community. There are numerous Working Groups, Advisory Committees, Independent Experts, and Monitoring Bodies operating at multiple levels of the international community (regional and global), and within different functional domains (e.g. peace and security; human rights; development and the environment). Even if the UN General Assembly decided to repudiate its 1992 Declaration on the Rights of Persons Belonging to National or Ethnic, Religious or Linguistic Minorities—itself an entirely unrealistic assumption—this would have no impact on the ways in which minority rights have permeated the operation of, say, the UNDP, the International Labour Organization, the World Bank, or UNESCO, not to mention the development assistance policies of individual countries around the world. Minority rights are here to stay, in one form or another.

The alternative, therefore, is to rethink the project of internationalizing minority rights to put it on a more stable footing, conceptually and politically. We need to show that there is a set of coherent goals and ideals here, and that there are feasible means to achieve them.

I believe that the most plausible basis for elaborating a coherent project of international minority rights lies in a conception of liberal multiculturalism. As I've argued throughout this book, liberal multiculturalism already operates as a powerful influence on the activities of IOs in the field of state-minority relations. This is reflected in the terminology and rhetoric used, in the examples which are selected as best practices, in the goal of formulating norms and standards of minority rights, and in the way these minority rights are seen as emerging from and embedded within larger frameworks of human rights and democratic constitutionalism. All of this bears the unmistakable imprint of liberal multiculturalism, and could not have emerged in its absence.

But to say that IOs have been influenced by liberal multiculturalism is not to say that there is an explicit global consensus on this approach, or a consistent application of it. On the contrary, as we've seen, the merits of liberal multiculturalism are deeply contested at the international level. Part of this opposition comes from state elites who do not wish to share power with minorities, or who maintain deep-seated prejudices against their 'backward' minorities. But much of the opposition comes from genuine doubts about the viability of liberal multiculturalism, or about the risks that it entails, particularly in conditions of geo-political insecurity or democratic transition.

As a result, the commitment to liberal multiculturalism remains largely implicit, and heavily qualified. According to some commentators, it would be more accurate to say that IOs are promoting a form of 'multi-culturalism light' (Skovgaard 2007), a watered-down version that seeks to avoid the more contested or risky aspects of liberal multiculturalism. But the commitments of IOs are more uneven and variable than this image suggests. Multiculturalism light may be all that is expected or encouraged for some minorities in some countries, but in other contexts a more robust form of multiculturalism is endorsed or even imposed, while in yet other contexts we see a retreat from even the most minimal forms of multiculturalism light. It is precisely this variability which is creating the conceptual and political instabilities I have traced in the previous two chapters.

The question, then, is whether we can stabilize this halting and uneven international commitment to liberal multiculturalism. Can we turn what is currently an implicit and uneven set of experiments in diffusing liberal multiculturalism into a more coherent legal and political project? The answer, I think, depends on whether we can address the basic dilemmas I raised at the start of the book: namely, (i) how do we combine generic and targeted minority rights?; (ii) how do we combine short-term conflict prevention with the long-term promotion of the highest standards of liberal-democratic multiculturalism?; and (iii) how do we combine the pursuit of ethnocultural justice with the protection of geo-political security?

It should be clear by now that there are no easy answers here. These dilemmas really are *dilemmas*: there are risks and trade-offs no matter how we proceed. Indeed, each of the three main strategies for diffusing liberal multiculturalism—publicizing best practices; formulating legal norms; and case-specific conflict-resolution interventions—has its own inherent dilemmas, and any attempt to combine the three immediately creates the potential for conflicting messages and perverse incentives. There will inevitably be reasonable disagreement about how to balance these risks, and so we should expect a range of alternative models to emerge. This indeed is precisely what we need: we need to get a range of contending approaches on the table, so that we can systematically evaluate their respective strengths and weaknesses.

It should also be clear, I hope, that the process of formulating and evaluating these alternatives must be a collaborative effort, drawing on the input of different academic disciplines, as well as different types of state and non-state actors, from different regions of the world. We have some of the building blocks for this effort: we have well-developed accounts by normative political theorists of the ideals and best practices of liberal multiculturalism, derived primarily from the experience of the consolidated Western democracies; we have well-developed accounts by political scientists of case-specific conflict resolution techniques in weak or divided societies, particularly in the post-communist and post-colonial world; and we have well-developed accounts by international lawyers of the existing concepts and categories used in various international conventions and declarations on minority rights. To date, however, these three building blocks exist in more or less splendid isolation from each other. We need to bring them together, constructing bridges between normative ideals of liberal multiculturalism, techniques of conflict prevention and resolution, and legal categories of minority rights.[1]

It would be premature to predict or prescribe the outcome of such an international and inter-disciplinary conversation. But in the rest of the conclusion, I will make a few preliminary speculations about how we might start the conversation, primarily to flag the sorts of issues we need to discuss collectively, and in the hope of encouraging others to develop other, better approaches. I will focus in particular on three questions: the categories of minority rights, the preconditions of minority rights; and the forum or arena for minority rights. The first two are questions about the substance or content of minority rights; the latter concerns the mechanisms or procedures by which these issues of substance are resolved.

The first question concerns the issue of categories. IOs have repeatedly struggled with the issue of whether to adopt targeted minority rights for specific categories of groups, such as national minorities and indigenous peoples. These struggles suggest a number of important lessons. The first is that some degree of targeting seems inevitable. As we've seen, many actors would prefer to stick to a purely generic minority rights approach that does not require putting ethnocultural groups into different categories for the purposes of international law. But in both the European and global contexts, a purely generic approach has proven insufficient. It is part of the very nature of ethnic conflict, and part of the very logic of liberal multiculturalism, that it raises group-differentiated issues. This suggests that some degree of targeting is essential if international norms are to play a constructive role.

Yet we are very far from having a coherent or systematic account of the kinds of targeting that are desirable or sustainable. The current use of targeted categories in international law—which is essentially limited to national minorities within Europe and indigenous peoples globally— is multiply flawed: it has emerged in an uncoordinated and ad hoc way, reflects an uneasy mix of security and justice considerations, has huge

---

[1] While liberal multiculturalism has been the most influential normative framework at the international level to date, we should not exclude the possibility that some other normative political theory can provide a better set of conceptual tools for addressing these dilemmas. It would indeed be very helpful if we had, say, a Buddhist or Islamic theory of international minority rights which explicitly addressed these issues of how to combine generic and targeted rights when formulating international legal norms and standards, or how to integrate short-term stability and long-term justice. To my knowledge, no such theories exist, although there are interesting discussions at the domestic level about the significance of such non-liberal traditions for minority issues. See, for example, the essays on China, Singapore, Indonesia, and Laos in Kymlicka and He 2005.

gaps in coverage, and a tendency to universalize what in fact are regional specificities. The result is growing pressure to abandon these targeted norms, or to re-interpret them in ways that subvert their original intent.

Is there a viable alternative? What would a more coherent or consistent liberal multiculturalist approach to the question of categories look like? From a liberal multicultural perspective, the rationale for targeting is to identify and remedy predictable patterns of injustice in state-minority relations. Just as traditional human rights can be understood as protecting individuals against 'standard threats' from the abuse of state power (Shue 1980), so we can think of targeted minority rights as an attempt to protect different types of minorities from the standard threats they face at the hands of modern nation states. As we saw in Chapter 3, these threats vary from group to group, depending in part on how they came to be part of the state: the policies that states have historically adopted towards colonized indigenous peoples differ from those adopted towards incorporated national minorities, which differ yet again from those adopted towards new minorities of immigrants and refugees. All of these policies have traditionally had the effect of imposing assimilation or exclusion on minorities, but the patterns of injustice involved, and the remedies needed, differ. The group-differentiated character of liberal multiculturalism can be understood as an attempt to identify and remedy these predictable patterns of injustice.

Viewed this way, we can begin to see, in embryonic form, the outlines of a justice-based system of international targeted norms. The clearest example concerns indigenous peoples in New World settler states, where emerging targeted norms arguably are designed precisely to remedy the predictable patterns of injustice they have suffered. There have also been serious proposals for adopting targeted norms for immigrant groups and for the Roma in Europe, for Afro-Latinos in Latin America, for hill tribes and for caste groups in Asia, and for pastoralists in Africa, amongst others, each premised on the assumption that there are standard threats or predictable patterns of injustice suffered by these types of minorities in various countries.

To date, most of these proposals have not been accepted, in part because they often appear as ad hoc, and as special pleading. There is no established procedure or criteria for evaluating proposals to establish new targeted categories, and no general theory of how and when targeted categories are needed to supplement generic minority rights.

In my view, this is an enormous gap in the current approach to minority rights. We need to think more systematically about the role of targeted minority rights. The experience to date suggests a few lessons. One thing we can safely say is that targeting only works if there is consistency between the form and content of targeted norms—i.e. if the distinctive set of rights being accorded to a particular type of group actually matches the distinctive needs or circumstances of that type of group. In the European context, a mismatch between form and content has emerged. European norms are formally targeted at national minorities, but are wholly generic in their substantive content, and the result is instability.

But even where there is a good match between targeted form and targeted content, as in the case of the UN's indigenous rights track, the result may still be unstable if this targeting exists in isolation from a more general framework or understanding of the role and function of targeted rights. To date, targeted norms have emerged in an ad hoc fashion, and are often presented as unique exceptions to the rule of generic minority rights. But this sort of ad hoc 'mono-targeting'—isolating one particular type of group for distinctive legal rights, while according all other groups only generic minority rights—is unlikely to be stable. If we start down the road of targeted norms, we may need to do it in a more self-conscious and systematic fashion. It may be that the only way to develop a sustainable set of targeted norms for indigenous peoples, say, is to make it part of a broader strategy of 'multi-targeting', operating in conjunction with sep-arate targeted norms for national minorities or other homeland groups, for immigrant groups, or for other types of groups with unique histo-ries and needs, such as the Roma or Afro-Latinos. Otherwise, any set of mono-targeted norms will face intense pressure to expand or redefine the category in ways that are unsustainable, as we are seeing both in Europe with respect to national minorities, and internationally with respect to indigenous peoples. Because these categories are the only available ones offering substantial protection, they are being pushed to cover an ever-expanding and increasingly heterogenous set of groups, to the point where the underlying logic behind the initial targeting is increasingly strained. If we wish to preserve the original intentions underlying a set of targeted rights designed for one type of group, we may need to ensure that other types of groups are able to appeal to their own targeted norms, as part of a larger framework of multi-targeted minority rights.

There have been few if any attempts to step back and ask what such a multi-targeted system of minority rights would look like. The categories of targeted rights need to be fine-grained enough to capture distinctive patterns of potential injustice, but not so fine-grained as to collapse into unique country-specific individual cases. And while there have to be enough categories to cover the major types of groups, there cannot be so many categories as to make the entire system unwieldy. It is not clear what mix of categories could serve as the basis for a sustainable global system of multi-targeted minority rights.

The intellectual task here is complicated by the fact that many of the categories currently in use, such as indigenous peoples or national minorities, are 'rooted in a particular time and space' (Lennox 2006: 4), and may not be globally applicable. They work well in some regions, but not in others. As we've seen, liberal multiculturalism in the West has relied on a specific set of categories—particularly immigrants, national minorities, and indigenous peoples—and the forty-year experience to date suggests that these do indeed capture predictable patterns of injustice in state-minority relations within the consolidated Western democratic nation-states. But it's less clear that these categories help identify or remedy standard threats involved in state–minority relations in Asia or Africa. Not only do minorities in these regions often differ in their histories, characteristics, and aspirations from minorities in the West, but so too do their states. As we've seen, many post-colonial states do not have a single dominant national group who can call the state their own, and so minorities do not face the same kind of nation-building. The threats of exclusion or marginalization differ, and so do the appropriate remedies.

In his influential *Minorities at Risk* study (see p. 47 above), Ted Gurr argues that we need new categories for classifying minorities in post-colonial states (Gurr 1993). For example, he employs the category of 'communal contenders' to capture a widespread type of diversity in post-colonial states that does not generally exist in the Western democracies. Like ethnonationalist groups in the West, communal contenders are powerful substate minorities with the capacity to challenge for state power, but they differ in their historic relations with the state, and in their current aspirations. Unlike substate ethnonational groups (or indigenous peoples) in the West, they are not the losers in the process of state formation and boundary-drawing. On the contrary, they often played an important role in fighting for independence, and indeed may view themselves as one of the founding peoples of the state. So they do not view themselves as having been involuntarily incorporated into someone else's state, and do not seek to escape from the state's authority. Rather, they fear that they may be losers in the day-to-day process of resource allocation and resource development. According to Gurr, the MAR database allows us to identify a predictable pattern of grievance and political mobilization associated with such groups, and also a range of appropriate policy responses, which differ from those associated with indigenous peoples, national minorities and immigrant groups. If so, this suggests that 'communal contenders' might provide an appropriate category for the construction of new targeted norms, particularly for Africa and Asia.

This is just one example of many one could give of groups in other regions of the world which do not fit established Western patterns or existing international legal categories. This example also suggests that the sorts of categories we need are likely to be regional rather than global in scope, to reflect the considerable variation between regions in the history and characteristics not only of their minorities, but also of their state structures. Indeed, even when the same legal category is used, as when hill tribes in south Asia or nomadic groups in Africa identify as indigenous peoples, it still may be useful to make regional distinctions. The historical relationship between indigenous peoples and New World settler states is quite different from the relationship between hill tribes or nomadic peoples and post-colonial states in Africa and Asia, and this may call for regional variations in their rights and remedies under international law. (This in turn raises the question of whether the task of formulating such region-specific categories is best left to regional organizations rather than to global organizations like the UN—I will return to this below).

In short, we have several unresolved questions about the categories of minority rights, and in particular about the role of targeted norms. The current use of targeted categories in international law is ad hoc and unstable, and we need to think of alternatives. I have suggested one possible approach, based on my reading of the logic of liberal multiculturalism. On this model, targeted rights are conceived as a means to identify and remedy standards threats of injustice, and hence are defined to track predictable patterns of state–minority relations. Compared to the status quo, such a model would make far greater use of targeted rights, and would be more sympathetic to region-specific rather than global categorizations.

Whether there is any realistic option of such a regional-specific system of multi-targeted rights being adopted is unclear, for reasons I will discuss below. But let's assume for now that we can come up with a compelling account of the appropriate categories for minority rights, based on predictable patterns and standard threats of injustice. This immediately leads us to the second major dilemma, which I will call the problem of 'conditions'. Put simply, the social and political factors that enabled the (uneven) adoption of liberal multiculturalism in the West as a remedy for minority group injustices are not present in much of the world. Even if we have identified appropriate categories, it would be unreasonable to expect liberal multiculturalist models to be adopted in contexts where states have a reasonable fear that it could lead to instability. As we've seen, models that have served the goal of citizenization in the West may simply reproduce relations of hierarchy and enmity under conditions of weak institutions and geo-political insecurity.

It is important therefore to distinguish what is feasible in the short-term from what is desirable in the long-term. Unfortunately, none of the existing strategies adopted by IOs to promote liberal multiculturalism have managed to successfully combine realism about short-term constraints with a coherent picture of our long-term goals. For example, the strategy of publicizing Western best practices often ignores the constraints on short-term feasibility, while the European legal norms that have been formulated for national minorities arguably go too far in the other direction, allowing short-term security concerns to crowd out any concern for liberal multiculturalist ideals.

Is there a viable alternative? From a liberal multiculturalist perspective, the goal would be to devise some sort of sequencing strategy that distinguishes short-term and long-term requirements. We might, for example, draw upon the ideas of 'progressive implementation' that have arisen in the broader human rights field. It has long been recognized that some of the social rights listed in the International Covenant on Economic, Social and Cultural Rights cannot immediately be implemented by some of the poorer countries (e.g. access to free university education). So it is common to distinguish those social rights that should be immediately and universally applied from those that we seek to achieve over time as the facilitating conditions are put in place. Although states in poor countries are not expected to fulfil the highest standards immediately, they are expected to explain what they are doing to put in place the conditions that would enable those standards to be progressively met.

We can similarly imagine a theory of the progressive implementation of liberal multiculturalism, with different minority rights provisions kicking in as the underlying conditions are established.[2] While states undergoing democratic transition or in unstable regions would not be expected to meet the highest standards of liberal multiculturalism, they would be

---

[2] A version of this idea is implicit in the Liechtenstein Draft Convention discussed earlier— see pp. 208 and 214 n 48 above. A related idea is the 'a la carte' menu approach adopted by the European Charter for Regional or Minority Languages. It offers states a long list of options for promoting minority languages in the fields of education, administration and the media, from which they are obliged to pick a minimum of thirty-five provisions. This allows states to avoid those options which are seen as the most controversial or risky.

expected to explain what they are doing to enable those standards to be progressively met over the long term.

To my mind, this is potentially an attractive model for linking short-term stability concerns with longer-term goals of justice. It would give states the breathing room they need to deal with their difficult circumstances, without giving them a free hand to suffocate the legitimate hopes and aspirations of minorities. For example, the model of progressive implementation would presumably not permit states to forbid peaceful and democratic forms of minority mobilization and expression, or to constitutionally entrench prohibitions on the future adoption of liberal multiculturalism (as several post-communist countries have done, often with the implicit blessing of European organizations). It would lower the immediate expectations put upon some states, but would not allow those states to fix in stone their preference to remain unitary, unilingual nation-states. On the contrary, it would impose a duty on such states to progressively put in place the conditions that would enable the peaceful and democratic pursuit of liberal multiculturalism over time.

If we combine this idea of progressive implementation with the idea of multi-targeted norms, the result would be a framework in which international norms would identify standard threats of injustice that affect particular types of minority groups, and would provide a series of benchmarks that states have a duty to meet over time to help achieve justice. These benchmarks would start with weak generic minority rights, but would then move into more robust models of targeted minority rights, as the various preconditions and risk factors are addressed.

That, at any rate, is one way of trying to move beyond our current impasse. If we were able to flesh it out with more detailed lists of categories and benchmarks, it might address many of the legitimate worries that are currently impeding and distorting international efforts at diffusing liberal multiculturalism. It would also reduce the potential inconsistencies within and between the three main strategies for diffusing liberal multiculturalism. It would not only put the legal norms track on a more consistent footing, but would also reduce the vast gulf that currently exists between the weak legal norms strategy and the more robust models of multiculturalism being promoted (in a selective and ad hoc way) through the publicizing of best practices and case-specific interventions.

Unfortunately, I do not believe that we actually have a workable theory of the proper sequencing of liberal multiculturalism. Indeed, I don't believe that we have the empirical basis needed to construct such a theory. We simply do not know which preconditions are needed to enable the successful operation of different aspects of liberal multiculturalism for different types of minority groups.

For example, the discussion in Chapters 6 and 7 might lead one to assume that some level of democratic consolidation should be in place before countries experiment with models of substate autonomy for national minorities. But that is far from clear. Consider the Spanish case. After the death of Franco, there was widespread agreement that the state needed to be both democratized and federalized. But there was an intense debate about the proper sequencing of these two tasks. Many democratic reformers argued that priority should be given to democratic consolidation, and only after that was secure should federalization take place. Many academics at the time agreed with this view. In the end, however, the decision was made to democratize and federalize simultaneously. And virtually every commentator today believes that this was the right choice, and that democratic consolidation would not have taken place if federalization had not occurred at the same time.

Spain may be an exception, and the presence of the EU and NATO undoubtedly played an important role in ensuring this successful double transition. But some international actors are hoping that a similar story will unfold in other countries, from Sudan to Iraq, where both the democratization and pluralization of the state are being undertaken simultaneously rather than sequentially.

We know that democratic consolidation assists in the successful operation of liberal multiculturalism, and that the latter is likely to be unstable without the former. That much, I think, is clear. But it does not follow that democratic consolidation should *precede* the adoption of liberal multiculturalist policies. Indeed, the former may not be possible without the latter, in at least some cases. We simply do not know enough about the sequencing here to make generalizations at a global scale about how to engage in the progressive implementation of minority rights.

A great deal of additional research is needed if we are to effectively address either the problem of categories or the problem of conditions. An attractive strategy for promoting liberal multiculturalism would involve a sequenced set of multi-targeted, regionally specific minority rights, but even if the political will existed for such an approach, it requires a degree of sophistication and knowledge that is several steps beyond our current level of academic research or public debate.

Perhaps in time we will develop the sort of conceptual tools and evidence that would enable us to formulate a plausible account of the targeting and sequencing of liberal multiculturalism. This would obviously be an ambitious undertaking, and would require a major invest-ment of time and resources, not only by IOs, but also by the global policy networks of academics, advocacy groups and philanthropic organizations that inform and sustain the work of IOs.

It is interesting to compare the situation here with other recent issues of global concern, where special efforts have been made to develop a stable and consensual framework for international action. Consider the 1993 Vienna World Conference on Human Rights, or the 1995 Beijing World Conference on Women. These involved massive consultations, research, debate and advocacy, over several years, at the national, regional and global levels, and were intended in part to address precisely the same sorts of dilemmas that affect the field of minority rights—e.g. how to combine universal norms with more targeted or context-specific norms, or how to engage in the long-term promotion of the highest standards of human rights while acknowledging the evident limitations on the capacities of weak states or transitional regimes to achieve these highest standards. The goal, in each case, was to develop a common conceptual framework that could guide and coordinate the activities of different international actors, and thereby push forward important agendas for change in a stable and coherent way. Something comparable—a World Conference or World Commission on Minority Rights—would probably be needed if there is to be any realistic prospect for significantly revising the current framework of international minority rights.

Unfortunately, there does not appear to be any enthusiasm for such a project today, either amongst IOs or their associated policy networks, at least at a global level. But perhaps that is the wrong level to look at. Regional organizations may offer a more promising forum for debates and experiments than global IOs. In principle, regional organizations should be better placed to develop appropriate categories and classifica-tions of minorities, rather than simply assuming that Western categories of indigenous peoples, national minorities and immigrants apply around the world. They should also be better able to understand the way different types of minority rights relate to broader patterns of regional security and democratization, so as to make better judgements about the sequencing of different types of reforms. Rather than treating minority rights in isolation from broader regional dynamics, as the current international discourse does, they could be integrated into larger processes of regional cooperation and development. And by devolving power to regional orga-nizations that are not dominated by Western states, the fear that the inter-nationalization of minority rights is simply a plot to maintain Western hegemony could perhaps be reduced. So there are several reasons why regional organizations might be better placed than global IOs to formulate norms and discourses of minority rights.

This has already happened to some extent. As we saw in Chapter 6, the Council of Europe and the OSCE have developed minority rights norms formulated specifically for the European context. Perhaps recognizing its own limited ability to generate effective global norms, the UN has repeatedly encouraged regional organizations elsewhere to follow the European example and develop their own regional norms (Hadden 2003; Packer and Friburg 2004). And some regional organizations have started to do so. The Organization of American States, for example, has drafted a declaration on the rights of indigenous peoples that is formulated specifically for the circumstances of the Americas. And the African Commission has recently set up a Working Group to consider drafting a declaration on indigenous and minority rights in Africa. Some commentators have encouraged ASEAN to do the same.

Unfortunately, the record to date of such regional initiatives is not encouraging. The regionalization of minority rights is most advanced within the West, in Europe and the Americas. By contrast, there is virtually no enthusiasm in Asia or the Arab/Muslim world to develop regional norms on minority rights. The whole issue remains essentially a taboo topic in many Asian and Middle Eastern countries.[3] Moreover, some minority rights advocates strongly oppose this idea of regionalization, on the (not unreasonable) expectation that such regional norms would at best be dramatically weaker than current global standards, and at worst would be mere camouflage for oppressive states.[4]

---

[3] Interestingly, the Organization of the Islamic Conference, representing Muslim-majority countries around the world, has a Department on Minority Affairs, but its formal resolutions focus exclusively on the rights of Muslim minorities living in non-Muslim majority countries (Khan 2002). (For a representative example, see the OIC's resolution 'On Safeguarding the Rights of Muslim Communities and Minorities in Non-OIC Member States'—Resolution No. 1/10-MM (IS), adopted at the 10th Session of the Islamic Summit Conference, 16–17 October 2003). The OIC has not attempted to codify norms, or to establish formal monitoring mechanisms, regarding the treatment of ethnic minorities within Muslim-majority countries, such as the oppression of the Kurds in Syria, the Ahwaz in Iran, the Hazars in Afghanistan, the Baluchs in Pakistan, the 'Al-Akhdam' in Yemen, or the Berbers in Algeria. (For the plight of Muslim ethnic minorities within Muslim-majority states, see, eg., Ibrahim 1995; Seif 2005; Grare 2006; Shatzmiller 2005; Bengio and Ben-Dor 1999).

[4] As one Sri Lankan human rights activist put it, 'One thing I don't want is Asian standards on how to deal with minorities. Nothing would be worse than India and Indonesia getting together and devising Bumiputra standards for Asia. This is not the time for Asian standards on minorities' (Radhika Coomaraswamy, in Steiner 2004: 102). For overviews of minority rights debates in Asia, and their relationship to international standards and practices, see Castellino and Redondo 2006; Kymlicka and He 2005; Pfaff-Czarnecka et al 1999.

And preliminary developments in the African Commission suggest that its proposed regional charter will simply reproduce existing international norms and discourses, rather than attempting to define categories and concepts of multiculturalism that are more truly reflective of African realities (Slimane 2003; Morawa 2002/3; Lennox 2006; Murray and Wheatley 2003). This may reflect the fact that Western-dominated organizations are a main source of the funding and expertise for the regional consultations on a pan-African charter.[5]

In short, there is little evidence that post-colonial states will take up the task of formulating regional norms of minority rights. Their attitude, by and large, has been one of hostility to the entire project of internationalizing minority rights, rather than attempting to develop more constructive versions of it.

So the prospects for significant innovation, at either the regional or global levels, are remote for the foreseeable future. We lack not only the political will, but also the sort of conceptual tools and empirical evidence needed to put the diffusion of liberal multiculturalism on a more stable and effective footing. Finding new ways of conceptualizing the categories and conditions of liberal multiculturalism at an international level is a worthwhile goal, but it is a distant one.

In the meantime, we have to work with what we have. And at the moment, the trend is, if anything, to move in the opposite direction. Rather than trying to elaborate a more complex model of targeted and sequenced minority rights that would attempt to track important differences across different types of groups and different circumstances, the trend today is to retreat to a more generic framework of minority rights that applies regardless of type of group or underlying conditions. As we've seen, none of the proposals for expanding the set of targeted categories— for example, to include targeted norms for immigrants or the Roma— have been accepted. And the two existing schemes of targeted norms, for national minorities and indigenous peoples, are under pressure.

Given the difficulties in identifying the appropriate categories or sequences for targeted rights, IOs have increasingly attempted to rely on generic minority rights. These generic rights include Article 27 rights of free association and expression, but may also include some minimal

---

[5] According to Lennox, 'the fact that the [African Commission's] Working Group relies on the international NGO the International Work Group on Indigenous Affairs for its funding may be decisive' in explaining their uncritical adoption of the category of indigenous peoples, and their lack of attention to alternative possible frameworks for categorizing minorities (Lennox 2006: 19–20).

level of 'effective participation', to help create a democratic space for states and minorities to slowly work out their own accommodations.[6] The increasing prominence of the idea of effective participation may reflect the belief that international intervention should be aimed at creating the conditions for societies to work out their own account of minority rights through peaceful and democratic deliberations, rather than seeking to impose some canonical set of internationally defined targeted minority rights.

This may be the direction we are headed in. And perhaps this is the most we can reasonably expect for now. Attempts to formulate international law principles to resolve deep conflicts over autonomy, power-sharing, land claims, language rights, naturalization rules, or religious accommodations may simply be unrealistic. Over time, we might hope and expect post-communist and post-colonial countries to generate their own trends towards liberal multiculturalism, but it may be difficult, and perhaps even counter-productive, to try to jump-start this process through the codification and imposition of international norms of substantive targeted minority rights.

However, if this is indeed the direction we are headed in, we need to be careful about how we characterize the resulting framework. In particular, it's essential that the minimal standards contained in the generic strategy be presented precisely as *minimum* standards. International norms must be seen as a floor from which minority rights should be domestically negotiated, not as a ceiling beyond which minorities must not seek to go.

The 'sequencing' strategy I mentioned earlier attempted to make this idea explicit: it would involve formally codifying the steps by which states should move from generic to more robust targeted norms, with explicit benchmarks and conditions along the way. As we have seen, this sort of formal codification of sequences and benchmarks is almost certainly too ambitious, at least for the foreseeable future. But even if we cannot codify such a sequencing strategy in formal legal rules, it is important

---

[6] While the Article 27 right to enjoy one's culture is now standardly interpreted as a generic minority right that applies to all minorities, including tourists and visitors, it's more difficult to view effective participation as a generic right, given that visitors are not citizens, and hence cannot exercise even the minimal right to vote. Effective participation therefore is often seen as a quasi-generic right—i.e. it applies to all members of minorities who are citizens, whether the minorities they belong to are old or new, large or small, concentrated or dispersed. But just for this reason, it can only be understood in a minimal sense: it cannot include the right to participate in self-governing institutions, or to have guaranteed representation on decisions affecting one's areas of traditional settlement, or to be able to use one's language in political institutions, since these clearly are not generic participation rights.

to insist that the basic goal remains the same. From the perspective of liberal multiculturalism, the hope and expectation is that states will build upon the minimum set of generic rights, with the goal of achieving more robust models of multiculturalism as the underlying preconditions and risk factors are addressed. If it proves impossible to codify sequenced substantive minority rights in international law, we must at least be clear that the meagre provisions currently codified in international instruments are the starting-point for democratic debate, not the end-point.

Unfortunately, this message is not always getting through. There is a concerted effort by many post-communist and post-colonial states to present minimum international norms as the outside limits of legitimate minority mobilization, and to silence or discredit minority leaders who ask for anything beyond these norms. Minimal international standards are not being treated as the preconditions needed to democratically negotiate the targeted forms of liberal multiculturalism appropriate to each country, but rather are seen as eliminating the need to adopt, or even to debate, forms of power-sharing, self-government, or official language status. When minority organizations raise questions about such substantive minority rights, states often respond 'we meet all international standards', as if that foreclosed the question of how states should treat their minorities. The statement that 'we meet all international standards' has become a mantra amongst post-communist states, taking the place of any serious debate about how to actually respond to minority claims regarding powers, rights, and status.

This attempt to treat weak generic rights as a ceiling rather than a floor is abetted by the confusing and ambivalent way IOs discuss the issue. As we have seen throughout this book, IOs have sent out mixed messages regarding the relationship between generic rights and the group-differentiated forms of liberal multiculturalism, such as the models of indigenous decolonization, multination federalism and immigrant multiculturalism that have emerged over the past forty years in the West. In many contexts, IOs endorse the latter as best practices and long-term goals, and present generic rights as a floor from which such group-differentiated rights can and should be negotiated. At other times, however, IOs seem to imply that generic rights are an alternative to group-differentiated rights, and that any minority claims that require targeting, particularly those that appeal to the relevance of history and territory, should be rejected on principle as inconsistent with norms of equality and liberal democracy.

For example, some actors have described the shift from robust targeted rights towards generic civil and participation rights as a victory for democracy and deliberation over judicialization and bureaucratization, or a victory for hybridity and fluidity over group reification and essentialism, or a victory for human rights and non-discrimination over tribalism and ethnic nationalism, or a victory for moral universalism over moral relativism, or a victory for liberal individualism over collective rights.[7] This sort of rhetoric, taken literally, not only delegitimizes the use of targeted norms at the international level, but also implicitly delegitimizes the use of group-differentiated rights at the domestic level, since they have the same logic and structure. Indeed, as we've seen, the development of targeted norms at the international level was in part an attempt to capture the group-differentiated logic of liberal multiculturalism as it has emerged in the West. It's as if IOs want to endorse the group-differentiated models of liberal multiculturalism while denying or disavowing their group-differentiated character.

Given these mixed messages, it is not surprising that many states have interpreted the shift to generic rights as a repudiation of the group-differentiated logic of liberal multiculturalism, and hence as setting a

---

[7] The legal and philosophical literature on minority rights is full of these sorts of oppositions (individual rights vs. collective rights; universalism vs. relativism; cultural fluidity vs. cultural essentialism; civic vs. ethnic nationalism; and so on). I have elsewhere discussed the multiple confusions involved in the way these tropes are deployed in the literature, and why they are often unhelpful in understanding the real issues (Kymlicka 1995; 2001). For present purposes, however, let me just point out that these oppositions shed no light on the evolution of international debates over the relationship between generic and targeted rights. Consider the recent shift away from robust targeted norms for national minorities (such as autonomy or official language status) in Europe. Some commentators view this retreat as a principled rejection of the very idea of collective rights, or as a rejection of ideologies of ethnic nationalism, moral relativism or cultural essentialism, in favour of individual rights, civic nationalism, moral universalism, and cultural fluidity. If this were true, IOs would be encouraging Western countries to abandon their models of territorial autonomy and of multination, multilingual federalism, since these were the precedent and inspiration for the targeted norms. In reality, however, IOs accept that these Western models have successfully combined the accommodation of ethnonational diversity with human rights norms, and have contributed to the replacement of historic relations of hierarchy and enmity with those of liberal-democratic citizenship. This is why IOs contemplated trying to codify these practices as legal norms in the early 1990s. They backed off this plan when it became clear that the underlying conditions for the successful adoption of these models were not present in many post-communist countries. We cannot begin to understand this set of developments if we insist on interpreting it as a debate between proponents and opponents of ideas of collective rights, relativism, essentialism, or ethnic nationalism. It would be absurd to suggest that Western states adopted and promoted models of multination federalism out of a commitment to collectivism, relativism, or essentialism, and that post-communist states resisted them out of a commitment to individualism, universalism, and fluidity. These were debates about the viability of different models of liberal multiculturalism under different circumstances, and whether they would contribute to or erode processes of citizenization. The shifts in the early 1990s reflected evolving judgements about this question, not a shifting balance of power between proponents and opponents of relativism, essentialism, collectivism and so on. Unfortunately, the prominence of these tropes in the literature generates misinterpretations of the rationale for the shift from targeted to generic norms.

ceiling on the legitimate claims of minorities. International action on minority rights is unlikely to be coherent or effective so long as such profound inconsistencies exist in the way the underlying goals are framed. Indeed, there is a danger that the international protection of generic minority rights will in fact be counter-productive: states will treat generic rights as an alternative to, rather than precondition for, the negotiation of liberal multiculturalism. If international norms are to play a useful role, we need to make clear that the retreat from targeted norms at the international level is not a retreat from the goal of promoting group-differentiated forms of liberal multiculturalism at the domestic level. And this in turn means acknowledging that the retreat from targeted norms is indeed a retreat, a regrettable recognition of our limited capacity to formulate workable categories and sequences, not a principled victory. And for that reason, it may not be a permanent retreat—we may want to revisit the role of targeted norms as our capacities for identifying categories and sequences improve, and as the limits of the generic approach resurface.[8]

This has implications not only for how we conceptualize international legal norms, but also for how we think about other activities of the international community in the field of state–minority relations. If generic rights are the floor from which more robust group-differentiated forms of multiculturalism are negotiated as the preconditions are put in place, then a crucial task for the international community is to help put those conditions into place. This means, for example, that it is not sufficient to simply publicize best practices—rather, we need to be conscious of the preconditions that that make those practices possible, and then think of the various ways that IOs can help achieve them. This may involve helping to build new regional security arrangements, to reduce the risk of the 'securitization' of minority issues. Or it may involve building considerations about the preconditions of liberal multiculturalism into international policies to promote democratization, the rule of law, or

---

[8] Recall that the whole experiment in formulating targeted norms arose in the early 1990s because the generic rights strategy had proven ineffective. Since generic rights do not provide guidance for addressing the actual issues at stake in destabilizing ethnic conflict, IOs were forced to rely heavily on case-specific interventions. These interventions typically promoted more robust minority rights, often based on Western theories and best practices of liberal multiculturalism, but did so in an ad hoc way that seemed to reward belligerence. The formulation of targeted minority rights was intended in part as a way of identifying consistent guidelines for addressing these real-world issues, and thereby replacing power politics with principle as a framework for international actions in the area of state-minority relations. This may have been an over-ambitious goal, given the difficulties in formulating targeted norms, and so we see a retreat to the generic strategy. But this simply returns us to the original dilemma: the generic strategy, on its own, is insufficient to deal with the real-world challenges of state–minority relations.

economic development, in order to reduce the likelihood that unresolved minority issues will derail these processes.

As we have seen, attention to minority rights has already entered into the discourses and policies of IOs involved in security, democratization, and development (such as the UNDP). But too often, this has simply meant attending to the protection of generic minority rights. If these policies are to genuinely help ensure peaceful development and democratization in multiethnic states—if they are to help enable states and minorities to overcome historic relations of hierarchy, exclusion and enmity and convert them into relations of democratic citizenship—then they will have to be attentive to more than generic minority rights. They will need to identify and promote the conditions that enable states to build up from the floor of generic rights towards more robust forms of liberal multiculturalism. And these factors, as we have seen, vary across different types of minorities and different geo-political conditions, in ways that require attending to issues of targeting and sequencing. The sorts of international programs and policies that will help build the preconditions for liberal multiculturalism for pastoralists in East Africa will not be the same as those that help build the preconditions for liberal multiculturalism for indigenous peoples in Latin America, ethnonationalist groups in South Asia, or immigrant groups in Western Europe. Both the nature of the multiculturalism being promoted, and the nature of the risk factors inhibiting it, vary significantly across these different groups and contexts.

Put another way, even if international legal norms of minority rights are largely generic, abstracting from differences in types of groups and geo-political conditions, the international community more generally needs to work with a more complex conception of the categories and conditions of liberal multiculturalism. Indeed, we might say that the more that international law avoids these issues, the more important it is that the other dimensions of international activity be sensitive to them. If we cannot build targeting and sequencing into international legal norms, we will have to build them into international democratization policies, development policies, peace and stability policies, and so on. These sorts of policies will play a decisive role in determining whether progress is made in creating the conditions needed to diffuse liberal multiculturalism.

In short, the shift to generic minority rights in international law displaces, but does not resolve or remove, the underlying questions about targeting and sequencing. We have no option but to try our best to think through the appropriate categories and conditions of liberal multiculturalism, and then use our findings wherever possible to inform the activities of IOs. If there are limits on the ability of international law at the global level to reflect these categories and conditions, then we need to look to other fields of international activity, and other levels of regional organizations. There is enormous scope for creative action here, but it is only possible if we view generic minority rights as the floor of a larger framework of liberal multiculturalism that relies on a complex set of targets and conditions.

* * * * *

Much work remains to be done to produce a stable and effective framework for the international diffusion of multiculturalism and minority rights. I have not tried to provide a blueprint for such a framework, but I have tried to identify the most important instabilities in the current approach, and to suggest various ways forward. The most ambitious proposal would be to entirely redesign the framework of international legal norms for minorities, supplementing or replacing the current system of weak generic rights with a more robust system of multi-targeted and sequenced minority rights. If that is too ambitious, I have suggested we can at least develop a more consistent and constructive account of the link between existing legal norms and the theory and practice of liberal multiculturalism. I hope that readers will come up with other, better, proposals for how to move forward.

However, to be honest, I am not particularly optimistic about the likelihood of a breakthrough, at least in the foreseeable future. The time for a real push on minority rights may have passed. The early 1990s offered an unprecedented window of opportunity for dramatic and creative innovations in the field of minority rights, but the window has gradually closed, with the job only half-done.[9] We may need to accept that this is as good as it gets, for now. If so, there are certainly grounds for supporting the current set of international norms and discourses, whatever their gaps and inconsistencies, and for welcoming their development over the past fifteen years. The best can be the enemy of the good, and the current framework has clearly done some good in helping to highlight the plight of many minorities around the world, and in helping to legitimize claims-making and political mobilization by ethnic political actors. It has

---

[9] In Andreas Wimmer's words, 'The hope for a new world order, in which governments, NGOs, and researchers would jointly work towards 'managing' and 'solving' ethnic conflicts around the world by spreading multicultural justice and democratic participation, has evaporated' (Wimmer 2004: 353).

helped make space at the table—indeed, at various tables, both domestic and international—for members of ethnic minorities to peacefully and democratically voice their concerns and aspirations, while simultaneously encouraging them to formulate their claims within the framework of human rights norms.

These are all significant accomplishments. My concern, however, is that the status quo is not only imperfect, but in fact unstable. The numerous inconsistencies and ambiguities in the current framework are under pressure, and we will either have to move forward or retreat. Unless we can think of intellectually compelling and politically viable ways of reconceptualizing the pursuit of multiculturalism and minority rights, the likely outcome will be a retreat from the more progressive aspects of the current system. Indeed as we have seen there is already evidence that this is taking place. And if so, the long-term prognosis for the global diffusion of liberal multiculturalism is poor indeed.

Bibliography

AAA (American Anthropological Association) Executive Board (1947) 'Statement on Human Rights Submitted to the Commission on Human Rights, United Nations', *American Anthropologist*, New Series 49: 539–43.

Abu-Laban, Yasmeen (2002) 'Liberalism, Multiculturalism and Essentialism', *Citizenship Studies*, 6/4: 459–82.

—— and Christina Gabriel (2002) *Selling Diversity: Immigration, Multiculturalism, Employment Equity and Globalization* (Broadview, Peterborough).

Adams, Michael (1997) *Sex in the Snow* (Penguin, Toronto).

—— (2000) *Better Happy Than Rich?* (Penguin, Toronto).

Addis, Adeno (1992) 'Individualism, Communitarianism and the Rights of Ethnic Minorities', *Notre Dame Law Review*, 67/3: 615–76.

Akermark, Sia Spiliopoulou (1997) *Justifications of Minority Protection in International Law* (Martinus Nijhoff, Dordrecht).

Albo, Xavier (1994) 'And from Kataristas to MNRistas? The Surprising and Bold Alliance between Aymaras and Neoliberals in Bolivia', in Donna Lee Van Cott (ed), *Indigenous Peoples and Democracy in Latin America* (St Martin's Press, New York), 55–82.

Aleinikoff, Alexander and Douglas Klusmeyer (eds) (2002) *Citizenship Policies for an Age of Migration* (Carnegie Endowment for International Peace, Washington).

Alemante, Selassie (2003) 'Ethnic Federalism: Its Promise and Pitfalls for Africa' *Yale Journal of International Law*, 28: 51–107.

Alesina, Alberto and Eliana LaFerrara (2005) 'Ethnic Diversity and Economic Performance', *Journal of Economic Literature*, 43: 762–800.

Alfonso Martinez, Miguel (1999) *Study on Treaties, Agreements and Other Constructive Arrangements between States and Indigenous Populations: Final Report by Special Rapporteur* (UN Sub-Commission on Prevention of Discrimination and Protection of Minorities, 51st Session, 22 June 1999, E/CN.4/Sub.2/1999/20).

Alfred, Gerald (1995) *Heeding the Voices of our Ancestors: Kahnawake Mohawk Politics and the Rise of Native Nationalism* (Oxford University Press, Toronto).

Alfredsson, Gudmundur and Erika Ferrer (eds) (1998) *Minority Rights: A Guide to United Nations Procedures and Institutions* (Minority Rights Group, London).

—— and Danilo Turk (1993) 'International Mechanisms for the Monitoring and Protection of Minority Rights: Their Advantages, Disadvantages and

Interrelationships', in Arie Bloed (ed), *Monitoring Human Rights in Europe: Comparing International Procedures and Mechanisms* (Kluwer, Norwell, Mass), 169–86.

Alston, Philip (ed) (2001) *People's Rights* (Oxford University Press, Oxford).

Anagnostou, Dia (2005) 'Deepening Democracy or Defending the Nation? The Europeanisation of Minority Rights and Greek Citizenship', *West European Politics*, 28/2: 335–57.

Anant, Arpita (2003) 'Group Rights in the Indian and International Discourses' (PhD thesis, School of International Studies, Jawaharlal Nehru University).

Anaya, S. James (1996) *Indigenous Peoples in International Law* (Oxford University Press, New York).

Anderson, Benedict (2004) 'The Future of Indonesia', in Michel Seymour (ed), *The Fate of the Nation-State* (McGill-Queen's University Press, Montreal).

Anderson, Carole (2003) *Eyes off the Prize: The United Nations and the African-American Struggle for Human Rights, 1944–55* (Cambridge University Press, Cambridge).

Anderson, Kenneth (1992) 'Illiberal Tolerance: An Essay on the Fall of Yugoslavia and the Rise of Multiculturalism in the United States', *Virginia Journal of International Law*, 33: 385–431.

Andreescu, Gabriel (1997) 'Recommendation 1201 and a Security (Stability) Network in Central and Eastern Europe', *International Studies* (Bucharest), 3: 50–63.

An-Na'im, Abdullahi (ed) (1992) *Human Rights in Cross-Cultural Perspectives* (University of Pennsylvania Press, Philadelphia).

Appadurai, Arjun (2006) *Fear of Small Numbers* (Duke University Press, Durham, NC).

Appiah, Anthony (2004) *The Ethics of Identity* (Princeton University Press, Princeton).

Ardrey, J. B. (2005) 'Minority Language Rights before and after the 2004 EU Enlargement: The Copenhagen Criteria in the Baltic States', *Journal of Multilingual and Multicultural Development*, 26/5: 453–68.

Armitage, Andrew (1995) *Comparing the Policy of Aboriginal Assimilation: Australia, Canada, New Zealand* (UBC Press, Vancouver).

Asiwaju, A. I. (ed) (1985) *Partitioned Africans: Ethnic Relations Across Africa's International Boundaries, 1884–1984* (Hurst, London).

Atanasoski, Neda (2006) 'Race toward Freedom: Post Cold War US Multiculturalism and the Reconstruction of Eastern Europe', *Journal of American Culture*, 29/2: 213–26.

Aukerman, Miriam (2000) 'Definitions and Justifications: Minority and Indigenous Rights in a Central/East European Context', *Human Rights Quarterly*, 22: 1011–50.

Azmi, Shaheen (1999) 'Wife Abuse and Ideological Competition in the Muslim Community of Toronto', in Harold Troper and Morton Weinfeld (eds), *Ethnicity, Politics and Public Policy* (University of Toronto Press, Toronto), 164–89.

Bach, Daniel (1997) 'Indigeneity, Ethnicity and Federalism', in L. Diamond (ed), *Transition without End: Nigerian Politics and Civil Society under Babangida* (Lynne Rienner, Boulder, Colo.), 333–49.

Bajpai, Kanti (1999) 'Majorities and Minorities in South Asia', in D. L. Sheth and Gurpreet Mahajan (eds), *Minority Identities and the Nation-State* (Oxford University Press, New Delhi), 220–41.

Banach, Edo (2002) 'The Roma and the Native Americans: Encapsulated Communities within Larger Constitutional Regimes', *Florida Journal of International Law*, 14: 353–95.

Banting, Keith and Will Kymlicka (eds) (2006) *Multiculturalism and the Welfare State: Recognition and Redistribution in Contemporary Democracies* (Oxford University Press, Oxford).

Banton, Michael (2002) *The International Politics of Race* (Polity Press, Cambridge).

Barkan, Elazar (2000) *The Guilt of Nations* (Johns Hopkins University Press, Baltimore).

Barnes, R. H. (ed) (1995) *Indigenous Peoples of Asia* (Association of Asian Studies, Ann Arbor).

Barnett, Michael and Martha Finnemore (2004) *Rules for the World: International Organizations in Global Politics* (Cornell University Press, Ithaca, NY).

Barry, Brian (2001) *Culture and Equality: An Egalitarian Critique of Multiculturalism* (Polity Press, Cambridge).

Barsh, Russel Lawrence (1994) 'Indigenous Peoples in the 1990s: From Object to Subject of International Law?', *Harvard Human Rights Journal*, 7: 33–86.

Batt, Judy and J. Amato (1998) 'Minority Rights and EU Enlargement to the East', European University Institute, Robert Schuman Centre Policy Paper No. 98/5.

Baubock, Rainer (1994) *Transnational Citizenship: Membership and Rights in Transnational Migration* (Edward Elgar, Aldershot).

—— (2000) 'Why Stay Together: A Pluralist Approach to Secession and Federation', in Will Kymlicka and Wayne Norman (eds), *Citizenship in Diverse Societies* (Oxford University Press, Oxford), 366–94.

—— (2001) 'Cultural Citizenship, Minority Rights and Self-Government', in Alex Aleinikoff and Douglas Klusmeyer (eds), *Citizenship Today: Global Perspectives* (Carnegie Endowment for International Peace, Washington), 319–48.

—— (2004) 'Territorial or Cultural Autonomy for National Minorities?' in Alain Dieckhoff (ed), *The Politics of Belonging: Nationalism, Liberalism and Pluralism* (Lexington Books, Lanham, Md.), 221–58.

—— (2006) 'Autonomy, Power-Sharing and Common Citizenship: Principles for Accommodating National Minorities in Europe', in John McGarry and Michael Keating (eds), *European Integration and the Nationalities Question* (Routledge, London), 85–102.

Bauer, Joanne and Daniel Bell (eds) (1999) *The East Asian Challenge for Human Rights* (Cambridge University Press, Cambridge).

Bayart, Jean-Françoise (2005) *The Illusion of Cultural Identity* (University of Chicago Press, Chicago).

Bayefsky, Anne (ed) (2000) *Self-Determination in International Law: Quebec and Lessons Learned* (Kluwer, The Hague).

Bell, Daniel A. (1999) *East Meets West: Human Rights and Democracy in East Asia* (Princeton University Press, Princeton).

—— (2004) 'Is Democracy the "Least Bad" System for Minority Groups?' in Susan Henders (ed), *Democratization and Identity: Regimes and Ethnicity in East and Southeast Asia* (Lexington, Lanham, Md.), 25–42.

Bell, Gary (2001) 'Minority Rights in Indonesia: Will Constitutional Recognition lead to Disintegration and Discrimination?' *Singapore Journal of International and Comparative Law*, 5: 784–806.

Bengio, Ofra and Gabriel Ben-Dor (eds) (1999) *Minorities and the State in the Arab World* (Lynne Reinner, Boulder, Colo.).

Bengoa, José (2000) 'Existence and Recognition of Minorities', Working Paper prepared for Working Group on Minorities, Sixth Session, 22–6 May 2000, United Nations document E/CN.4/Sub.2/AC.5/2000/WP.2

Benhabib, Seyla (2002) *The Claims of Culture: Equality and Diversity in the Global Era* (Princeton University Press, Princeton).

Bermeo, Nancy (2002) 'The Import of Institutions', *Journal of Democracy*, 13/2: 96–110.

Berry, John, Jean Phinney, David Sam, and Paul Vedder (2006) 'Immigrant Youth: Acculturation, Identity and Adaptation', *Applied Psychology: An International Review*, 55/3: 303–32.

Bessenyey-Williams, Margit (2002) 'European Integration and Minority Rights: The Case of Hungary and its Neighbours', in Ron Linden (ed), *Norms and Nannies: The Impact of International Organizations on the Central and East European States* (Rowman and Littlefield, Lanham, Md.), 227–58.

Béteille, André (2000) 'On the Concept of Indigenous Peoples', *Current Anthropology*, 19/2: 187–97.

Bibo, Istvan (1991) 'The Distress of East European Small States' in Karoly Nagy (ed), *Democracy, Revolution, Self-Determination* (Social Science Monographs, Boulder, Colo.), 13–86; 1st pub. 1946.

Billig, Michael (1995) *Banal Nationalism* (Sage, London).

Birnbaum, Pierre (2004) 'Between Universalism and Multiculturalism: The French Model in Contemporary Political Theory', in Alain Dieckhoff (ed), *The Politics of Belonging* (Lexington, Lanham, Md.), 177–94.

Bissoondath, Neil (1994) *Selling Illusions: The Cult of Multiculturalism in Canada* (Penguin, Toronto).

Bloed, Arie and Pieter van Dijk (eds) (1999) *Protection of Minority Rights through Bilateral Treaties: The Case of Central and Eastern Europe* (Kluwer, The Hague).

Bloemraad, Irene (2002) 'The Naturalization Gap: An Institutional Approach to Citizenship Acquisition in Canada and the United States', *International Migration Review*, 36/1: 194–229.

—— (2005) 'The Limits of de Tocqueville: How Government Facilitates Organizational Capacity in Newcomer Communities', *Journal of Ethnic and Migration Studies*, 31: 865–87.

—— (2006) *Becoming a Citizen: Incorporating Immigrants and Refugees in the United States and Canada* (University of California Press, Berkeley).

Bonnett, Alistair (2000) *Anti-Racism* (Routledge, London).

—— (2006) 'The Americanisation of Anti-Racism: Global Power and Hegemony in Ethnic Equity', *Journal of Ethnic and Migration Studies*, 32/7: 1083–103.

Booth, Ken (1999) 'Three Tyrannies', in Tim Dunne and Nicholas Wheeler (eds), *Human Rights in Global Politics* (Cambridge University Press, Cambridge), 31–70.

Borgwardt, Elizabeth (2005) *A New Deal for the World: America's Vision for Human Rights* (Harvard University Press, Cambridge, Mass.).

Borrows, John (2000) ' "Landed Citizenship": Narratives of Aboriginal Political Participation', in Will Kymlicka and Wayne Norman (eds), *Citizenship in Diverse Societies* (Oxford University Press, Oxford), 326–42.

Borstelmann, Thomas (1993) *Apartheid's Reluctant Uncle: The United States and Southern Africa in the Early Cold War* (Oxford University Press, Oxford).

—— (2001) *The Cold War and the Color Line: American Race Relations in the Global Arena* (Harvard University Press, Cambridge, Mass.).

Bourdieu, Pierre and Loïc Wacquant (1999) 'On the Cunning of Imperialist Reason', *Theory, Culture and Society*, 16/1: 41–58.

Bowen, John (2000) 'Should We Have a Universal Concept of "Indigenous Peoples Rights"? Ethnicity and Essentialism in the Twenty-First Century', *Anthropology Today*, 16/4: 12–16.

Bowring, Bill and Deirdre Fottrell (eds) (1999) *Minority and Group Rights in the New Millennium* (Martinus Nijhoff, The Hague).

Breuning, Maruke (1999) 'Ethnopolitical Parties and Development Cooperation: The Case of Belgium', *Comparative Political Studies*, 32/6: 724–51.

Brölmann, Catherine, René Lefeber, and Marjoleine Zeick (eds) (1993) *Peoples and Minorities in International Law* (Martinus Nijhoff, Dordrecht).

Brooks, Roy (2004) *Atonement and Forgiveness: A New Model for Black Reparations* (University of California Press, Berkeley).

Brubaker, Rogers (1996) *Nationalism Reframed: Nationhood and the National Question in the New Europe* (Cambridge University Press, Cambridge).

—— (2001) 'The Return of Assimilation?' *Ethnic and Racial Studies*, 24/4: 531–48.

Brusis, Martin (2003) 'The European Union and Interethnic Power-Sharing Arrangements in Accession Countries', *Journal of Ethnic and Minority Issues in Europe*, Issue 2003/1 (<http://www.ecmi.de/jemie>).

Brysk, Alison (2000) *From Tribal Village to Global Village: Indian Rights and International Relations in Latin America* (Stanford University Press, Stanford, Calif.).

Buchanan, Allen (2004) *Justice, Legitimacy and Self-Determination* (Oxford University Press, Oxford).

Bulbeck, Chilla (2004) 'The "White Worrier" in South Australia: Attitudes to Multiculturalism, Immigration and Reconciliation', *Journal of Sociology*, 40/4: 341–61.

Bunce, Valerie (1999) *Subversive Institutions: The Design and Destruction of Socialism and the State* (Cambridge University Press, Cambridge).

—— and Stephen, Watts (2005) 'Managing Diversity and Sustaining Democracy in the Post Communist World', in Philip Roeder and Donald Rothchild (eds), *Sustainable Peace: Power and Democracy after Civil War* (Cornell University Press, Ithaca, NY).

Burgess, Adam (1999) 'Critical Reflections on the Return of National Minority Rights to East/West European Affairs', in Karl Cordell (ed), *Ethnicity and Democratisation in the New Europe* (Routledge, London), 49–60.

Burns, M. (1996) 'Disturbed Spirits: Minority Rights and the New World Orders, 1919 and the 1990s' in S. F. Wells and P. Bailey-Smith (eds), *New European Orders: 1919 and 1991* (Woodrow Wilson Center Press, Washington), 41–61.

Byman, Daniel (1997) 'Rethinking Partition: Lessons from Iraq and Lebanon', *Security Studies*, 7/1: 1–32.

Cairns, Alan (2000) *Citizens Plus: Aboriginal Peoples and the Canadian State* (University of British Columbia Press, Vancouver).

—— (2005) *First Nations and the Canadian State: In Search of Coexistence* (Institute for Intergovernmental Relations, Kingston).

Caplan, Richard (2005) *Europe and the Recognition of New States in Yugoslavia* (Cambridge University Press, Cambridge).

Caputo, Richard (2001) 'Multiculturalism and Social Justice in the United States: An Attempt to Reconcile the Irreconcilable with a Pragmatic Liberal Framework', *Race, Gender and Class*, 8/1: 161–82.

Carens, Joseph (ed) (1995) *Is Quebec Nationalism Just?* (McGill-Queen's University Press, Montreal).

—— (2000) *Culture, Citizenship and Community* (Oxford University Press, Oxford).

Cashaback, David (2005) 'Accommodating Multinationalism in Russia and Canada: A Comparative Study of Federal Design and Language Policy in Tatarstan and Quebec', Ph.D. Thesis, London School of Economics and Political Science.

Cassese, Antonio (1995) *Self-Determination of Peoples: A Legal Reappraisal* (Cambridge University Press, Cambridge).

Castellino, Joshua (2000) *International Law and Self-Determination* (Martinus Nijhoff, Dordrecht).

—— and Elvira Dominguez Redondo (2006) *Minority Rights in Asia: A Comparative Legal Analysis* (Oxford University Press, Oxford).

Ceuppens, B. and P. Geschiere (2005) 'Autochthony, Local or Global? New Modes in the Struggle over Citizenship and Belonging in Africa and Europe', *Annual Review of Anthropology*, 34: 385–428.

Chandler, David (1999) 'The OSCE and the Internationalisation of National Minority Rights', in Karl Cordell (ed), *Ethnicity and Democratisation in the New Europe* (Routledge, London), 61–76.

—— (2000) *Bosnia: Faking Democracy after Dayton* (Pluto, London).

Chandler, Michael and Christopher Lalonde (1998) 'Cultural Continuity as a Hedge against Suicide in Canada's First Nations', *Journal of Transcultural Psychiatry*, 35/2: 191–219.

Chapman, Chris (2005) 'Conflict Prevention and the Rights of Minorities and Indigenous Peoples', *Human Rights Tribune des droits humains*, 11/2 (<http://www.hri.ca/tribune/onlineissue/25_05-2005/contents.html>).

Chartrand, Paul (1995) 'The Aboriginal Peoples of Canada and Renewal of the Federation', in Karen Knop (ed), *Rethinking Federalism: Citizens, Markets and Governments in a Changing World* (University of British Columbia Press, Vancouver).

Checkel, Jeffrey (1999) 'Norms, Institutions, and National Identity in Contemporary Europe', *International Studies Quarterly*, 43: 83–114.

Chesterman, Simon (2001) 'Minority Protection, Conflict Prevention, and the UN System' (Presented at meeting of the Rockefeller Foundation, October), available at <http://www.ipacademy.org/PDF_Reports/minority_protection_for_web.pdf>.

Chua, Amy (2003) *World on Fire: How Exporting Free Market Democracy Breeds Ethnic Hatred and Global Instability* (Doubleday, New York).

Cilevics, Boris (2005) 'Modern Nation-State and European Standards of Minority Rights', in *State Consolidation and National Identity* (Council of Europe Publishing, Science and Technique of Democracy Series No. 38, Strasbourg), 15–24.

Claude, Inis (1955) *National Minorities: An International Problem* (Harvard University Press, Cambridge, Mass.).

Cocen Group (1999) 'Guiding Principles for Improving the Situation of the Roma Based on the Recommendations of the Council of Europe's Specialist Group on Roma/Gypsies and on the Recommendations of the OSCE High Commission on National Minorities', adopted by the European Union (Cocen Group) at the Tempere Summit, December 1999 (<http://www.CoE.int/T/DG3/RomaTravellers/documentation/recommendations/MiscCOCENguidelineseu_eg.asp>).

Collier, Paul (2000) 'Ethnicity, Politics, and Economic Performance', *Economics and Politics*, 12/3: 225–46.

—— Lani Elliot, Havard Hegre, Anke Hoeffler, Marta Reynal-Querol, and Nicholas Sambanis (2003) *Breaking the Conflict Trap: Civil War and Development Policy* (World Bank, Washington).

Commission on Systemic Racism in the Ontario Criminal Justice System (1995), *Racism behind Bars: The Treatment of Black and other Racial Minority Prisoners in Ontario Prison* (Interim Report, Toronto).

Commission on the Future of Multi-Ethnic Britain (2000) *The Future of Multiethnic Britain* (Profile Books, London).

Connor, Walker (1993) *Ethnonationalism* (Princeton University Press, Princeton).

Connor, Walker (1999) 'National Self-Determination and Tomorrow's Political Map', in Alan C. Cairns, John C. Courtney, Peter Mackinnan, Hans J. Michelmann, and David E. Smith (eds), *Citizenship, Diversity and Pluralism: Canadian and Comparative Perspectives* (McGill-Queen's University Press, Montreal), 163–76.

Coppieters, Bruno (2004) *Europeanization and Conflict Resolution: Case Studies from the European Periphery* (Academia Press, Ghent).

Cornell, Stephen and Joseph Kalt (1995) 'Where Does Economic Development Really Come From? Constitutional Rule among the Contemporary Sioux and Apache', *Economic Inquiry*, 33: 402–26.

—— —— (1998) 'Sovereignty and Nation-Building: The Development Challenge in Indian Country Today', *American Indian Culture and Research Journal*, 22: 187–214.

—— —— (2000) 'Where's the Glue? Institutional Bases of American Indian Economic Development', *Journal of Socio-Economics*, 29: 443–70.

Cornell, Svante (2002) 'Autonomy as a Source of Conflict: Caucasian Conflicts in Theoretical Perspective', *World Politics* 54/2: 245–76.

Cornwall, Mark (1996) 'Minority Rights and Wrongs in Eastern Europe in the Twentieth Century', *The Historian*, 50: 16–20.

Council of Europe (2004) *Mechanisms for the Implementation of Minority Rights* (Council of Europe Publishing, Strasbourg).

—— (2005) *Framework Convention for the Protection of National Minorities: Collected Texts*, 3rd edn (Council of Europe Publishing, Strasbourg).

Cowan, Jane (2001) 'Ambiguities of an Emancipatory Discourse: The Making of a Macedonian Minority in Greece', in Cowan et al (eds) (2001).

—— Marie-Bénédicte Dembour, and Richard Wilson (eds) (2001) *Culture and Rights: Anthropological Perspectives* (Cambridge University Press, Cambridge).

Cowan, Klint (2006) 'International Responsibility for Human Rights Violations by American Indian Tribes', *Yale Human Rights and Development Law Journal* 9. (Available at http://islandia.law.yale.edu/yhrdlj/)

Crawford, James (ed) (1988) *The Rights of Peoples* (Oxford University Press, Oxford).

Crepaz, Markus (2006) ' "If You are My Brother, I May Give You a Dime!" Public Opinion on Multiculturalism, Trust and the Welfare State', in Banting and Kymlicka (eds) (2006), 92–118.

Cumper, Peter and Steven Wheatley (eds) (1999) *Minority Rights in the 'New' Europe* (Kluwer, The Hague).

Daes, Erica-Irene (1996) 'Working Paper on the Concept of "Indigenous people" ', prepared for the UN Working Group on Indigenous Populations (UN Doc. E/CN.4/Sub.2/AC.4/1996/2).

Danspeckgruber, Wolfgang (ed) (2002) *The Self-Determination of Peoples: Community, Nation, and State in an Interdependent World* (Lynne Reinner, Boulder, Colo.).

—— and Arthur Watts (eds) (1997) *Self-Determination and Self-Administration: A Sourcebook* (Lynne Reinner, Boulder, Colo.).

Das Gupta, Tania (1999) 'The Politics of Multiculturalism: "Immigrant Women" and the Canadian State', in Enakshi Dua and Angela Robertson (eds), *Scratching the Surface: Canadian Anti-Racist Feminist Thought* (Women's Press, Toronto).

Dasko, Donna (2005) 'Public Attitudes towards Multiculturalism and Bilingualism in Canada', in Margaret Adsett, Caroline Mallandain, and Shannon Stettner (eds), *Canadian and French Perspectives on Diversity: Conference Proceedings* (Department of Canadian Heritage, Ottawa), 119–25.

Davies, Scott (1999) 'From Moral Duty to Cultural Rights: A Case Study of Political Framing in Education', *Sociology of Education*, 72: 1–21.

De La Pena, Guillermo (2002) 'Social Citizenship, Ethnic Minority Demands, Human Rights, and Neoliberal Paradoxes: A Case Study in Western Mexico', in Rachel Sieder (ed), *Multiculturalism in Latin America: Indigenous Rights, Diversity and Democracy* (Palgrave, London), 129–56.

Deets, Stephen and Sherrill Stroschein (2005) 'Dilemmas of Autonomy and Liberal Pluralism: Examples Involving Hungarians in Central Europe', *Nations and Nationalism*, 11/2: 285–305.

Delanty, Gerard (2003) *Community* (Routledge, London).

Dembour, Marie-Benedicte (2001) 'Following the Movement of a Pendulum: Between Universalism and Relativism', in Cowan et al (eds) (2001), 56–79.

Deveaux, Monique (2000) 'Conflicting Equalities? Cultural Group Rights and Sex Equality', *Political Studies*, 48/3: 522–39.

DeWitte, Bruno (1993) 'The European Community and its Minorities', in C. Brölmann et al (eds), *Peoples and Minorities in International Law* (Martinus Nijhoff, Dordrecht), 167–85.

—— (2002) 'Politics versus Law in the EU's Approach to Ethnic Minorities', in Jan Zielonka (ed), *Europe Unbound: Enlarging and Reshaping the Boundaries of the European Union* (Routledge, London), 137–60.

—— (2004) 'The Constitutional Resources for an EU Minority Protection Policy', in Toggenburg (ed), 109–24.

Dezalay, Yves and Bryant Garth (2002) *The Internationalization of Palace Wars: Lawyers, Economists, and the Contest to Transform Latin American States* (University of Chicago Press, Chicago).

Dharmadase, K. N. O. (1992) *Language, Religion and Ethnic Assertiveness: The Growth of Sinhalese Nationalism in Sri Lanka* (University of Michigan Press, Ann Arbor).

Diaz Polanco, Hector (1997) *Indigenous Peoples in Latin America: The Quest for Self-Determination* (Westview, Boulder, Colo.).

Dimitras, Panayote (2004) *Recognition of Minorities in Europe: Protecting Rights and Dignity* (Minority Rights Group, London).

Dinstein, Yoram (ed) (1992) *The Protection of Minorities and Human Rights* (Martinus Nijhoff, Dordrecht).

Ditchev, Ivaylo (2004) 'Monoculturalism as Prevailing Culture' (trans. from the original Bulgarian on <http://www.eurozine.com>).

Dobre, Ana-Marie (2003) 'EU Conditionality and Romanian Minority Rights Policy: Towards the Europeanisation of the Candidate Countries', *Perspectives on European Politics and Society*, 4/1: 55–83.

Dolowitz, David and David Marsh (1996) 'Who Learns What from Whom? A Review of the Policy Transfer Literature', *Political Studies*, 44: 353–57.

—— —— (2000) 'Learning from Abroad: The Role of Policy Transfer in Contemporary Policy-Making', *Governance: An International Journal of Policy and Administration*, 13/1: 5–24.

Dorff, Robert (1994) 'Federalism in Eastern Europe: Part of the Solution or Part of the Problem?', *Publius*, 24: 99–114.

Dorowszewska, Ursula (2001) 'Rethinking the State, Minorities and National Security', in Kymlicka and Opalski (eds) (2001), 126–34.

Drake, St Clair (1951) 'The International Implications of Race and Race Relations', *Journal of Negro Education*, 29: 261–78.

Druviete, Ina (1997) 'Linguistic Human Rights in the Baltic States', *International Journal of the Sociology of Language*, 127: 161–85.

Drzewicki, Krzysztof (2005) 'A Constitution for Europe: Enshrining Minority Rights', *OSCE Magazine*, 11/1: 19–21.

Easterly, William and Ross Levine (1997) 'Africa's Growth Tragedy: Policies and Ethnic Division', *Quarterly Journal of Economics*, 112: 1203–50.

Economist The, (1995) 'A Question of Colour', *The Economist*, 15 April, 13–14.

Ehmann, Annagret (1998) 'From Colonial Racism to Nazi Population Policy', in Michael Berenbaum and Abraham Peck (eds), *The Holocaust and History* (Indiana University Press, Bloomington, Ind), 115–33.

Eide, Asbjorn (1993) 'In Search of Constructive Alternatives to Secession', in Tomuschat (ed) (1993), 136–76.

—— (2004) 'The Role of the United Nations Working Group in Minorities', in Council of Europe (2004), 55–70.

—— and Erika-Irene Daes (2000) 'Working Paper on the Relationship and Distinction between the Rights of Persons Belonging to Minorities and those of Indigenous Peoples', prepared for the UN Sub-Commission on Promotion and Protection of Human Rights (UN Doc. E/CN.4/Sub.2/2000/10).

Eisenberg, Avigail and Jeff Spinner-Halev (eds) (2005) *Minorities within Minorities: Equality, Rights and Diversity* (Cambridge University Press, Cambridge).

Ejobowah, John Boye (1998) 'The Political Public and Difference: The Case of Nigeria' (PhD Thesis, Department of Political Science, University of Toronto).

Entzinger, Han (2003) 'The Rise and Fall of Multiculturalism in the Netherlands', in Christian Joppke and Ewa Morawska (eds), *Toward Assimilation and Citizenship: Immigrants in Liberal Nation-States* (Palgrave, London), 59–86.

—— (2006) 'The Parallel Decline of Multiculturalism and the Welfare State', in Banting and Kymlicka (eds) (2006), 177–201.

Eriksen, Thomas Hylland (2001) 'Between Universalism and Relativism: A Critique of the UNESCO Concept of Culture', in Cowan et al (eds) (2001), 127–48.

Estebanez, Maria (1997) 'The High Commissioner on National Minorities: Development of the Mandate', in Michael Bothe, Natalino Rouzitti, and Allan Rosas (eds), *The OSCE in the Maintenance of Peace and Security* (Kluwer, The Hague), 123–66.

EUMAP (2001) *Monitoring the EU Accession Process: Minority Protection* (European Union Accession Monitoring Program, Open Society Institute, Budapest).

European Commission (2004) 'Handbook on Integration for Policy-Makers and Practitioners' (Directorate-General, Justice, Freedom and Security, European Communities) <http://www.europa.eu.int/comm/justice_home/>.

European Commission for Democracy through Law (1994) *The Protection of Minorities: Collected Texts of the European Commission for Democracy through Law* (Council of Europe Publishing, Strasbourg).

—— (1996) 'Opinion of the Venice Commission on the Interpretation of Article 11 of the Draft Protocol to the European Convention on Human Rights appended to Recommendation 1201'.

European Council (2004) 'Common Basic Principles for Immigrant Integration Policy in the European Union', Document 14615/04, adopted 19 November 2004.

Evans, Geoffrey (2006) 'Is Multiculturalism Eroding the Welfare State? The British Case', in Banting and Kymlicka (eds) (2006), 152–76.

Evers, Pieter (1995) 'Preliminary Policy and Legal Questions about Recognizing Traditional Land in Indonesia', *Ekonesia*, 3: 1–24.

Eyoh, Dickson (2004) 'Contesting Local Citizenship: Liberalization and the Politics of Difference in Cameroon', in Bruce Berman, Dickson Eyoh, and Will Kymlicka (eds), *Ethnicity and Democracy in Africa* (James Currey Ltd, Oxford), 96–112.

Falk, Richard (1999) *Predatory Globalization: A Critique* (Polity Press, Cambridge).

—— (2000) *Human Rights Horizons: The Pursuit of Justice in a Globalizing World* (Routledge, New York).

Favell, Adrian (2001) *Philosophies of Integration: Immigration and the Idea of Citizenship in France and Britain*, rev. edn. (St Martin's Press, New York).

Fearon, James and David Laitin (1996) 'Explaining Interethnic Cooperation', *American Political Science Review*, 90/4: 715–35.

—— —— (2000) 'Violence and the Social Construction of Ethnic Identity', *International Organization*, 54/4: 845–77.

—— —— (2003) 'Ethnicity, Insurgency and Civil War', *American Political Science Review*, 97/1: 75–90.

Feldman, Alice (2002) 'Making Space at the Nations' Table: Mapping the Transformative Geographies of the International Indigenous Peoples' Movement', *Social Movement Studies*, 1/1: 31–46.

Fink, Carole (2004) *Defending the Rights of Others: The Great Powers, the Jews, and International Minority Protection, 1878–1938* (Cambridge University Press, Cambridge).

Finkielkraut, Alain (1988) *The Undoing of Thought*, trans. Dennis O'Keefe (Claridge Press, London).

Fish, Steven and Robin Brooks (2004) 'Does Diversity Hurt Democracy?' *Journal of Democracy*, 15/1: 154–66.

Fleras, Augie and Jean Elliot (1992) *The Nations Within: Aboriginal–State Relations in Canada, the United States and New Zealand* (Oxford University Press, Toronto).

Forbes, Donald (1994) 'Canada: From Bilingualism to Multiculturalism', in Larry Diamond and Marc Plattner (eds), *Nationalism, Ethnic Conflict and Democracy* (Johns Hopkins University Press, Baltimore), 86–101.

Ford, Stuart (1999) 'OSCE National Minority Rights in the United States: The Limits of Conflict Resolution', *Suffolk Transnational Law Review*, 23/1: 1–55.

Fraser, Nancy (1995) 'From Redistribution to Recognition? Dilemmas of Justice in a "Post-Socialist" Age', *New Left Review*, 212: 68–93.

—— (1998) 'Social Justice in the Age of Identity Politics: Redistribution, Recognition and Participation', in Grethe Peterson (ed), *The Tanner Lectures on Human Values*, 19 (University of Utah Press, Salt Lake City), 1–67.

—— (2000) 'Rethinking Recognition', *New Left Review*, 3: 107–20.

—— (2003) 'Social Justice in the Age of Identity Politics', in Nancy Fraser and Axel Honneth, *Redistribution or Recognition? A Political-Philosophical Exchange* (Verso, London), 7–109.

Freeman, Michael (2002) 'Anthropology and the Democratisation of Human Rights', *International Journal of Human Rights*, 6/3: 37–54.

Frideres, James (1997) 'Edging into the Mainstream: Immigrant Adult and their Children', in S. Isajiw (ed), *Multiculturalism in North American and Europe: Comparative Perspectives on Interethnic Relations and Social Incorporation* (Canadian Scholar's Press, Toronto), 537–62.

Füredi, Frank (1998) *The Silent War: Imperialism and the Changing Perception of Race* (Pluto, London).

Gagnon, Alain and James Tully (eds) (2001) *Multinational Democracies* (Cambridge University Press, Cambridge).

Gal, Kinga (1999) *Bilateral Agreements in Central and Eastern Europe: A New Inter-State Framework for Minority Protection* (European Centre for Minority Issues, Working Paper No. 4, Flensburg).

Galbreath, David (2003) 'The Politics of European Integration and Minority Rights in Estonia and Latvia', *Perspectives on European Politics and Society*, 4/1: 35–53.

—— (2006) 'European Integration through Democratic Conditionality: Latvia in the Context of Minority Rights', *Journal of Contemporary European Studies*, 14/1: 69–88.

Galston, William (1991) *Liberal Purposes* (Cambridge University Press, Cambridge).

Ganguly, Sumit (1997) 'Ethnic Policies and Political Quiescence in Malaysia and Singapore', in Michael Brown and Sumit Ganguly (eds), *Government Policies and Ethnic Relations in Asia and the Pacific* (MIT Press, Cambridge), 233–72.

Garet, Ronald (1983) 'Communality and Existence: The Rights of Groups', *Southern California Law Review*, 56/5: 1001–75.

Gayim, Eyassu (2001) *The Concept of Minority in International Law: A Critical Study of the Vital Elements* (University of Lapland Press, Rovaniemi).

Geschiere, P. (2005) 'Autochthony and Citizenship: New Modes in the Struggle over Belonging and Exclusion in Africa', *Forum for Development Studies*, 32/2: 371–84.

Ghai, Yash (1999) 'Universalism and Relativism: Human Rights as a Framework for Negotiating Interethnic Claims', *Cardozo Law Review*, 21: 1095–140.

Ghanea, Nazila and Alexandra Xanthaki (eds) (2005) *Minorities, Peoples and Self-Determination: Essays in Honour of Patrick Thornberry* (Martinus Nijhoff, Leiden).

Giroux, Henry (1994) *Disturbing Pleasures: Learning Popular Culture* (Routledge, London).

Glazer, Nathan (1997) *We Are All Multiculturalists Now* (Harvard University Press, Mass., Cambridge).

Glendon, Mary Ann (2001) *A World Made New: Eleanor Roosevelt and the Universal Declaration of Human Rights* (Random House, New York).

Global Commission on International Migration (2005) *Migration in an Interconnected World: New Directions for Action* (United Nations, New York—posted at <http://www.gcim.org>).

Goodwin, Morag (2004) 'The Romani Claim to Non-territorial Nation Status: Recognition from an International Legal Perspective', *Roma Rights*, 2004/1: 54–64.

Government of Canada (1995) 'Female Genital Mutilation: Report on Consultations Held in Ottawa and Montreal' (Report WD1995-8e, Department of Justice, Research and Statistics Section, Ottawa).

Grabb, Edward and James Curtis (2005) *Regions Apart: The Four Societies of Canada and the United States* (Oxford University Press, Toronto).

Grare, Frederic (2006) *Pakistan: The Resurgence of Baluch Nationalism* (Carnegie Papers No. 65, Carnegie Endowment for International Peace, Washington).

Gray, Andrew (1998) 'Development Policy—Development Protest: The World Bank, Indigenous Peoples, and NGOs', in Jonathan Fox and David Brown (eds), *The Struggle for Accountability: The World Bank, NGOs, and Grassroots Movements* (MIT Press, Cambridge, Mass.), 267–302.

Green, Joyce and Ian Peach (2007) 'Beyond "Us" and "Them": Prescribing Postcolonial Politics and Policy in Saskatchewan', in Keith Banting, Thomas Courchene, and Leslie Seidle (eds), *Belonging? Diversity, Recognition and Shared Citizenship in Canada* (Institute for Research on Public Policy, Montreal), 263–84.

Grin, François (1999) *Language Policy in Multilingual Switzerland: Overview and Recent Developments* (ECMI Brief No. 2, European Centre for Minority Issues, Flensburg).

Grin, François (2004) 'On the Costs of Cultural Diversity', in Philippe Van Parijs (ed), *Cultural Diversity versus Economic Solidarity* (Deboeck Université Press, Brussels), 189–202.

Guglielmo, Rachel (2004) 'Human Rights in the Accession Process: Roma and Muslims in an Enlarging EU', in Toggenburg (ed) (2004), 39–58.

—— and Timothy William Waters (2005) 'Migrating Towards Minority Status: Shifting European Policy Towards Roma', *Journal of Common Market Studies*, 43/4: 763–86.

Guibernau, Montserrat (1999) *Nations without States: Political Communities in a Global Age* (Polity Press, Cambridge).

Guilhot, Nicolas (2005) *The Democracy Makers: Human Rights and International Order* (Columbia University Press, New York).

Gurr, Ted (1993) *Minorities at Risk: A Global View of Ethnopolitical Conflict* (Institute of Peace Press, Washington).

—— (2000) *Peoples versus States: Minorities at Risk in the New Century* (Institute of Peace Press, Washington).

Gustafson, Bret (2002) 'Paradoxes of Liberal Indigenism: Indigenous Movements, State Processes, and Intercultural Reform in Bolivia', in David Maybury-Lewis (ed), *The Politics of Ethnicity: Indigenous Peoples in Latin American States* (Harvard University Press, Cambridge, Mass.), 267–306.

Gwyn, Richard (1995) *Nationalism without Walls: The Unbearable Lightness of Being Canadian* (McClelland and Stewart, Toronto).

Hadden, Tom (2003) 'Towards a Set of Regional Guidelines or Codes of Practice on the Implementation of the Declaration' (Working Paper prepared for 9th Session of the UN Working Group on Minorities, E/CN.4/Sub.2/AC.5/2003/WP.1).

—— (2004) 'The Pendulum Theory of Individual, Communal and Minority Rights', in Simon Caney and Peter Jones (eds), *Human Rights and Global Diversity* (Frank Cass, Portland, Ore.), 77–90.

Hale, Charles (2002) 'Does Multiculturalism Menace? Governance, Cultural Rights, and the Politics of Identity in Guatemala', *Journal of Latin American Studies*, 34: 485–524.

Hannikainen, Lauri (1996) 'The Status of Minorities, Indigenous Peoples and Immigrant and Refugee Groups in Four Nordic States', *Nordic Journal of International Law*, 65: 1–71.

—— (1998) 'Self-Determination and Autonomy in International Law', in Marku Suksi (ed), *Autonomy: Applications and Implications* (Kluwer, The Hague), 76–95.

Hannum, Hurst (1990) *Autonomy, Sovereignty and Self-Determination: The Accommodation of Conflicting Rights* (University of Pennsylvania Press, Philadelphia).

Hansen, Randall (2007). 'Diversity, Integration and the Turn from Multiculturalism in the United Kingdom', in Keith Banting, Thomas Courchene, and Leslie Seidle (eds), *Belonging? Diversity, Recognition and Shared Citizenship in Canada* (Institute for Research on Public Policy, Montreal), 35–86.

Harles, John (2004) 'Immigrant Integration in Canada and the United States', *American Review of Canadian Studies*, 34/2: 223–58.

Harty, Siobhan and Michael Murphy (2005) *In Defense of Multinational Citizenship* (UBC Press, Vancouver).

Havemann, Paul (ed) (1999) *Indigenous Peoples' Rights in Australia, Canada and New Zealand* (Oxford University Press, Oxford).

He, Baogang (1998) 'Can Kymlicka's Liberal Theory of Minority Rights be Applied in East Asia?', in Paul van der Velde and Alex McKay (eds), *New Developments in Asian Studies* (Kegal Paul International, London), 20–44.

—— (2004) 'Confucianism versus Liberalism over Minority Rights: A Critical Response to Will Kymlicka', *Journal of Chinese Philosophy*, 31/1: 103–23.

Heintze, H. J. (1998) 'On the Legal Understanding of Autonomy', in Marku Suksi (ed), *Autonomy: Applications and Implications* (Kluwer, The Hague).

Henrard, Kristin (2000) *Devising an Adequate Scheme of Minority Protection: Individual Human Rights, Minority Rights and the Right to Self-Determination* (Martinus Nijhoff, Dordrecht).

—— (2005) 'Ever-Increasing Synergy towards a Stronger Level of Minority Protection between Minority-Specific and Non-Minority-Specific Instruments', *European Yearbook of Minority Issues*, 3: 15–42.

Henry, Frances (1994) *The Caribbean Diaspora in Toronto: Learning to Live with Racism* (University of Toronto Press, Toronto).

Hero, Rodney and Robert Preuhs (2006) 'Multiculturalism and Welfare Policies in the US States: A State-Level Comparative Analysis', in Banting and Kymlicka (eds) (2006), 121–51.

Hewitt, Roger (2005) *White Backlash and the Politics of Multiculturalism* (Cambridge University Press, Cambridge).

Hillard, Pierre (2002) *Minorités et Régionalismes dans l'Europe Fédérale des Régions: Enquête sur le plan allemand qui va bouleverser l'Europe*, 3rd edn (Editions François-Xavier de Guibert, Paris).

Ho, Chin Ung (2000) *The Chinese of South-East Asia* (Minority Rights Group, London).

Hobsbawm, Eric and Terence Ranger (eds) (1983) *The Invention of Tradition* (Cambridge University Press, Cambridge).

Hoffman, Rainer (2002) 'Protecting the Rights of National Minorities in Europe: First Experiences with the Council of Europe Framework Convention for the Protection of National Minorities', *German Yearbook of International Law*, 44: 237–69.

Hooker, Juliet (2005) 'Indigenous Inclusion/Black Exclusion: Race, Ethnicity and Multicultural Citizenship in Contemporary Latin America', *Journal of Latin American Studies*, 37/2: 285–310.

Housden, Martyn (2006) 'Ewald Ammende, the Congress of European Nationalities and the Rise of Nazism' (Paper presented at conference on 'The Theory and

Practice of Cultural Autonomy in Central and Eastern Europe: Historical and Contemporary Perspectives', University of Glasgow, July).

Howard-Hassmann, Rhoda (2003) *Compassionate Canadians: Civic Leaders Discuss Human Rights* (University of Toronto Press, Toronto).

Hughes, James and Gwendolyn Sasse (2003) 'Monitoring the Monitors: EU Enlargement Conditionality and Minority Protection in the CEECs', *Journal on Ethnopolitics and Minority Issues in Europe*, 1: 1–36.

Hum, Derek and Wayne Simpson (2007) 'Revisiting Equity and Labour: Immigration, Gender, Minority Status and Income Differentials in Canada', in Sean Hier and Singh Bolaria (eds) *Race and Racism in 21st Century Canada* (Broadview, Peterborough).

Huntington, Samuel (1996) *The Clash of Civilizations and the Remaking of World Order* (Simon & Schuster, New York).

Hussain, Asaf, Bill Law, and Tim Haq (2006) *Engagement with Culture: From Diversity to Interculturalism* (Institute of Lifelong Learning, University of Leicester, Leicester).

Ibrahim, Saad Eddin (1996) 'Management and Mismanagement of Diversity: The Case of Ethnic Conflict and State-Building in the Arab World' (MOST Discussion Paper No. 10, UNESCO—posted at <http://www.unesco.org/most/ibraeng.htm>).

ICES (International Centre for Ethnic Studies) (1995) *Minorities in Cambodia* (Minority Rights Group Report 95/2, London).

Ignatieff, Michael (1993) *Blood and Belonging: Journeys into the New Nationalism* (Farrar, Straus and Giroux, New York).

—— (2000) *The Rights Revolution* (Anansi Press, Toronto).

Inglehart, Ronald, Miguel Basanez, and Alejandro Moreno (1998) *Human Values and Beliefs: A Cross-Cultural Sourcebook* (University of Michigan Press, Ann Arbor).

—— and Christian Welzel (2005) *Modernization, Cultural Change and Democracy: The Human Development Sequence* (Cambridge University Press, Cambridge).

IOG (Institute on Governance) (2000) *Governance Models to Achieve Higher Levels of Aggregation: Literature Review* (<http://www.iog.ca>).

Ivison, D., Patton, P., and Sanders, W. (eds) (2000) *Political Theory and the Rights of Indigenous Peoples* (Cambridge University Press, Cambridge).

Jabareen, Hassan (2002) 'The Future of Arab Citizenship in Israel', in Daniel Levy and Yfaat Weiss (eds), *Challenging Ethnic Citizenship* (Berghahn, New York), 196–220.

—— (2005) 'Collective Rights and Reconciliation in the Constitutional Process: The Case of Israel', *Adalah Newsletter*, 12 (April) (<http://www.adalah.org>).

Jackson, Robert (1993) 'The Weight of Ideas in Decolonization: Normative Change in International Relations', in Judith Goldstein and Robert Keohane (eds) *Ideas and Foreign Policy* (Cornell University Press, Ithaca), 111–38.

Jackson Preece, Jennifer (1998) *National Minorities and the European Nation-States System* (Oxford University Press, Oxford).

—— (2005) *Minority Rights* (Polity Press, Cambridge).

Jain, Pratibha (2005) 'Balancing Minority Rights and Gender Justice: The Impact of Protecting Multiculturalism on Women's Rights in India', *Berkeley Journal of International Law*, 23: 201–22.

Jamal, Amal (2005) 'On the Morality of Arab Collective Rights in Israel', *Adalah Newsletter*, 12 (April) (<http://www.adalah.org>).

James, Estelle (1987) 'The Public/Private Division of Responsibility for Education in International Comparison', *Economics of Education Review*, 6/1: 1–14.

—— (1993) 'Why Do Different Countries Choose a Different Public/Private Mix of Education Services?', *Journal of Human Resources*, 28/3: 531–92.

James, Matt (1999) 'Redress Politics and Canadian Citizenship', in Harvey Lazar and Tom McIntosh (eds), *How Canadians Connect* (Institute of Intergovernmental Affairs, Kingston), 247–81.

—— (2006) 'Do Campaigns for Historical Redress Erode the Canadian Welfare State?' in Banting and Kymlicka (eds) (2006), 222–46.

James, Oliver and Martin Lodge (2003) 'The Limitations of "Policy Transfer" and "Lesson Drawing" for Public Policy Research', *Political Studies Review*, 1: 179–93.

Jaworsky, John (1998) 'Nationalities Policy and Potential for Interethnic Conflict in Ukraine', in Magda Opalski (ed), *Managing Diversity in Plural Societies: Minorities, Migration and Nation-Building in Post-Communist Europe* (Forum Eastern Europe, Ottawa), 104–27.

Jedwab, Jack (2005) 'Muslims and Multicultural Futures in Western Democracies: Is Kymlicka's Pessimism Warranted?', *Canadian Diversity*, 4/3: 92–6.

Johns, Martin (2003) 'Do As I Say, Not As I Do: The European Union, Eastern Europe and Minority Rights', *East European Politics and Society*, 17/4: 682–99.

Johnson, Carter (2006) 'The Use and Abuse of Minority Rights: Assessing Past and Future EU Policies towards Accession Countries of Central, Eastern and South-Eastern Europe', *International Journal on Minority and Group Rights*, 13: 27–51.

Johnston, Darlene (1989) 'Native Rights as Collective Rights: A Question of Group Self-Preservation?', *Canadian Journal of Law and Jurisprudence*, 2/1: 19–34.

Johnston, Kara (2006) 'Letter', *Herizons*, 20/2: 2.

Joppke, Christian (2002) 'Multicultural Citizenship', in B. S. Turner (ed), *Handbook of Citizenship Studies* (Sage, London), 245–58.

—— (2004) 'The Retreat of Multiculturalism in the Liberal State: Theory and Policy', *British Journal of Sociology*, 55/2: 237–57.

Jung, Courtney (2007) 'Democratic Engagement with Ethnic Minority Claims: A Methodological Intervention into a Normative Debate, in Omid Payrow Shabani (ed) *Multiculturalism and the Law* (University of Wales Press, Cardiff), 263–79.

Jupp, James (1995) 'The New Multicultural Agenda', *Crossings*, 1/1: 38–41.

Karmis, Dimitrios (1993) 'Cultures autochtones et libéralisme au Canada: les vertus mediatrices du communautarisme libéral de Charles Taylor', *Canadian Journal of Political Science*, 26/1: 69–96.

Kate, Mary-Anne (2005) 'The Provision of Protection to Asylum-Seekers in Destination Countries' (Working Paper No. 114, New Issues in Refugee Research, Evaluation and Policy Analysis Unit, UNHCR).

Kauffman, Paul (2004) 'Diversity and Indigenous Policy Outcomes: Comparisons between Four Nations', *International Journal of Diversity in Organizations, Communities and Nations*, vol. 3 (<http://ijd.cgpublisher.com/product/pub.29/prod.3A.20>).

Kaufmann, Chaim (1996) 'Possible and Impossible Solutions to Ethnic Civil Wars', *International Security*, 20/4: 136–75.

—— (1998) 'When All Else Fails: Ethnic Population Transfers and Partitions in the Twentieth Century', *International Security*, 23/2: 120–56.

Kawczynski, Rudko (2000) 'Report on the Condition of the Roma in Europe' (Background paper commissioned for OSCE/ODIHR International Consultation on Roma Refugees and Asylum-Seekers, Warsaw, October), available at <http://www.romnews.com/a/RKreport.htm>.

Kay, Barbara (2006) 'The Rise of Quebecistan', *National Post* (Toronto), 9 August.

Keal, Paul (2003) *European Conquest and the Rights of Indigenous Peoples: The Moral Backwardness of International Society* (Cambridge University Press, Cambridge).

Keating, Michael (2001) *Plurinational Democracy: Stateless Nations in a Post-Sovereignty Era* (Oxford University Press, Oxford).

—— and McGarry, J. (eds) (2001) *Minority Nationalism and the Changing International Order* (Oxford University Press, Oxford).

Keck, Margaret and Kathryn Sikkink (1998) *Activists beyond Borders: Transnational Advocacy Networks in International Politics* (Cornell University Press, Ithaca, NY).

Keitner, Chimène (2004) *UNESCO and the Issue of Cultural Diversity: Review and Strategy 1946–2004* (Division of Cultural Policies and Intercultural Dialogue, UNESCO, Paris).

Keller, Perry (1998) 'Rethinking Ethnic and Cultural Rights in Europe', *Oxford Journal of Legal Studies*, 18: 29–59.

Kelley, Judith (2004*a*) *Ethnic Politics in Europe: The Power of Norms and Incentives* (Princeton University Press, Princeton).

—— (2004*b*) 'International Actors on the Domestic Scene: Membership Conditionality and Socialization by International Institutions', *International Organization*, 58: 425–57.

Kemp, Walter (2002) 'Applying the Nationality Principle: Handle with Care', *Journal on Ethnopolitics and Minority Issues in Europe*, Issue 4.

Khan, Sa'ad (2002) 'The Organization of the Islamic Conference (OIC) and Muslim Minorities', *Journal of Muslim Minority Affairs*, 22/2: 351–67.

Kingdon, John (1997) *Agendas, Alternatives, and Public Policies*, 2nd edn (Longman, New York).

Kingsbury, Benedict (1995) ' "Indigenous Peoples" as an International Legal Concept', in R. H. Barnes (ed), *Indigenous Peoples of Asia* (Association of Asian Studies, Ann Arbor), 13–34.

—— (1998) ' "Indigenous Peoples" in International Law: A Constructivist Approach to the Controversy', *American Journal of International Law*, 92/3: 414–57.

—— (1999*a*) 'The Applicability of the International Legal Concept of "Indigenous Peoples" in Asia', in Joanne Bauer and Daniel Bell (eds), *The East Asian Challenge for Human Rights* (Cambridge University Press, Cambridge), 336–77.

—— (1999*b*) 'Operational Policies of International Institutions as Part of the Law-Making Process: The World Bank and Indigenous Peoples', in Guy Goodwin-Gill and Stefan Talmon (eds), *The Reality of International Law* (Oxford University Press, Oxford), 330–42.

—— (2001) 'Reconciling Five Competing Conceptual Structures of Indigenous Peoples' Claims in International and Comparative Law', in Alston (ed) (2001), 69–110.

Klausen, Jytte (2005) *The Islamic Challenge: Politics and Religion in Western Europe* (Oxford University Press, Oxford).

Klebes, Heinrich (1995) 'The Council of Europe's Framework Convention for the Protection of National Minorities', *Human Rights Law Journal*, 16/1: 92–8.

Klimová-Alexander, Ilona (2005) *The Romani Voice in World Politics: The United Nations and Non-State Actors* (Ashgate, Aldershot).

—— (2006) 'Transnational Romani and Indigenous Non-Territorial Self-Determination Claims' (Presented at conference on 'The Theory and Practice of Cultural Autonomy in Central and Eastern Europe: Historical and Contemporary Perspectives', University of Glasgow, July).

Knop, Karen (2002) *Diversity and Self-Determination in International Law* (Cambridge University Press, Cambridge).

Kolsto, Pal (2001) 'Territorial Autonomy as a Minority Rights Regime in Post-Communist Countries', in Kymlicka and Opalski (eds) (2001), 200–19.

Koopmans, Ruud and Paul Statham (1999) 'Challenging the Liberal Nation-State? Postnationalism, Multiculturalism and the Collective Claims-Making of Migrants and Ethnic Minorities in Britain and Germany', *American Journal of Sociology*, 105/3: 652–96.

—— —— (2003) 'How National Citizenship Shapes Transnationalism: A Comparative Analysis of Migrant and Minority Claims-Making in Germany, Great Britain and the Netherlands', in Christian Joppke and Ewa Morawska (eds), *Toward Assimilation and Citizenship: Immigrants in Liberal Nation-States* (Palgrave, London), 195–238.

—— —— Macro Guigni and Florence Passy (2005) *Contested Citizenship: Immigration and Cultural Diversity in Europe* (University of Minnesota Press, Minneapolis).

Koulish, Robert (2005) 'Hungarian Roma Attitudes on Minority Rights: The Symbolic Violence of Ethnic Identification', *Europe-Asia Studies*, 57/2: 311–26.

Kovacs, Maria (2003) 'Standards of Self-Determination and Standards of Minority Rights in the Post-Communist Era: A Historical Perspective', *Nations and Nationalism*, 9/3: 433–50.

Krasner, Stephen (1999) *Sovereignty: Organized Hypocrisy* (Princeton University Press, Princeton).

Krishna, Sankaran (1999) *Postcolonial Insecurities: India, Sri Lanka and the Question of Nationhood* (University of Minnesota Press, Minneapolis).

Kristol, Irving (1991) 'The Tragedy of Multiculturalism', *Wall Street Journal*, 31 July, p. 15.

Kunz, Jozef (1954) 'The Present Status of the International Law for the Protection of Minorities', *American Journal of International Law*, 48/2: 282–7.

Kuper, Adam (2003) 'The Return of the Native', *Current Anthropology*, 44/3: 389–402.

Kuzio, Taras (2001) 'Nationalising States or Nation-Building? A Critical Review of the Theoretical Literature and Empirical Evidence', *Nations and Nationalism*, 7/2: 135–54.

Kymlicka, Will (1989) *Liberalism, Community, and Culture* (Oxford University Press, Oxford).

—— (1995) *Multicultural Citizenship: A Liberal Theory of Minority Rights* (Oxford University Press, Oxford).

—— (1998) *Finding Our Way: Rethinking Ethnocultural Relations in Canada* (Oxford University Press, Oxford).

—— (2001) *Politics in the Vernacular: Nationalism, Multiculturalism, Citizenship* (Oxford University Press, Oxford).

—— (2002) 'The Impact of Group Rights on Fear and Trust: A Response to Offe', *Hagar: International Social Science Review*, 3/1: 19–36.

—— (2004*a*) 'Marketing Canadian Pluralism in the International Arena', *International Journal*, 59/4: 829–52.

—— (2004*b*) 'Universal Minority Rights? The Prospects for Consensus', in Morigiwa Yasutomo, Ishiyama Fumihiko, and Sakurai Tetsu (eds), *Universal Minority Rights, A Transnational Approach* (Archiv für Rechts- und Sozialphilosophie No. 96, Franz Steiner Verlag, Stuttgart), 13–57.

—— (2004*c*) 'Culturally Responsive Policies' (Background paper prepared for the 2004 United Nations Human Development Report, posted at <http://hdr.undp.org/publications/papers.cfm>).

—— (2005*a*) 'Testing the Bounds of Liberal Multiculturalism? The Sharia Debate in Ontario', presented at the conference on 'Muslim Women's Equality Rights in the Justice System: Gender, Religion and Pluralism' (Canadian Council of Muslim Women, April 2005). Forthcoming in *Ethique publique*, 9/1 (2007).

—— (2005*b*) 'Renner and the Accommodation of Substate Nationalisms', in Ephraim Nimni (ed), *National Cultural Autonomy and its Contemporary Critics* (Routledge, London), 137–49.

—— (2006*a*) 'The Evolving Basis of International Norms of Minority Rights: Rights to Culture, Participation and Autonomy', in John McGarry and Micheal Keating (eds), *European Integration and the Nationalities Question* (Routledge, London), 35–63.

—— (2006b) 'Emerging Western Models of Multination Federalism: Are they Relevant for Africa?' in David Turton (ed), *Ethnic Federalism: The Ethiopian Experience in Comparative Perspective* (James Currey Ltd, Oxford), 32–64.

—— (2007) 'Ethnocultural Diversity in a Liberal State: Making Sense of the Canadian Model(s)', in Keith Banting, Tom Courchene, and Leslie Seidle (eds), *Belonging? Diversity, Recognition and Shared Citizenship in Canada* (Institute for Research on Public Policy, Montreal), 39–86.

—— and Baogang He (eds) (2005) *Multiculturalism in Asia* (Oxford University Press, Oxford).

—— and Magda Opalski (eds) (2001) *Can Liberal Pluralism be Exported? Western Politicial Theory and Ethnic Relations in Eastern Europe* (Oxford University Press, Oxford).

Laitin, David (1998) *Identity in Formation: The Russian-Speaking Populations in the Near Abroad* (Cornell University Press, Ithaca, NY).

—— and Robert Reich (2003) 'A Liberal Democratic Approach to Language Justice', in Will Kymlicka and Alan Patten (eds) *Language Rights and Political Theory* (Oxford University Press, Oxford), 80–104.

Lam, Maivan (2000) *At the Edge of the State: Indigenous Peoples and Self-Determination* (Transnational Publishers, Ardsley).

Lamming, Lord (2003) *The Victoria Climbie Inquiry Report* (HMSO, London).

Landry, Rodrigue (2005) 'Challenges Facing Canada's Francophone Minority: A Macroscopic Perspective', in Margaret Adsett et al (eds), *Canadian and French Perspectives on Diversity: Conference Proceedings* (Department of Canadian Heritage, Ottawa), 75–86.

Lauren, Paul Gordon (1996) *Power and Prejudice: The Politics and Diplomacy of Racial Discrimination*, 2nd edn (Westview, Boulder, Colo.).

Layachi, Azzedine (2005) 'The Berbers in Algeria: Politicized Ethnicity and Ethnicized Politics', in Maya Shatzmiller (ed), *Nationalism and Minority Identities in Islamic Societies* (McGill-Queen's University Press, Montreal), 195–228.

Layton, Azza Salama (2000) *International Politics and Civil Rights Policies in the United States* (Cambridge University Press, Cambridge).

Leff, Carole (1999) 'Democratization and Disintegration: Federalism and the Break-Up of the Communist Federal States', *World Politics*, 51/2: 205–35.

Lemarchand, Rene (1997) 'Ethnic Conflict Resolution in Contemporary Africa: Four Models in Search of Solutions', in Gunther Bachler (ed), *Federalism against Ethnicity* (Verlag Ruegger, Zurich), 95–106.

Lennox, Corinne (2006) 'The Changing International Protection Regimes for Minorities and Indigenous Peoples: Experiences from Latin America and Africa' (presented to Annual Conference of International Studies Association, San Diego, March 2006).

Lerner, Natan (1991) *Group Rights and Discrimination in International Law* (Martinus Nijhoff, Dordrecht).

Letschert, Rianne (2005) *The Impact of Minority Rights Mechanisms* (Asser Press, The Hague).

Levine, Alissa (1999) 'Female Genital Operations: Canadian Realities, Concerns and Policy Recommendations', in Harold Troper and Morton Weinfeld (eds), *Ethnicity, Politics and Public Policy* (University of Toronto Press, Toronto), 26–53.

Levy, Jacob (2000*a*) 'Three Modes of Incorporating Indigenous Law', in Will Kymlicka and Wayne Norman (eds), *Citizenship in Diverse Societies* (Oxford University Press, Oxford), 297–325.

—— (2000*b*) *The Multiculturalism of Fear* (Oxford University Press, Oxford).

—— (2004) 'Liberal Jacobinism', *Ethics*, 114: 318–36.

Lewis-Anthony, Sian (1998) 'Autonomy and the Council of Europe—With Special Reference to the Application of Article 3 of the First Protocol of the European Convention on Human Rights', in Suksi (ed) (1998), 317–42.

Lian, Brad and John Oneal (1997) 'Cultural Diversity and Economic Development: A Cross-National Study of 98 Countries, 1960–85', *Economic Development and Cultural Change*, 46: 61–77.

Libal, Michael (1997) *Limits of Persuasion: Germany and the Yugoslavia Crisis, 1991–1992* (Praeger, Westport, Conn.).

Liddle, Rod (2004) 'How Islam has Killed Multiculturalism', *Spectator*, 1 May, 12–13.

Liebich, André (1995) 'Nations, States and Minorities: Why is Eastern Europe Different?', *Dissent* (summer): 313–17.

—— (2004) 'The Old and the New: Historical Dimensions of Majority-Minority Relations in an Enlarged Union', presented at ECMI conference on 'An Ever More Diverse Union?', Berlin).

Lindquist, Sven (1996) *Exterminate all the Brutes* (New Press, New York).

Lupul, Manoly (2005) *The Politics of Multiculturalism: A Ukrainian-Canadian Memoir* (Canadian Institute of Ukrainian Studies Press, Edmonton).

Luttwak, Edward (1999) 'Give War a Chance', *Foreign Affairs*, 78/4: 36–44.

Lyons, Gene and James Mayall (eds), *International Human Rights in the 21st Century: Protecting the Rights of Groups* (Rowman and Littlefield, Lanham, Md).

McCormick, Neil (2004) 'The European Constitutional Convention and the Stateless Nations', *International Relations*, 18/3: 331–44.

McCorquodale, Robert (ed) (2000) *Self-Determination in International Law* (Ashgate, Aldershot).

McCrudden, Christopher (2007) 'Consociationalism, Equality and Minorities in the Northern Ireland Bill of Rights Debate: The Inglorious Role of the OSCE High Commissioner for National Minorities', in J. Morison, K. McEvoy, and G. Anthony (eds), *Judges, Transition and Human Rights Cultures* (Oxford University Press, Oxford).

Macdonald, Lindsay Te Ata O Tu and Paul Muldoon (2006) 'Globalisation, Neo-liberalism, and the Struggle for Indigenous Citizenship', *Australian Journal of Political Science*, 41/2: 209–23.

McDonald, Michael (1991) 'Should Communities Have Rights? Reflections on Liberal Individualism', *Canadian Journal of Law and Jurisprudence*, 2/1: 217–37.

MacFarlane, Neil (2001) 'The Internationalization of Ethnic Strife', in Jan Zielonka and Alex Pravda (eds), *Democratic Consolidation in Eastern Europe*, ii (Oxford University Press, Oxford), 139–62.

McGarry, John and Michael Keating (eds) (2006) *European Integration and the Nationalities Question* (Routledge, London).

MacKay, Fergus (2002) 'Universal Rights or a Universe unto Itself: Indigenous Peoples' Human Rights and the World Bank's Operational Policy 4.10 on Indigenous Peoples', *American University International Law Review*, 17: 527–624.

McMahon, Patrice (2006) 'Ethnic Peace in the East? Transnational Networks and the CSCE/OSCE', *Ethnopolitics*, 5/2: 101–24.

MacMillan, Margaret (2001) *Paris 1919: Six Months that Changed the World* (Random House, New York).

McRoberts, Kenneth (2001) *Catalonia: Nation Building without a State* (Oxford University Press, Toronto).

Mahajan, Gurpreet (1998) *Identities and Rights: Aspects of Liberal Democracy in India* (Oxford University Press, Delhi).

Malksoo, Lauri (2000) 'Language Rights in International Law: Why the Phoenix is Still in the Ashes', *Florida Journal of International Law*, 12/3: 431–65.

Malloy, Tove (2005) *National Minority Rights in Europe* (Oxford University Press, Oxford).

Mamdani, Mahmood (1996) *Citizen and Subject* (Princeton University Press, Princeton).

—— (ed) (2000) *Beyond Rights Talk and Culture Talk* (St Martin's Press, New York).

Manas, Jean (1996) 'The Council of Europe's Democracy Ideal and the Challenges of Ethno-National Strife', in Abram Chayes and Antonia Chayes (eds) *Preventing Conflict in the Post-Communist World* (Brookings Institution, Washington), 99–144.

Manning, Nicole (2002) 'US Companies Support Gender Segregation in Saudi Arabia', *National NOW Times*, summer (<http://www.now.org/nnt/summer-2002/gender.html>).

Marc, Alexandre (2005) 'Cultural Diversity and Service Delivery: Where Do We Stand?' (Working paper prepared for World Bank conference on 'New Frontiers of Social Policy: Development in a Globalizing World', Arusha, Tanzania, December 2005).

Margalit, Avishai and Joseph Raz (1990) 'National Self-Determination', *Journal of Philosophy*, 87/9: 439–61.

Markell, Patchen (2003) *Bound by Recognition* (Princeton University Press, Princeton).

Marples, David and David Duke (1995) 'Ukraine, Russia and the Question of Crimea', *Nationalities Papers*, 23/2: 261–89.

Mascarenhas, Tomas Bril (2006) 'The Privatization of Patagonia', *New Internationalist*, No. 392 (August): 30–1.

Matustik, M. (1998) 'Ludic, Corporate, and Imperial Multiculturalism: Imposters of Democracy and Cartographers of the New World Order', in Cynthia Willett (ed), *Theorizing Multiculturalism: A Guide to the Current Debate* (Blackwell, Oxford), 100–17.

May, Stephen (ed) (1999) *Indigenous Community-Based Education* (Multilingual Matters, Clevedon).

—— (2001) *Language and Minority Rights: Ethnicity, Nationalism and the Politics of Language* (Longman, London).

Medda-Windischer, Roberta (2004) 'Historical Minorities and Migrants: Foes or Allies?', *eumap.org Online Journal* (July 2004)—available at: <http://www.eumap.org/journal/features/2004/migration/pt1/minmigrants>.

Meijknecht, Anna (2001) *Towards International Personality: The Position of Minorities and Indigenous Peoples in International Law* (Intersentia, Antwerp).

Meyer, John (2001) 'Globalization, National Culture, and the Future of the World Polity', Wei Lun Lecture, Chinese University of Hong Kong (November).

Michaels, Walter Benn (2006) *The Trouble with Diversity: How We Learned to Love Identity and Ignore Inequality* (Metropolitan Books, New York).

Mihalikova, Silvia (1998) 'The Hungarian Minority in Slovakia: Conflict Over Autonomy', in Magda Opalski (ed), *Managing Diversity in Plural Societies: Minorities, Migration and Nation-Building in Post-Communist Europe* (Forum Eastern Europe, Ottawa), 148–64.

Miller, David (1995) *On Nationality* (Oxford University Press, Oxford).

—— (2000) *Citizenship and National Identity* (Polity Press, Cambridge).

—— (2006) 'Multiculturalism and the Welfare State: Theoretical Reflections', in Banting and Kymlicka (eds) (2006), 232–38.

Minority Protection Association (1995) *The Slovak State Language Law and the Minorities: Critical Analyses and Remarks* (Minority Protection Association, Budapest).

Mitchell, Katharyne (1993) 'Multiculturalism, or the United Colors of Benetton?', *Antipode* 25: 263–94

Mitnick, Eric (2006) *Rights, Groups, and Self-Invention: Group-Differentiated Rights in Liberal Theory* (Ashgate, Aldershot).

Modood, Tariq (1996) 'The Changing Context of "Race" in Britain', *Patterns of Prejudice*, 30/1: 3–12.

—— (2003) 'Muslims and the Politics of Difference', in Sarah Spencer (ed), *The Politics of Migration* (Blackwell, Oxford) 100–15.

Moodley, Kogila (1992) 'Ethnicity, Power, Politics and Minority Education', in K. Moodley (ed), *Beyond Multicultural Education: International Perspectives* (Detselig, Calgary), 79–94.

Moore, Margaret (2001) *The Ethics of Nationalism* (Oxford University Press, Oxford).

Morawa, Alexander (2002–3) 'The Jurisprudence of the American and African Regional Human Rights Bodies', *European Yearbook of Minority Issues*, 2: 537–76.

—— (2004) 'The United Nations Treaty Monitories Bodies and Minority Rights', in Council of Europe (2004), 29–53.

Morsink, Johannes (1999) 'Cultural Genocide, the Universal Declaration, and Minority Rights', *Human Rights Quarterly*, 21/4: 1009–60.

Moynihan, Daniel (1993) *Pandaemonium: Ethnicity in International Affairs* (Oxford University Press, New York).

Mozaffar, Shaheen and James Scarritt (2000) 'Why Territorial Autonomy is Not a Viable Option for Managing Ethnic Conflict in African Plural Societies', in William Safran and Ramon Maiz (eds), *Identity and Territorial Autonomy in Plural Societies* (Frank Cass, London), 230–53.

MRG (1997) *World Directory of Minorities* (Minority Rights Group International, London).

—— (1999) *Forests and Indigenous Peoples of Asia* (Minority Rights Group, Report 98/4, London).

—— (2003) 'Possible New United Nations Mechanisms for the Protection and Promotion of the Rights of Minorities' (Working Paper submitted to UN Working Group on Minorities, 9th Session, May: E/CN.4/sub.2/AC.5/2003/WP.3).

—— (2004) 'Submission to the UN High-Level Panel on Threats, Challenges and Change: Conflict Prevention and the Protection of Minorities' (Minority Rights Group, London).

—— (2005) 'The Millennium Development Goals: Helping or Hurting Minorities?' (Working Paper submitted to the UN Working Group on Minorities, 11th Session, 31 May–3 June).

Muehlebach, Andrea (2003) 'What Self in Self-Determination: Notes from the Fronteirs of Transnational Indigenous Activism', *Identities: Global Studies in Culture and Power*, 10: 241–68.

Mukarji, Nirmal and Balveer Arora (1992) 'Introduction', in N. Mukarji and B. Arora (eds), *Federalism in India: Origins and Development* (Vikas Publishing, Delhi).

Murray, Rachel and Steven Wheatley (2003) 'Groups and the African Charter on Human and Peoples' Rights', *Human Rights Quarterly*, 25: 213–36.

Musgrave, Thomas (1997) *Self-Determination and National Minorities* (Oxford University Press, Oxford).

Nanda, Meera (2003) *Prophets Facing Backwards: Critiques of Science and Hindu Nationalism in India* (Rutgers University Press, New Brunswick, NJ).

Nandy, Ashis (1992) 'Federalism, the Ideology of the State and Cultural Plrualism', in Mukarji and Arora (eds) (1992).

Nelson, Daniel (1998) 'Hungary and its Neighbours: Security and Ethnic Minorities', *Nationalities Papers*, 26/2: 314–30.

Neukirch, Claus, Katrin Simhandl, and Wolfgang Zellner (2004) 'Implementing Minority Rights in the Framework of the CSCE/OSCE', in Council of Europe (2004), 159–81.

Newman, Saul (1996) *Ethnoregional Conflict in Democracies: Mostly Ballots, Rarely Bullets* (Greenwood Press, Westport, Comm).

Nietschmann, Bernard (1987) 'The Third World War', *Cultural Survival Quaterly*, 11/3: 1–16.

Niezen, Ronald (2003) *The Origins of Indigenism: Human Rights and the Politics of Identity* (University of California Press, Berkeley).

Nimni, Ephraim (2005) 'Introduction: The National Cultural Autonomy Model Revisited', in E. Nimni (ed) *National Cultural Autonomy and its Contemporary Critics* (Routledge, London), 1–14.

Nissan, Elizabeth (1996) *Sri Lanka: A Bitter Harvest* (Minority Rights Group, London).

Norman, Wayne (2006) *Negotiating Nationalism: Nation-Building, Federalism and Secession in the Multinational State* (Oxford University Press, Oxford).

Offe, Claus (1993) 'Ethnic Politics in East European Transitions', in Jody Jensen and Ferenc Miszlivetz (eds), *Paradoxes of Transition* (Savaria University Press, Szombathely), 11–40.

—— (1998) ' "Homogeneity" and Constitutional Democracy: Coping with Identity Conflicts with Group Rights', *Journal of Political Philosophy*, 6/2: 113–41.

—— (2001) 'Political Liberalism, Group Rights and the Politics of Fear and Trust', *Studies in East European Thought* 53: 167–82.

OHRC (1996) *Policy on Female Genital Mutilation* (Ontario Human Rights Commission, Toronto).

Okin, Susan (1999) *Is Multiculturalism Bad for Women?* (Princeton University Press, Princeton).

Opalski, Magda (2001) 'Can Will Kymlicka be Exported to Russia?', in Kymlicka and Opalski (eds) (2001): 298–319.

OSCE (1997) *Report on the Linguistic Rights of Persons Belonging to National Minorities in the OSCE Area: Annex: Replies from OSCE Participating States* (Office of the High Commissioner on National Minorities, Organization for Security and Cooperation in Europe, The Hague).

—— (1999) 'Lund Recommendations on Effective Participation of National Minorities', available at <http://www.osce.org/item/2929.html>

—— (2006) 'Policies on Integration and Diversity in some OSCE Participating States' (prepared by the Migration Policy Group for the High Commissioner on National Minorities, OSCE, June 2006) <http://www.osce.org/item/19961.html>.

Packer, John and Erik Friberg (2004) 'Submission to the UN High-Level Panel on Threats, Challenges and Change: Conflict Prevention and the Protection of Minorities' (Minority Rights Group, London).

Papillon, Martin (1999) 'Mouvement de Protestation et Représentation Identitaire: L'émergence de la Nation Crié Entre 1971 et 1995', *International Journal of Canadian Studies*, 20: 101–25.

Parekh, Bhikhu (2000) *Rethinking Multiculturalism: Cultural Diversity and Political Theory* (Harvard University Press, Cambridge, Mass.).

Paris, Roland (2004) *At War's End: Building Peace after Civil Conflict* (Cambridge University Press, Cambridge).

Passy, Florence (1999) 'Supranational Political Opportunities as a Channel of Globalization of Political Conflicts: The Case of the Rights of Indigenous Peoples', in Donatella della Porta, Hanspeter Kriesi, and Dieter Rucht (eds), *Social Movements in a Globalizing World* (Macmillan, London), 148–69.

Patil, S. H. (1998) 'State Formation in Federal India', in Abdulrahim Vijapur (ed) *Dimensions of Federal Nation Building* (Manak, Delhi), 148–59.

Pentassuglia, Gaetano (2002) *Minorities in International Law* (Council of Europe Publishing, Strasbourg).

Pettai, Vello (1998) 'Emerging Ethnic Democracy in Estonia and Latvia', in Magda Opalski (ed), *Managing Diversity in Plural Societies: Minorities, Migration and Nation-Building in Post-Communist Europe* (Forum Eastern Europe, Ottawa), 15–32.

Pfaff, William (1993) *The Wrath of Nations: Civilization and the Furies of Nationalism* (Simon & Schuster, New York).

Pfaff-Czarnecka, Joanna, Darini Rajasingham-Senanayake, Ashis Nandy, and Edmund Terence Gomez (eds) (1999) *Ethnic Futures: The State and Identity Politics in Asia* (Sage, New Delhi).

Phillips, Alan and Allan Rosas (eds) (1995) *Universal Minority Rights* (Abo Akademi University, Turku and Minority Rights Group, London).

Phillips, Anne and Moira Dustin (2004) 'UK Initiatives on Forced Marriage: Regulation, Dialogue and Exit', *Political Studies*, 52/3: 531–51.

Pieterse, Jan Nederveen (2005) 'The *Human Development Report* and Cultural Liberty: Tough Liberalism', *Development and Change*, 36/6: 1267–73.

Postero, Nancy Grey and Leon Zamosc (eds) (2004) *The Struggle for Indigenous Rights in Latin America* (Sussex Academic Press, Eastbourne).

Prins, Baukje and Sawitri Saharso (2006) 'Cultural Diversity, Gender Equality: The Dutch Case' (Paper for workshop on 'Gender Equality, Cultural Equality: European Comparisons and Lessons', Vrije Universiteit Amsterdam, 8–9 June).

Pritchard, Eleonar (2000) 'A University of their Own', *Central Europe Review*, 2/24 (19 June).

Puri, Sunita (2005) 'Rhetoric v Reality: The Effect of "Multiculturalism" on Doctors' Responses to Battered South Asian Women in the United States and Britain', *Patterns of Prejudice*, 39/4: 416–30.

Quane, Helen (2005) 'The Rights of Indigenous Peoples and the Development Process', *Human Rights Quarterly*, 27/2: 652–82.

Ram, Melanie (2001) 'Minority Relations in Multiethnic Societies: Assessing the EU Factor in Romania', *Romanian Journal of Society and Politics*, 1/2: 63–90.

—— (2003) 'Democratization through European Integration: The Case of Minority Rights in the Czech Republic and Romania', *Studies in Comparative International Development*, 38/2: 28–56.

Ratner, Steven (2000) 'Does International Law Matter in Preventing Ethnic Conflicts', *New York University Journal of International Law and Politics*, 32/3: 591–698.

Raz, Joseph (1994) 'Multiculturalism: A Liberal Perspective', *Dissent*, (winter): 67–79.

Rehman, Javaid (2000) *The Weakness in the International Protection of Minority Rights* (Kluwer, The Hague).

Requejo, Ferran (2005) *Multinational Federalism and Value Pluralism: The Spanish Case* (Routledge, London).

Resnick, Philip (1994) 'Towards a Multination Federalism', in Leslie Seidle (ed), *Seeking a New Canadian Partnership: Asymmetrical and Confederal Options* (Institute for Research on Public Policy, Montreal), 71–90.

Richards, John (2006) *Creating Choices: Rethinking Aboriginal Policy* (C. D. Howe Institute, Toronto).

Richardson, Rudy (2004) 'Multiculturalism in the Dutch Armed Forces' (presented at the International Seminar on 'Leadership, Education and the Armed Forces: Challenges and Opportunities', La Paz, Bolivia, 13–15 September).

Riggs, Fred (1994) 'Ethnonationalism, Industrialism and the Modern State', *Third World Quarterly*, 15/4: 583–611.

Ringold, Dena (2005) 'Accounting for Diversity: Policy Design and Maori Development in New Zealand' (Working paper prepared for World Bank conference on 'New Frontiers of Social Policy: Development in a Globalizing World', Arusha, Tanzania, December).

Roach, Steven (2005) *Cultural Autonomy, Minority Rights and Globalization* (Ashgate, Aldershot).

Roberts, Adam (1994) 'Ethnic Conflict: Threat and Challenge to the UN', in Anthony McDermott (ed), *Ethnic Conflict and International Security* (Norwegian Institute of International Affairs, Oslo), 5–36.

Robinson, Andrew (2003) 'Cultural Rights and Internal Minorities: On Protestants and Pueblos', *Canadian Journal of Political Science*, 36/1: 107–27.

Robinson, Randall (2000) *The Debt: What America Owes to Blacks* (Dutton, New York).

Rodriguez-Pinero, Luis (2005) *Indigenous Peoples, Postcolonialism, and International Law* (Oxford University Press, Oxford).

Roeder, Phillip (2004) *Where Nation-States Come From: Soviet Lessons, Global Implications* (University of California at San Diego, San Diego).

—— (2005) 'Power-Dividing as an Alternative to Power-Sharing', in Philip Roeder and Donald Rothchild (eds), *Sustainable Peace: Power and Democracy after Civil War* (Cornell University Press, Ithaca, NY).

Rooker, M. (2002) *The International Supervision of the Protection of Romany People in Europe* (Nijmegen University Press, Nijmegen).

Rosenblum, Nancy (1998) *Membership and Morals: The Personal Uses of Pluralism in America* (Princeton University Press, Princeton).

Rotberg, Robert (ed) (2004) *When States Fail: Causes and Consequences* (Princeton University Press, Princeton).

Rudge, Philip (1998) 'Reconciling State Interests with International Responsibilities: Asylum in North America and Western Europe', *International Journal of Refugee Law*, 10/1: 7–20.

Saideman, Stephen and William Ayres (2001) 'Determining the Sources of Irredentism: Logit Analyses of Minorities at Risk Data', *Journal of Politics*, 63/4: 1126–44.

—— David Lanoue, Michael Campenni, and Samuel Stanton (2002) 'Democratization, Political Institutions, and Ethnic Conflict: A Pooled Time-Series Analysis, 1985–1998', *Comparative Political Studies*, 35/1: 103–29.

Sarfaty, Galit (2005) 'The World Bank and the Internalization of Indigenous Rights Norms', *Yale Law Journal*, 114: 1791–818.

Sasse, Gwendolyn (2004) 'Minority Rights and EU Enlargement: Normative Overstretch or Effective Conditionality?', in Toggenburg (ed) (2004), 61–83.

—— (2005) 'Securitization or Securing Rights? Exploring the Conceptual Foundations of Policies towards Minorities and Migrants in Europe', *Journal of Common Market Studies*, 43/4: 673–93.

—— (2006) 'National Minorities and EU Enlargement: External or Domestic Incentives for Accommodation?', in John McGarry and Michael Keating (eds), *European Integration and the Nationalities Question* (Routledge, London), 64–84.

Schain, Martin (1999) 'Minorities and Immigrant Integration in France', in Christian Joppke and Steven Lukes (eds), *Multicultural Questions* (Oxford University Press, Oxford), 199–223.

Schauer, Frederick (2000) 'The Politics and Incentives of Legal Transplantation', in Joseph Nye and John Donahue (eds), *Governance in a Globalizing World* (Brookings Institution Press, Washington), 253–68.

Scheinin, Martin (2005) 'What are Indigenous Peoples?' in Nazila Ghanea and Alexandra Xanthaki (eds), *Minorities, Peoples and Self-Determination* (Martinus Nijhoff, Leiden), 3–13.

Schouls, Tim (2003) *Shifting Boundaries: Aboriginal Identity, Pluralist Theory, and the Politics of Self-Government* (UBC Press, Vancouver).

Schwellnus, Guido (2005) 'Operation Successful, Patient Dead? The Impact of Effective EU Conditionality on Consolidating a European Minority Rights Standard', (Paper presented at DVPW Sektionstagung Internationale Beziehungen, Mannheim, 6–7 October.).

Schwittay, Anke (2003) 'From Peasant Favors to Indigenous Rights: The Articulation of an Indigenous Identity and Land Struggle in Northwestern Argentina', *Journal of Latin American Anthropology*, 8/3: 127–54.

Scott, James (1998) *Seeing Like a State* (Yale University Press, New Haven).

Seif, Huda (2005) 'Accursed Minority: The Ethno-Cultural Persecution of the Al-Akhdam in the Republic of Yemen', *Muslim World Journal of Human Rights*, 2/1 (<http://www.bepress.com/mwjhr/vol2/iss1/art9/>).

Semb, Anne Julie (2005) 'Sami Self-Determination in the Making?', *Nations and Nationalism*, 11/4: 531–49.

Sen, Amartya (2006) *Identity and Violence: The Illusion of Destiny* (Norton, New York).

Shachar, Ayelet (2001) *Multicultural Jurisdictions: Cultural Differences and Women's Rights* (Cambridge University Press, Cambridge).

—— (2006) 'The Race for Talent: Highly Skilled Migrants and Competitive Immigration Regimes', *New York University Law Review*, 81/1: 148–206.

Sharp, A. (1996) 'The Genie that Would Not Go Back into the Bottle: National Self-Determination and the Legacy of the First World War and the Peace Settlement', in S. Dunn and T. G. Fraser (eds), *Europe and Ethnicity: The First World War and Contemporary Ethnic Conflict* (Routledge, London), 10–29.

Shastri, Amita (1997) 'Government Policy and the Ethnic Crisis in Sri Lanka', in Michael Brown and Sumit Ganguly (eds), *Government Policies and Ethnic Relations in Asia and the Pacific* (MIT Press, Cambridge, Mass.), 129–63.

Shatzmiller, Maya (2005) 'Conclusion', in Maya Shatzmiller (ed), *Nationalism and Minority Identities in Islamic Societies* (McGill-Queen's University Press, Montreal), 283–7.

Shue, Henry (1980) *Basic Rights: Subsistence, Affluence and U.S. Foreign Policy* (Princeton University Press, Princeton).

Sieder, Rachel (1997) *Customary Law and Democratic Transition in Guatemala* (Institute of Latin American Studies, London).

—— (1999) 'Rethinking Democratisation and Citizenship: Legal Pluralism and Institutional Reform in Guatemala', *Citizenship Studies*, 3/1: 103–18.

—— (2001) 'Advancing Indigenous Claims through the Law', in Cowan et al (eds) (2001): 201–25.

—— (ed) (2002) *Multiculturalism in Latin America: Indigenous Rights, Diversity and Democracy* (Palgrave, London).

Simhandi, Katrin (2006) ' "Western Gypsies and Travellers"—"Eastern Roma": The Creation of Political Objects by the Institutions of the European Union', *Nations and Nationalism*, 12/1: 97–116.

Sisk, Tim (1996) *Power Sharing and International Mediation in Ethnic Conflicts* (US Institute of Peace Press, Washington).

Skovgaard, Jakob (2007) 'Preventing Ethnic Conflict, Security Ethnic Justice? The Council of Europe, the EU and the OSCE High Commissioner on National Minorities' Use of Contested Concepts in their Responses to the Hungarian Minority Policies of Hungary, Romania and Slovakia' (Ph.D. thesis, Department of Political and Social Science, European University Institute, Florence).

Skurbaty, Zelim (ed) (2005) *Beyond a One-Dimensional State: An Emerging Right to Autonomy?* (Martinus Nijhoff, Leiden).

Slimane, S. (2003) 'Recognizing Minorities in Africa' (Minority Rights Group, London)—available at: (<http://www.minorityrights.org/Advocacy/africa2003.htm>).

Smith, Anthony (1981) *The Ethnic Revival in the Modern World* (Cambridge University Press, Cambridge).

Smith, Rogers (2003) *Stories of Peoplehood: The Politics and Morals of Political Membership* (Cambridge University Press, Cambridge).

Sniderman, Paul and Louk Hagendoorn (2007) *When Ways of Life Collide: Multiculturalism and its Discontents in the Netherlands* (Princeton University Press, Princeton).

Snyder, Jack (2000) *From Voting to Violence: Democratization and Nationalist Conflict* (Norton, New York).

Solchanyk, Roman (1994) 'The Politics of State-Building: Centre-Periphery Relations in Post-Soviet Ukraine', *Europe-Asia Studies*, 46/1: 47–68.

Soroka, Stuart, Richard Johnston, and Keith Banting (2007) 'Ties that Bind: Social Cohesion and Diversity in Canada', in Keith Benting, Tom Courchene, and Leslie Seidle (eds), *Belonging? Diversity, Recognition and Shared Citizenship in Canada* (Institute for Research on Public Policy, Montreal), 561–600.

Speed, Shannon and Jane Collier (2000) 'Limiting Indigenous Autonomy in Chiapas, Mexico: The State Government's Use of Human Rights', *Human Rights Quarterly*, 22: 877–905.

Spinner, Jeff (1994) *The Boundaries of Citizenship: Race, Ethnicity and Nationality in the Liberal State* (Johns Hopkins University Press, Baltimore).

Srinivasavaradan, T. C. A. (1992) 'Pluralistic Problems in the Federal System', in Mukarji and Arora (eds) (1992), 127–57.

Stavenhagen, Rodolfo (ed) (1996) *Ethnic Conflicts and the Nation State* (Macmillan, Basingstoke).

Steiner, Henry (ed) (2004) *Ethnic Conflict, Minority Protection and Conflict Resolution: Human Rights Perspectives* (Harvard Law School Human Rights Program, Cambridge, Mass.).

Stepan, Alfred (1999) 'Federalism and Democracy: Beyond the US Model', *Journal of Democracy*, 10/4: 19–34.

Stone, Diane (2004) 'Transfer Agents and Global Networks in the "Transnationalization" of Policy', *Journal of European Public Policy*, 11/3: 545–66.

Strazzari, Francesco (1998) 'Macedonia: State and Identity in an Unstable Regional Environment', in Magda Opalski (ed), *Managing Diversity in Plural Societies: Minorities, Migration and Nation-Building in Post-Communist Europe* (Forum Eastern Europe, Ottawa), 165–90.

Suksi, Marku (ed) (1998) *Autonomy: Applications and Implications* (Kluwer, The Hague).

Svensson, Frances (1979) 'Liberal Democracy and Group Rights: The Legacy of Individualism and its Impact on American Indian Tribes', *Political Studies*, 27/3: 421–39.

Tamir, Yael (1993) *Liberal Nationalism* (Princeton University Press, Princeton).

Taras, Raymond and Rajat Ganguly (1998) *Understanding Ethnic Conflict: The International Dimension* (Longman, New York).

Taylor, Charles (1992) 'The Politics of Recognition', in Amy Gutmann (ed), *Multi-culturalism and the 'Politics of Recognition'* (Princeton University Press, Princeton), 25–73.

—— (1996) 'A World Consensus on Human Rights?', *Dissent* (summer): 15–21.

Tennant, Chris (1994) 'Indigenous Peoples, International Institutions, and the International Legal Literature from 1945-1993', *Human Rights Quarterly*, 16: 1–57.

Thiele, Carmen (2005) 'Citizenship as a Requirement for Minorities', *European Human Rights Law Review*, 3: 276–89.

Thio, Li-Ann (2003) 'Developing a 'Peace and Security' Approach towards Minorities' Problems', *International and Comparative Law Quarterly*, 52: 115–50.

Thornberry, Patrick (1991) *International Law and the Rights of Minorities* (Oxford University Press, Oxford).

—— (1995) 'The UN Declaration on the Rights of Persons Belonging to National or Ethnic, Religious and Linguistic Minorities: Background, Analysis, Observations and an Update', in Phillips and Rosas (eds) (1995), 13–76.

—— (1998) 'Images of Autonomy and Individual and Collective Rights in International Human Rights on the Rights of Minorities', in Suksi (ed) (1998), 97–124.

—— (2002) *Indigenous Peoples and International Law* (Manchester University Press, Manchester).

—— and Maria Estebenez (eds) (2004) *Minority Rights in Europe: A Review of the Work and Standards of the Council of Europe* (Council of Europe Publishing, Strasbourg).

Tierney, Stephen (ed) (2000) *Accommodating National Identity: New Approaches in International and Domestic Law* (Kluwer, The Hague).

—— (2004) *Constitutional Law and National Pluralism* (Oxford University Press, Oxford).

Tilley, Virginia (2002) 'New Help or New Hegemony? The Transnational Indigenous Peoples' Movement and "Being Indian" in El Salvador', *Journal of Latin American Studies*, 34: 525–54.

Tilly, Charles (1975) 'Reflections on the History of European State-Making', in C. Tilly (ed), *The Formation of National States in Western Europe* (Princeton University Press, Princeton), 3–83.

Toggenburg, Gabriel (2004) 'Minority Protection in a Supranational Context: Limits and Opportunities', in Toggenburg (ed) (2004), 1–36.

—— (ed) (2004) *Minority Protection and the Enlarged European Union: The Way Forward* (Open Society Institute, Budapest).

—— (2005) 'Who is Managing Ethnic and Cultural Diversity in the European Condominium? The Moments of Entry, Integration and Preservation', *Journal of Common Market Studies*, 34/4: 717–38.

Tomei, Manuela (2005) *Indigenous and Tribal Peoples: An Ethnic Audit of Selected Poverty Reduction Strategy Papers* (International Labour Organization, Geneva).

Tomova, Ilona (1998) 'The Migration Process in Bulgaria', in Magda Opalski (ed), *Managing Diversity in Plural Societies: Minorities, Migration and Nation-Building in Post-Communist Europe* (Forum Eastern Europe, Ottawa), 229–39.

Tomuschat, Christian (ed) (1993) *Modern Law of Self-Determination* (Martinus Nijhoff, Dordrecht).

Torbisco Casals, Neus (2006) *Group Rights as Human Rights: A Liberal Approach to Multiculturalism* (Springer, Dordrecht).

Torpey, John (2006) *Making Whole What Has Been Smashed: On Reparations Politics* (Harvard University Press, Cambridge, Mass.).

Toyota, Mika (2005) 'Subjects of the Nation Without Citizenship: The Case of 'Hill Tribes' in Thailand', in Will Kymlicka and Baogang He (eds), *Multiculturalism in Asia* (Oxford University Press, Oxford), 110–35.

Trifunovaska, Snezana (1997) 'One Theme in Two Variations—Self-Determination for Minorities and Indigenous Peoples', *International Journal on Minority and Group Rights*, 5: 175–97.

Tronvoll, Kjetil (2000) *Ethiopia: A New Start?* (Minority Rights Group, London).

Trudeau, Pierre (1971) 'Statement to the House of Commons on Multiculturalism', House of Commons, *Official Report of Debates*, 28th Parliament, 3rd Session, 8 October 1971, pp. 8545–46.

UN (2000) *We the Peoples: The Role of the United Nations in the 21st Century* (United Nations, Department of Public Information, New York).

—— (2004) *A More Secure World: Our Shared Responsibility: Report of the Secretary-General's High-Level Panel on Threats, Challenges and Change* (United Nations, New York).

UNDP (2000) *Overcoming Human Poverty* (United Nations Development Program, New York).

UNHDR (2004) *Cultural Liberty in Today's Diverse World: Human Development Report 2004* (United Nations Development Programme, New York).

Vallieres, Pierre (1971) *White Niggers of America* (McClelland and Stewart, Toronto).

Van Cott, Donna Lee (1996) *500 Years of Confrontation: Indigenous Rights and State Security Policy in Latin America* (Institute for National Strategic Studies, McNair Paper No. 53).

—— (2000) *The Friendly Liquidation of the Past: The Politics of Diversity in Latin America* (University of Pittsburgh Press, Pittsburgh).

—— (2006) 'Multiculturalism versus Neo-liberalism in Latin America', in Banting and Kymlicka (eds) (2006), 272–96.

Van der Stoel, Max (1999) *Peace and Stability through Human and Minority Rights: Speeches by the OSCE High Commissioner on National Minorities* (Nomos Verlagsgesellschaft, Baden-Baden).

Van Dyke, Vernon (1977) 'The Individual, the State, and Ethnic Communities in Political Theory', *World Politics*, 29/3: 343–69.

—— (1982) 'Collective Rights and Moral Rights: Problems in Liberal-Democratic Thought', *Journal of Politics*, 44: 21–40.

Varshney, Ashutosh (2002) *Ethnic Conflict and Civic Life* (Yale University Press, New Haven).

Vasilyeva, Olga (1995) 'Has Ethnic Federalism a Future in Russia?', *New Times*, March 1995, 34–7.

Vermeersch, Peter (2002) 'Ethnic Mobilisation and the Political Conditionality of European Union Accession: The Case of the Roma in Slovakia', *Journal of Ethnic and Migration Studies*, 28/1: 83–101.

—— (2003) 'EU Enlargement and Minority Rights Policies in Central Europe: Explaining Policy Shifts in the Czech Republic, Hungary and Poland', *Journal on Ethnopolitics and Minority Issues in Europe* 1 (<http://www.ecmi.de/jemie/>).

—— (2005) 'Marginality, Advocacy and the Ambiguities of Multiculturalism: Notes on Romani Activism in Central Europe', *Identities: Global Studies in Culture and Power*, 12: 451–78.

Verstichel, Annelies (2004) 'Elaborating a Catalogue of Best Practices of Effective Participation of National Minorities'. *European Yearbook of Minority Issues*, 2: 165–96.

Vizi, Balázs (2005) 'The Unintended Legal Backlash of Enlargement? The Inclusion of the Rights of Minorities in the EU Constitution', *Regio: Minorities, Politics, Society* (Budapest), 8: 87–106.

Von Eschen, Penny (1997) *Race against Empire: Black Americans and Anti-Colonialism 1937–57* (Stanford University Press, Stanford, Calif.).

Waever, Ole (1995) 'Securitization and Desecuritization', in Ronnie Lipschutz (ed), *On Security* (Columbia University Press, New York), 46–86.

Waldron, Jeremy (1995) 'Minority Cultures and the Cosmopolitan Alternative', in Will Kymlicka (ed), *The Rights of Minority Cultures* (Oxford University Press, Oxford), 93–119.

—— (2000) 'Cultural Identity and Civic Responsibility', in Will Kymlicka and Wayne Norman (eds), *Citizenship in Diverse Societies* (Oxford University Press, Oxford), 155–74.

Walker, Samuel (1998) *The Rights Revolution: Rights and Community in Modern America* (Oxford University Press, New York).

Walker, Scott and Steven Poe (2002) 'Does Cultural Diversity Affect Countries' Respect for Human Rights?', *Human Rights Quarterly*, 24/1: 237–63.

Walzer, Michael (1983) *Spheres of Justice* (Basic Books, New York).

Warren, Kay and Jean Jackson (2002) 'Introduction' in K. Warren and J. Jackson (eds), *Indigenous Movements, Self-Representation and the State in Latin America* (University of Texas Press, Austin).

Watts, Arthur (2002) 'The Liechtenstein Draft Convention on Self-Determination through Self-Administration: A Commentary', in W. Danspeckgruber (ed), *The Self-Determination of Peoples: Community, Nation, and State in an Interdependent World* (Lynne Reinner, Boulder, Colo.), 365–81.

Weiner, Brian (2005) *Sins of the Parents: The Politics of National Apologies in the United States* (Temple University Press, Philadelphia).

Weiner, Myron (1998) *Sons of the Soil* 2nd edn (Oxford University Press, Delhi).

Weldon, Steven (2006) 'The Institutional Context of Tolerance for Ethnic Minorities: A Comparative, Multilevel Analysis of Western Europe', *American Journal of Political Science*, 50/2: 331–49.

Welhengama, Gnanapala (1998) 'The Legitimacy of Minorities' Claim for Autonomy through the Right to Self-Determination', *Nordic Journal of International Law*, 68: 413–38.

—— (2000) *Minorities' Claims: From Autonomy to Secession, International Law and State Practice* (Ashgate, Aldershot).

Weller, Marc (2003) 'Filling the Frame: 5th Anniversary of the Entry into Force of the Framework Convention for the Protection of National Minorities' (Conference Report, Council of Europe, Strasbourg: 30–1 October).

—— (2005a) 'Towards a General Comment on Self-Determination and Autonomy', (Working paper submitted to UN Working Group on Minorities, 11th Session, 25 May 2005, E/CN.4/Sub.2/AC.5/2005/WP.5)

—— (ed) (2005b) *The Rights of Minorities in Europe: A Commentary on the European Framework Convention for the Protection of National Minorities* (Oxford University Press, Oxford).

—— and Stefan Wolff (eds) (2005) *Autonomy, Self-Governance and Conflict Resolution* (Routledge, London).

Welsh, David (1993) 'Domestic Politics and Ethnic Conflict', in Michael Brown (ed), *Ethnic Conflict and International Security* (Princeton University Press, Princeton), 43–60.

Weyland, Kurt (2005) 'Theories of Policy Diffusion: Lessons from Latin American Pension Reform', *World Politics*, 57: 262–95.

Wheatley, Steven (1997) 'Minority Rights and Political Accommodation in the "New" Europe', *European Law Review*, 22 (Supplement), pp. HRC63–HRC81.

—— (2005) *Democracy, Minorities and International Law* (Cambridge University Press, Cambridge).

Wikan, Unni (2002) *Generous Betrayal: Politics of Culture in the New Europe* (University of Chicago Press, Chicago).

Wilkinson, Steven (2005) 'Conditionality, Consociationalism, and the European Union', in Sid Noel (ed), *From Power-Sharing to Democracy: Post-conflict Institutions in Ethnically Divided Societies* (McGill-Queen's University Press, Montreal), 239–62.

Williams, Charlotte and Haluk Soydan (2005) 'When and How Does Ethnicity Matter? A Cross-National Study of Social Work Responses to Ethnicity in Child Protection Cases', *British Journal of Social Work*, 35: 901–20.

Williams, Melissa (1995) 'Justice Towards Groups: Political not Juridical', *Political Theory*, 23/1: 67–91.

Wilson, R. A. (ed) (1997) *Human Rights, Culture and Context: Anthropological Perspectives* (Pluto Press, London).

351

Wimmer, Andreas (2002) *Nationalist Exclusion and Ethnic Conflict: Shadows of Modernity* (Cambridge University Press, Cambridge).

—— (2003) 'Democracy and Ethnoreligious Conflict in Iraq', *Survival*, 45/4: 114–34.

—— and Nina Glick Schiller (2002) 'Methodological Nationalism and Beyond: Nation-State Building, Migration and the Social Sciences', *Global Networks*, 2/4: 301–34.

—— Richard Goldstone, Donald Horowitz, Ulrike Joras, and Conrad Schetter (eds) (2004) *Facing Ethnic Conflict: Toward a New Realism* (Rowman and Littlefield, Lanham, Md.).

Wippman, David (ed) (1998) *International Law and Ethnic Conflict* (Cornell University Press, Ithaca, NY).

Woehrling, Jean-Marie (2005) *The European Charter for Regional and Minority Languages: A Critical Commentary* (Council of Europe Publishing, Strasbourg).

Wolton, Suke (2000) *Lord Hailey, the Colonial Office and the Politics of Race and Empire in the Second World War: The Loss of White Prestige* (Macmillan, Basingstoke).

World Bank (2003) *Implementation of Operational Directive 4.20 on Indigenous Peoples: An Independent Desk Review* (Operations Evaluation Department, Report 25332, World Bank, Washington).

—— (2005) 'Legal Note on Indigenous Peoples' (World Bank Legal Department, 8 April).

Wright, Jane (1996) 'The OSCE and the Protection of Minority Rights', *Human Rights Quarterly*, 18/1: 190–205.

Yashar, Deborah (2005) *Contesting Citizenship in Latin America: The Rise of Indigenous Movements and the Postliberal Challenge* (Cambridge University Press, Cambridge).

Young, Crawford (ed) (1998) *Ethnic Diversity and Public Policy: A Comparative Enquiry* (Macmillan, Basingstoke).

—— (ed) (1999) *The Accommodation of Cultural Diversity: Case Studies* (Macmillan, Basingstoke).

—— (2002) 'Deciphering Disorder in Africa: Is Identity the Key?', *World Politics*, 54/4: 532–57.

Yousif, Ahmad (2000) 'Islam, Minorities and Religious Freedom: A Challenge to Modern Theory of Pluralism', *Journal of Muslim Minority Affairs*, 20/1: 29–40.

Zaagman, Rob (1997) 'Commentary', in Danspeckgruber and Watts (eds) (1997) 248–54.

—— (1999) *Conflict Prevention in the Baltic States: The OSCE High Commissioner on National Minorities in Estonia, Latvia and Lithuania* (ECMI Monograph No. 1, European Centre for Minority Issues, Flensburg).

Žižek, Slavoj (1997) 'Multiculturalism, Or, the Cultural Logic of Multinational Capitalism', *New Left Review*, 225: 28–51.

Index